Baedeker's
California

Baedeker's

CALIFORNIA

Imprint

251 colour photographs, 17 line drawings, 14 special plans,
13 general plans, 11 town plans, 9 ground plans, 1 large area map (with special maps of the conurbations of Los Angeles, Sacramento, San Diego and San Francisco).

Research and text: Henry Marx, New York
Illustration lay-out: Carin Drechsler-Marx, New York
Climate: Dr Wolfgang Hassenpflug, Kiel

Editorial work and completion: Baedeker-Redaktion (Astrid Feltes)
English Language edition: Alec Court

Cartography: Gert Oberländer, Munich; Christoph Gallus, Hohberg-Niederschopfheim
Hallweg AG, Bern (area map)

General direction: Dr Peter H. Baumgarten, Baedeker Stuttgart

Source of illustrations: Bickel (2), Drechsler-Marx (190), Feltes(1), Frick (24), Historia-Photo (5), Hottmann (1), Institute of Foreign Relations Stuttgart (1), Klepiszewskii (2), Messerschmidt (5), Möhle (2), Scherm (6), Ullstein (10), US Embassy Bonn (1)

English Translation: David Cocking, Julie Waller, Alec Court

Following the tradition established by Karl Baedeker in 1844, sights of particular interest and hotels and restaurants of particular quality are distinguished by either one or two asterisks.

To make it easier to locate the various places listed in the "A to Z" section of the Guide, their coordinates on the large city map are shown at the head of each entry: e.g. Sacramento G/H 2/3

Only a selection of hotels, restaurants and shops can be given; no reflection is implied therefore on establishments not included.

In a time of rapid change it is difficult to ensure that all the information given is entirely accurate and up-to-date, and the possibility of error can never be entirely eliminated. Although the publishers can accept no responsibility for inaccuracies and omissions, they are always grateful for corrections and suggestions for improvement.

1st edition

© Baedeker Stuttgart: original German edition

© 1991 Jarrold and Sons Ltd: English language edition worldwide

© 1991 The Automobile Association:
United Kingdom and Ireland

US and Canadian edition: Prentice Hall Press

Distributed in the United Kingdom by the Publishing Division of The Automobile Association, Fanum House, Basingstoke, Hampshire, RG21 2EA.

The name *Baedeker* is a registered trademark
A CIP catalogue record for this book is available from the British Library.

Licensed user: Mairs Geographischer Verlag GmbH & Co.,
Ostfildern-Kemnat bei Stuttgart

Reproductions: Eder Repro GmbH, Ostfildern-Scharnhausen

Printed in Italy by G. Canale & C. S.p.A – Borgaro T.se – Turin

0–13–094731–8 US & Canada
0 7495 0289 4 UK

Contents

Anaheim, Anza-Borrego State Park, Auburn, Baja California, Bakersfield, Barstow, Benicia, Berkeley, Big Bear Lake, Big Sur, Bishop, Bodega Bay, Bodie State Historic Park, Buena Park, Calistoga, Cambria, Carlsbad, Carmel, Channel Islands National Park, Coloma, Costa Mesa, Crescent City, Dana Point, Davis, Death Valley National Monument, Donner Pass, Dutch Flat, El Camino Real, Eureka, Ferndale, Fort Bragg, Fort Ross State Historic Park, Fresno, Garberville, Geyserville, Glen Ellen, Grass Valley, Healdsburg, Indio, Inyo National Forest, Irvine, Joshua Tree National Monument, Laguna Beach, Lake Tahoe, Lassen Volcanic National Park, Lava Beds National Monument, Lompoc, Lone Pine, Long Beach, Los Angeles, Los Gatos, Los Padres National Forest, Malibu, Mammoth Lakes, Mendocino, Merced, Mission Stations, Modesto, Mojave Desert, Mono Lake State Reserve, Monterey, Morro Bay, Mother Lode County, Mount Shasta, Muir Woods National Monument, Napa, Newport Beach, Oakland, Ojai, Oroville, Oxnard, Palm Springs, Palo Alto, Pasadena, Petaluma, Pinnacles National Monument, Pismo Beach, Placerville, Point Lobos State Reserve, Point Reyes National Seashore, Red Bluff, Redding, Redwood Highway, Riverside, Sacramento, St Helena, Salinas, Salton Sea, San Bernadino, San Diego, San Francisco, San José, San Luis Obispo, San Simeon, Santa Barbara, Santa Catalina Island, Santa Clara, Santa Crux, Santa Monica, Santa Rosa, Sausalito, Sequoia & Kings Canyon National Parks, Silicon Valley, Solvang, Sonoma, Sonora, Stockton, Tijuana, Truckee, Ukiah, Vallejo, Ventura, Weaverville, Yosemite National Park

Air travel, Art Galleries, Bathing Beaches, Boat Excursions, Bookshops, Buisness Hours, Car Rental, Chemists, Clothing, Consulates, Crime, Currency, Customs Regulationsm, Emergencies, Events, Food and Drink, Getting to California, Hotels and Motels, Information, Insurance, Language, Medical Assistance, Motoring Assistance, Museums, Newspapers and Periodicals, Post, Telephone and Telegraph, Public Holidays, Radio and Television, Railways, Restaurants, Shopping, Sport, Taxis, Time, Tipping, Travel Documents, Weather Reports, Wine, Youth Hostels

The Principal Sights at a Glance

Foreword

This pocket guide to California is one of the new generation of Baedeker guides.

Baedeker pocket guides, illustrated throughout in colour, are designed to meet the needs of the modern traveller. They are quick and easy to consult, with the principal places of interest described in alphabetical order, and the information is presented in a format that is both attractive and easy to follow.

The present guide is concerned with the entire state of California, in particular with the Federal US State, but also included are the two parts of the Mexican State of Baja (lower) California – B.C.Norte and B.C.Sur.

The guide is in three parts. The first part gives a general account of California, its climate, flora and fauna, population and religion, economy, notable personalities, history, art and architecture. and suggested itineraries. In the second part towns, villages, scenery, national parks, etc. which are of interest to the tourist are described in some detail. The third part consists of practical information arranged in alphabetical order.

The new guides are abundantly illustrated and contain many newly drawn plans and numerous colour photographs. Each entry in the A to Z section gives the co-ordinates of the square on the map in which the particular feature can be located. Users of this guide, therefore, will have no difficulty in finding what they want to see.

Facts and Figures

Note

California lies on the Pacific coast of North America and consists basically of the US Federal State of California (originally Alta California), but also includes the adjoining narrow peninsula of Lower California to the south; this consists of the two Mexican states of Baja California Sur and Baja California Norte.

General

Position and extent

California, after Alaska and Texas, is the third largest of the 50 American federal states, and covers an area of 156,297 sq. miles/404,808 sq. km. – almost twice as large as Great Britain. It lies between latitudes 32° and 42° north and longitudes 114° and 124° west. In the north it is bounded by the state of Oregon, in the east by Nevada and Arizona, and in the south by the Mexican province of Baja California. The Pacific Ocean forms the western boundary. Its length from north to south as the crow flies is 780 miles/1248 km, and the coast has a length of 1224 miles/2024 km. The width from east to west is 150–350 miles/240–560 km.

Natural Divisions

Geological faults

It has been said that the physical picture of California is as restless as the inhabitants of its towns. The reason for this is primarily the 560 mile-/900 km-long San Andreas fault which extends from Mexico to Point Reyes north of San Francisco. Since the western side of the fault moves every year about 3 cm to the north, California is in great danger from earthquakes. This danger is increased by numerous other faults.

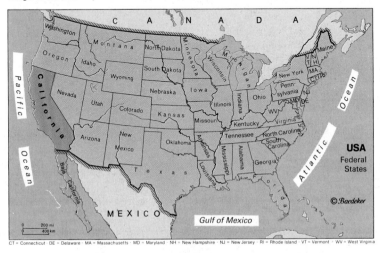

CT = Connecticut · DE = Delaware · MA = Massachusetts · MD = Maryland · NH = New Hampshire · NJ = New Jersey · RI = Rhode Island · VT = Vermont · WV = West Virginia

◀ In the Mojave Desert

9

In the High Sierra

The Sierra Nevada fault caused the most extensive earthquake in California in 1872, particularly in Owen's Valley. The so-called white wolf fault was the cause of the earthquake at Bakersfield in 1952. The Santa Inez fault was responsible for the earthquake which devastated Santa Barbara in 1925. Movement of the Newport Inglewood fault destroyed Long Beach in 1933. In addition the San Jacinto fault, a southern extension of the San Andreas depression mentioned above, and the Garlook fault were responsible for minor earthquakes.

Surface

Three mountain ranges and two great valleys characterise the central geography of California. Parallel to the coast runs the Coastal Range which reaches a height of 8861 ft/2700 m. To the east, in the north of the state, rises the Cascade Range up to a height of 14,408 ft/4390 m, and along the frontier of Nevada extends the Sierra Nevada which can only be crossed by passes and which has a maximum height of 13,500 ft/4418 m. Between the two mountain ranges stretches the great valley of California, called the Great Californian Long Valley, with a length of almost 435 miles/700 km and a width of 37 miles/60 km. It is formed by the Sacremento Valley in the north and the San Joaquin Valley in the south. The other great valley, Imperial Valley, is one of the most important territories of the state and extends from the Salton Sea as far as Mexico.

Lakes

The lakes in the north of California were formed more than 20,000 years ago by glacial water rushing down into the valleys of the Sierra Nevada. These include Lake Almanor, Honey Lake and Eagle Lake. One of the largest is Lake Tahoe which is shared by California and Nevada. The most southerly of these lakes is Mono Lake, not far from the Yosemite National Park. The inland lakes cover an area of more than 2162 sq. miles/5600 sq. km. In addition to the natural lakes there are others which have been formed by the construction of dams and these include Lake Oroville, Lake Beryessa, Lake Shasta and Lake Clair Eagle.

Wilderness areas

A particular feature of California are the four great wilderness areas which

Parched landscape in the "Valley of Death"

are not covered with sand but in places have rich animal life and vegetation, and which cover more than a quarter of the entire surface of the state. The Colorado Desert in the south-east of the state is partially used for agriculture (Imperial Valley, Coachella Valley) and provides space for recreational centres (especially in Palm Springs).

The Mojave Desert, which borders the Colorado Desert at the Joshua Tree National Monument, occupies one sixth of the area of California. Thanks to irrigation there are also extremely fertile areas here.

Contrasting areas such as Owen's Valley or Death Valley are part of the Trans-Sierra Desert.

Because of its extent and soil conditions California has extremely varying climatic zones and the expression "twelve Californias" is often used:

Regions

The north coast with its rock formations, giant redwood trees and vineyards.

North coast

To the east lies the Shasta Cascade territory where the mountain tops are always covered with snow, where there are forests, caves and innumerable mountain lakes.

Shasta Cascade

The territory of the high Sierra Nevada adjoins to the south-east with the Yosemite National Park, the Kings Canyon and Sequoia National Park and probably the most popular skiing areas of the state especially around Lake Tahoe and the Mammoth Lakes.

High Sierra

In the west is "Goldland" where there are still remains of the gold digging centres of the nineteenth century, and where you can see the spot on the American River where in 1848 the first gold was found.

"Goldland"

South of "Goldland" lies Central Valley, one of the most fertile regions in

Central Valley

Roaring spray on the Pacific Coast

the United States, with the towns of Sacramento, Fresno and Bakersfield. The last named being the centre of the traditional American rodeo.

San Francisco

The sixth region is San Francisco with the entire great bay territory. In addition to this, perhaps the most attractive town in the state, there are other places which are worth visiting, such as San Jose or the university town of Santa Clara.

Central Coast

South of San Francisco lies the central coastal area with the picturesque peninsula of Monterey, Carmel, Point Lobos and the massive castle which the newspaper proprietor Hurst had built in San Simeon. The area extends as far as Santa Barbara with its Spanish-Mexican atmosphere and the finest of all the mission churches.

Los Angeles

From here it is only a short drive to the area of Los Angeles with Hollywood and Beverly Hills, museums and theatres and an almost one-hundred-mile-long unbroken sandy beach.

Wildernesses

Although Los Angeles is situated in the desert, the actual great desert area begins to the east of the town. Here are the Joshua Tree National Monument, Death Valley and Palm Springs, the haunt in the season from December to May of many rich Americans.

Inland Empire

Typical of the contrasts in California is the fact that nearby can be found the Inland Empire where the first orange trees were planted and which is today the major region for the growing of citrus fruit. Here there are lakes and alpine resorts: theoretically it should be possible to indulge in water-skiing and land-skiing on one and the same day!

Orange County

West of the Inland Empire extends Orange County with its many exclusive residential places and the playground of the nation: the amusement parks

State flag of California

of Knott's Berry Farm and Disneyland, a motor museum, one of the largest waxworks in the world and probably the most fashionable bathing resort in the state, Newport Beach.

The most southern of the "Twelve Californias" is the region around San Diego, which was discovered by the Spaniards 50 years before the east coast of the United States was discovered by the English. Balboa Park, San Diego zoo with its enclosure for game, sailing regattas, one of the finest aquaria and the most elegant suburb La Jolla are the attractions of this region. You can go from here to Tijuana by tram and enjoy in the largest town of Baja California the atmosphere of Mexican life.

San Diego

Administration

Like all the federal states California, which in 1850 became the 31st state of the USA, is divided into counties (numbering 58). San Bernardino County with one eighth of the total area is the largest. With an area of 20,226 sq. miles/52,400 sq. km it is not only one third as large again as Switzerland but is the largest county in the United States. Its total population is around one million, and the county town of the same name has 130,000 inhabitants. The smallest county is San Francisco, with 44 sq. miles/113 sq. km and barely 700,000 inhabitants: it consists only of the city of San Francisco and is the only county which coincides in area with a single town. The county with the largest population (7.7 million) is Los Angeles; it covers an area of some 6,245 sq. miles/16,180 sq. km. Alpine County which borders Nevada has the smallest population; with an area of 679 sq. miles, 1760 sq. km, it has less than 1200 inhabitants.

Counties

At the head of the state is a Governor who with his deputy and the Minister of Justice is elected every four years by popular vote. He names the other members of the cabinet who need approval by the Senate. This consists of

Government

Counties

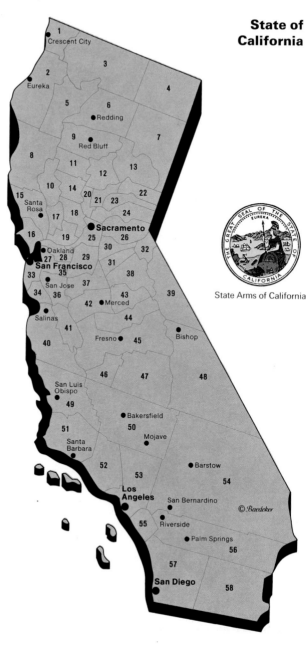

State Arms of California

1 Del Norte
2 Humboldt
3 Siskiyou
4 Modoc
5 Trinity
6 Shasta
7 Lassen
8 Mendocino
9 Tehama
10 Lake
11 Glenn
12 Butte
13 Plumas
14 Colusa
15 Sonoma
16 Marin
17 Napa
18 Yolo
19 Solano
20 Sutter
21 Yuba
22 Sierra
23 Nevada
24 Placer
25 Sacramento
26 El Dorado
27 San Francisco
28 Contra Costa
29 San Joaquin
30 Amadora
31 Calaveras
32 Alpine
33 San Mateo
34 Santa Cruz
35 Alameda
36 Santa Clara
37 Stanislaus
38 Tuolumne
39 Mono
40 Monterey
41 San Benito
42 Merced
43 Mariposa
44 Madera
45 Fresno
46 Kings
47 Tulare
48 Inyo
49 San Luis Obispo
50 Kern
51 Santa Barbara
52 Ventura
53 Los Angeles
54 San Bernardino
55 Orange
56 Riverside
57 San Diego
58 Imperial

40 members of which half are elected every two years, so that a continuous process of law-making can be effected. The second chamber, called the "Assembly", consists of 80 members who are elected every two years. Laws which have been accepted by both chambers can be vetoed by the Governor, but his veto can be overturned by a majority of two thirds in both chambers.

In the Congress in Washington California is represented by 47 members of Congress and two Senators. A total of one tenth of the total population of America lives in California which has approximately the same proportion of the total number of Congressmen (435); however, in the Senate, like all other states, California has only two representatives. Numerous legislative proposals, especially for alterations to the Constitution, are decided by referendum, as they are in Switzerland. These referenda take place annually on American election day, the Tuesday after the first Monday in November.

The famous Californian poppy, which grows principally on the eastern slopes of the Central Valley, has been adopted as the state flower. "Golden Poppy Day" is held in April, although the flower blooms almost throughout the year.
State symbols

The chosen state fish is not from the Pacific Ocean; it is the Californian golden trout which is only found in this part of America, especially in the High Sierra and the Shasta Cascade area.

The official state bird is the Californian tree-quail which is found all over the state.

The grey bear appears on the state seal and on the Californian flag, but the animal has been extinct for a very long time.

The state flag dates from the foundation of the short-lived independent Republic of California and was raised for the first time on June 18th 1846 at Sonoma. The present state flag was approved by parliament in 1911. On a white background is a red star in the upper left-hand segment; in the middle is a brown bear on a green strip, moving towards a star; below in black are the words "California Republic" with a red strip along the bottom of the flag.

Climate

Central California around San Francisco enjoys a pleasant climate with dry summers and rain in winter, corresponding to the Mediterranean climate in Europe. Northern and Southern California, the interior and the mountains each have their own distinct climatic zones:
General

Coast Range (including the adjoining Klamath Range)
Central Valley
Sierra Nevada
Southern California
Mojave Desert
Climatic Zones

Together with Florida, California is the part of the USA with the least climatic stress, i.e. its summers are neither too hot or oppressive nor its winters too cold. For this reason it is favoured by winter holidaymakers and as a retirement home for older citizens, except for the most northern and eastern regions.

The climates of the individual zones of California can be more precisely described by means of climatic graphs for typical locations. The temperature and precipitation levels throughout the year can be read from left to right (J = January to D = December). The blue rainfall columns show the monthly precipitation (in mm) according to the blue scale at the side. Temperatures are indicated by the orange-red band. The upper line represents the average highest day temperature, the lower line the average lowest night temperature. Temperature figures are given on the red scale at
Climatic graphs

Climate

Explanation in text

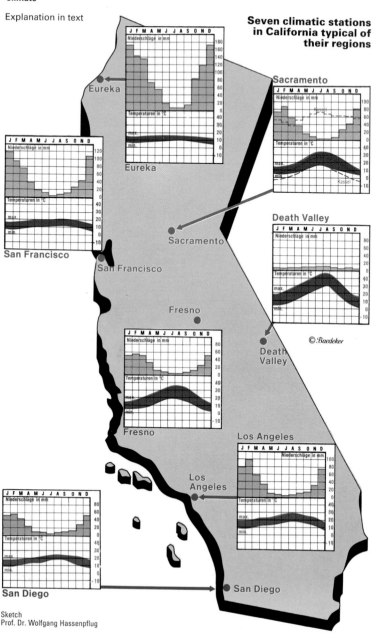

© Baedeker

Sketch
Prof. Dr. Wolfgang Hassenpflug

the side. The peculiarities of California's individual climatic zones are apparent when compared to the climatic conditions of Central Europe. There are even differences within the regions.

Coast Range

The climate is warm temperate with rain in winter and dry in summer, similar to the Mediterranean climate. In contrast, however, the maximum average summer temperatures seldom rise above 22° C; the highest summer temperatures are in September and, in Point Reyes, even in November. The graph shows that temperatures during the preceding months are not much lower. The diurnal and annual range of temperatures is quite small. In August the temperature in San Francisco is 12° at night and 18° at noon.

Climatic stations San Francisco and Eureka

This is due to the California Current which flows south. It brings cold water from sub-Arctic latitudes and at the same time stirs up the cold deep water off the coast. The centre of this cold water zone lies north of San Francisco. In August temperatures of 11° are recorded, almost 7° lower than in the open sea far off the coast. To the north as far as the Oregon coast the temperatures reach 17° and 18° C at the Mexican border. In winter the water temperature graduates from 16° at the Mexican border to 10° at the border with Oregon. The prevailing west winds (sea winds) in summer cool the damp sea air above the cold water. Fog regularly forms as far as the southern outskirts of San Francisco, drifting inland and hardly rising above 500 m.

During the dry summer the trees on the coast range absorb this dampness, so that the grass below them which would otherwise dry up stays green. The sea mist penetrates up to 15 miles/30 km inland to the north of San Francisco where the redwoods (Sequoia sempervirens) grow.

In autumn the sea breezes diminish and mainland temperatures are lower causing the mists to be less frequent.

Above the mist the air is normally warmer and drier. Point Reyes on the coast has an average July temperature of 12° C, compared with nearby Mount Tamalpais (2376 ft/724 m). 19.6° C Relative humidity in Point Reyes in July is 90%, in Tamalpais 39%. From June to September it is on average 4° C warmer on Mount Tamalpais than in San Francisco. If the temperature difference between the two stations is more than 4° by morning then mist will probably form on the coast in the afternoon.

Storms are extremely rare; it is said that an earthquake is more probable than a storm.

A comparison of the San Francisco and Eureka stations illustrates the regular variations from north to south. Towards the south amounts of precipitation and the number of days of rainfall decrease (975 mm on 118 days in Eureka; 529 mm on 67 days in San Francisco). Temperature and hours of sunshine increase (average annual temperature in Eureka 11.3° C, in San Francisco 13.8°C; hours of sunshine 2198 and 2959 respectively). North of Eureka the winter precipitation levels increase further, the climate is maritime with very mild winters and summers which are only moderately warm and dry.

Sierra Nevada

The mountain climate of the Sierra Nevada in common with the low lying areas is marked by maximum precipitation in winter, but because of the altitude (over 4000 m) it falls mostly as snow (hence its name!). At Tamarack station (8000 ft/2438 m) for five months the average temperature is below freezing and 88% of the precipitation of 1314 mm falls as snow. This area gets the most snow in the USA (over 6 m), providing the basis for extensive winter sports, e.g. Squaw Valley (Olympic Games 1960). Despite the high snowfall there is a lot of fine weather, mostly of over a week's duration, 40% of winter days and 47% of spring days.

No climatic station

Inyo County: "Land of eternal sun"   *and "Death Valley"*

In summer the snow virtually disappears. The snowfalls of the Sierra Nevada are more important than the precipitation of the Coastal Range in providing the source of California's water supply, especially that of Southern California. In nearly all the valleys on its western slopes dams have been constructed. The Sequoia gigantea grows at an altitude of 2200 m; at 3000 m the forest gives way to sub-alpine meadows.

Southern California

Southern California is considerably warmer and drier than Central California. In Los Angeles the annual precipitation is lower and less frequent than in San Francisco (373 mm on 37 days). Lowest night temperatures are somewhat higher than in San Francisco and the highest daytime temperatures are much higher; at 3284 hours annually the amount of sunshine is 300 hours greater than in San Francisco.

Climatic stations Los Angeles and San Diego

Towards the south it gets progressively drier. Los Angeles has a Mediterranean type climate, whereas San Diego has a prairie climate. The overall higher temperatures mean that in the Salton depression at the southern state boundary even the winters are mild.

The dry climate and clear air made Los Angeles the ideal location at the beginning of the century for the Hollywood film studios, as filming could nearly always take place outdoors. Since then, however, the quality of the air has very much deteriorated. Smog forms when warm air from the Mojave Desert meets the cool sea air. As soon as the lowest level of warm air drops to 500 m in the Los Angeles basin it prevents the movement of air. Even when the light wind off the land blows the polluted air partly out to sea at night, it usually returns again in the morning with the sea breeze.

Usually, and ideally, the wind in Los Angeles blows from the west; a light

◀ *Morning mist over the Golden Gate*

Redwoods

Fan palm

"Teddy-bear" Cholla

Joshua tree

sea breeze brings cooling air into the city. Occasionally, however, the wind changes direction. Winds from the south-east not only bring the danger of fog but also of heatwaves. Coming from the hot desert across the Santa Ana mountains they introduce oppressively hot air into the city. Then the temperatures can exceed 40° C (as recently as April 1989) and are higher than in Death Valley.

Mojave Desert

In the interior or Southern California a veritable hot desert climate prevails owing to its southerly location. Extreme temperatures are reached in the lee of the Sierra Nevada and in the lowest locations in Death Valley (up to 86 m below sea level). The distance from the Pacific and the drop in relative humidity associated with falling air lead to only relatively low and very irregular precipitation levels (average 41 mm annually on 9 days and 334 cloudless days). Heavy rain of more than 10 mm can fall suddenly in any month and leave furrows on the land which remain for years or even decades. The aridity gives rise to great discrepancies in daily and annual temperatures. The highest air temperature on earth was recorded here on July 10th 1913 – 56.7° C (a disputed rival measurement of 58° was taken in Libya in 1922).

Climatic stations Greenland Ranch, Death Valley

The average maximum summer temperatures exceed 45° C. In contrast in winter there are frequent temporary but heavy night frosts, while the average night temperatures do not fall below 3° C.

The extreme conditions of this desert climate make it absolutely essential that adequate clothing is worn (protection against the sun and the cold) and that water supplies are carried. Even without feeling thirsty the human body requires so much water in dry air and high temperatures that a lack of it can quickly lead to collapse.

Flora and Fauna

Thanks to its many natural resources California has a rich panoply of animal and plant life which is spread throughout the various climatic zones and which varies according to the amounts of rainfall.

General

Flora

Despite large areas having been cleared in earlier times, two thirds of California remains forested. There are still considerable tracts of virgin wilderness which are officially protected. The Great Californian Valley between the two mountain ranges belongs to the vegetation zone designated as prairie. However, these fertile valleys were extensively converted for cultivation and are now among the most productive areas of fruit, vegetable and wine producing areas in the USA.

Differences of habitat

The arid deserts of Southern California have primarily a flora with machia-like scleophyllous scrub (chaparral) as a typical example.

Some of its native species of trees, especially the giants (see "Redwood Highway"), have made California world-famous. The fan-palm or Washington filifera, growing exclusively in the south of the state, is one of the 1200 species of palm in the world. In the numerous coniferous forests there are several common indigenous varieties of fir and pine, as well as the famous Monterey pine in and around Monterey, the Torrey pine, found only in San Diego County especially in La Jola, and the ancient gnarled bristlecones in upland areas. Apart from the Joshua Tree National Monument in the Mojave Desert, this indigenous tree is also found in parts of Arizona, Nevada and Utah.

Trees

In addition, most other trees that exist in the world thrive here, especially in

Cormorants at Point Lobos

the northern mountain area. Significant stands of eucalyptus which originated in Australia are to be found, and the oak in at least a dozen of its various varieties is so widespread that its Spanish name "poble" has persisted in over 130 place names.

Other commonly found arboreal species include cedar, cypress, juniper, poplar and willow.

Desert vegetation

Approximately one quarter of California is covered by the Southern Desert. In the barren, sometimes wildly romantic strips of land such as Death Valley National Monument, only creosote bushes thrive in patches, their poisonous roots killing all surrounding vegetation which might compete for the minute quantities of life-giving water.

Cacti are indigenous and numerous in the desert, conserving water in their stems and leaves. Most cacti belong to the opuntia family. There are nine distinct types of cholla, one of which, the snake cholla, is found only between San Diego and the Mexican border. One species of opuntia is the platyopuntia, to which belong the nine varieties of prickly pear; these have blossom in many colours following a wet winter, and their fruit is highly prized.

Fauna

Mammals

The grey or grizzly bear, the emblem on the state flag, has been extinct in California since the beginning of the twenties. Much of the land has been enclosed by man, leaving little space for the vast territory which is a precondition for the grizzly's existence. However, his smaller relative, the chiefly plant-eating black bear, is to be found in the Sierra Nevada between Siskiyou and Kern County.

The coyote, another mammal which played an important role in Indian mythology, is widespread all over the state and can be hunted throughout the year. The pronghorned antelope, living in the mountains of the north,

"El Capitan"; rock mass in the Yosemite National Park

was almost extinct ten years ago but now numbers about 5000 thanks to a hunting ban. Elk, another species threatened with extinction but now protected, can also be found here. Raccoons, badgers, hares, foxes, otters, oppossum and numerous species of squirrel are common. The wolf appears to have become extinct in California.

Of the many golden eagles which must have existed here in past times, as many place names and geographical references suggest, only a few remain today; the condor can only be seen in the zoos of San Diego and Los Angeles. Nevertheless wild ducks, jays, ptarmigans, owls, quails, herons and many other birds are everywhere.

There are large numbers of sea birds and waders on the Californian beaches and in the bays, lagoons and estuaries. Several types of seagulls, pelicans, cormorants (especially on Point Lobos), black-tailed godwits, avocets, terns, redshanks, pondskaters and oystercatchers are the most notable.

Birds

The varieties of fish in Californian waters include sole, perch, salmon, halibut, cod, mackerel, tuna, shark, sea and river trout, pike and marlin. The sea holds other delicacies, such as the clawless Californian lobster and the oysters in the beds of Moro Bay, Point Reyes and Humboldt Bay. In San Francisco Bay oyster fishing had to be abandoned some 50 years ago because of the polluted water. Abalone mussels, with their mother-of-pearl shells, are found in southern waters. These large molluscs are an expensive gastronomic delicacy.

Fish

National Parks and similar areas

The extensive exploitation of the past soon had negative consequences. In the USA the necessity to conserve at least parts of the natural environment from further destruction was realised earlier than in other countries. In the

General

**National Parks
and similar
Institutions in
California**

1 Redwood
   National
   Park
2 Lava Beds
   National
   Monument
3 Shasta National
   Recreation
   Area
4 Trinity National
   Recreation
   Area
5 Whiskeytown
   National
   Recreation Area
6 Humboldt Red-
   woods State
   Park
7 Lassen Volca-
   nic National
   Park
8 Point Reyes
   National Sea-
   shore Park
9 Muir Woods
   National
   Monument
10 Golden Gate
   National
   Recreation
   Area
11 Yosemite
   National
   Park
12 Devils Postpile
   National
   Monument
13 Pinnacles
   National
   Monument
14 Kings Canyon
   National Park
15 Sequoia
   National Park
16 Death Valley
   National
   Monument
17 Santa Monica
   Mountains
   National
   Recreation
   Area
18 Channel Islands
   National Park
19 Cabrillo
   National
   Monument
20 Anza-Borrego
   Desert State
   Park
21 Joshua Tree
   National
   Monument

Crescent City

Eureka

Redding

Red Bluff

Santa
Rosa

Sacramento

Oakland

San Francisco

San Jose

Merced

Salinas

Fresno

Bishop

San Luis
Obispo

Bakersfield

Mojave

Santa
Barbara

Barstow

**Los
Angeles**

San Bernardino

Riverside

**San
Diego**

© *Baedeker*

face of great resistance this idea led to the establishment of extensive areas of protected countryside, the so-called National Parks, where typical regions of outstanding beauty are preserved in their original form.

The National Park Service is responsible to the State Department of External Affairs and adminsters all protected areas, nature monuments, places of historical interest and long-distance footpaths.

National Park Service

In California there are six parks under the auspices of this department. In order of their establishment these are: Yosemite (1890), Sequoia (1890), Lassen Volcanic (1916), Kings Canyon (1940), Redwood (1968) and Channel Island (1980).

The same department also controls eight so-called National Monuments: Muir Woods (1908), Devil's Postpile (1911), Cabrillo (1913), Lava Beds (1925), Death Valley (1933), Joshua Tree (1936). In addition there are: Port Reyes National Seashore (1962), three national recreation areas – Golden Gate, Santa Monica Mountains and Whiskey-town Trinity Shasta – and six national wild and scenic rivers – American River, Eel River, Feather River, Klamath River, Smith River and Trinity River.

There are also 20 national wildlife refuges in California controlled by the Federal Government, covering a million hectares (2471 million acres), 18 national forests with a total area of nine million hectares (22,240 million acres) and two so-called national resource lands – Kings Range in the north-west and Owens Valley in the south-east.

The various Indian reserves have been taken out of the control of the State of California and are now the responsibility of the Indian Affairs Bureau of the State Department. The largest, with an area of approximately 35,000 hectares (86,485 acres) is that of the Hoopa Indians in Humboldt County in the north-east of the state.

Indian Affairs Bureau

Population

California's population consists of many races and nationalities. During the 1840s, when California became one of the American states, it was inhabited by approximately 100,000 Indians and about 14,000 others. The gold rush which was soon to follow brought an influx of people from many different countries; towns such as Sacramento and San Francisco experienced a real population explosion, while the gold towns were soon abandoned after the gold seams were exhausted and became genuine ghost towns. In the following years the European settlers were joined by Blacks, Mexicans, Chinese, Japanese, Koreans and more recently other Asians such as Vietnamese and Cambodeans.

"Melting pot"

Indians are supposed to have lived on California soil over 7000 years ago. The first mission stations were founded to convert the pagan inhabitants, consisting of about 300,000 Indians of whom around one sixth went over to Christianity. Maltreatment and torture by the whites together with imported disease reduced their numbers to almost 58,000. By 1913 the decimation of the Indian population had reached its peak. There were still about 13,000 distributed among a multiplicity of tribes. With the establishment of Indian reserves and increasing state protection their numbers increased gradually; in 1928 there were 23,000, in 1970 91,000 and 200,000 by 1980 when the last census took place. This is still less than 1% of the total population and only about one fifth live in reserves. Numerous places and rivers in California have Indian names.

Indians

The first Chinese arrived in California around 1850. They were engaged in gold-mining and treated almost like slaves by their employers. In former gold-mining towns such as Dutch Flat or Weaverville, which are relatively unknown today, as many as 2000 Chinese were employed. Later thousands worked on building the trans-continental railway line (for a dollar a day). By 1875 50,000 Chinese were living in the Chinese quarter of San Francisco.

Chinese

Population

Californian faces

Japanese

The Japanese first came to America in 1868, as emigration was not allowed before then. In 1942 they were interned, including those born in the USA, the so-called Nisei, and those with Japanese citizenship. Not until 1988 were they awarded damages from the US government for the injustice they suffered.

Other Asians

About 170,000 Vietnamese and Cambodians emigrated to California at the end of the Vietnam War (1975) and live exclusively in and around Los Angeles. Koreans, some of whom came to California at the beginning of the 20th century, arrived in greater numbers following the Korean War and then again after 1976; their total number is estimated at 150,000, of whom the majority live in Los Angeles.

Blacks

Before 1850 there were at the most 1000 Blacks in California, and even at the beginning of the 20th century there were only about 11,000. In 1920 their numbers rose to 38,000, 20 years later to 124,000 and by 1950 to 462,000. Another 20 years later 1,400,000 were counted, and in the last population census in 1980 there were about 1,819,000. They formed 7.7% of the total population, while the Asians constituted 5%.

The largest proportion of the non Anglo-Saxon population consists of the Mexicans with about 19%; in 1980 there were around 4½ million, of whom about one quarter were born outside the USA. The number of Mexicans in the cities is as follows: 816,000 in Los Angeles, 140,000 in San Jose, 130,000 in San Diego and 83,000 in San Francisco.

Mexicans

In 1985 the total population of California was estimated at 26,365,000, of whom less than half (45%) were born in the state. A further increase in population to over 28 million is anticipated in the next census in 1990; the continued annual increase of more than 400,000 people shows that the attraction of California for Americans from the other 49 states and from abroad remains undiminished.

Population growth

California has been the most populated state since 1963 when it overtook New York. While it had only 5 million inhabitants in 1930, that is about two thirds of the population of New York City, it reached 9 million after the Second World War and has since risen to over 25 million. The growth is primarily due to immigrants from other parts of the USA who were attracted by the prosperous economy and the "eternal spring" of the coastal area. Los Angeles and San Diego – the two cities with a population of over one million – and their suburbs were the most popular areas and experienced tremendous growth. By 1982 Los Angeles has become the second largest city in the United States, overtaking Chicago which had been second since 1890.

Religion and Cults

Christianity – or more precisely Catholicism – was introduced into California by the Spanish missionaries and spread widely following the first wave of immigrants with the 1848 Gold Rush. The fortune hunters were accompanied into the promised land by Protestant priests – Baptists, Congregationalists, Methodists and Presbyterians. By 1900 almost half the population were adherents of the Christian faith.

Denominations

Despite the rise of various sects at the beginning of the 20th c. the traditional churches remained the dominant force. In 1980 they had more than eight million members: 3,322,117 Protestants, the Mormons (Church of Jesus Christ of Latter Day Saints) having the largest number, followed by the Baptists, Methodists and Presbyterians. In 1984 almost 5½ million belonged to the Roman Catholic Church.

The Jewish population of 792,515, of whom some two-thirds live in the metropolis of Los Angeles, is the second largest in the USA, and this is also true of the Catholics.

As well as the expansion of the established Churches, the last one and a half centuries has seen the growth of every possible type of cult in California – perhaps for the same reasons which make the state so attractive to other Americans and foreigners: the hope of an easier and more fulfilled life. When demagogues promise the new arrivals heaven on earth under the guise of alternative religions, they are more likely to be believed here than in other parts of the country. The fact that most of these movements are only short-lived has not deterred the introduction of new cults.

Cults

Most of these cults were only of interest to the sociologist. The most notable were the Theosophists, led by Anny Besant and Katherine Tingley, who founded a secret society in Point Lorna, the Canadian Aimee Semple McPherson, whose Angelus Temple in Los Angeles had many adherents, and more recently Jim Jones, whose People's Temple, first in Ukiah and subsequently in San Francisco, abused the blind faith of thousands of followers, driving about 900 of them to commit mass suicide in Guayana in 1978.

Theosophists, Angelus and People's Temple

Los Angeles: a soaring city

Utopian and Communist communities

There has been no shortage of Utopian societies in California. One of the first was founded in Anaheim by the Polish author Henryk Sienkiewicz and the actress Helena Modjeska, but it disintegrated in 1878 after only two years. Sienkiewicz returned to Poland while Modjeska began a successful stage career. A mountain close to Anaheim and an island off the coast of Newport are named after her.

Socialist and communist communities also had a following in California but lasted only a short time. Among them were the Kaweah Cooperative Commonwealth (1885–1892), near the present-day Sequoia National Park and the Llano-del Rio (plain by a stream) Commune (1914–1918), between the Mojave Desert and the San Gabriel Mountains, which in its heyday had 900 members.

Beat and Hippy Movement

In 1956 the Beat movement started in San Francisco, followed a few years later by the Hippies. Both movements sought happiness through alcohol and drugs, and rejected the establishment completely. Allan Ginsberg, Jack Kerouac and Lawrence Ferlinghetti were poets of the Beat generation, but the Hippies left behind no such talent. With the grisly murders of the rich and famous by the Manson family (originally with 26 members, 20 of them women) in 1969, the movement degenerated into an anti-social lifestyle without any ideals. The San Francisco suburb of Haight-Ashbury, which was home to the Hippies 20 years ago, has again become a very middle-class area.

Bodybuilding

This decidedly harmless cult which began in California has gradually spread over the whole of the country. Male and female bodybuilders alike, for whom obsessive physical training often degenerates into exhibitionism, are active all over California. In particular these muscle-men and women frequent the beaches of central and southern California, where the sun nearly always shines, and can even be seen demonstrating their prowess in front of the Mission Church at Santa Barbara.

Economy

Industry

About half of California's gross national product comes from industry. The most important sectors are aerospace, electronics, metallurgy and chemicals, with food-processing (preserves and deep-frozen food) overlapping both agriculture and industry. The production of television and cinematic films is concentrated on Hollywood. Tourism is of increasing importance; the number of visitors to California each year from other states of the USA and from abroad can be counted in millions. Both the state and individual towns actively promote tourism.

General

The origins of the aerospace industry go back to the time before the First World War, when pilots such as Glenn Martin, Allan Lockheed (actually Loughead), Donald Douglas and John K. Northrop founded small firms bearing their own names. With the exception of Martin, who settled in Baltimore, the remaining pioneers remained loyal to California and others joined them. In 1939 no more than 20,000 people were employed in the industry, but this number increased tenfold over the following four years. After the Second World War a slump set in, which, however, was soon overcome owing to the increase in civilian air traffic.

Since then the Californian aerospace industry has inexorably expanded, not least because it has received almost a quarter of government armaments contracts. This industry now employs more than 650,000 people. The Californian firm of McDonnell-Douglas has become within the space of a few decades the world's leading aircraft manufacturer.

Aerospace Industry

Whereas the aircraft industry is concentrated in southern California, the newer electronics industry has developed almost exclusively in Silicon Valley, in the region between Palo Alto and San Jose, to the south of San Francisco. Although the first of the firms had sprung up by 1920, the real boom did not begin until after the Second World War. In addition to major concerns, such as Hewlett-Packard and Fisher, there are countless smaller firms specialising in the latest electronic developments.

The concentration of these firms in a relatively restricted space is due to the proximity of Stanford University, where Frederick E. Terman, who was responsible for the electronics department, placed engineers trained by him to combine research and its practical application. He supported the creation of Stanford Industrial Park on sites owned by the university, where factories could be built near the university laboratories. Terman died in 1982 but he was able to witness the results of his endeavours.

Electronics Industry: Silicon Valley

The oil industry's modest beginnings date back to just after 1860 when the first oil was found in Ojay Valley. It really expanded with the discovery of oil in several parts of the state towards the end of the 19th century. The first oil in Los Angeles was found in 1892, soon followed by oil fields in Santa Barbara, in Ventura, Kings and Kern County. From four million barrels in 1900 the annual quota rose to 105 million barrels in 1920. Oil was also discovered off the coast in the Pacific Ocean, especially around the Channel Islands. But since large quantities of oil were washed up on the coast from an accident in 1969, an influential ecological movement has been formed which has been successful in campaigning against further drilling for oil. As a result of this the planned drillings around the coast of Mendocino and Fort Bragg have been postponed.

Large quantities of natural gas, found in all oil fields and also on its own (a distinction is made between "wet" and "dry" natural gas), are obtained in California but not sufficient for domestic demand, so that additional gas has to be imported from Texas and Canada.

Oil Industry

Apart from the almost exhausted gold reserves there are other minerals

Minerals

Fruit in abundance

important to industrial processes. These are borax, especially in Death Valley, gypsum, molybdenum, tungsten, antimony, lead, manganese, mercury and potash. Iron and copper are scarce.

Prosperity

The state of California has the highest gross national product in the USA, and if it were an independent country it would be in sixth position in the world after the USA, the Soviet Union, Japan, West Germany and Great Britain.

Agriculture

Importance

Agriculture owes its importance to the fertile soils and favourable climatic conditions widespread throughout the state. Some statistics illustrate this: in 1988 about 78,000 farms earned more than 16 thousand million dollars. No less than 250 different agricultural products are grown, more than in any other state. Almost half of the fruit and vegetables in the US comes from California, which is also the leading producer of cotton, eggs and greenhouse vegetables.

Fruit and Vegetable produce

With the exception of coffee and bananas every conceivable type of fruit and vegetable is grown here, and wheat production is only surpassed by the Mid-West states.

Apples, apricots, cherries, dates, figs, grapes, melons, nectarines, nuts, peaches, pears, plums and especially citrus fruit are harvested in almost wasteful quantities. Tomatoes are the most important vegetables, followed by asparagus, carrots, lettuce, cauliflower, sprouts, spinach and broccoli.

Flowers

The warm climate is conducive to horticulture with the result that California is the main area of flower-growing in the country. The chief areas of cultivation are the counties of Monterey and Santa Clara, the valleys north of Santa Barbara and Orange, Ventura and San Diego counties. Until about

60 years ago France was the main supplier of seeds to the USA. Lompoc in Santa Barbara County has now taken over this position.

Cultivated areas

Agriculture is concentrated in Imperial Valley, but from the economic viewpoint equally as important as fruit and vegetable production (especially oranges and lemons) is the cotton-growing industry in San Joaquin Valley. Almost the total US production of sultanas, dates, figs, olives and walnuts comes from the south. Peaches, almonds, cherries and apricots are produced in the north. Timber production is of only limited importance today, whereas the fishing industry remains buoyant.
Around 80% of all American wines originate in California. Chief growing areas include the Nappa and Sonoma Valleys north of San Francisco, Santa Clara and Joaquin Valley, the region around Monterey, and Cucamonga south of San Francisco. There are also vineyards further east of Los Angeles and further south in the region of Temecula, halfway between Los Angeles and San Diego. There are some 400 wine-producing concerns in the USA.

Irrigation

Water supply is of concern to agriculture, as rainfall has been unusually low in recent years. Californian agriculture needs 80% of all water which, because of the dry summers, has to be imported from further afield. The cotton planters are accused of using too much water for a product for which there is little demand worldwide. However, California has succeeded in recent years in producing new markets for its products in Japan.

Water supply

Water reserves

The very existence of California with its big cities and agriculture depends upon an adequate water supply. One problem is caused by the northern part of the state with most of the rivers and lakes having a small percentage of the population, whilst the majority of the population is concentrated in the desert areas of the south. In other words 70% of the water supply is in areas which are thinly populated, whereas 80% of the water is required by the south. Redirecting water from the north to the south is no solution owing to the occasional extremely low amounts of rain and snow in the north. This was the case in 1976 and 1977 and again a decade later in 1987 and 1988. It is only a small consolation that in 1978 and 1979 so much rain fell that drought-stricken Los Angeles was threatened with flooding! San Francisco, which introduced water-rationing in May 1988 in anticipation of a hot summer, "helped itself" to water from Hetch-Hetchy Valley at the beginning of the century. Los Angeles built a 250-m-long aqueduct to direct water south from the Owens River.

Hoover Dam

With the rapid growth of Los Angeles the water from the Owens River no longer sufficed. A second aqueduct, not quite so long, was built from Colorado, using water belonging to the neighbouring state of Arizona which finally agreed to the building of the Hoover Dam for electricity production, flood control and irrigation. The "All American Canal" irrigated the Imperial and Coachella Valleys. Other rivers which have been tapped for the south's water include the Sacramento, Joaquin, McCloud, Pit, Feather and Stanislaus rivers. Hundreds of dams and reservoirs have been built and new water projects are constantly being considered to appease the insatiable thirst of Southern California.

Water projects

Massive amounts of money have been invested in these water projects to provide at any cost all taxpayers of Southern California with cheap water. The major investor is the Federal Government with the state also involved. The state has to strike a balance between the arid but rich and powerful south and the well-watered but under-populated north. Finally it is not only the cities which benefit from this, as 80% of the water required is used in cattle rearing and agriculture which is concentrated in the south.

Rush-hour in Los Angeles

Traffic

Age of the car

Nothing symbolises the life of the Californian better than the automobile, without which the steady economic prosperity of the state would have been inconceivable. On the other hand it has meant that the development of a good public-transport network was neglected in the built-up cities. There are no underground railways, except in San Francisco, and even here only five stations link the city centre with the network to Oakland, Berkeley and other nearby towns. Back in the twenties Los Angeles planned the construction of an underground railway, yet has never realised the plan, and not until the last decade of this century will an underground railway, at present under construction, open in San Fernando Valley.

Los Angeles

Los Angeles is a typical example of a city which developed during the age of the motor vehicle. Automobile clubs, which were founded at the beginning of the 20th century encouraged the development of roads, with the result that two decades later one in three of the population was a car owner. In 1950 three million cars were registered in the state, in the following 30 years this number quadrupled to reach 13.3 million. In 1982 17 million of California's population of 25 million had driving licences, a proportion which no other state even approaches.

Freeways

The dramatic rise in car ownership led to the development of the highways and so-called "freeways", which are toll-free throughout the state. California has over 180,000 miles of metalled roads, of which almost 39,000 miles were built by the government and 15,000 by the state. The first enormous highway was not constructed until 1940; this is the Pasadena freeway from Los Angeles to Pasadena, with fly-overs instead of intersections. Nowadays such dense road networks can be found everywhere, especially on the approaches to large cities, with as many as twelve lanes in each direction, as in Los Angeles.

The most important roads are:

No. 1 along the coast from Eureka to San Juan Capistrano;
No. 5 from the Oregon border via Los Angeles and San Diego to the Mexican frontier;
No. 10 from Santa Monica via Indio and Blythe to the border with Arizona;
No. 15 between San Diego and Las Vegas (Nevada) via San Bernadino and Barstow;
No. 80 from San Francisco via Sacramento to Reno (Nevada) and thence to the east coast of the USA;
No. 101 from the Oregon border via Eureka, San Francisco, San Jose, San Luis Obispo and Santa Barbara to Los Angeles;
No. 280 from San Bruno connects with No. 101 at San José, it is an award-winning scenic highway.
No. 395 from San Bernadino via Lone Pine and Bishop past the Yosemite National Park to Carson City (Nevada).

Before 1973 low fuel prices made the automobile not only the most convenient but also the cheapest form of transport. Since then increased prices have not hindered the unrestrained increase in car ownership. Even in recent years the environmentalists' strong objections that cars are the principal contributors to smog have had little impact. The speed limit on motorways (in some places 65 miles/100 km per hour, generally 55 miles/83 km per hour) has helped to restrict pollution.

History

1510	The name "California" meaning "land of fantasy" appears for the first time in "Las Sergas de Esplandián", a work by the Spaniard Garcí Ordóñez de Montalvo.
1533	Fortún Jiménez discovers the peninsula of Baja California on behalf of Hernando Cortes.
1540	Hernando de Alarcón discovers the Colorado River and is the first white man to set foot on Alta California, which today is the Federal State of California.
1542	Juan Rodriguez Cabrillo is the first to enter San Diego Bay and discovers the offshore islands.
1579	Sir Francis Drake lands his ship the "Golden Hind" in an unidentified harbour, probably north of present-day San Francisco and claims the country for Queen Elizabeth I as Nova Albion.
1601	Sebastian Vizcaíno sails along the coast and lands where San Diego, San Pedro and Monterey Bay are situated today.
1613	Juan Torquemada believes that California is an island.
1697	The Jesuit Juan Maria Salvatierra founds the first mission station in Baja California.
1701	The Jesuit Eusebio Francisco Kino is the first to cross the Colorado and reach Alta California.
1769	The Spanish government replaces the Jesuits with Franciscans.
1769	Junípero Serra, the chief missionary in Alta California, founds the first of Alta California's 21 missions in San Diego.
1770	Founding of the San Carlos Mission in Monterey. Pedro Fages becomes the first "Commandante militar" and "gobernante" of the two Californias.
1775	Monterey is proclaimed the capital of Alta California.
1776	Founding of the mission stations Dolores (in what was later San Francisco) and San Juan Capistrano. At the head of a Mexican overland expedition Bautista de Anza reaches the area of San Francisco.
1781	Los Angeles is established by Felipe de Neva as El Pueblo de Nuestro Señora de la Reine de Los Angeles de Porciúncula with 44 settlers.
1784	Serra dies and Francesco Paulo is named as head of the mission stations in Alta California, but only one year later he is succeeded by Fermín Francisco de Lasuén who remains in charge until his death in 1803.
1786	Founding of the Santa Barbara Mission, followed one year later by the mission La Purísima Concepción at Lompoc.
1791	Mission stations are founded at Santa Cruz and Soledad. The English captain George Vancouver arrives on the first of four journeys to California to chart a map of the coast.

Covered wagons en route to the West

Four mission stations – San José, San Juan Bautista, San Miguel Arcangel   1797
and San Fernando Rey de España – are founded, followed the next year by
the San Luis Rey de Francia Mission.

Estevan Tapis is the new head of the mission stations. An earthquake   1803
destroys the San Diego Mission.

California is divided into two provinces: Alta California and Baja California.   1804
José Joaquin de Arrillaga is the first governor of Alta California

The Russian Nikolai Petrovich Rezanow, founder of the Russian-American   1806
Company, sails into the bay of San Francisco, becomes engaged for politi-
cal reasons to the 16-year-old daughter of the second governor, José Dario
Arguella, but dies in Siberia on the return journey to St Petersburg.

Russians begin to settle at Bodega Bay.   1809

Four mission stations, Santa Barbara, La Puísima Concepcíon, San Buen-   1812
ventura and San Juan Capistrano, are destroyed by an earthquake; the
Russians establish the fortified trading post of Fort Ross.

John Gilroy is the first non-Spaniard to settle in California.   1814

A Russian expeditionary fleet under the command of a German, Otto von   1816
Kotzebue, spends a month in San Francisco Bay; among those on board is
Adelbert von Chamisso, who described his Californian experiences in
"Reise um die Welt" (Journey around the World; 1836).

The non-Indian population is estimated to be around 3500, 650 of whom   1820
live in Los Angeles.

Gold diggers working by a river

1822	Mexico gains independence from Spain; Emperor Agustin I proclaims Alta California to be a province of the Mexican Empire.
1823	The last of 21 mission stations, San Francisco Solano, is founded in Sonoma.
1827	Jehedia S. Smith, leading a group of trappers, is the first white man to conquer the peaks of the Sierra Nevada.
1833	Governor José Figueroa proclaims the secularisation of the mission stations.
1838	Rosalia Leese is the first white child to be born in what is to become San Francisco.
1839	Johann August Sutter (later calling himself John Augustus Sutter) arrives in California from Germany, becomes a Mexican citizen and receives from the governor Juan Bautista Alvarado a vast territory at the confluence of the American and Sacramento Rivers, which he names Nueva Helvetia. He establishes a fort here and buys
1841	Fort Ross from the Russians, thereby ending the Russian attempt to colonize California.
1844	Thomas Oliver Larkin is named first US consul of Alta California.
1845	Pio Pico, the first native born governor, becomes the last Mexican governor of California.
1846	On May 13th war breaks out between Mexico and the USA; from June 10th to July 9th California is a republic under the flag of the bear. War ends in

1847. Captain George Stock and John Charles Frémont conquer Los Angeles; the US flag is raised over Yerba Buena ("good pasture") and its name is changed to San Francisco, with Washington A. Bartlett as the first American "alcalde" (mayor). California becomes one of the United States of America.

1848

The loss of California is recognised by Mexico in the Treaty of Guadalupe Hildalgo. James W. Marshall, a partner of Sutter, discovers gold during the construction of a sawmill near Coloma on the southern fork of the American River.

1849/1850

The state constitution is ratified in 1849 and on September 9th 1850 California is accepted as the 23rd state of the Union. Its first capital is San José. The population of the new state is estimated at 92,597; in Los Angeles there are 1611 inhabitants, while San Francisco, attracting thousands of golddiggers, has a population of 24,000.

1851

The capital is transferred to Vallejo. The first universities are founded: Santa Clara and the University of the Pacific in San Jose.

1852

The population of the state reaches 255,000.

1853

Benicia, only founded in 1847, becomes the third capital within a year. Foundation of the Californian Academy of Sciences. Opening of San Quentin Prison.

1854

Sacramento is the fourth and final capital of California.

1857

The first overland stagecoaches arrive in San Diego.

1859

Discovery of the Comstock Lode, an area about 2 miles/3 km wide and not quite 62 miles/100 km in length near Virginia City, abundant in gold and silver deposits.

1860

The population rises to almost 360,000 (52,802 in San Francisco, 4385 in Los Angeles).

1862

Transcontinental telegraph line from New York to San Francisco is finished.

1867

Outbreak of anti-Chinese demonstrations in San Francisco.

1868

University of California is founded. Naturalist John Muir arrives in California.

1869

Central Pacific and Union Pacific railway lines meet at Promontory Point (Utah), thereby establishing transcontinental transport between the east and west coasts.

1870

State population is now 560,000; 150,000 of whom live in San Francisco but only 5700 in Los Angeles.

1871

Serious anti-Chinese disturbances in Los Angeles. California Historical Society and San Francisco Art Institute are founded.

1873

First of the cable-cars comes into service in San Francisco.

1879

The second meeting of the Constitutional Assembly. Foundation of the University of Southern California in Los Angeles. Tennis is introduced into California.

1880

State population rises to 865,000; 234,000 live in San Francisco and 11,200 in Los Angeles.

History

1885	The Santa Fe Railroad reaches Los Angeles. Competition between railway companies leads to price cuts, attracting many people to the south and causing real-estate sales to flourish.
1890	The population reaches 1,200,000; San Francisco is the largest city with 300,000 inhabitants, followed by Los Angeles with 50,000. Congress establishes the National Parks of Yosemite and Sequoia.
1891	Oil is discovered in Los Angeles. Opening of Stanford University in Palo Alto. Throop Institute, the forerunner of the California Institute of Technology, is founded in Pasadena.
1892	The Sierra Club is founded.
1893	Stephen M. White is the first federal senator born in California.
1900	Population of California reaches 1,485,053; 343,000 live in San Francisco, and Los Angeles exceeds 100,000 for the first time.
1903	The yellow poppy is declared the state flower; Chamisso gave it its scientific name "Eschscholtzia California" in honour of Johann Freidrich Eschscholtz, the doctor on the Kotzebue expedition (see 1816).
1906	Earthquake followed by fire destroys large areas of the city of San Francisco. Founding of the the Los Angeles suburb of Beverly Hills. First film studio comes into operation in Los Angeles.
1910	Population now numbers 2,377,549; almost a third live in San Francisco (416,912) and Los Angeles (319,198). First film studio in Hollywood comes into operation.
1915	Panama-Pacific International Exposition takes place in San Francisco. First trans-continental telephone conversation between San Francisco and New York.
1919	Founding of Hoover Institution in Palo Alto. Hearst begins to build his castle in San Simeon.
1920	For the first time the population of Los Angeles (576,673) exceeds that of San Francisco (506,676); total population is 3,426,861.
1921	Huge oil reserves are discovered at Signal Hill, Long Beach.
1922	The Hollywood Bowl is opened.
1924	First airmail letters sent from San Francisco to New York.
1925	Serious earthquake in Santa Barbara
1928	A regular air connection is established between San Francisco and Los Angeles.
1929	First Academy Award (to Emil Jannings and Janet Gaynor, and to the film "Wings").
1930	Population reaches 5,677,251, of whom 1.2 million live in Los Angeles and 634,000 in San Francisco.
1932	Olympic Games in Los Angeles.
1933	Earthquake hits Long Beach.

The Golden Gate Bridge in San Francisco is acclaimed at its opening as a new wonder of the world.	1935, 1936, 1937
Within a decade the population has increased by a million to 6,907,000; Los Angeles has 1,504,277 inhabitants and San Francisco 634,536. The Pasadena freeway, the first motorway in Los Angeles, is completed.	1940
Japanese submarines attack an oil field near Goleta. A detention camp is set up for Japanese nationals.	1942
The All American Canal providing irrigation for Imperial Valley is completed, and is extended to Coachella Valley in 1948.	1943
United Nations Organisation (UNO) founded in San Francisco.	1945
Population has risen to 10,586,223; Los Angeles 1,970,000 and San Francisco 775,000.	1950
"I love you California", a song by F.B. Silverwood (words) and A.F. Frankenstein (music) published in 1913, becomes the official state anthem.	1951
The redwood tree and the grey bear become new state emblems.	1953
Disneyland is opened at Anaheim.	1955
Approval is given for a water supply system to ensure provision of water throughout the state, and for the building of the Oroville Dam to begin.	1957
The move from New York by the Giants and the Dodgers means that California has the two leading baseball teams playing in one of the two main leagues.	1958
In ten years the population has increased by 50% to 15,717,000, with 2,480,000 living in Los Angeles and 740,000 in San Francisco.	1960
California overtakes New York state as the most populated state in the USA, with 17.3 million inhabitants. John Steinbeck is the first native Californian to receive the Nobel Prize for Literature.	1963
Serious disturbances in Watts, a suburb of Los Angeles predominantly inhabited by blacks.	1965
In Oakland Bobby Seale and Huey Newton found the militant Black Panther organisation; Eldridge Cleaver joins soon after its foundation and becomes its spokesman.	1966
Ronald Reagan is elected 33rd governor of the state and re-elected four years later.	1967
International attention is aroused by a series of murders committed by the Manson family who, on two consecutive days in Los Angeles, kill seven strangers.	1969
The ever increasing population reaches almost 20 million, with 2,809,000 inhabitants in Los Angeles and 715,000 in San Francisco. Indians occupy Alcatraz Island off San Francisco.	1970
San Fernando Valley is affected by a serious earthquake.	1971
In San Francisco the BART rapid transport system for local traffic is opened.	1972

1974	The Symbionese Liberation Army, an underground terrorist group, kidnaps Patty Hearst a student at the University of California in Berkeley. The granddaughter of the newspaper magnate William Randolph Hearst joins her kidnappers, participating in their crimes and, after being in hiding for a year and a half, is sentenced to seven years' imprisonment.
1977	Second year of low rainfall levels leads to a drought and water rationing in several regions of the state. Parliament reintroduces the death penalty.
1978	Floods and landfalls cause severe damage around Los Angeles. Voters decide on an addition to the constitution "Proposition 13" which restricts ground taxes and requires spending cuts in many counties and throughout the state.
1980	Population has risen to 23.6 million, a fivefold increase in 50 years.
1981	The state parliament passes a law to make all houses in the earthquake zone proof against future quakes.
1982	The "Peripheral Canal" is rejected in a referendum.
1984	23rd Olympic summer games in Los Angeles.
1987	According to the latest demographic census the Californian population will reach 33.5 million by the year 2000.
1988	Contrary to the Indians' wishes the Franciscan father Junípero Serra, who founded the first mission stations in the 18th c., is canonized; the Indians regard him as an oppressor of their forefathers. Many communities oppose further growth; the electors support about half the initiatives which are necessary for a referendum
1989	On October 17th the Bay of San Francisco is hit by the most severe earthquake (6.9 on the Richter scale) since 1906 (8.3 on the Richter scale) at 5.04 p.m. during the rush hour. It causes serious damage in San Francisco, Oakland, Santa Cruz and in Silicon Valley. The epicentre of the quake lies about 80 km south of San Francisco in the mountains between Santa Cruz and San José. Tremors are felt as far away as Nevada in the north and Los Angeles in the south. After being in the forefront of economic development for six years (1982–1988) California faces a recession and economic growth is expected to slow down over the coming years.

Serious earthquakes in California since the 19th century

(reading on the Richter scale given in brackets)

South California (7.2)	1812	Kern County (7.7)	1952
San Francisco (7.0)	1838	Eureka (6.6)	1954
South California (8.3)	1857	Borrego Mountain (6.4)	1968
Hayward (6.8)	1868	San Fernando (6.6)	1971
Owens Valley (8.0)	1872	Eureka (7.2)	1980
San Francisco (8.3)	1906	Coalinga (6.7)	1983
Santa Barbara (6.3)	1925	Whittier Narrows (5.9)	1987
Lompoc (7.5)	1927	Santa Cruz, San Francisco,	
Long Beach (6.3)	1933	Oakland (6.9)	1989
Imperial Valley (7.1)	1940		

Famous Personalities

The following alphabetical list of names consists predominantly of people connected with California through birth, residence, influence or death, who have achieved national, even international importance.

Note

Born in California, Adams became famous chiefly for his clear and sympathetic photographs of the Yosemite National Park and other protected areas, nearly all of which are in the west of the United States. Together with several books about the Sierra Nevada, the Californian desert and the National Parks, he also published photographic text-books and a book about the Nisei (the Japanese born in California). His photographs can be seen in nearly every museum in the US which has a photographic collection. Prints made by him fetch high prices at auction. He died in Monterey, not far from his last home in Carmel.

Anselm Adams
Photographer
(20. 2. 1902–
22. 4. 1984)

It is impossible to discuss the early theatre in America without mentioning Belasco – actor, producer, director, theatre owner and playwright. Born in San Francisco, he went as a child with his parents to Canada and then at 20 to New York to try his luck on Broadway. After a few difficult years he found success and played an active role in the American theatre for almost the next half-century. His distinctive style of direction was apparent even in his plays, two of which – "Madame Butterfly" and "The Girl of the Golden West" – formed the basis for the libretti of two of Puccini's operas. There is a theatre named after him in a side-street off Times Square in New York.

David Belasco
Theatre director
(25. 7. 1859–
14. 5. 1931)

Burbank was 26 when he came from Masssachusetts to California, where three of his brothers were already living. Influenced by the ideas of Darwin, he tried to grow new plants by cross-fertilisation. His experiments were so successful that he almost achieved mythical status in Santa Rosa, where he lived until his death. He succeeded in growing no less than 40 new varieties of plums and damsons, ten new berries, and new strains of tomatoes, peas, maize, roses, lilies and poppies. As well as his memoirs he wrote several books recording his successful work.

Luther Burbank
Botanist
(7. 3. 1849–
11. 4. 1926)

Whereas many famous Californians came from the north-east or the mid-west of the US to the "Golden State", the composer John Cage arrived from the other direction. He was a student at Pomona College (the town of the same name is situated in the outskirts of Los Angeles) and studied musical theory under Arnold Schönberg and Henry Cowell. Cage taught for a period at Mills College in Oakland. For decades he has been known as the "enfant terrible" of the contemporary music scene, which he continues to surprise with new and difficult compositions. His own piano concertos often give the impression of being "happenings". He has published numerous books on ballet and the theatre.

John Cage
Composer
(born 5. 9. 1912)

James J.Corbett, the first world heavyweight boxing champion (known as "Gentleman Jim"), began his career as a bank employee in San Francisco. He won his world title there in 1892; after his victory over John L.Sullivan he lost the title five years later to Bob Fitzsimmons. It is said that he never fought unfairly.

James J.Corbett
World champion
boxer
(1. 9. 1866–
18. 12. 1933)

Cowell's career soon took him from his birthplace of Mento Park near Palo Alto to the east, where he lived until his death in New York. His study of comparative musical theory at the University of Berlin from 1931 to 1932 gave him new inspiration for his individual compositions. He taught at several of the universities of California, including Stanford, Mills College and the University of California. He left behind a comprehensive collection

Henry Cowell
Composer
(11. 3. 1897–
10. 12. 1965)

Famous Personalities

Cecil B. DeMille

Walt Disney

Isadora Duncan

of works which contributed to his reputation of being distinctly avant-garde; they are difficult to perform and not much of his output has been published.

Alan Cranston
Politician
(born 19. 6. 1924)

Born in Pala Alto, Alan Cranston is one of the two men who have represented California in the Senate in Washington since 1949. He attended Stanford University, became involved in the real estate business shortly afterwards, and was active in the Democratic Party. He was financial controller of the state from 1959 until 1967.

Cecil B. DeMille
Producer and film director.
(12. 8. 1881–21. 1. 1959)

Born in Ashfield (Massachusetts), DeMille is one of the legendary film pioneers who made Hollywood famous. Following in his parents' footsteps, he joined the theatre as an author, producer, actor and manager. Soon after starting a production company in 1912 and making his first film "The Squaw Man", his fame spread. Owing to vehement criticism of the alleged immoraltity of his earlier social comedies, such as "Male and Female", he turned his attention to higher budget films with patriotic and religious themes, their exciting and sometimes superficial storyline having a wider public appeal.

Joan Didion
Writer
(born 5. 12. 1934)

Novels, essays and film scripts – the latter co-written with her husband John Gregory Dunne – have contributed to the fame of this writer from Sacramento, the capital of California. She attempts to capture the atmosphere of the 60s and 70s in the form of a social critique. Her meticulous stylistic detail is especially evident in "Run River", one of her most important novels, which shows the changes which have affected her home town where the 1849 Gold Rush began. In contrast, her novel "Play it as it Lays" is set in southern California.

Joe DiMaggio
Baseball player
(born 24. 11. 1914)

Hardly known outside America, the 75-year-old former baseball player DiMaggio, Marilyn Monroe's second husband, is still an idol. He comes from the small town of Martinez to the east of San Francisco; he began his career in 1932 as a national player in that town but was soon to become a member of the Yankee team in New York. He holds the unbroken record of having scored in 56 consecutive games.

Walt Disney
Cartoonist and film producer
(5. 12. 1901–15. 12. 1966)

Born in Chicago, Walt Disney began his career as an advertising artist, and after his first attempts at film cartoons he drew the popular "Mickey Mouse" series in 1928. He developed colour cartoon films ("Snow White" 1937; "Bambi" 1942) and produced adventure films ("Treasure Island") and award-winning nature films ("The Desert is Alive" 1953; "The Wonders of the Prairie" 1954) as well as films for television ("Mickey Mouse Club", "Davy Crockett", "Walt Disney's Wonderful World of Colour"). In

Jack London

Marilyn Monroe

George S. Patton

1955 he set up the ever-popular recreational fairytale park "Disneyland" at Anaheim near Los Angeles and planned the larger than life amusement centre "Walt Disney World" at Orlando, Florida (opened 1971).

Born in San Francisco, Isadora Duncan had her first real breakthrough in Europe, because the reactionary Americans disapproved of her carefree lifestyle and were opposed to her sympathy for the Russians. Living most of the time in Paris, she opened her first school in Berlin in 1904 and another school in Moscow in 1921 which lasted only a short time. She distanced herself from traditional classical ballet and sought inspiration in the free movements of ancient Greek dances. The importance of her pioneering work was only recognised after her premature death, as a result of a car accident in Nice.

Isadora Duncan
Dancer
(27. 5. 1878–
13. 9. 1927)

Ferlinghetti, born in New York, had a lasting influence on the cultural life of San Francisco and California. A member of the "Beat generation", he helped its poets to gain recognition by publishing their works and selling them in his City Lights Bookshop in San Francisco. He was, for example, the first to publish Allen Ginsberg. His own work is notable for having peculiar speech rhythms and unusual typography.

Lawrence Ferlinghetti
Poet and publisher
(born 24. 3. 1919)

Francis, from San Mateo, is considered one of the most important of present-day artists. His works can be seen in every museum of contemporary art. he was educated at the University of California in Berkeley and at the Californian School of Fine Arts (now San Francisco Art Institute). His mostly large abstract paintings stand out for their richness of colour and for their distinct feeling of space.

Sam Francis
Artist
(born 25. 7. 1923)

Hearst's father came to California on foot from the mid-west in 1850, and within a decade he was one of the nouveau riche of San Francisco, thanks to acquiring silver mines in Nevada as well as other mines. His only son, William Randolph, born with the proverbial silver spoon in his mouth, was made publisher at the age of 24 of the daily newspaper "San Francisco Examiner" by his father, but built up his newspaper and magazine empire from New York. Hearst's publications were characterised by sensationalism and patriotism; it was also he who introduced comics into the daily press. Later he bought up radio stations and film companies, as well as real estate, yet he did not neglect his father's mines. He lived in grand style, had a castle built at San Simeon, where his lover Marion Davies was mistress. Orsen Wells paid a not exactly flattering tribute to Hearst in the film "Citizen Kane".
His granddaughter Patricia (Patty) Hearst, born in 1954, was kidnapped by terrorists in 1974. She was seized by the FBI in 1975 and sentenced to

William Randolph Hearst
Newspaper magnate
(29. 4. 1863–
14. 8. 1951)

several years' imprisonment in 1976 for involvement in her kidnappers' crimes. She was reprieved in 1979.

Herbert C. Hoover
(10. 8. 1874–
20. 10. 1964)
US President

Hoover was the first of three presidents of the USA who lived in California. He came as a young man from Iowa in the mid-west and studied engineering science at Stanford University. He had a successful career as a mining engineer and expert on international mining problems behind him when he enlisted for official duties in the First World War. At first he organised aid for Belgian and French civilians; on America's entry into the war he became responsible for food supplies to his own country, and after the war he despatched food to young people in countries in need. He was Minister of Trade from 1921 to 1928 and in the latter year, as the Republican candidate, was elected President. The Stock Exchange crash of 1929 occurred during his presidency and the ensuing economic depression ruined his political reputation, with the result that Franklin D. Roosevelt won the 1932 election.

Robinson Jeffers
Poet
(10. 1. 1887–
20. 1. 1962)

At the age of sixteen Jeffers came to Pasadena with his family from Pittsburgh where he was born. He attended the Occidental College in Los Angeles where he studied medicine and forestry science. From 1916 to the end of his days he lived in Carmel and helped to give the town its reputation as a favoured residence for writers, up-and-coming artists and leading retired academics. Much of his philosophical and complex work reflects the ambience of Carmel and its surroundings, where "for the first time he saw people living in the midst of magnificent unspoiled countryside, as in the idylls and legends of Homer's Ithaca". He wrote more than a dozen volumes of poetry and a few adaptations of Euripides' tragedies. The interpretation of the poems, most of which do not rhyme, is made more difficult by ambiguous poetic images and symbols. His works, published during the Second World War, are filled with hatred of civilisation and social criticism.

Jesse Lasky
Film producer
(13. 9. 1880–
13. 1. 1958)

Of the numerous early film producers Lasky is the only native Californian (he came from San Francisco). With his brother-in-law Samuel Goldwyn he founded his first film company which became Paramount Pictures. After losing control of the biggest film concern of its time, he remained active as a producer for other companies, such as Fox, Warner and RKO. His most successful films include "Sergeant York", "The Adventures of Mark Twain", "Rhapsody in Blue" and "The Great Caruso". Shortly before his death at Beverly Hills he published his memoirs.

Jack London
Writer
(12. 1. 1876–
22. 11. 1916)

The illegitimate son of an itinerant astrologer and of a mother who was not over-concerned for him, London was born in San Francisco. At fourteen he left school and made his way as a fisherman, harbour policeman (in Oakland) and sailor. He was first arrested for vagrancy and again for making an inflammatory Socialist speech. He was also among those who searched for gold on the Canadian River Klondike. He began his work as an author by writing short stories reflecting his varied experiences; these were first published separately in magazines and in 1900 in a book edition entitled "The Son of the Wolf". Over the course of the next fifteen years he wrote 40 novels. "The Call of the Wild" became his most famous work worldwide. Jack London had a house built in Glen Ellen which, however, burnt down as soon as it was completed in 1913. During the last years of his life he became a depressive and at 40 he committed suicide.

Marilyn Monroe
Film actress
(1. 6. 1926–
2. 2. 1957)

Born Norma Jean Baker or Mortenson in Los Angeles, Marilyn Monroe began her heady career as a photographic model, was then discovered as a "sex-bomb" in Hollywood and marketed in almost 30 films. After playing mainly minor roles from 1948 to 1952, she became famous overnight by her part in the film "Niagara". "Gentlemen Prefer Blondes", "The Prince and the Showgirl" and above all "Some Like It Hot" were among her best-known films. This undoubtedly talented actress became a tragic, frustrated victim of Hollywood's idol factory. Several biographies of her have appeared. Her third and final marriage was to the author Arthur Miller.

Julia Morgan, born in San Francisco, was the first Californian woman to qualify in engineering, and to graduate as an architect at the Ecole des Beaux Arts in Paris. In 1905 she opened her own architect's office in San Francisco and in the course of her long career designed about 600 blocks of flats. Her most important achievement was the planning and completion of the castle built for William Randolf Hearst in San Simeon. She worked on this project from 1919 until 1947.

Julia Morgan
Architect
(26. 1. 1872–
2. 2. 1957)

John Muir came with his family to the United States as an eleven-year-old from Scotland. He grew up in Winsconsin and first visited California in 1868, where he found his life's work, and where he stayed until his death. (He died in Martinez.) Muir had studied chemistry, geology and botany, and first ran a fruit farm for ten years near Martinez, east of San Francisco. Then he devoted his attention to the preservation of forests, and played a decisive role in the creation of the Yosemite National Park (1890). It was due to his initiative that dozens of forest reserves were created in California. Many places of interest are named after him: the Muir Woods near San Francisco, the John Muir Trail through the High Sierra, the Muir Ravine in the Yosemite National Park, the Muir Grove in Sequoia National Park and the Muir Pass in Kings Canyon National Park.

John Muir
Naturalist
(21. 7. 1838–
24. 12. 1914)

Of the three Presidents of the USA who lived in California, Nixon is the only one who was born in the state. His birthplace was Yorba Linda, east of Anaheim, now a town with 36,000 inhabitants. His family was quite poor, but he had the opportunity to attend a college and then to study law at Duke University in North Carolina. He settled down as a lawyer in Whittier, served in the navy in the Second World War and was elected to the House of Representatives in 1946. Four years later he was elected senator, and in 1952 became Vice-President under Eisenhower. In 1960 he lost the presidential election to John F. Kennedy and in 1962 he was also defeated in the election for State Governor in California. Not until 1968 did he fulfil his life's ambition to become President, and four years later he was re-elected. Nixon advocated detente between the great powers, recognition of the People's Republic of China and the introduction of a ceasefire in the Vietnam War. His increasingly authoritarian style of government and finally his involvement in the Watergate affair forced him to resign, the only one of 40 US Presidents to do so.

Richard M.Nixon
US President
(born 9. 1. 1913)

Born in Los Angeles the son of a Japanese lyric poet and an American authoress, Noguchi went to school in Japan and returned to the USA in 1918, where he received his artistic education. He worked for six months in Paris as a Guggenheim scholar and assistant to Brâncusis. In his buildings (for example the UNESCO Building in Paris and the Billy Rose Sculpture Gardens in Jerusalem) he combines oriental and surrealist elements with his teacher's initiatives, and he achieves elegant abstractions and an integration of architecture and sculpture. Active until the end of his life, he lived in the USA, Japan and Italy. In 1985 he created the Isamo Noguchi Garden Museum in New York City, the place where his productive life ended.

Isamo Noguchi
Architect and
sculptor
(17. 11. 1904–
30. 12. 1988)

Patton was a controversial figure but this never worried him. Born in San Gabriel, he grew up on his maternal grandfather's ranch, attended the military academy of West Point and commanded a tank brigade in the First World War. During the Second World War he was commander of the US Third Army which advanced from France as far as Czechoslovakia. His attacks which were often improvised have become almost legendary. Patton was killed in a road accident in Heidelberg shortly after the end of the war.

George S. Patton
Military
commander
(11. 11. 1885–
11. 12. 1945)

Peck is one of the few film stars who were born in California. He comes from La Jolla, a suburb of San Diego, studied at the University of California in Berkeley, was a successful actor on Broadway, yet in 1944 decided to concentrate on the cinema. He became known for his reserved and cool

Gregory Peck
Actor
(born 3. 4. 1916)

Famous Personalities

William Saroyan

Upton Sinclair

John Steinbeck

acting, as in his most famous films "Duel in the Sun" and "To Kill a Mockingbird". From 1967 to 1970 he was president of the Academy of Motion Picture Arts and Sciences.

Ronald Reagan
Governor,
US President
(born 6. 2. 1911)

The 33rd Governor of California (1967–1975) and the 40th President of the United States was born in the state of Illinois. He was for five years a sports announcer with a radio station in Iowa before coming to Hollywood in 1937 where he had a rapid career in B films. After the war, during which he served in the air force, he was president of the Film Actors' Union for twelve years, became a Republican in 1962, and was elected governor four years later without ever having held office previously. In 1976 he was defeated in the Republican primaries for the presidency, but was elected four years later and re-elected in 1984. He now lives in Bel Air, probably the most prestigious suburb of Los Angeles.

William Saroyan
Writer
(31. 8. 1908–
19. 5. 1981)

Born to Armenian parents in Fresno, William Saroyan spent part of his childhood in an orphanage as his widowed mother was too poor to keep him. He left school at the age of twelve; his first job was as a telegraph messenger and he only had casual work over the next 20 years, although he wrote short stories on the side, which he completed in the edition "The Man of the Flying Trapeze" in 1934. His works are renowned for their often excessively optimistic style which is not always without sentimentality, and they frequently contain autobiographical material. He has also written half a dozen novels as well as several plays. He was awarded the Pulitzer Prize in 1939 for the play "The Time of Your Life", but he did not accept it. Sarayon's uncritical belief in the "American Dream" and the naive viewpoint of his characters have received a mixed critical response. He died in Fresno.

Upton Sinclair
Writer
(20. 9. 1878–
25. 11. 1968)

After a successful career in the east of the country, this Baltimore-born writer first came to California in 1909 and settled in Pasadena in 1917. Among his earlier successes was "The Jungle" (1906), a novel which portrayed the atrocities of the slaughterhouse of Chicago. After settling in the west he wrote almost 100 works in which he criticised the inadequacies of American society. He still found time, however, for political activity, applying as a socialist in 1920, 1922 and 1926 for several positions without success. In 1934 he stood as a Democratic candidate for governor but was defeated by his Republican opponent. He described himself as a religious socialist.

Lincoln Steffens
Writer
(6. 4. 1866–
9. 8. 1936)

He was born in San Francisco, and grew up in Sacramento in a gabled Victorian house which later became the residence of the governor. Steffens gained an international outlook through studying in several European countries, which stood him in good stead as a journalist. His struggle was

Levi Strauss   *Johann A. Sutter*   *Orson Welles*

primarily against corruption in the big American cities, San Francisco being no exception at the turn of the century. His book "The Shame of the Cities" not only created a sensation, but also had practical consequences for some of the cities that were the subject of his criticism. His most widely read book is his autobiography which appeared in 1931, in which he openly expresses his scepticism about the structure of American society, and which has much to say about the introduction of a different economic and political system. Steffens died in Carmel.

Like so many American writers Steinbeck cannot get away from his roots. Those who know his birthplace Salinas and the surrounding Monterey Peninsula will keep finding references to his home among the best pages of his books. He studied at Stanford University without taking his finals, and had several short-term jobs before publishing the novel "Cup of Gold" in 1929. He wrote his most important works during the thirties: "Of Mice and Men" (later adapted for the stage) and "The Grapes of Wrath" which represented the tragedy of people driven from their land by economic depression and drought. He was awarded the Nobel Prize for Literature in 1962 for his collected works.

John Steinbeck
Writer
(17. 2. 1902–
20. 12. 1968)

Irving Stone, another writer born in San Francisco, is famous for biographical novels of famous people. Works connected with California include "Sailor on Horseback" (about Jack London), "Immortal Wife" (about Jessie Frémont, whose husband was a soldier of fortune, a Californian senator and a major-general in the Civil War) as well as the novel "Men to Match My Mountain" about Californian pioneers.

Irving Stone
Writer
(born 14. 7. 1903)

Levi Strauss, whose jeans produced in San Francisco since 1850 have achieved world fame, came to America from Bavaria when he was fourteen. Before setting off on a three-month sea journey around Cape Horn he laid in, from his brother's textile business in New York, a store of various types of material and some rolls of canvas for stage-coaches. Even before he arrived in San Francisco he had sold all his wares except the canvas. One day a gold miner complained that his trousers tore so easily because of his strenuous work, and Strauss hit upon the idea of making trousers from the canvas; these were an immediate success. In 1853 he founded with his brother the firm which is still in existence today. The idea of reinforcing the pockets with copper studs was that of a local tailor (patented in 1878). Later, instead of canvas, resistant cotton drill was used and was named after its French town of origin, "serge de Nímes" which became known as "denim".

Levi Strauss
Textile merchant
(1829–1902)

Famous Personalities

Johann August Sutter
Landowner
(15. 2. 1803–18. 6. 1880)

An unhappy marriage and the failure of his haberdashery business led Sutter to emigrate to America, the paradise at that time for "black sheep". He was born in Germany and grew up in Switzerland. Johann August Sutter arrived in 1839 after adventures which had taken him to Alaska and Hawaii. He became a Mexican citizen and received the largest possible grant of land from the Mexican governor of that time, and farmed it with the help of Indian slaves. Sutter built a fort on the land and called his empire "Nueva Helvetia". He bought the Russian owned Fort Ross and Bodega Bay, and supported the Americans in conquering California. He became a delegate to Congress and from then on called himself John Augustus Sutter. Near Sacramento, the capital of California, which was founded by Sutter, James W. Marshall discovered in 1848 the first Californian gold. Gold was also discovered in 1949 during the construction of a saw mill on Sutter's land and soon his property was overrun with fortune hunters who destroyed everything that was not nailed down. Sutter lost everything, lived sixteen years on a small pension which the Senate allowed him, but his claims for compensation were never recognised by the Federal Government. He died penniless and in obscurity.

Shirley Temple
Actress
(born 23. 4. 1928)

The actress from Santa Monica was only three years old when she first faced the camera. By the age of six she was a favourite with audiences both young and old with her winning smile, blond curly hair and indisputable talent. The success of her earlier films ("Little Miss Marker", "The Littlest Rebel" and "Rebecca of Sunnybrook Farm") made between 1934 and 1938 was not to be repeated. At 22, an age when many are just beginning, she gave up her film career, married a rich businessman and joined the diplomatic service, becoming ambassador to Ghana.

Earl Warren
Governor
(19. 3. 1891–9. 7. 1974)

Earl Warren studied law in Los Angeles where he was born, and took part in the First World War. After returning to civilian life and a short spell as a lawyer, he was elected district attorney, i.e. chief prosecutor, of Alameda County in Oakland. As state Justice Minister (attorney general), the next rung on his ladder to success, he was a successful campaigner against organised crime. Contrary to his otherwise liberal outlook, one of his last official acts was to sanction the internment of the Japanese in the coastal areas. Elected governor of California in 1943 and twice re-elected, his twelve years of service meant he was in office longer than any other governor. President Eisenhower appointed him to the Supreme Federal Court in 1953. During his sixteen years in office he made important judgements in favour of minorities; he declared racial segregation in schools to be unconstitutional.

Orson Welles
Actor and director
(16. 5. 1915–10. 10. 1985)

Orson Welles, born in Kenosha (Wisconsin), thrilled his theatre audiences from the beginning with his distinctive individual productions. His realistic radio production of H.G. Welles "War of the Worlds" caused mass hysteria and brought him the unique contract for Hollywood of making a completely independent film every year. His first film was "Citizen Kane" which with its editing and lighting techniques, together with the alienating perspective, broke new ground. However, interference and disputes caused him to leave Hollywood in 1947. Often supported by patrons, he experimented as a director in different countries and as an actor – he normally played the leading role in his films – with different kinds of artistic forms. "Macbeth" (1947) and "The Third Man" (1949) are two of his best known films.

Edward Weston
Photographer
(1886–1. 1. 1968)

Edward Weston was born in the state of Illinois and came to California at nineteen where he went about knocking on doors to get portrait commissions. As well as portraits of people he also photographed landscapes, nudes, plants and vegetables. He also used to earn money making prints in his laboratory. During the twenties he spent several years in Mexico but in 1928 he settled in Carmel where he spent the last 30 years of his life, paralysed from 1958 by Parkinson's disease. Like Adams he captured on camera the beauty of the coast of California, especially Point Lobos, rather than the mountains and forests.

Art and Culture

Education System

Beginnings

A rudimentary education system became established in California in the middle of the last century. Whereas the Franciscan monks were making efforts even earlier to educate those Indians who were willing to learn, neither the Spanish nor the Mexican colonial governments provided schools for their people. The American settlers who had been coming to California since the early 1840s opened the first school in 1846 at the Santa Clara Mission; another appeared a year later in Monterey. San Francisco got its first school in 1850, about the time when California was accepted into the Union. Chinese, Indian and Black children were excluded from lessons. The legal requirement to establish a school providing three months' teaching in every school district was only gradually complied with, and it was decades later before a higher education system existed throughout the state.

Secondary

The first high schools were private institutions of a religious nature. In 1851 the Jesuits founded Santa Clara College (Santa Clara University from 1885) in the town of the same name, and the Methodists founded the College of the Pacific in neighbouring San José. The latter was transferred to Stockton in 1961 and is now called the University of the Pacific. Both institutions are open to members of other denominations.

State universities

The extensive network of the University of California, now famous throughout the world, had its origins in 1873 in the College of California in Oakland. The State University was founded in 1868 and moved to Berkeley in 1873, where in the same year the first class of twelve men received their diplomas. Three decades later the first branches were founded in Riverside, La Jolla, San Francisco (the Foundation for Medical Research was taken over) and Los Angeles. Later the Universities of Davis, Santa Barbara, San Diego, Santa Cruz and Irvine were added. The network of state universities had now spread throughout the whole state. The Universities of Berkeley and Los Angeles rank among the most pioneering of all the higher education establishments of America. The State also maintains a separate system of state colleges, of which there are currently nineteen with over 320,000 students. A college is the equivalent of an English sixth-form and the foundation year of a university course, and it attendance is a prerequisite for a university place. Not until this stage has been reached does specialisation in individual subjects begin.

Private universities

Some private universities also enjoy an outstanding reputation. These include the University of Southern California in Los Angeles, founded in 1880 by the Methodists and today the largest private university in the State. Others are the world-famous Stanford University in Palo Alto (1891), created by one man, the "railway king" Leland Stanford, the Occidental College in Los Angeles, founded by the Presbyterian religious community, and, last but not least, the Californian Institute of Technology in Pasadena, which owns the Palomar Observatory. This institute is noted for its high staffing ratio – 800 university lecturers to 1800 students.
In the south-east of Los Angeles County at the foot of the San Gabriel Mountains, in the town of Claremont with only 35,000 inhabitants, there is a noteworthy group of six colleges which originated between 1887 and 1946: Pomona College, Claremont Graduate School, Scripps College, Claremont McKenna College, Harvey Mudd College and Pitzer College.

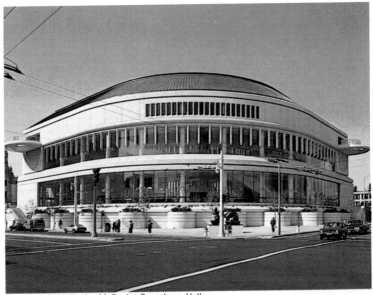

San Francisco: Louise M. Davies Symphony Hall

The Arts

The cultural life of California has developed in less than a century. Although folk music and folk dancing were practised in the 1850s and there were even early dramatic performances, these were put on by amateurs and lacked suitable premises. However, as long ago as the 1860s some of the most prominent American actors of the time, including Edwin Booth, Edwin Forrest and Laura Keene, came to California. Even Lola Montez, the mistress of Ludwig I of Bavaria, appeared in San Francisco and some gold-mining towns after her expulsion from Munich.

Beginnings

California's first theatre was built in 1869 in Bath Street and held an audience of between 1478 and 2150. Seven years later there followed the Baldwin Academy of Music, converted from part of an hotel and accommodating 2100, and Wade's Opera House for an audience of 2234.

Theatre

In Los Angeles theatrical life first began in the nineties with the building of the Majestic and Burbank Theatres, which at first only featured guest productions from New York with such famous stars as Joseph Jefferson, James O'Neill (the father of Eugene O'Neill), Sarah Bernhardt, Julia Marlowe and Ellen Terry. Only gradually did Californian actors, such as David Belasco and David Warfield make a name for themselves, but they soon tried their luck on the stages of New York.

The development of theatrical life began to stagnate with the arrival of the cinema. Even in the early days of motion pictures (around 1917) there were more picture houses than theatres in San Francisco. Today the theatrical landscape has radically changed. Not only San Francisco but also Los Angeles have dozens of large and small theatres; San Diego, Sacramento, San José, Santa Barbara, Monterey and numerous other towns can also

◀ *Palo Alto: Stanford University, tower of the Green Library*

San Diego: Old Globe Theatre

accommodate permanent theatrical ensembles. The American Conservatory Theatre in San Francisco, the Mark Taper Forum in Los Angeles and the Old Globe Theatre in San Diego now rank among the leading theatres in the country.

Music

The development of musical life was also slow at first, even with the establishment of a philharmonic orchestra in San Francisco as long ago as 1852, which was subsidised mainly by German clubs. Regular operatic performances began in 1877 with mostly Italian opera in the Tivoli Opera House and the Grand Opera House, both of which disappeared in rubble and ashes in the 1906 earthquake. It was 1919 before a new start was made with the San Francisco Opera Company which still exists today.

The first symphony orchestra came into being in San Francisco and from the outset it was able to call on famous conductors. It was followed in 1919 by the Symphony Orchestra of Los Angeles. The construction of the Music Centre for the Performing Arts (completed in 1967) provided a permanent home for the Los Angeles opera which had existed since 1919 in the Dorothy Chandler Pavilion. Summer concerts in the enormous Hollywood Bowl, "Symphony under the Stars", can accommodate an audience of 20,000 sitting and a further 10,000 standing. Today other Californian towns have their own orchestras, including Oakland, San José, San Diego, Fresno, Stockton and Sacramento. Music concerts are frequently held in other towns, such as Carmel and Ojay.

The founding of the first conservatory of music (San Francisco Conservatory) in 1917 gave a vital impulse to musical life. The exodus of renowned composers from Europe in the years following 1933 brought world-famous musicians to Californian universities; a representative selection include the Swiss Ernest Block (University of California in Berkeley), Arnold Schönberg (University of California in Los Angeles where there is also a Schönberg research centre), and Darius Milhaud (Mills College in Oakland).

The importance of popular music in recent times, especially rock music, is worth mentioning. Groups such as "The Grateful Dead", "Jefferson Airplane" and "Beach Boys" have left their mark on the American popular music scene.

Museums appeared in California even later than theatres and concert halls, indeed not until the present century. The fact that they are among the most important in the world is a reflection of the great hunger for culture of this young state. In this area, too, San Francisco took the lead. In 1916 the M. H. de Young Museum received a purpose-built extension. In 1960 there was added the Asian Art Museum to house the exhibits from the collection of Avery Brundage, the long-serving Chairman of the Olympic Committee. The San Francisco Museum of Modern Art and the California Palace of the Legion of Honour (containing exclusively French works of art) were founded in the twenties.

Museums

The most significant Los Angeles museum, the County Museum of Art, was not built until 1965, yet in less than a quarter of a century it has acquired an enviable collection. This was followed by the opening of the Museum of Contemporary Art in 1967 and this is still being extended. The Southwest Museum ranks as one of the best museums with exhibits illustrating Indian culture. Close to Los Angeles are the Henry E. Huntington Library and Art Gallery (opened 1919) and the Norton Simon Museum of Art (opened 1974) in Pasadena, and the J. Paul Getty Museum in Malibu (opened 1973).

Other notable museums are the Stanford University Museum in Palo Alto, the E. B. Crocker Art Gallery in Sacramento, the Berkeley University Art Museum, the Oakland Museum, the Santa Barbara Museum of Art, the Museum of Art in Long Beach, the Museum of Contemporary Art in La Jolla, together with the Fine Arts Gallery and the Timken Art Gallery in San Diego. There are also numerous museums of local history and science throughout the state.

During the 19th century a whole range of painters lived in California. They were either European immigrants, such as the German Albert Bierstadt and the British-born Thomas Hill, or artists who had at least studied in Europe. Not until after the Second World War did native painters or those working in the state make a name for themselves; these include Clyfford Still, Mark Rothko, Richard Diebenkorn, Robert Motherwell and Sam Francis.

Painters

Architecture

Californian architecture is as varied as the countryside. It ranges from the adobe houses with flat roofs dating from the colonial period to the sky-scrapers which have dominated the outlines of San Francisco, San Diego and Los Angeles for the last decades. Nothing remains of the skittle-shaped huts of the Yurok Indians.

General

Spanish missionaries came from Mexico to California. They built their mission stations to match the local building style of the pueblo (village). Building materials used were wooden beams and adobe, which consists of a mixture of dried clay and vegetable fibres and was used by the Indians. With this method of building the characteristic adobe architecture developed, and this can be seen throughout California. As well as the special materials used, the main features of this building style, which is still popular today, are a crude, castle-like appearance, façades without windows, and rounded corners.

Adobe style

The mission stations built in the second half of the 18th c. were the first Californian buildings not intended solely for habitation. A right-angled inner courtyard ("patio") was enclosed by the church and the domestic and residential buildings of the monastery. The builders of the mission stations, the Franciscan fathers, basically followed essentially Mexican models, although occasionally Roman architects such as Vitruvius were copied, for example in the construction of the façade of Santa Barbara Mission Station. The work was frequently carried out by the Indians.

Malibu: J. P. Getty Museum

Santa Barbara Mission

Los Angeles: Hotel Bonaventura

With the arrival of the Americans from the east coast of the United States, a mixture of New England style and Spanish-Mexican elements developed which is referred to in architectural history as Monterey Colonial style.

The construction of the saw-mills led to an increased number of shingle-built houses and to various kinds of wood being used in construction work. As a result of the fire hazard shops and offices soon came to be built of brick or stone, but wooden houses continued to be constructed for private use until late in the 19th century. Eclectism reigned in Californian architecture; there are examples of Neo-Classicism, Romanesque and Renaissance in the cities, particularly in San Francisco. Whole suburbs were characterised by the large number of Victorian wooden houses from around 1870 until the earthquake of 1906. The architects did not shy from exaggeration as the "San Francisco Stick" proves. The wooden decorations of these houses could be bought ready-made. The "Eastlake" style can be traced back to England furniture designs, and the Queen Anne style is typified by asymmetrical houses with high gabled roofs and decorated towers. One of the best examples of this style is the Carson House in Eureka.

Los Angeles, having no more than 10,000 inhabitants in 1880, was untouched by these architectural trends. As the town expanded the number of architects who settled there and who influenced the town's appearance grew. In any case it was some time before a distinctive style emerged. At first the mission style was recreated, then the Beaux Arts style spread, of which there are many examples to be found in Los Angeles. Art Nouveau is more prevalent in Los Angeles than in other Californian towns. The influence of the Austrian architects Richard Neutra and Rudolph Schindler who worked there is still of paramount importance today. Numerous private houses in and around Los Angeles, as well as some public buildings by the American Frank Lloyd Wright, seem to indicate an original style.

By American standards skyscrapers came late to San Francisco and Los Angeles, not least because of the continued threat of earthquakes. In Los Angeles from the end of the twenties blocks of flats were not allowed to be built. Not until the advent of earthquake-resistant buildings could skyscrapers be constructed in California, and even today, particularly in downtown Los Angeles, this trend still continues.
San Francisco with its many hills did not appear to be a favourable site for skyscrapers; gradually they came into being but are not as high as in Manhattan. A referendum prevented the unrestricted construction of high-rise buildings after building restrictions had been over-ruled three times during the seventies.

Quotations

Ethel Barrymore
American actress
(1879–1959)

The people (in Hollywood) are unreal, they don't smell. The fruit is unreal, it doesn't taste of anything. The whole place is a glaring, gaudy, nightmarish set, built up in the desert.

Vicky Baum
German author
(1888–1960)

Sometimes when I think of what the polyp of a town (Los Angeles) was like thirty years ago, I get a bit sentimental. Since we have been living in this stifling, evil-smelling khaki-coloured smog, we scarcely know what it was once like; a gentian-blue sky, cold nights with the heavens filled with stars, and the smell of jasmine . . . the air so pure that you could not only breathe it, you could even have drunk it.

Adalbert von Chamisso
German author
(1781–1838)

The mist which the mighty winds from the sea blow over the coast dissolves in summer over the hot thirsty land, and in autumn the landscape has the appearance of bare space, burned brown by the heat and broken by sparse stunted bushes and dazzling deserts of quicksand. Here and there on the crests of the mountains dark pine forests can be seen.

John Gunther
American journalist
(1901–1970)

California, the most spectacular and most diversified American state. California so ripe, golden, yeasty, churning in a flux, is a world of its own . . . It contains both the most sophisticated and the most bigoted community in America; it is a bursting cornucopia of peoples as well as of fruit, glaciers, sunshine, desert and petroleum. There are several Californias, and the state is at once demented and very sane, adolescent and mature, depending on the point of view.

Johan Huizinga
Dutch historico-cultural writer
(1872–1945)

The feeling of the sanctity of science and of a true communal spirit in the service of an ideal was never so clear to me as on the day I spent with the workers on Mount Wilson, the great observatory at Pasadena in California. In Europe art has taken over the functions once fulfilled by religion; in America this position appears to have been assumed by science.

Rudyard Kipling
British author
(1865–1936)

Remember that the men who stocked California in the 50s were physically and as far as certain tough virtues are concerned, the pick of the earth . . . To this nucleus were added all the races of the continent – French, Italian, German, and, of course, the Jews. The result you can see in large-boned, deep-chested, delicate handed women and long, elastic, well-built boys. It needs no little golden badge . . . to mark the native son of the Golden West . . . Him I love because he is devoid of fear, carries himself like a man, and has a heart as big as his boots.

Wolfgang Koeppen
German author
(born 1906)

Broadway in L.A. was no shopping street for the rich; it belonged to the people and never before did I see such folk. Whites of all shades, Blacks both light and dark, Asians both yellow and brown, Filipinos, Mexicans, Latin-Americans, Indians; old races, new races, who worked and walked handsomely, proudly, uninhibited and free.

D. H. Lawrence
British author
(1885–1930)

California is a queer place – in a way it has turned its back on the world, and looks into the void Pacific. It is absolutely selfish, very empty but not false, and at least not full of false effort . . . It is sort of crazy-sensible. Just the moment: hardly as far ahead as "carpe diem".

Carey McWilliams
American Sociologist
(1905–1960)

Nature in California is neurotic, its apparent stability a mask for anguish and anxiety; drought and fire are her most frequent aggressions, but earthquake her constant menace.

Nineteen suburbs in search of a metropolis (description of Los Angeles). The Californian climate makes the sick well and the well sick, the old young and the young old.

H. L. Mencken
American author
(1880–1956)

Big Sur is the California that men dreamed of years ago, this is the Pacific that Balboa looked at from the peak of Darien, this is the face of the earth as the Creator intended it to look.

Henry Miller
American author
(1891–1980)

It (California) is the land of perpetual pubescence, where cultural lag is mistaken for Renaissance.

Ashley Montagu
Anthropologist
(b. 1905)

The Pacific coast in general is the paradise of conifers. Here nearly all of them are giants, and display a beauty and magnificence unknown elsewhere. The climate is mild, the ground never freezes, and moisture and sunshine abound all the year. Nevertheless, it is not easy to account for the colossal size of the sequoias. The largest are about 300 feet high and 30 feet in diameter.

John Muir
American
naturalist
(1838–1914)

California, the advance post of our civilization, with its huge aircraft factories, TV and film studios, automobile way of life . . . its flavourless cosmopolitanism, its charlatan philosophies and religions, its lack of anything old and well-tried, rooted in tradition and character.

J. B. Priestley
British author
(1894–1984)

I am struck in California by the deep and almost religious affection people have for nature . . . it is their spontaneous substitute for articulate art and articulate religion.

George Santayana
Spanish author
(1865–1952)

The spring is beautiful in California. Valleys in which the fruit blossoms are fragrant pink, and white waters in a shallow sea. The first tendrils of the grapes swelling from the old gnarled vines, cascade down to cover the trunks.

John Steinbeck
American author
(1902–1968)

California is an Italy without its art. There are subjects for the artist, but it is universally true that the only scenery which inspires utterance is that which man feels himself the master of. The mountains of California are so gigantic that they are not favourable to art or poetry. There are good poets in England, but none in Switzerland. There the mountains are too high. Art cannot add to nature.

Oscar Wilde
Irish author
(1854–1900)

California, since we took it from the Mexicans, has always presented itself to Americans as one of the strangest and most exotic of their exploits.

Edmund Wilson
American author
(1895–1972)

California Dreamin'

John Phillips
Michelle Gillian

All the leaves are brown and the sky is grey
I've been for a walk on a winter's day
I'd be safe and warm if I was in L.A.
California dreamin' on such a winter's day.

At the beginning of the 60s the Hippy movement spread from California. The song "California dreamin'", made popular by the American pop-group "The Mamas & the Papas" is an expression of this philosophy.

Suggested Itineraries

Preliminary

The following suggested itineraries are intended to help the motorist touring California, without denying him freedom to make his own plans and choice of route. The routes have been chosen so that the principal places of interest in the state are visited. However, not all the places of interest in this guide can be covered without making detours. The proposed routes can be followed on the map at the back of this book.

Note

Departure points, to which the motorist will return at the end of each tour, are principally the towns of San Francisco, Los Angeles and San Diego.
For most journeys several days are needed and the overnight stops must be planned in advance.
Places and areas which are covered in the A to Z section under a main heading are printed in **bold**.
All the towns, villages, areas, rivers, etc. mentioned in the routes, as well as individual sights, whether they are under main headings or in the surroundings, can be found in the index at the end of the guide.

1: From San Francisco along the Pacific coast to the north and into the vine-growing area

Leaving San Francisco on Highway 101 over the Golden Gate Bridge you first reach the picturesque town of **Sausalito**, and from there go north on the CA 1 to **Muir Woods National Monument** where there is a fine stand of giant redwoods. Continue along the coast road to Inverness and Point Reyes peninsula with **Point Reyes National Seashore** at its south-west end (February to July flowers; 50 miles/80 km of footpaths), then via **Bodega Bay** to **Mendocino**, originally a fishing village which has interesting traces of its past.
From there go inland on the CA 20 and CA 29 via Willits to Clear Lake, which is popular with local people, and past the south end of the lake as far as **Calistoga**, continuing via **St Helena**, Rutherford, Oakville and Yountville, where there are numerous wineries, to **Vallejo** and then along the 1-80 to the university town of **Berkeley**.
From Calistoga an alternative route can be followed back to San Francisco: go north-west on the CA 128 to **Geyserville** and **Healdsburg**, both centres of viniculture, and then on the US 101 to **Santa Rosa**. Continue south on the CA 12 to the Jack London State Historic Park about 1½ miles/2½ km west of **Glen Ellen**. Here can be seen the ruins of burnt-out houses which the author Jack London had built, and also his grave. From here you drive to **Sonoma** once the capital of the short-lived Californian Republic and now the headquarters of numerous wine-producing firms. Continue south along the CA 121 and then take the CA 37 to the west; at San Rafael you turn on to the US 101 and finally arrive back at San Francisco.

Distance and road conditions

This entire route is 342 miles/537 km long. If you choose the alternative return route from Calistoga this adds another 40 miles/64 km to the journey. The roads are all good but the CA 1 coastal road is extremely winding.

2: From San Francisco into Goldland, to Lake Tahoe and into the Yosemite National Park.

This route starts on the US 80 crossing the San Francisco Oakland Bay Bridge, with a view of the hilly island of Yerba Buena. It then goes via

Oakland and Berkeley from where there are beautiful views over San Francisco Bay and of the silhouette of **San Francisco**. Continue along San Pablo Bay via Richmond to **Vallejo** where the Napa River flows into San Pablo Bay. To the north-west extend the well-known Californian vine-growing valleys of **Napa** and **Sonoma**. You then drive via Fairfield through the fertile Sacramento Valley (fruit, citrus fruits) and the northern part of the Great Californian longitudinal valley between the Sierra Nevada and the Coast Range to the capital **Sacramento**. From there take the US 80 to **Auburn** and then the CA 49 to **Grass Valley** and Nevada City. Return to Grass Valley, on the CA 174 via Colfax to **Dutch Flat**. All these places were once gold-mining towns which still bear traces of their past. Continuing on the US 80 you come to Donner Lake and the Donner Memorial State Park (a memorial to the "Donner Party") and crossing the once important **Donner Pass**, the scene of a tragedy in 1846 when settlers were surprised by an early winter, you come to the pleasant winter sports resort of **Truckee**. Following the CA 89 southwards you arrive at the well-known **Lake Tahoe** one of the finest mountain lakes in the world, part of which is in the neighbouring state of Nevada. From here a short detour can be made to the casinos of Nevada.

From South Lake Tahoe first follow the CA 89 and then roads CA 89/US 50 and 395 to Bridgeport and to the **Bodie State Historic Park**, a ghost town from the end of the 19th c. which has not been restored. The road continues beyond Lee Vining and the attractive **Mono Lake State Reserve** to the east entrance of the **Yosemite National Park**. You then take the CA 120 over the 9846 ft/3000 m-high Tioga Pass, the highest in California which can be crossed by cars, to Yosemite Village 75 miles/120 km further on in the centre of the national park. Leaving Yosemite on the CA 120 you reach Mariposa where can be seen the oldest Californian law court which is still in use and which dates from 1854. You now traverse the Merced Canyon on the CA 49 to Chinese Camp, where in the 1850s thousands of Chinese prospected for gold, and reaches **Sonoro** which was founded by Mexican gold diggers. The road now continues through numerous gold prospecting places such as Mokelumne Hill, Jackson, Sutter Creek and Amador City, to **Placerville**, **Coloma** and the Marshall Gold Discovery State Park where in 1848 on the American River the first gold in California was discovered. The return journey is along the US 50 to Sacramento and from there the US 80 goes back to San Francisco.

This route is 775 miles/1240 km long. The roads are almost all in good condition. To the Bodie State Historic Park there are 12 miles/20 km of partially unmade road, and when traversing the Merced Canyon you are advised to drive carefully.

Distance and road conditions

3: From San Francisco along the Pacific Coast to Los Angeles

Driving south from San Francisco on Highway 101 you first come to the university town of **Palo Alto**, the seat of the renowned Stanford University. Then you pass through the very fertile Santa Clara Valley, fringed by hills, which today is better known as **Silicon Valley**. You soon reach **Santa Clara**, one of the universities founded by the Jesuits, and **San Jose**, which is the fastest growing industrial town in the USA (micro-electronics), the population of which will soon exceed that of San Francisco. The CA 717 takes you south to **Santa Cruz** at the north end of Monterey Bay, a fishing port, market town (vegetables, fruit) and seaside resort. Continue along US 1 and CA 152 to Gilroy, from where you can make a short detour to the San Juan Bautista Mission (CA 156) and to the industrial and commercial town of **Salinas** (wine), the birthplace of John Steinbeck. It is only a few minutes drive along CA 68 to **Monterey**, the port on the south side of Monterey Bay (viniculture), which has a Spanish atmosphere and where there is a mission station.

From Monterey you can take a 17-mile-drive around the picturesque

Monterey Peninsula past Pacific Grove, Seal Rocks, Cypress Point, Pebble Beach and **Carmel**. The last named has a beautiful situation and is popular with artists. The drive continues on the US 1 along the coast to **Point Lobos**, to the artists' colony of **Big Sur** and to **San Simeon** where the notable mansion of William Randolph Hearst is situated. Via **Cambria** and **Morro Bay** you reach **San Luis Obispo**.

From this trading centre, lying a short way inland, you continue south on the coastal road 101 at first some distance from the sea. You come to Buellton from where the CA 246 branches off to **Solvang**, founded by the Danes and still having a Danish character, and to the Santa Ines Mission (**Mission Stations**). From Buellton continue south over the Gaviota Pass in the Santa Ynéz Mountains back to the sea. There is a view of Santa Barbara Island which is bounded on the south by the Santa Barbara Channel and which with Santa Catalina Island south of Los Angeles forms the Channel Islands (**Channel Islands National Park**).

On the CA 154 you drive to the trading and industrial town of **Santa Barbara** (electronics, computer manufacture) with its beautiful mission stations which, after a severe earthquake in 1925, were extensively rebuilt in Spanish and Mexican style. Now you pass the harbour towns of Carpinteria and **Ventura**, both of which have extensive beaches; from the latter you can make a detour along CA 33 to **Ojai** which attracts many visitors to California because of its sophisticated atmosphere. From Ventura or from **Oxnard**, a few miles further south, you are recommended to make a boat trip to the Channel Islands. From Oxnard continue along the US 101 direct to Los Angeles.

Distance and road conditions

The total distance is 478 miles/750 km all the roads mentioned are in good condition.

4: From Los Angeles into Orange County

You leave Los Angeles on US 5 going south through the industrial suburbs to **Buena Park** (Knott's Berry Farm) and to **Anaheim** (Disneyland), and via Santa Ana to **San Juan Capistrano** with its charming mission station of the same name. From here the tour continues on CA 74, crossing the Cleveland National Forest to Lake Elsinore, another favourite excursion venue of the Californians. From here you continue on US 15 as far as the south of Temecula, through the most southerly vine-growing area of California, until you reach the intersection with CA 46 which leads west to Oceanside, near which is the huge Camp Pendelton, the largest base of the US Marine Corps. Continuing north on US 5 you pass several beaches before reaching San Clemente, a town in which many retired people have made their home. A few miles further north lies **Dana Point**, which was well-known as a port in the early history of California; now it is the surfing "capital". Here the US 1, also called the Pacific Coast Highway, begins again and runs past well-known coastal resorts, including **Laguna Beach, Newport Beach** and Huntington Beach, to **Long Beach** where the luxury liner "Queen Mary", now a hotel, lies at anchor. Beyond **San Pedro** – from where you can take a boat to **Santa Catalina Island** – are other coastal places, including Palos Verdes, Redondo Beach, Venice and **Marina del Rey**, before you reach **Santa Monica** and return to **Los Angeles** along the Santa Monica Freeway (US 10) and the Harbor Freeway (US 110).

Distance and road conditions

This tour is 263 miles/420 km long, but to be able to see all the sights you will need more time on this relatively short route than on several of the longer ones.

All the roads mentioned are in good condition; on CA 74 you should drive with care, owing to the sharp curves on certain stretches in the Cleveland National Forest.

5: From Los Angeles into the Desert

From Los Angeles you take the US 10 (now called the San Bernadino Freeway), drive east to **San Bernadino** and then take US 215 and US 15, passing the San Gabriel Mountains in the north and the San Bernadino Mountains (with Mount San Antonio 10,082 feet/3072 m) in the south, to Victorville, once the setting for many western films. Continue through the Mojave Desert with its dried-up salt lakes and sparse vegetation (yucca, cactus, juniper, wormwood) to **Barstow** and the neighbouring ghost town of Calico, an abandoned silver-mining town. You continue on US 15 to Baker, where you take the CA 127 to Shoshone; a few miles to the north you turn on to the CA 178 leading into **Death Valley** which you cross in a northerly direction. To reach the most important sights in this desert region which extends over an area of some 3000 square miles, it is necessary to make use of a number of by-roads.

You leave Death Valley on CA 190 and drive west; if you wish to see Scotty's Castle which lies to the north you will have to make a detour of about 62 miles/100 km. CA 190 and CA 136 take you to **Lone Pine**, from where it is about 12 miles/20 km west to the foot of Mount Whitney, which at 14,800 feet/4418 m is the highest mountain on the mainland of the United States. The long return journey begins on CA 395 and CA 14, first to Mojave and then east on CA 58, and via Kramer Junction on CA 395, US 15 and US 215 to **San Bernadino**. From here you drive back to Los Angeles on US 10.

This route, covering 717 miles/1150 km – not counting the detours in Death Valley and to Mount Whitney – is one of the longest tours and makes the visitor realise the huge distances which must be covered in California. Moreover on this trip you get a good impression of the extent and emptiness of the desert area still crossed by only a few roads, which are nevertheless generally well-maintained.

Distance and road conditions

Because of the remoteness of many places – it is often 100 miles/150 km between filling stations – you must make sure that you have enough fuel, oil and water with you. Moreover, owing to the restricted accommodation facilities in several areas the trip must be planned with care and rooms reserved in good time.

It should also be noted that hotels in Death Valley National Monument are closed from mid May to mid October. Because of the extreme heat in summer you should not attempt this tour during these months.

Warning

6: From Los Angeles to San Diego

This route also uses the US 10 from Los Angeles to **San Bernardino** – you can also make a short detour to **Pasadena** – and continues on the US 10 to Banning; about eight miles east of Banning you turn on to the CA 62 which takes you to Yucca Valley and Twenty-nine Palms, from where you traverse the very interesting **Joshua Tree National Monument** until you reach the US 10 and **Indio**, the "date"-capital of the country, continuing to **Palm Desert** and **Palm Springs**. You return to Palm Desert, follow CA 74, CA 371 and CA 7 and then, south of Temecula, take US 215. This joins US 15 which leads direct to San Diego.

The total trip is 386 miles/620 km long. Most roads are in good condition, except that traversing the Joshua Tree National Monument.

Distance and road conditions.

7: From San Diego to the southern outskirts.

This trip begins on US 8 in San Diego and leads east as far as CA 54 and then follows CA 94 to Campo, close to the Mexican frontier. ¾ mile/1.5 km from here lies Cameron Corners, where the county road S 1 leads back to US 8; shortly before reaching Descanso this crosses CA 79 which you follow as far as Julian. From here you take CA 78 to the **Anzo-Borrego State Park**. The county road S 3, a very attractive desert road, leads to Borrego Springs Oasis. You now drive west on S 22 as far as the CA 79 which you follow for about 4 miles/6 km to the CA 76 and continue along this road for about another 4 miles north-west to the S 7 which you follow to its intersection with the S 6. You take this road and reach the Palomar Obervatory (Pasadena). From here you drive 6 miles/10 km south along the S 6, then 5 miles/8 km west on CA 79 and then south again to Escondido, where a visit to the San Diego Wild Animal Park **(San Diego)** should on no account be missed. You take S 6 via Rancho Santa Fe to Del Mar, with its famous horse-racing course, and from there the S 21 and the North Torrey Pines Road to La Jolla, an exceptionally fine suburb of San Diego, and finally the US 8 back to the starting point.

Mileage and road conditions

This 255 mile/410 km-long journey offers no problems, except on the mountain roads (CA 94, CA 79 and S 6) where speed must be kept well down.

Point Loma (San Diego), Cabrillo National Monument ▶

Sights from A to Z

Anaheim Q 3

Orange County
Altitude: 160 ft/49 m. Population: 220,000

How to get there	By air, Anaheim can be reached from Los Angeles airport (40 miles/64 km away) and from John Wayne Orange County Airport (14 miles/22 km to the south). There are direct coach connections from both airports (free information on 800/962-1976). By car, you can drive to Anaheim from Los Angeles via Freeway No. 5 (Exit 78, Katella Ave. and Anaheim Blvd. lead direct to Disneyland).
Location and origin	Until about thirty years ago Anaheim was a rather unremarkable, sleepy place in the slowly developing Orange County, which takes in a 40 miles/64 km stretch of coastline, and reaches almost 25 miles/40 km inland. It was founded in the year 1857 by German immigrants, who decided to cultivate grapes and produce wine there – the name is derived from the river Santa Ana and the German word "Heim" (home) – and in a few years they succeeded in making Anaheim the leading wine-producing area of the United States. However, in the 1880s all the vines were destroyed by a leaf disease.
Citrus fruits	The cultivation of citrus fruits, especially oranges, proved so successful that this stretch of country became one of the most important orange-growing regions in the USA. So it is not surprising that the county founded in 1889 – an offshoot of Los Angeles County – should be named "Orange County". However, Santa Ana (see entry) was nominated as the capital of the area, not little Anaheim.
"Utopian" colony	In the year 1876 Anaheim attracted a group of Polish intellectuals, whose intention was to found here one of the many "Utopian Communities" found in the United States in the 19th c. The writer Henryk Sienkiewicz (later a Nobel Prizewinner for his novel "Quo Vadis") and the actress Helena Modjeska and her husband were at the head of the group. However, their dreams quickly vanished; only two years later the author returned to his homeland. Modjeska remained, however, and started a successful theatre career (there is even a town in Orange County which bears her name).
Upswing	Not until 1955 when Walt Disney decided to choose Anaheim as the site for his Disneyland Pleasure and Leisure Park, did Anaheim develop rapidly into an industrial town. Since then the number of visitors annually has been in the millions. Hotels have mushroomed, some with over 1000 rooms, and there is also plenty of accommodation for meetings and congresses.
Sport	Anaheim is the smallest of the 20 American towns which have a first-class baseball team. The Angels play there from the middle of April until the beginning of October; from August until December there are also matches involving the Los Angeles Rams, a football team, being played in the Anaheim stadium. (Information on 634-2000 for baseball, 937-6767 for football.)
Note	Coach tours: "Gray Line" (tel. 778-2770) and "Pacific Coast Sightseeing" (tel. 978-8855). Further information: Anaheim Area Visitor & Convention Bureau, 800 West Katella Avenue; tel. 999-8999.
Surroundings	Buena Park, Costa Mesa and Santa Ana (see entries).

Annual Disney Parade

** Disneyland

From Los Angeles the US 5 (Santa Ana Freeway) leads direct to Disneyland (exit Katella Avenue).

How to get there

When Walt Disney opened his first pleasure park in Anaheim in the year 1955 he could not have foreseen that others would follow some years later, namely, in Florida ("Disneyworld"), in Tokyo (opened 1983) and then in Pussta (Hungary) and near Paris. In the 34 years of its existence, Disneyland itself has been extended and adapted to the needs of the time. On many a Sunday in summer 70,000 people pass through the turnstiles of the park, and 50,000 to 60,000 on other days of the week, to enjoy Mickey Mouse – who "celebrated" his 60th birthday in 1988 – and the other figures from Disney's fantasy world.

Importance

In Disneyland, everything appears colossal: the size often confuses car drivers who, in spite of the good direction signs, cannot find their cars again on the giant car-parks (some with over 11,000 spaces). However, zealous officials in mini-cars always succeed in finding the vehicles, even with the barest of details. Tourists who have drifted away from their party can be reunited with it if they report to the City Hall in "Main Street USA", near the entrance to the park.

Scale

Large, too, are the hotels in the immediate vicinity, three of which can offer overnight accommodation to more than a thousand people: "Hilton", with 1600 rooms, "Disneyland" with 1174 and "Marriott" with 1043.

Walt Disney and his successors (Disney died in 1966) have invested well over 200 million dollars in this project, which can prove fascinating to all

Pleasure park

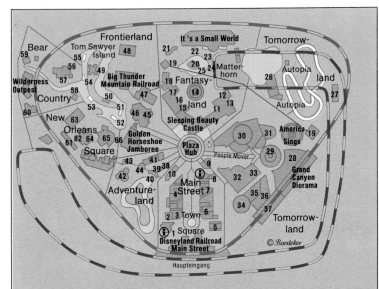

Haupteingang

Disneyland

Anaheim

1 City Hall
2 Fundbüro
3 The Emporium & Shops
4 Penny Arcade
5 The Walt Disney Story
6 Main Street Shops Cinema
7 Main Street Shops
8 Erste Hilfe
9 Plaza Inn
10 Plaza Pavilion
11 Peter Pan's Flight
12 Mr. Toad's Wild Ride
13 Alice in Wonderland
14 King Arthur Carousel
15 Tinker Bell Toy Shoppe
16 Snow White's Scary Adventures
17 Pinocchio's Daring Jorney
18 Village Haus
19 Skyway to Tomorrowland
20 Dumbo – the Flying Elephant
21 Videopolis
22 Casey Junior Circus Train
23 Motor Boat Cruises
24 Matterhorn Bobslids
25 Storybookland Canal Boats
26 Tomorrowland Monorail Station
    Submarine Voyage
27 Disneyland Railroad Tomorrowland
28 Mission to Mars
29 Rocket Jets
30 World Premier Circle-Vision
31 Tomorrowland Terrace
32 Star Tours
33 Star Traders & Star Arcade

Railway
Monorail
Skyway

34 Space Mountain
    Space Stage
35 Magic Eye Theater Captain Eo
36 Space Place
37 Primeval World
38 Enchanted Tiki Room
39 Tahiti Terrace
40 Jungle Cruise
41 Adventureland Bazaar
42 Swiss Family Tree House
43 The Blue Bayou Restaurant
44 River Belle Terrace
45 Frontier Trading Post & Arcade
46 Columbia & Mark Twain Landing
47 Casa Mexicana
48 Big Thunder Ranch
49 Fort Wilderness
50 Barrel Bridge
51 Mark Twain Steam Boat
52 Tom Sawyer Island Rafts
53 Mike Fink Keel Boats
54 Davy Crockett's Explorer Canoes
55 Columbia Sailing Ship
56 Hungry Bear Restaurant
57 Country Bear Playhouse
58 Indian Trading Post
59 Mile Long Bar
60 Restroom
61 Disneyland Railroad New Orleans
62 French Market
63 Haunted Mansion
64 New Orleans Square Shops
65 Café New Orleans
66 Pirates of the Caribbean

"Mickey's Birthday"

Snow White Fountain

age groups. Dozens of shops, from cheap souvenir stalls to elegant specialist stores, will suit all tastes. Every kind of food at all price levels is available, from fast food to French cuisine. There is only one thing you will not find in Disneyland, and which must not be brought in: alcoholic drinks.

A first general view of the park, which has already been visited by well over 100 million people, is obtained from the "Santa Fe & Disneyland Railroad", which passes through a diorama of the Grand Canyon. It is also worth taking a trip on the "Disneyland Alweg Monorail" (2½ miles/4 km).
How long a visit should last depends on the stamina of the visitors, their number and on the weather. However, a minimum of six hours is necessary to cover the total area of 77 acres/31 hectares, and to view the most interesting attractions from the inside (the entrance fee includes, among other things, free visits to all roundabouts, rides, boats and film-shows).

Overall view

Sectors

At the entrance on the right is a street built in the style of a small American town at the turn of the century, with horse-drawn trams, double-decker buses and a fire-engine; in the "theatre" old films are shown, including "Great Moments with Mr. Lincoln".

1. Main Street USA

On the left lies Adventure Land, where you can go by boat on a "jungle cruise" through the jungle with its tropical animals (alligators, hippos, gorillas, water buffaloes and elephants).
In the so-called Tiki Room this exotic world is provided with background music in the shape of "South Sea Fantasies".

2. Adventure Land

Adjoining Adventure Land lies New Orleans Square, its streets typical of a French-influenced town of about 1850, with shops, restaurants, cafés and balconies. Boats (bateaux), such as are used in the swamps of Louisiana,

3. New Orleans Square

67

ply from the square. On the trip you are treated to a colourful revue in the form of a battle between a pirate ship and a coastal fort ("Pirates of the Caribbean") and a ghost scene in an enchanted house, which is a copy of a public building in Baltimore.
From here it is possible to take a train ride to the last sector, Tomorrowland, or else you can walk to

4. Bear Country

This newest section was not built until after Walt Disney's death, but is based largely on his characters, and its best attractions are an original bear revue, the "Country Bear Jamboree" Wild West Show, and a trip in an old-fashioned boat.
Since the summer of 1989 it has been possible to go on a canal trip ("Splash Mountains") through Critter County (previously Bear Country); at a speed of 40 m.p.h., it is the fastest trip in Disneyland.

5. Frontierland

In the adjoining Frontierland you can get an idea of the gold-digging period of the Wild West: a mining-railway runs through the desert and the Rainbow Caverns; the paddle-steamer "Mark Twain" takes you back into the 19th c. On the reproduction of the "Columbia Rediviva", the first American sailing vessel to circumnavigate the world at the end of the 18th c., you can either make a trip on the boat or be taken to visit a farmhouse on Tom Sawyer Island.

6. Fantasyland

In the heart of Disneyland is Fantasyland, where the familiar characters from Disney's productions are brought to life. These include Snow White and the Seven Dwarfs, Mickey Mouse and Alice in Wonderland. Since reconstruction of this section in 1983 the setting for Disney's fairytale world now includes a European village, an imitation of the Castle of Neuschwanstein and a steel-framed "Matterhorn" (sledge rides available). On festive summer nights firework displays add to the atmosphere of make-believe.

7. Tomorrowland

Tomorrowland adjoins Main Street USA. A 2½-mile-/4-km-long cable railway ("Skyway") leads through the "Matterhorn", along the winding "Autopia" motor-racing circuit and the submarine-lake ("Submarine Voyage"). After passing the space travel control centre, a "Saturn" rocket-trip takes you into "space" for several minutes. Most impressive is the "Roundabout of Progress" (General Electric). In the circular Bell Telephone Theater ("Circle Vision 360"), you can experience "The Beautiful America", as in the present day, and the "Wonders of China".

Notes

Please note!

The best time to visit Disneyland is in the months of June to September when opening times are longest. The usual queues at the individual attractions in summer – especially at week-ends – can best be avoided on week-days such as Tuesday and Wednesday when there are fewer visitors.

Opening times

In Jan. and Feb.: Wed.–Fri. 10 a.m.–6 p.m., Sat. 9 a.m.–9 p.m., Sun. 9 a.m.–7 p.m.; Mon. and Tue. closed.
Mar., Apr. and May: daily 10 a.m.–6 p.m., Sat. and Sun. 9 a.m.–9 p.m., in May Sat.until midnight.
June: daily 9 a.m.–9 p.m., Sat. 9 a.m.–midnight, Sun. 9 a.m.–10 p.m.
July, Aug. and the first week of Sept.: daily 9 a.m.–midnight, Sat. 9 a.m.–1 a.m., Sun. 9 a.m.–midnight.

Mid Sept. to end Dec.: Wed.–Sun. 10 a.m.–6 p.m., Sat. and Sun. 9 a.m.–
9 p.m. in Nov. and Dec. 10 a.m.–7 p.m., Mon. and Tue. closed.
On some public holidays (President's birthday, Easter, Memorial Day,
Independence Day, Columbus Day, Thanksgiving week-end and from
20th–30th Dec.) opening times are longer than they would otherwise be at
the time of year.
The Disneyland telephone no. for further information is 714/999-4565.

Anza-Borrego Desert State Park
R/S 5

San Diego County
Altitude: 16–7780 ft/5–2370 m

About 85 miles/136 km north-east of San Diego, and reached via Highways
8, 79 and 78, is the entrance to the biggest state Park in California, which
covers an area of about 600,000 acres/242,200 hectares, and is one of the
most beautiful desert landscapes in the state. Dunes, alluvial land, canyons, palm groves, flowers and cacti (which flower in March and April), as
well as fantastic views, represent only some of the attractions of this area
on the edge of the Colorado Desert.

Location and
* importance

The more than 500 miles/805 km of road are mainly unmetalled, and can be
negotiated only in a cross-country vehicle. Apart from Route 78 (with some
hotels) which runs past Borrego Springs, only the S2, S3 and S22 are
made-up.
Information about the condition of the roads and informative brochures
can be obtained from the Visitor Center west of Borrego Springs (tel. (619)
767-5311).

The park was named after the priest Juan Bautista de Anza, who, in the
course of 2½ months in 1774, crossed the Colorado desert with a small
group from Sonora (Mexico) and reached the Californian mission stations
(see entry).

Name

The Spanish name "Borrego" (year-old ram) refers to the thick-horned
sheep which at one time lived in this wasteland region, but which are
seldom encountered today.

Auburn
R/S 5

Placer County
Altitude: 1300 ft/395 m
Population: 7950

Auburn, founded by inhabitants of the town of the same name in New York
State in the year the gold rush started (1849), lies on the Transcontinental
Highway 80, about 30 miles/50 km north of Sacramento (see entry). Its
carefully restored old town, with houses from the middle of the 19th
century – including an interesting fire-station and the oldest post-office in
continuous use in California – reminds us of the gold rush era.

Location and
origin

Of interest is the Placer County Museum (1273 Placer Street), in which the
early times of this region are documented, for example by means of old
gold-digging tools, as well as Indian and Chinese artefacts.

Placer County
Museum

Open Tues-Sun (Closed holidays) 10 a.m.–4 p.m. In Bernhard House,
which adjoins the museum, Victorian furniture and old photographs are
on display.

Wagons of the first pioneers in Anza-Borrego Desert State Park

Auburn: Fire-brigade House

Vintage car

A romantic bay in Baja California

Avalon

See Santa Catalina Island.

Baja California off the map below S/T 3–7

Mexican State
Population: 2,300,000

By air from Mexico City and other Mexican airports to Tijuana and La Paz (see entries); by ferry; by rail from Mexico City in about 60 hours to Mexicali; by coach from Mexico City in about 44 hours; from the USA by air, by Greyhound coach and by car.

How to get there

The 775 miles/1250 km long and, on an average, 56 miles/90 km wide peninsula of Baja California (Lower California), which consists of two federal states, borders the USA (California) in the north. Its shores are lapped by the Pacific in the west and the Golfo de California in the east. The border between Baja California Norte and Baja California Sur runs along the 28th degree of latitude. The peninsula is a hot, dry area with mountain ranges and richly contoured coasts.

Location and description

The most important chain of mountains is the Sierra de Pedro Mártir, running roughly from north to south, its highest peak being the Cerro de la Encantada (10,100 ft/3080 m above sea level). The border with the state of Sonora is formed by the Rio Colorado, which runs into the northernmost point of the Gulf of California.

Surf breaking in Baja California

The peninsula, which obtained a north to south road connection with the building of the Carretera Transpeninsular in 1974, offers little that is typically Mexican, apart from some mission stations. As a result of its proximity to the USA and the great stream of tourists from the north, its towns and villages have largely assumed an American character. The tourist charm lies in the desert flora (cacti), the impressive silhouettes of the bare mountain regions and the endless coasts, with their mixture of sandy beaches, cliffs and lagoons. Apart from a few places overrun with tourists, in Baja California you can find barren, isolated countryside.

The original Indian population, made up of the Cucapá, Kiliwa, Pai-pai, Cochimí and Ki-nai tribes, numbers scarcely 1000 today.

Fauna

Baja California is rich in varieties of animal life. On the peninsula still live the puma, coyote, fox, red deer, hare, wild goose, wild duck and sea-birds of all kinds; grey whales frolic in the sea and can be watched in the Bay of San Ignacio from December to February; sea-lions, seals, swordfish, dolphins, barracudas and tuna-fish also can be seen.

Archaeological sites

Apart from some rock-paintings, such as those at San Boritja, San Ignacio and Calimalí, Baja California holds little of archaeological interest. Caves have been found in Caguama, Metate Comondú and on the Isla de Cedros.

History

Traces of settlements from pre-Columbian times, going back as far as 7500 B.C., have been found. Almost nothing is known of the little developed culture of the early Indian tribes of the peninsula.

In search of a legendary Amazonian paradise ruled over by a black queen named Calafia, Hernán Cortés landed in the La Paz region in 1535. The Spaniards who followed later met with strong resistance from the Indios, and were unable to gain a foothold there. Embittered by their lack of success, they named the area "California", after the queen who had never been found. Not until after 1697, when the Jesuit missionaries Francisco Eusebio Kino, Juan Maria de Salvatierra and Juan de Ugarte arrived, were

Baja California Norte
Baja California Sur

States
Estados

1a Baja California Sur	12 Aguascalientes	
1b Baja California Norte	13 Jalisco	
	14 Guanajuato	
2 Sonora	15 Querétaro	
3 Chihuahua	16 Hidalgo	
4 Sinaloa	17 Colima	
5 Durango	18 Michoacán	
6 Coahuila	19 México	
7 Nuevo León	20 Morelos	
8 Zacatecas	21 Tlaxcala	
9 San Luis Potosí	22 Puebla	26 Chiapas
10 Tamaulipas	23 Veracruz	27 Tabasco
11 Nayarit	24 Guerrero	28 Campeche
	25 Oaxaca	29 Yucatán
		30 Quintana Roo

D.F. Distrito Federal (Federal district)

© *Baedeker*

they successful in colonising parts of the country. After the expulsion of the Jesuits in 1767, the Franciscans took over this task, until the Dominicans superseded them in 1772. In 1804 Lower California was separated from California, and during the war with the USA the peninsula was occupied by American troops in 1847/1848. In 1931 the division into northern and southern territories took place. Finally in 1952 Baja California Norte, and in 1974 Baja California Sur, were declared independent federal states.

As well as a considerable tourist industry, the cultivation of cotton, maize, wheat, alfalfa, vegetables and fruit is carried on with the aid of artificial irrigation. The processing of agricultural and fishing products, and the mining of gold, copper, iron, silver and salt are worthy of mention. Fishing could be a good source of income but it lacks a strong fleet and processing facilities.

Economy

In addition to Tijuana (see entry), the most important destinations to aim for in Baja California Norte, which do not lie on the Carretera Transpeninsular, are Tecate, Mexicali and San Felipe (for all these see the entry for Tijuana).

Destinations

On the Carretera Transpeninsular from Tijuana to Cabo San Lucas

Baja California's largest town, Tijuana (see entry), on the border with the USA, is the starting point of the 1056 miles/1700 km long MEX 1 (Carretera Transpeninsular), which runs the whole length of the peninsula.

After 19 miles/30 km, the first place you come to is El Rosarito. The next town of any size, after 50 miles/80 km, is Ensenada (population 225,000). This fishing port, now a favourite tourist spot (water sports, deep-sea fishing), extends along the beautiful bay of Todos los Santos, which was discovered in 1542 by the Portuguese seafarer Rodríguez Cabrillo. After the

Ensenada

separation of the northern part of the peninsula from the southern part, Ensenada was the capital of the northern part from 1888 until 1910, when Mexicali took over this position.

In addition to tourism, the town lives mainly from fishing and its deep-water harbour. In the town is the biggest wine-cellar in all Mexico, the "Bodegas Santo Tomás".

"La Bufadora"

10 miles/16 km south of Ensenada, near Maneadera, a road branches off to the north-west to the tip of land known as Cabo Punta la Banda (14 miles/22 km), where you can witness a natural spectacle frequently found on the Pacific coast, in the form of "La Bufadora" (from "bufar" = to snort). The sea water is squeezed with terrific force through a narrow opening in the rocks, and hurled upwards with a mighty roar to a height of 70 feet/20 m. After returning to the main road continue along the 110 miles/175 km stretch to San Quentin; along this stretch you can visit some old mission stations, such as Santo Tomás, San Vicente and Vicente Guerrero, and Orte La Huerta and San Miguel, which are inhabited by Cochimí Indios. The

San Quintín

farming and fishing village of San Quintín, lying in a fertile valley on the flat bay of the same name has beautiful white beaches.

The road to the south leaves the coast near El Rosario and now runs inland. In addition to El Rosario, there are further mission stations along the road, including San Fernando, San Agustín and Cataviña, which lies in the midst of impressive, rocky scenery.

Bahía de los Angeles

The road leads past the Laguna Chapala and 30 miles/50 km further on there is a turn off to the left, which leads to the beautiful Bahía de los Angeles (Bay of Angels), about 43 miles/70 km away.

Border

After returning to the MEX 1, the first place you will come to is Rosarito. Shortly before the Guerrero Negro, a 130 ft/40 m high steel eagle (Monumento Aguila) marks the 28th degree of latitude, the border between the federal states of Baja California Norte and Baja California Sur, and also the boundary between the time-zones Hora del Pacifico in the north and Hora de las Montanas in the south (+ one hour). In the vicinity of Guerrero Negro are huge salt-deposits caused by evaporation, which are among the largest in the world.

Grey whales

The quiet waters of the lagoons by the Bahía Sebastián Vizcaíno (Laguna Scammon, Laguna Ojo de Liebre) as well as the more easily accessible lagoon San Ignacio, south of the Sierra Vizcaíno, offer each year, from the end of December until March, the unique spectacle of the grey whales (Spanish "ballena gris") mating and bringing their young into the world. In and around Guerrero there are several points from which you can observe the whales. About 2 miles/3 km south of the town a road, marked with road signs showing symbols of grey whales, turns off to the nature park (Parque Natural de la Ballena Gris), which is about a further 17 miles/27 km. Tourist visits by boat are at present very restricted.

The grey whales (eschrichtius gibbosus), weighing up to 25 tons and measuring 30 to 45 ft/10 to 15 m in length, begin their long journey in the autumn, in the arctic waters of the Bering Sea. As grey whales have a gestation period of 13 months, the pregnant whales give birth while the other animals are preparing to mate. Two males and one female are involved in the mating. The dominant whale does the actual mating, while the other male helps the female into a suitable position. Having been seriously decimated by hunting, they have been a protected species since 1947.

San Ignacio
* Jesuit Church

From Guerrero Negro the road leads inland and, after about 78 miles/126 km, it reaches the pretty town of San Ignacio. With its Jesuit church, begun in 1728 and completed in 1786 by Juan Crisóstomo Gómez, it possesses the best preserved place of worship in Baja California. For those interested it is worthwhile making the three or four hour trip from here, under expert guidance, to see the cave paintings of Cueva de la Cuesta del

Palmerito. These portray large impressions of animals and men, the origin and age of which have not yet been researched. Other caves in the vicinity should be visited only if, in addition to a guide, you have some days to spare and are suitably equipped.

On the left, on the road to the coast, stands the still active volcano Las Tres Virgenes (7150 ft/2180 m above sea-level).

46 miles/74 km further on from San Ignacio you come to the little port of Santa Rosalía (population 14,000). The little town was founded in the middle of the 19th c. The French, to whom the copper mines of the region previously belonged, built the church of Santa Rosalía, which was constructed of imported iron sections and was reputedly based on a design by Gustave Eiffel, the constructor of the Eiffel Tower. Further items of interest are the anthropological museum in the Casa de Cultura, and at the northern entrance a mining museum with an old train used for transporting ore. There is a ferry link to Guaymas (Sonora).

Santa Rosalía

Continuing the journey from Santa Rosalía, after about 25 miles/40 km you come to a turning on the right to the Hacienda Baltasar leading by way of a track to the great caves of San Borjita (some 14 miles/22 km), where you can see colourful wall-paintings of hunting and warlike scenes. This trip can be made only in a vehicle suitable for cross-country work, and the last mile-and-a-half or so (2 or 3 km) must be covered on foot. In the vicinity there are are a number of other caves (La Trinidad, San José de los Arce, El Coyote, La Esperanza) with similar but less impressive paintings.

Caves of San Borjita

The next place of any size is the little town of Mulegé (population 5000), on the Gulf of California, with the Jesuit mission of Santa Rosalía de Mulegé (1705). This is a copy of the Cananea Prison (Sonora) which has neither bars nor locked doors and which was made famous in folk-songs and street-ballads. There is a lovely walk along the river through the groves of date palms. The town also has several beaches and opportunities for fishing and boating.

Mulegé

About 6 miles/10 km past Mulegé, in a particularly charming coastal region, stretches Bahía Concepcíon, with beautiful beaches such as Punta Arena, Santiapac, El Coyote, El Requesón and Los Muertos.

*Bahía Concepción

84 miles/135 km from Mulegé you come to the picturesque little town of Loreto (population 11,000; fiesta: 8th September, Dia de Nuestra Señora de Loreto), which was founded by the Jesuits in 1697 when they built the now restored mission church, and is thus the oldest Jesuit foundation on the peninsula. Loreto was the setting-off point for the exploration and Christianisation of Lower California, which is well documented in the mission museum. Between 1776 and 1830 the town was also the capital of Lower California. This coastal town on the Gulf of California is popular as a base for trips to the offshore islands and for deep-sea fishing and diving.

Loreto

A detour from Loreto over 25 miles/40 km of mainly poor roads (cross-country vehicle neccesary) leads to San Javier, where you can visit the well-preserved mission church, dedicated to San Francisco Javier and dating from the first half of the 18th c.; it has a fine Baroque façade and guilded high altar.

San Francisco Javier

16 miles/26 km south of Loreto, in magnificent natural surroundings, the new seaside resort of Puerto Escondido is developing.

Some 25 miles/40 km out of Loreto the road again turns inland, and after 50 miles/80 km reaches the town of Villa Insurgentes. From here, a turn-off leads to Puert A. López Mateos, situated on the long Bahía de Magdalena (Pacific coast). Like that of Sebastián Vizcaíno this bay is the place to watch the mating and breeding of the many grey whales, which winter here every year. An equally well situated place to watch the whales from a boat is the little harbour town of Puerto San Carlos to the south, best reached by going 35 miles/55 km in a westerly direction from Ciudad Constitución. The Isla de Santa Margarita in the bay is inhabited by numerous sea-lions.

If you turn back near Ciudad Constitución onto the Carretera Transpeninsular it is then about a further 130 miles/210 km to La Paz.

From La Paz, MEX 1 leads via San Pedro (after 16 miles/26 km there is a turn-off to Todos Santos and Cabo San Lucas) and El Triunfo (former mining town) to the fishing village and seaside resort of Los Barriles (65 miles/104 km). After a further 4 miles/6 km you come to Buenavista, visited mainly by sporting fisherman and sailors.

San José del Cabo   From Buenavista, via Miraflores, a former settlement of Pericúe Indians, now known for its beautiful leatherwork, it is another 47 miles/75 km or so to San José del Cabo (population 23,000; fiesta; 19th March, Día de San José). This old fishing and mission village is now an important agricultural centre for the region. In addition, it possesses several beaches, some with strong waves, and good facilities for fishing. In the Culture House is a small museum and a library.

South of San José del Cabo there are good opportunities for surfing at various points.

In another 22 miles/35 km you reach Cabo San Lucas, the terminus of the Carretera Transpeninsular.

Bakersfield N 3

Kern County
Altitude: 407 ft/124 m
Population; 118,600

Location and origin   Bakersfield is easy to reach by road, along one of the great motorways of California, the US 5; it is 111 miles/179 km from Los Angeles and about 290 miles/465 km from San Francisco. Founded by Colonel Thomas Baker in the seventies of the last century, it first came to life in 1885, when – almost 40 years later than in the actual gold area to the north – gold was discovered in the Kern River Canyon. Major roles in the development of this town were played by the discovery of oil, by agriculture and wine production (about 1/4 of the wine of the US is pressed here). However, in 1889 a fire destroyed the old town; the 1952 earthquake also caused great damage. Nevertheless, the population increased considerably in the years that followed; with an annual growth rate of some 7% Bakersfield stands at the head of all Californian towns.

Pioneer Village; Kern County Museum   About 3 miles/5 km east of Bakersfield, on the CA 99 (3801 Chester Avenue) and covering an area of about 15 acres/6 hectares, stands Pioneer Village, with 60 restored houses from the second half of the 19th century. In its museum, the main branch of which is in Bakersfield, exhibitions alternating between natural and cultural history are held. (Open: weekdays 8 a.m.–5 p.m., weekends 10 a.m.–5 p.m.; tel. (805) 861-2132.)

Barstow P 5

San Bernardino County
Altitude: 2100 ft/642 m
Population; 19,500

Location and origin   Barstow lies north-east of San Bernardino, at the foot of the Calico Mountains and at the intersection of the US 15, US 40 and CA 58 highways. Founded in the year 1880, it did not attain economic importance until a decade later, when gold and silver was found in the hills. This upsurge was further fostered by the nearby military no-go area of Fort Irwin, with its weapon testing grounds, and by its favourable position as a setting-off point for expeditions and trips into Death Valley National Monument (see entry) as well as into the Mojave Desert (see entry; US 15).

The ghost town of Calico lies 10 miles/17 km east of Barstow, near the US 15. From 1881 to 1896 it was one of the most important US-American towns, from where thousands set off to prospect for silver in the nearby mountains. When the price of silver fell in 1895 the silver mines closed and Calico went into decline. In 1954 the ghost town was restored by the owner of Knott's Berry Farm.
(Open: daily 9 a.m.–5 p.m.; admission free; tel. (619) 254-2122.)

Ghost town of Calico

This museum lies 14 miles/23 km east of Calico, on the US 15 not far from the unmetalled Minneola Road. It was opened a quarter of a century ago by the renowned archaeologist Dr Louis Leakey, who excavated more than 12,000 stone-age implements dating back some 200,000 years. These are the oldest artefacts to prove the existence of man in the western hemisphere.
(Open: Wed.–Sun. 8.30 a.m.–4.30 p.m.; tours each hour on the half-hour until 3.30 p.m. except at 12.30 p.m.; tel. (619) 256-3591.)

Calico Early Man Archaeological Site

In the Mojave Valley Museum (270 East Virginia Way) minerals from the Calico Mountains, archaeological finds, Indian artefacts and photos are on display. (Open: daily 9 a.m.–5 p.m.; admission free; tel. (619) 256-5452.)

Mojave River Valley Museum

Benicia   H 1/2

Solano County
Altitude: 8 ft/2.5 m
Population: 18,250

Benicia lies on the north coast side of the road from Carquinez which connects San Pablo Bay with Suisun Bay. Founded in the year 1847 – before California became a member of the United States – Benicia is one of the oldest towns in the federation. However, the hopes of its founders to build a large harbour there, have not been been fulfilled; nevertheless, Benicia was the capital of the state between 1853/1854. Here, too, the first Protestant church was built (1859), and the first Masonic Lodge in California came into being. Two camel stalls, a beautiful bell-tower and a Dominican cemetery bear witness to the early history of the town. It is also known that Jack London caught oysters in Benicia.

Location and origin

Berkeley   H 1

Alameda County
Altitude: 150 ft/46 m
Population: 106,000

At the northern end of the San Francisco–Oakland Bay Bridge are the outskirts of Berkeley which was always intended to be a university town even at the time it was founded as a ranch in 1866. Only some 12 miles/ 19 km from San Francisco and easily reached from there by car via the Golden Gate Bridge or by the BART underground railway, the town bears the name of the Irish bishop George Berkeley, responsible for the saying "The Empire is spreading westwards". The University of California was founded as early as 1873. Today, the second largest campus of that university (31,000 students) is to be found here. Since a raging fire destroyed whole residential areas of Berkeley in 1923, the town has had one of the most efficient fire-protection systems.

Location and origin

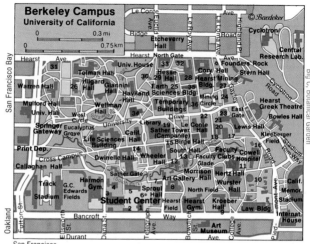

1 Student Union (Visitor Center)
2 Eshleman Hall
3 Zellerbach Hall
4 Alumni House
5 Dining Commons (Mensa)
6 Ludwig's Fountain
7 Architects & Engineers Building
8 Barrows Hall
9 Lowie Museum of Anthropology
10 Calvin Laboratory
11 Minor Hall
12 Moses Hall
13 Stephens Hall
14 Durant Hall
15 Placement Center
16 Girton Hall
17 Hildebrand Hall
18 Gilman Hall
19 Bancroft Library
20 Glauque Hall
21 Latimer Hall
22 Campbell Hall
23 Physical Sciences
24 Stanley Building
25 McLaughlin Hall
26 Morgan Hall
27 Donner Laboratory
28 Davis Hall
29 Seismograph (Earth Sciences Building)
30 Leuschner Observatory
31 Biochemistry Building
32 Naval Architecture Building
33 North Gate Hall
34 Moffitt Library
35 Bechtel Building
36 Evans Building

Places of interest

Worth seeing are Charles Lee Tilden Regional Park and Bancroft Way, with its pubs and shops much favoured by the students.

The main attraction, however, is the world-famous University of California. An excursion to Berkeley enables the visitor to appreciate the very special campus atmosphere of an American university.

A further attraction is provided by the University Art Museum, with a collection of paintings by 19th and 20th c. artists and an important film archive.

*University of California

Location and origin

In the eastern part, some 5 miles/8 km north-east of the bridge across the bay, lie the extensive grounds of the University of California (Telegraph Avenue and Bancroft Way), whose world reputation results not only from its numerous Nobel Prize winners, but also, inter alia, from the student unrest in the sixties which spread from here to the whole western world.

Guided tours

Guided tours of the campus take place from Monday to Friday at 1 p.m. from the Visitor Center in the Student Union building on the southern edge of the campus. Group tours, lasting an hour and a half, can be arranged by appointment each day at 1 p.m. (tel. (415) 642-5215).

Sather Tower (bell tower)

The symbol of the university is the bell tower known as Sather Tower, a 1914 reproduction of the St Marc's Tower in Venice (open: daily 10 a.m.–4.15 p.m.). Being 308 ft/94 m high, it towers over all the other buildings on the spacious and park-like university grounds. From the top

Berkeley: University of California, Sather Tower

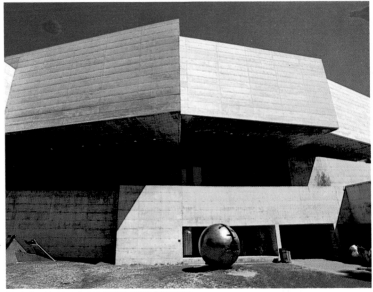

Berkeley University: exterior of Art Museum

(lift) there is a magnificent view of the campus, San Francisco Bay and the Golden Gate Bridge. Also worthy of mention is the peal of bells, which can be heard on weekdays at 7.50 a.m., noon and 6 p.m. (except during examination times), Saturdays at 6 p.m. and Sundays at 2 p.m.

Other buildings

South-west of the bell tower stands South Hall, built in 1873 in the Tudor style, and the oldest building on the campus. Further south-west is the Sather Gate which together with the Plaza forms the centre of the student quarter.

The Earth Sciences Building, not far from the north gate, contains palaeontological and mineralogical collections, as well as an interesting seismograph on the ground floor. (Open 8 a.m.–noon; admission free; tel. 642-1827.)

In the chapel of the Pacific School of Religion (1198 Scenic Avenue) can be seen one of the largest stained-glass windows in the world. (Open: Mon.–Fri. 8.30 a.m.–4.30 p.m.)

The Cyclotron (particle accelerator) in the north-east and the California Memorial Stadium, a sports arena with 76,500 seats, in the south-east, are also of interest.

Lawrence-Berkeley Laboratory

Something of a special nature which is worth a visit is the Lawrence-Berkeley Laboratory, in which the Nobel Prizewinner Ernest O. Lawrence pioneered new developments in the field of atomic research. His assistants included, among others, J. Robert Oppenheimer who did important preparatory work in developing the first atomic bomb. When Oppenheimer opposed the making of the hydrogen bomb investigations were made on the grounds of his alleged Communist views, and President Eisenhower withdrew his permission for him to work on any further secret projects.

A guided tour through this extremely interesting research station is possible on Tuesdays at 2 p.m. if a prior appointment is made by telephone (tel. 486-4000, ext. 5611; not on public holidays or during university vacations).

Museums

In addition to the University Art Museum, there are the following museums on the campus:

The collection in the Judah L. Magnes Memorial Museum (2911 Russell Street; admission free) includes mainly Jewish ritual items. Two libraries adjoin it. (Open: Sun.–Thur. 10 a.m.–4 p.m.; tel. (415) 849-2710.)

The Palestine Institute exhibits archaeological finds from Palestine, from the time of the Old Testament up to the fifth century B.C. (Open: daily 9 a.m.–5 p.m.)

The Robert H. Lowie Museum of Anthropology displays anthropological collections to visitors. (Open Mon.–Fri. 10 a.m.–4 p.m., Sat.–Sun. noon–4 p.m., closed Weds.)

University Art Museum

Foundation

This museum, situated on the university campus, 2626 Bancroft Way (open: Wed.–Sun. 11 a.m.–5 p.m.; admission free on Thur.) was built in 1970 to the design by Mario Campi, and in the following two decades has earned a good reputation. The surprisingly large stocks held by this young museum stem from works of art collected at the time the university was founded (1873).

Hans Hofmann

The decisive impetus leading to the building of the museum came from the German painter Hans Hofmann, who lived in America from 1932 and had already held summer courses at the University of California in Berkeley from 1930 to 1931.

As a teacher (he opened his own art schools) he had a great influence on young American painters, such as Louise Nevelson, Helen Frankenthaler and Larry Rivers.

In 1963 he presented 45 of his paintings to the university and promised to donate money for the building of a museum.

Seven years passed before it was completed. Today, about a half of all Hofmann's works to be found here are displayed in one big hall, so that in no other museum can you get a better view of the work of this painter. The museum also has a big collection of orientalia, as well as numerous paintings from the 19th c. Special exhibitions are often held, particularly of painters, sculptors and photographers of the 20th c. (tel 642-1207).

The University Art Museum is also the home of the Pacific Film Archive, which continually offers interesting productions in its 200-seat auditorium. It possesses a stock of about 5000 films, including the greatest number of copies of Japanese films outside Japan; there are also numerous avant-garde and experimental US films, as well as a collection of 35 mm copies of Soviet silent films (tel. 642-1412).

Pacific Film
Archive

Beverly Hills

See Los Angeles

Big Bear Lake   Q 5

San Bernardino County
Altitude: 6750 ft/2059 m
Population: 3300

Big Bear Lake, on Highway 18, some 30 miles/48 km north east of San Bernardino in the San Bernardino Mountains, is situated in the centre of an increasingly popular area for summer and winter sports (swimming in the lake is prohibited). Not far away is the start of the Gold Fever Trail, a car journey of some three hours through a number of places which still remain from the second Californian gold-rush in the years 1860 to 1875. A brochure giving more detailed descriptions is available free of charge from the Ranger Station, 4 miles/6½ km east of Fawnskin, on Highway 38.

Location and
importance

Ski-slopes in the immediate vicinity are:
Snow Summit, 1 mile/1.6 km south of the lake, reached via a turn-off from Highway 18;
Goldmine, 2 miles/3.2 km south-east of the lake, reached via a turn-off from Highway 18.
Snow Forest, ½ mile/800 m away, on Pine Knot Avenue. Further information from the Chamber of Commerce, 41647 Big Bear Blvd., Big Bear Lake 92315, tel. 866-4607.

Ski-slopes

Big Sur   K O

Monterey County
Altitude: 154 ft/47 m
Population: about 1000

Big Sur – the name originates from Rio Grande del Sur, the biggest river in the South – is one of the most beautiful wooded coastal regions in northern California. It begins about 4 miles/6½ km south of Carmel (see entry) in Yankee Point, and stretches along the coast-road No. 1 as far as Salmon Cove, some 17 miles/26 km north of San Simeon (see entry). From Highway 1 there are splendid views over the picturesque coastal region. To the east, however, stretches a true wilderness; the Santa Lucia Mountains and Ventana Forests, with more than 220 miles/350 km of trails, are ideal for

Location and
origin

Coast near Big Sur

experienced walkers. The long-lasting dispute between those supporting further economic development of the area and the nature conservationists ended with the compromise that they would agree to the building of only 850 new houses here, none of which could be seen from the coast road. In addition, only small hotels with less than 300 rooms may be added to the 165 hotels already there. The main objective is to leave untouched the natural beauty of this region.

Artists

The name of Big Sur is linked with numerous artists; the writer Henry Miller lived in Big Sur in 1944 when it had only 60 inhabitants. At that time a friend of Miller's intended to set up a Henry Miller museum. John Kerouac, one of the "beat" literary figures, wrote the novel "Big Sur" about a "beat" leader who settled here. Robinson Jeffers immortalized the area in his poems; Joan Baez organised a festival here for many years called "Celebration at Big Sur"; since 1962 the Esalen Institute has had its home here; its aim is to help people to a new feeling of awareness by means of meditation and psychedelic insight.

State Park

In the close vicinity of Big Sur lies Pfeiffer-Big Sur State Park, with bathing facilities, the most southerly redwood grove in California, and further south the Julia Pfeiffer Burns State Park, a setting-off point for numerous walks in the Ventana Wilderness.

Bishop   K 5

Inyo County
Altitude: 4150 ft/1264 m
Population: 3300

Location and importance

Bishop lies at the north end of Owens Valley, between the two highest mountain chains in the state. From here, climbers set out on extended

Seals wallowing in Bodega Bay

climbs in the eastern part of the Sierra Nevada; in particular, Bishop is the best starting point from which to reach the Bristlecone Pine Forest (Inyo National Forest), which has the oldest trees in California. One of these trees, which has been named Methuselah, is, according to the findings of Dr Louis Schulman of Washington University in St Louis, more than 4600 years old, and another, "Pine Alpha", bears this name because it was the first pine over 4000 years old which Schulman could definitely identify.

To reach this rough terrain is far from simple: from Bishop you take Route 395 southwards as far as Big Pine, then turn east on to Route 168. About 13 miles/20 km from Big Pine, a wide road climbs up to a height of 11,500 ft/3500 m into the Bristlecone Pines region. The total distance from Big Pine to Schulman or Methuselah Grove is 35 miles/54 km, quite a difficult stretch, but you will not need a cross-country vehicle.
After a further 14 miles/22 km you come to Patriarch Grove, containing more examples of ancient Bristlecone pines. Only rarely do they exceed 23 ft/7 m tall; the trunks are gnarled and shine from afar. In the raw climate, and in view of the low rainfall, they probably reach such a great age only because they do not have to share the meagre water supplies with animals or plants. From Schulman Grove it is possible to do a 4 mile/6½ km tour on foot; in view of the height and the rough climate great care should be taken. The best time for a visit are the summer months.

Routes: pine groves

Also worth seeing is the Laws Railway Museum, lying about 5 miles/8½ km south-east on Route 6. Here the once bustling but now silent Laws Southern Pacific railway station dating from 1883, as well as a post-office more than 100 years old and other artefacts from that period have been lovingly restored. (Open: daily Mar. 1st–mid Nov.; at other times only on Sat. and Sun. 10 a.m.–4 p.m.; admission free; tel. (619) 873-5950.)

Place of interest

Old railway engine at Knott's Berry Farm

Bodega Bay   G 1

Sonoma County
Altitude: 120 ft/37 m
Population: 300

Location and
origin

Little Bodega Bay is part of Point Reyes National Seashore (see entry) and
lies roughly on the spot where Francis Drake dropped anchor in the year
1579. In 1809 Ivan Kusko of the Russian-American Co. established a settlement here for the purpose of growing wheat and catching otters. In order to
halt the Russian advance the Mexican governor Vallejo gave three American sailors some land on the borders of the Russian settlement. After the
Russians had withdrawn the land was sold to John A. Sutter.

Importance

Bodega Bay, where Alfred Hitchcock shot the film "The Birds", is today an
important fishing-port. The University of California also has a laboratory of
marine biology here.

Bodie State Historic Park   J 5

Mono County
Altitude: 8530 ft/2600 m

Location and
general comments

This ghost town, situated 20 miles/32 km south-east of Bridgeport on
Routes 395 and 270 (the final three miles are not made-up) once boasted
10,000 gold diggers, who were a particularly corrupt and disreputable
bunch. Until about 1876 large amounts of gold were mined here; then the
town fell into decay. The remaining 170 houses have not been fully restored, but were kept from further decay by the creation of a state park in

1964. As a result of the efforts to retain the gold digging atmosphere of the previous century, it represents a place of interest unique in California. In the winter months, the unmetalled stretch of the approach road is often barred to traffic (tel. 525-7232).

Borrego Springs

See Anza-Borrego Desert State Park

Buena Park   P 3

Orange County
Altitude: 75 ft/23 m
Population: 64,200

Buena Park is one of those towns on the US 5 Highway south of Los Angeles which follow one another without any clear boundaries, namely, Norwalk, Buena Park, Anaheim (see entry) and Santa Ana (see entry). This town, which has quickly shot up without any particular character, is typical of suburban development in the larger conurbations of California. In addition to Knott's Berry Farm, the oldest Californian pleasure park, Buena Park also offers other attractions;

Location and origin

8039 Beach Boulevard (2 miles/3 km south of the US 5 on Route CA 39): in the year 1920 Walter Knott opened a fruit-stall here. Shortly afterwards he added a restaurant, in which at first he served only chicken dishes. The jams his wife made were a further speciality. In the course of time the farm developed into the present pleasure park to which new attractions are constantly being added. The emphasis here is on the re-awakening of the themes of the American past; the gold rush, a Spanish-American fiesta village, the "Roaring Twenties", a 19th century railway which runs round a large part of the grounds, a reproduction of the Independence Hall in Philadelphia with its Liberty Bell in its original size, and roundabouts.
In the latest section ("Wild Water Wilderness") you take a white-water trip ("Big Foot Rapid") in original surroundings. (Open: Sun.–Fri. 9 a.m.– midnight, Sat. 9 a.m.–1 a.m.; closed at Christmas; tel. (714) 220-5200.)

∗ Knott's Berry Farm

7711 Beach Boulevard: in this museum are more than 200 life-size wax figures of film and television stars, some in authentic-looking scenes, ranging from Charlie Chaplin to "Star Wars". There is also a fine collection of bioscopes (the first film projection equipment), props from old films, rare film posters and Hollywood photos. (Open: Sun.–Thur. 9 a.m.–11 p.m., Fri. and Sat. 10 a.m.–10 p.m.; tel. (714) 522-1154.)

Six Flags Movieland Wax Museum

7884 E. La Palma Avenue (corner of Beach Boulevard): here will be found dioramas amd military memorabilia from Europe (including the biggest military uniform collection in North America) – from the antique to the Second World War. The most famous exhibits are some of Hermann Goering's uniforms. (Open: in summer daily except Mon.; in the remaining months daily except Mon. and Tue.; tel. 952-1776.)

Museum of World Wars

Further information about Buena Park can be obtained from the Chamber of Commerce: tel. 521-0261.

Information

Burbank

See Los Angeles

Calistoga   G 1

Napa County
Altitude: 360 ft/110 m
Population: 4220

Calistoga lies at the northern end of the Napa Valley, on Highways 29 and 128, some 75 miles/120 km from San Francisco. The town was founded in 1859 by Sam Brannan who sensed in the hot springs, the natural mud and the geysers the ideal requirements for building Cambria into a spa. Calistoga (the name is a combination of California and Saratoga, an important spa in New York State) reached its peak in the seventies and eighties of the last century. Since then vine cultivation together with some large wine-cellars has been the main source of income.
Location and origin

About 8 miles/13 km north of Calistoga, on the CA 29, stands the extinct volcano Mount St Helena where Robert Louis and Fanny Stevenson spent part of their honeymoon in 1880 (Robert Louis Stevenson State Park near Mount St Helena with a statue of the poet).
Mount St Helena

Only 1 mile/1.6 km away between Routes 29 and 128 can be seen the "Old Faithful Geyser of California", one of the few geysers in the world which at regular intervals shoots some 98 ft/20 m high fountains into the air. (Open: daily in summer 9 a.m.–6 p.m., at other times 9 a.m.–5 p.m.)
Old Faithful Geyser

Some 5 miles/9 km to the west by Petrified Forest Road you can see fossilised redwoods and a museum. (Open: daily in summer 9 a.m.–6 p.m., at other times 9 a.m.–5 p.m.)
Redwoods Petrified Forest

In the main street of Calistoga (1411 Washington Street) is the Sharpsteen Museum, with photos, dioramas and other artefacts from the town's early days when it was still a spa. The wood cabin near the museum, which was built for those visiting the spa is another reminder of these days.
(Museum open: May to Oct. 10 a.m.–4 p.m., at other times noon–4 p.m.; tel. 942-5911. Further information: Calistoga Chamber of Commerce, 1458 Lincoln Avenue; tel. (707) 942-6333.)
Sharpsteen Museum

Cambria   *Blue Whale Inn*   L 1

San Luis Obispo County
Altitude: 66 ft/20 m
Population: 3000

Only 6 miles/10 km south of San Simeon (see entry), the site of the castle built by William Randolph Hearst, and not far from Highway US 1, lies the little town of Cambria, which offers a welcome change. It is built almost entirely in the English style, and because of its quiet atmosphere and its beautiful beach, numerous artists have chosen to live there. The short detour before going on to Morro Bay (see entry) and San Luis Obispo (see entry) is worthwhile, not least because of the many interesting shops. In an historical schoolhouse dating from 1881 the Cambria Allied Arts Association offers an insight into the work of native artists. (Open: daily noon–3.30 p.m.; tel. (805) 927-8190.)
Location and general comments

Carlsbad   R 4

San Diego County. Altitude: 40 ft/12 m. Population: 36,000.

◀ *"Old Faithful" geyser near Calistoga*

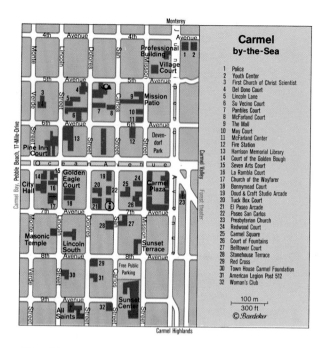

Monterey

Carmel
by-the-Sea

1 Police
2 Youth Center
3 First Church of Christ Scientist
4 Del Dono Court
5 Lincoln Lane
6 Su Vecino Court
7 Panties Court
8 McFarland Court
9 The Mall
10 May Court
11 McFarland Center
12 Fire Station
13 Harrison Memorial Library
14 Court of the Golden Bough
15 Seven Arts Court
16 La Rambla Court
17 Church of the Wayfarer
18 Bonnymead Court
19 Doud & Craft Studio Arcade
20 Tuck Box Court
21 El Paseo Arcade
22 Paseo San Carlos
23 Presbyterian Church
24 Redwood Court
25 Carmel Square
26 Court of Fountains
27 Belltower Court
28 Stonehouse Terrace
29 Red Cross
30 Town House Carmel Foundation
31 American Legion Post 512
32 Woman's Club

100 m
300 ft
©Baedeker

Carmel Highlands

Location and general comments

Although it bears no resemblance at all to the famous Bohemian spa of the same name (now Carlovy Vary), it must be explained that Carlsbad owes its name to mineral springs which are no longer used, but whose healing properties are every bit as good as those of Karlsbad. Established in 1889, Carlsbad has developed into one of the favourite water-sports resorts in southern California, where a lot of golf and tennis is also played. Today Carlsbad has merged with Oceanside, the town to its north which was twice as large, to form one town.

Carmel

J 1

Monterey County
Altitude: 220 ft/67 m
Population: 4800

Location and origin

Carmel, a favourite resort of artists, is charmingly situated south of San Francisco on the Monterey peninsula. The Spanish seafarer Sebastian Vizcaino named the river flowing past Carmel after the three Carmelite monks who in 1603 landed with him not far from the second Californian mission which was originally built in Monterey (see entry). On instructions from the Mexican viceroy, he pushed on from here to Monterey, the northernmost point of his journey. Carmel grew only slowly; at the beginning of the 20th c. it was still an unimportant village with cattle grazing nearby.

*Importance

Carmel was then discovered by painters, writers and photographers, who chose to live there, but its fame had not yet spread beyond the borders of California. It did not fully develop into a mass-tourist attraction until after

Carmel: Serra sculpture

Carmel: shops

the Second World War. Today it is world famous. The election of Clint Eastwood as mayor (1986) contributed to this in no small way.

The long-lasting struggle between those advocating increased growth and those supporting the status quo finally led to a compromise, as a result of which Carmel changed only slightly and was able to retain its distinctive charm, with its houses clearly influenced by English village architecture. You will look in vain here for street lights or neon signs; there are still only very few pavements; the houses have no numbers (directions read "north of Ocean Avenue" or "west of San Carlos"); Monterey pines grow in the centre; no post is delivered (all the inhabitants collect it from the post office at the south-east corner of 5th and Dolores Street); there is a law against wearing high heels; eating in the street is forbidden; there are no parking meters, no large garages and no high-rise buildings; parking in the streets is restricted to one or two hours, and the streets are patrolled by 26 local policemen and policewomen.

Tradition

Carmel has more than 50 restaurants (fast-food restaurants such as McDonalds and Kentucky Fried Chicken are not allowed), about 70 galleries and 40 real-estate agents. The total of some 1200 shops and service establishments are in a ratio of one to every four inhabitants, but are aimed at the large number of tourists who spend many millions of dollars here every year. In the high season especially – some 50,000 cars drive through Carmel in one day at the weekend – the stream of visitors is overwhelming. This combination of cosy informality and mass tourism is Carmel's unique secret. The bulk of the visitors stay in the square mile of the town centre. Only a few venture out into the residential areas or on to the small but beautiful beach

Tourism

In contrast to many other places in California, Carmel does not depend on outstanding individual attractions, but rather on its effect as a whole, and this is what makes a visit there worthwhile. The weather is mild all the year. 300 days of sunshine each year is the norm. However, there is often a

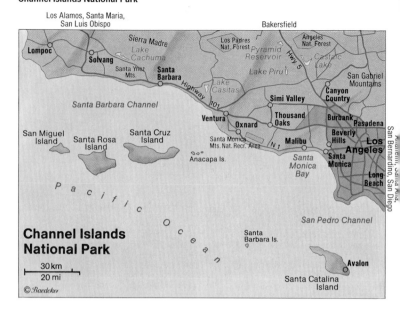

Los Alamos, Santa Maria, San Luis Obispo

Bakersfield

Lompoc

Sierra Madre

Solvang

Lake Cachuma

Santa Ynez Mts.

Santa Barbara

Los Padres Nat. Forest

Pyramid Reservoir

Angeles Nat. Forest

Castaic Lake

Hwy 5

Santa Barbara Channel

Lake Casitas

Highway

101

Lake Piru

San Gabriel Mountains

Canyon Country

Simi Valley

Ventura

Oxnard

Thousand Oaks

Burbank

Pasadena

San Miguel Island

Santa Rosa Island

Santa Cruz Island

Santa Monica Mts. Nat. Recr. Area

N 1

Malibu

Beverly Hills

Los Angeles

Anacapa Is.

Santa Monica Bay

Santa Monica

Long Beach

San Bernardino, San Diego

Pacific

Ocean

Channel Islands National Park

Santa Barbara Is.

San Pedro Channel

30 km
20 mi

© Baedeker

Avalon

Santa Catalina Island

morning mist in the months of July (21 days), August (22) and September (16).

Mission

Nobody should fail to visit the mission of San Carlos Borromeo del Rio Carmelo, where Peter Junipero Serra is buried (see entry for Mission Stations). The Bach Festival, which takes place every year in the second half of July, brings together prominent soloists and chamber music ensembles. You reach it via Seventeen Mile Drive which leads from Monterey (see entry) to Carmel.

Information

Monterey Peninsula Visitors and Convention Bureau, Monterey; tel. (408) 649-1770. Carmel Business Association, Carmel; tel. 624-2522.

In the vicinity

Anybody who wishes to escape the mist in Carmel can pitch his tent in Carmel Valley, a few miles to the south-east (reached by Route G 16, a turn-off from the US 1). Situated by the River Carmel, quite apart from its proximity to the town, Carmel Valley offers many sporting facilities, such as fishing and swimming. Here, too, you will find the largest Zen monastery in the United States of America.

Channel Islands National Park

Location and
*importance

The Channel Islands National Park is famous for its sea-lions, colonies of sea-birds and over 800 endemic plant varieties.
Of the eight islands forming this archipelago, five – Anacapa, Santa Barbara, San Miguel, Santa Rosa and Santa Cruz – have been declared a national park. They are situated off the coast of South California between Point Conception, west of Santa Barbara (see entry) and Oxnard (see entry). Only two of these islands are accessible by ship from Ventura (see entry): Anacapa all the year round, and Santa Barbara only between the

end of May and the beginning of September. A third island, Santa Rosa, was purchased a short time ago by the federal government, and should soon be accessible by boat (Island Packers Co. in Ventura; tel. 805/644-8262).
Before visiting the islands you are recommended to call in at the National Park Visitor Center (1901 Spinnaker Drive, Ventura), where you can see a half-hour film of the islands, photographs and other documents as well as utensils and ritual objects used by the Chumash Indians, the original inhabitants of these now almost uninhabited islands.

11 miles/18 km from the mainland is Anacapa, a group of three islands, connected only by boat. From Ventura you can get to East Anacapa. All three islands cover an area of one square mile (about 290 hectares). Near the landing-stage is the start of a 1½ mile/2.4 km nature path, which opens up the beauties of the island. From January to March you can watch from here the migration of the grey whales from Alaska to Mexico. There is a camp-site on East Anacapa for which you must get a permit in advance from the park headquarters in Ventura.

Anacapa

Santa Barbara, the other island which can be reached by ship, is the southernmost one and, covering an area of 640 acres/260 hectares, is the smallest island on the archipelago. It was not inhabited until the 1920s; prior to that it served as grazing land, but the vegetation was seriously damaged by fires and the mass invasion of wild hare. The island possesses tracks totalling 6 miles/9 km in length. A favourite setting-off point is Canyon View, south of the landing-stage. There is a camp-site here for which you need a permit. You must bring food and water with you. There is no shade on Anacapa or on Santa Barbara, so you must take precautions to protect yourself from the sun.

Santa Barbara

San Miguel (8 miles/13 km long and 4 miles/6 km wide) is a plateau about 400–500 ft/120–150 m high. Here there is no public transport and no camp-site. If you wish to get there in your own boat you will need a special permit. This also applies to Santa Cruz – the biggest of the islands, which is 24 miles/39 km in length and covers an area of 37 sq. miles/96 sq. km – as well as to the 15 mile/24 km long and 10 mile/16 km wide island of Santa Rosa.

San Miguel

All five islands offer a rare opportunity of getting to know a small part of California in its original state, with rich fauna and flora.

Coloma

G 3/4

Placer County
Altitude: 900 ft/275 m
Population: 300

Coloma lies on Highway CA 49, between Auburn (see entry) and Placerville (see entry). This little settlement has found a place in California's history for one reason only: here is the actual spot where James W. Marshall (1810–1885) found the first gold in the American River in the year 1848.

Location and importance

Today, the whole area in which Marshall, a partner of John A. Sutter, worked has been incorporated into the Marshall Gold Discovery State Park. On a hill stands a statue of Marshall, pointing a finger at the spot where the gold was found.
On instructions from Sutter a saw-mill was built there (about 50 miles/80 km from Fort Sutter in Sacramento; see entry), a reproduction of which stands in State Park. Some of the older houses have been preserved, and a museum in the State Park Building displays artefacts of the great gold rush. The park is open daily 8 to sunset, museum daily 10 a.m.–5 p.m., tel. (916) 622-3470 for information.

Marshall Gold Discovery Park

Coloma: Sutter's Mill

Coloma: Monument to J. W. Marshall

Corona del Mar

See Newport Beach

Coronado

See San Diego

Costa Mesa

Q 3

Orange County
Altitude: 100 ft/31 m
Population: 82,500

Location and importance

Costa Mesa forms part of the chain of middle-sized towns which lie one after the other south-east of Los Angeles on both sides of the US 405, the so-called San Diego Freeway. Costa Mesa, Huntington Beach, Fountain Valley, Santa Ana and Newport Beach (see entry) run almost imperceptibly one into the other. Costa Mesa takes precedent over the other towns in Orange County because of its commitment to culture.

Performing Arts Center

Here in 1986 the Orange County Performing Arts Center was first set up, where the Los Angeles Philharmonic Orchestra and the New York City Opera Company are regular guests, as well as numerous other orchestras and soloists. Rock concerts are no rarity here either. (600 Town Center Drive; tel. 556-2787.)

Fair

In Costa Mesa, too, are the Orange County Fair Grounds, where in July each year the Orange County Fair which is worth a visit is found (tel. (714) 751-3247). Within the Fair Grounds stands the Pacific-Amphitheater where open-air performances are held all the year round.

Costa Mesa is also notable in the theatrical sphere. The South Coast Repertory Company (655 Town Center Drive), quite close to the Cultural Center, is one of the best theatres in California. In its two auditoria, main stage (seating 500) and second stage (seating 160), five to six premières are presented every year (season tickets are obtainable). Californian authors are often asked to speak here; tel. 957-2602.

South Coast Repertory Company

Crescent City

A 2

Del Norte County
Altitude: 43 ft/13 m
Population: 3200

This town, situated on the Pacific in the "High North" not far from the border with Oregon, was founded by gold-seekers in 1851, and gets its name from the horn-shaped bay. Point St George, the headland immediately north of the harbour, protects the town from the cold north winds. The paddle-steamer "Brother Jonathan" sank off this coast in 1885 with the loss of 265 lives. The victims of the catastrophe are buried in the Brother Jonathan Cemetery (9th St, Pebble Beach). A further disaster, a tidal wave, destroyed a large part of the town in 1964.

Location and origin

Redwood National Park, covering an area of 1,070,000 acres/434,000 hectares, begins in Crescent City and runs south for 46 miles/74 km, 30 miles/48 km of which border the Pacific coast. As well as the beautiful redwood trees, the park offers numerous walks and picnic-sites. The headquarters of the park are in Crescent City (corner of 2nd and K Street; tel. (707) 464-6101) where further information can be obtained.

Redwood National Park

Inside Redwood National Park, which was created in 1868, lie three State Parks, all on or near Highway 101: Jedediah Smith Redwoods State Park, Del Norte Redwoods State Park and Prairie Creek Redwoods State Park. The latter possesses the tallest redwoods; it lies about 33 miles/53 km south of Crescent City.

State Parks

Crescent City, with its seven motels (about 300 rooms), offers adequate accommodation, whereas near the US 101, also known as Redwood Highway, there is little to be found.

Accommodation

Dana Point

Q 3

Orange County
Altitude: 33 ft/10 m
Population: 14,000

In the last few years Dana Point has developed into one of the major water-sports resorts between San Diego and Los Angeles, its proximity to the better known and often overcrowded Laguna Beach (see entry) being instrumental in this. During the 19th century Dana Point was one of the few natural harbours between San Diego and Santa Barbara; today this bay has a marina which can accommodate up to 25,000 motor-boats and sailing-boats.

Location and importance

The name Dana Point can be traced back to the sailor, writer and lawyer Richard Henry Dana who in 1834 as a simple seaman made the trip round

How it got its name

Mighty lunar landscape in Death Valley

Cape Horn to California and stayed here for sixteen months in the years 1835/1836. His adventures, including an act of heroism in the harbour later named Dana Point, are described in his novel, later to become a classic, "Two Years Before The Mast", which had a big influence on later travel literature. He thus became a champion of the rights of seamen, "that race of men with whom my fate was linked for so long".

Places of interest

From December to March Dana Point is an ideal spot from which to observe the whales migrating north. Here, too, can be found the Orange County Marine Institute, a reproduction of the ship "Pilgrim" which plied along the Californian coast, and the Dana Point Lighthouse with some interesting artefacts.

Davis

G 2

Yolo County
Altitude; 50 ft/15 m
Population: 38,000

Location and origin

Davis, a suburb of Sacramento situated on the US 80 going towards San Francisco, bears the name of its founder Jerome C. Davis who planted wheat, barley, vines and fruit trees on a 400 acre/162 hectare holding here. Today this now urbanised town still lies in the middle of a rich agricultural area.

University of California

The campus of the University of California can be traced back to an agricultural school founded in 1907, which for 15 years was transferred to Berkeley (see entry) as a branch of the University of California. In 1961 Davis obtained its own campus, whose total area of 1000 acres/400 hectares makes it the third largest site of the University of California, after Los

Angeles and Berkeley (20,000 students), and which dominates the town. Davis has also made a name for itself in California through its energy-saving programme and its research projects in the sphere of solar energy.

Death Valley National Monument

Inyo County
Altitude: 280 ft/86 m–11,050 ft/3368 m

The valley can be reached from three sides: From Los Angeles it is 300 miles/480 km, via the US 15 Highway as far as Baker, then via the CA 127 and 190 or the CA 405, 14 and 395 as far as Olancha, thence by Route No. 190. From Las Vegas in Nevada, 140 miles/224 km away, you take the US 15, then the 127 to Death Valley Junction and the 190 direct to the Visitor Center in Furnace Creek. From Lone Pine (see entry) on the CA 395, you drive direct to Death Valley on the CA 136 and 190.

How to get there

The Death Valley region, low in rainfall and protected as a national monument, (land area 3000 sq. miles/7770 sq. km), lies in central south-east California, extending slightly into the US federal state of Nevada, and includes the 140-mile (225 km)-wide and 4–16-mile (6–26 km)-wide desert valleys of the Amargosa River and Salt Creek, as well as the surrounding chains of mountains known as the Panamint Range in the west, and the Amargosa Range in the east.

*Location and ** importance*

The impressive scenery of this geologically multiform desert (maximum temperature 56.7°C), with its wondrous rocky wastes and sand-dunes, conceals numerous streams and a rich animal and plant life including succulents of all kinds. 21 species of plants and trees found here are unique to the valley.

Rock-drawings, hearths and supply trails have all been found, providing evidence of pre-historic settlements in almost all parts of Death Valley.

History

Death Valley is a harsh wilderness, with high mountain peaks and deep valleys, sand dunes like those in the Sahara, oases where date-palms grow, water courses below sea level, and a rich flora, especially in spring, which belies the name given to the whole region. Death Valley is also of great geological interest. Many years ago it was an inland lake; the mountains were formed as the result of mighty land eruptions, and the water evaporated under the merciless sun. The formation of the mountains was accompanied by a lowering of the valley bottom; the valley came into being not through erosion, as most did, but as a result of a shift in the earth's crust. Thus Telescope Peak was raised from 280 ft/86 m below sea level to 11,050 ft/3368 m above. What we see in many parts today is a world of rock in every colour imaginable which never fails to amaze the visitor.

Origin

This wonder of nature was discovered more or less by chance in 1849 when some adventurers, wanting to find their way as quickly as possible to the land of the gold-rush to the west, wandered into the unhospitable desert from which they escaped again only after considerable hardship and difficulty. They had to abandon their wagons and eat the oxen which pulled them in order not to starve – they also gave the area its present name. A few years later they were followed by men who believed they would find gold and silver. It is true that they found a few veins of these valuable metals but their labours were scarcely worthwhile and they soon moved on to pastures new.

When discovered

Then, however, "white gold" was discovered in the desert – borax, an important chemical used in many branches of industry. At the start teams

"White gold" (borax)

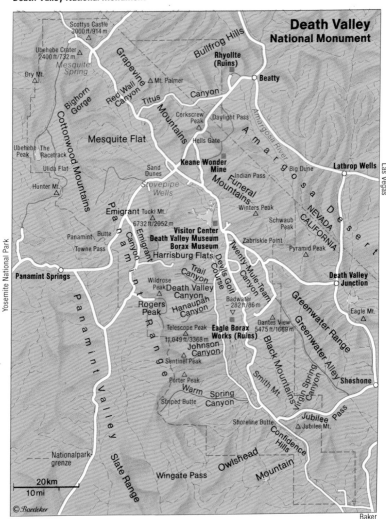

Death Valley National Monument

Scottys Castle 3000 ft/914 m
Ubehebe Crater 2400 ft/732 m
Mesquite Spring
Dry Mt.
Bullfrog Hills
Rhyolite (Ruins)
Beatty
Grapevine Mountains
Red Wall Canyon
Bighorn Gorge
△ Mt. Palmer
Titus Canyon
Cottonwood Mountains
Ubehebe Peak
The Racetrack
Ulida Flat
Hunter Mt. △
Corkscrew Peak
Daylight Pass
Mesquite Flat
Hells Gate
Amargosa River
Keane Wonder Mine
Sand Dunes
Stovepipe Wells
Indian Pass
Funeral Mountains
Big Dune
Lathrop Wells
Las Vegas
NEVADA
CALIFORNIA
Amargosa Desert
Emigrant Tucki Mt. 6732 ft/2052 m
Panamint Butte
Towne Pass
Panamint Canyon
Emigrant Canyon
Winters Peak
Schwaub Peak
Visitor Center
Death Valley Museum
Borax Museum
Harrisburg Flats
Zabriskie Point
Pyramid Peak
Panamint Springs
Yosemite National Park
Trail Canyon
Devils Golf Course
Twenty-Mule-Team Canyon
Death Valley Junction
Wildrose Peak
Death Valley Canyon
Rogers Peak
Hanaupah Canyon
Badwater 282 ft/86 m
Dantes View 5475 ft/1669 m
Eagle Mt.
Telescope Peak 11,049 ft/3368 m
Eagle Borax Works (Ruins)
Johnson Canyon
Greenwater Range
Greenwater Alley
Sentinel Peak △
Porter Peak △
Black Mountains
Shoshone
Striped Butte
Warm Spring Canyon
Smith Mt.
Virgin Spring Canyon
Shoreline Butte
Jubilee Mt. △
Jubilee Pass
Confidence Hills
Nationalpark-grenze
Slate Range
Wingate Pass
Owlshead Mountain

20 km
10 mi
©Baedeker

Baker

of two horses and eighteen mules (not just mules, as the legendary description of 20-mule teams would have us believe) had to pull their load over a distance of 165 miles/264 km to Mojave which took them ten days. Eventually, a railway was built. In 1881 Harmony Borax Works (near Furnace Creek), which is now partly restored and open to visitors, came into operation; others followed and the quantities of borax, which is still mined to some extent in Death Valley today, increased within a few years to hundreds of thousands of tons. Today borax is used mainly in the production of glass and glass-fibres, as well as in the soap industry.

Death Valley: "Dante's View"

Although Death Valley has been a "National Monument" since 1933, borax can still be mined within its boundaries, but only underground. There are also still optimists who climb around in the deep canyons of Death Valley in the mostly vain hope of stumbling upon a vein of gold. However, the many thousands who come to Death Valley year after year (in the season, there are sometimes as many as 10,000 in one day) do so because of the unique scenery.

Sights

Can one "do" Death Valley in a day? It is possible if you arrive in the evening, stay there overnight (facilities only from the middle of October until the end of May), and then follow a definite plan. In Furnace Creek, the centre of Death Valley which lies below sea level, there is a hotel and a motel (for both it is essential to book in advance; tel. 800/528-6367). Here also there is a National Park Service information office tel. (619) 786-2331, a post office (closed in summer) and a filling station.

Furnace Creek

From Furnace Creek you should start the tour as early as possible the next morning, first going in a southerly direction for 4 miles/6.4 km to Zabriskie Point, from where there is a fantastic view of the western part of Death Valley and the Panamint Mountains. Here you are surrounded by gold-coloured rocks; in the foreground is Manly Bacon Peak, named after one of the men who were the first to cross the desert in 1849, the first white people to do so. Indians of the Shoshone tribe, who called the area "tomesha" or "fiery earth", had been there for 7000 years.

From Zabriskie Point, return to the CA 190, and then drive a further 4 miles/6.4 km along a one-way road to 20-Mule-Team Canyon, a very winding stretch which is not easy to negotiate, then 19 miles/30 km up to the viewing platform Dante's View (an allusion to hell as described by the Italian poet. You are now at a height of 5478 ft/1669 m and the temperature is considerably cooler than in Furnace Creek.

* Dante's View:
Ryan Borax Mine

Death Valley National Monument

Badwater: the lowest point in the United States

On the way, you will pass the still active Ryan Borax Mine. From here you can look down onto the lowest point of the American continent, Badwater, which lies 280 ft/86 m below sea level. A mere ten miles/sixteen km away you can see the 10,380 ft/3300 m high Telescope Peak, which is often snow-capped until June.

Devil's Golf Course
Artist's Drive

Via East Side Road you now come to Devil's Golf Course, a giant flat area covered in sharp salt crystals. The nearest approach is Artist's Drive, a winding one-way road, the most beautiful part of which bears the description "Painter's Palette", because perhaps nowhere else in Death Valley do the rocks glow in so many colours as they do here.

Badwater

South of Furnace Creek, there only remains the drive to Badwater. It is not possible to reach the lowest point by car; you must be satisfied with going down to a depth of 277 ft/85 m. While it was about 20° cooler on Dante's Point and more windy than in Furnace Creek, here it is 6–8°C warmer. In Badwater there is a small salt lake which does not dry up even in the hot months, and which is surrounded by white salt. Only small insects and algae of various colours live in the sour, warm water.

Harmony Borax Works

From Badwater you should return to Furnace Creek for a rest and to recuperate, perhaps also have a refreshing swim in the pool which is fed by a stream, and then you are off again to see the sights to the north. The nearest is the Harmony Borax Works, which has already been mentioned; from there you can make a small detour to the sand dunes on the road leading to Stove Pipe Wells, which are most beautifully illuminated towards sunset.

Ubehebe Crater

Then it is northwards to the Ubehebe Crater, measuring about 0.6 mile/1 km wide and 400 ft/122 m deep, the only crater in the area which resulted from a volcanic explosion.

Steam tractor in Furnace Creek

So far in Death Valley you have only seen what nature has provided. Now, however, you come to Scotty's Castle, probably the strangest building you could expect to find in this part of the country. You can only visit it as part of a guided tour. It was built in the twenties by a Chicago businessman named Albert Johnson, about a decade before Death Valley was declared a national monument. At the time there were still no roads, and all building materials had to be obtained the hard way. In addition to the main house with its 50-ft/15-m-high living-room, in which the Johnsons only stayed for one month in the year, there are stables, a guest-house, a house for the staff, and a bell-tower, all maintained in the Hispano-Moorish style. The contents of the house are original; furniture, books and paintings are those owned by the Johnsons.

Scotty's Castle

On the upper floor are the bedrooms and an unusual music room with a magnificent organ (1600 pipes) which is also fitted with self-playing musical cylinders as Mrs Johnson was not a very good organist. The house was never completed, however; before the garden, swimming pool and illuminated tiled courtyard could be finished, the Wall Street Crash of 1929 came and Johnson lost almost all his money. The house went to a religious institution from whom the National Park acquired it in 1970.

"Scotty's Castle" was the unofficial name for this strange building. It comes from "Death Valley Scotty", an adventurer who was also a confidence trickster and who bore the same name as the writer Walter Scott. Although not as much as one single brick belonged to him, he told anyone who would listen that the house was his and that Johnson was only his "banker"! In time people believed him.

Notes

Of course, anybody with more than a day to spare can see much more of Death Valley. Perhaps it is then a good idea to make use of one of the ten camping sites, the biggest of which is Sunset Camp with 1000 pitches

Camping sites

(open only from November to April). Contrary to some other camping sites, you cannot book in advance in Death Valley; the maxim "first come, first served" applies here. With the exception of Furnace Creek camping site, where you can only stay for a maximum of 14 days, the period is 30 days on all the others.

Temperatures

When should you visit Death Valley? If possible not in the months of June to September when the great heat does not make it an ideal holiday spot for people (or for cars). During these months the average maximum temperatures are 42–46°C, and some 6–8° hotter in the parts which lie below sea level. In Death Valley on one July day in 1913 the temperature was measured as 57°C (in the shade!), the highest ever recorded in the western hemisphere. In the other eight months, however, pleasant summer weather prevails with only very occasional rain (the average annual rainfall is only 2 in/50 mm).

Rules to be followed

Anyone wishing to visit Death Valley during the summer heat should take certain precautionary measures: you should take at least 1 gallon/4 litres of water with you; do not switch the air-conditioning on in the car to avoid overheating the engine; wear a large hat with a brim and a long-sleeved white shirt which will reflect the sun; although there are several places in Death Valley where you can fill up with fuel (Furnace Creek, Stove Pipe Wells and Scotty's Castle), it is best to start with a full tank, as distances are fairly great; remember in summer especially never to stray from the made-up roads!

Information

The Visitor Center in Furnace Creek is open every day. Guided tours are organised from there; from November to April slide-shows and other performances are given in the auditorium in the evenings. The Visitor Center can be contacted by telephone (619) 786-2331.

Disneyland

See Anaheim, Disneyland

Donner Pass   G 5

Location and importance

This pass in the Sierra Nevada, west of Truckee (see entry), over which the Transcontinental Highway US 80 now runs, was the scene of a great tragedy in California's early history, and also the only authenticated case of cannibalism in the history of the US.

Trek to the west

In April 1846 a group of 89 people from Illinois, led by the brothers Georg and Jacob Donner who probably originated from Germany, set off for California. The covered wagons, pulled by oxen, were supposed to follow a route which promised to be 350 miles/560 km shorter than those known at the time. However, they had to cross over high passes and a 36 mile/57 km stretch of desert. In the attempt some of their draught animals died and they had to abandon some wagons which was to cost them almost three weeks loss of time.

Natural obstacles

It was the end of October before they reached the area now known as Reno, exhausted, embittered, demoralised and molested by Paiute Indians. After a short rest they continued their trek, but winter set in early at the beginning of November. The pass, which now bears the name of the Donner brothers, became snow-bound and they were unable to cross it. They had to pitch their tents on the lower shores of the lake, which now also bears their name and forms the centre of the Donner Memorial State Park. One of the members pressed on to Fort Sutter (now Sacramento; see entry). As he had

Old hotel in Dutch Flat

to cover a rough stretch of almost 100 miles/160 km rendered almost impassable by heavy snow-drifts, it was March 1st before he could get back with the provisions they so desperately needed.

In the meantime some members of the Donner group had died of starvation. The others could stay alive only by eating the flesh of the dead men. Even after months of waiting, they could not all escape from this wilderness at the beginning of March; those left behind continued to starve. It is said that in April Louis Keseberg murdered Georg Donner's wife in order to get her money and consume the corpse. In all, 42 of those who had left Illinois perished, only 47 survived and settled in the Sacramento Valley.

Cannibalism

In the Donner Memorial State Park can be seen the spot where the Donner group camped; this tragic episode in American history is remembered in the Emigrant Trail Museum two miles west of Truckee.

Donner Memorial State Park

Dutch Flat

G 4

Placer County
Altitude: 1346 ft/410 m
Population: 800

The place name Dutch Flat derives from the "Dutch" which has been introduced into America as a phonetic form of "Deutsch" (German), but has no connection at all with the English word "Dutch". Today it is a forgotten former gold-mining town near the US 80, some 18 miles/30 km north-east of Auburn (see entry). It was founded in 1851 by German immigrants, the brothers Carl and Josef Dornbach. Countless adventurers streamed to Dutch Flat, which developed into one of the richest gold-mining towns in the whole of the state and provided a home for one-tenth

Location and origin

of the inhabitants of the whole of Placer County. In addition, some 2000 Chinese settled here to assist in digging for gold, initially as paid workers, but rapidly becoming almost slaves. The advertisements in the newspaper of the time, the "Dutch Flat Enquirer", show that at the beginning of the 1860s there were seventeen bars, two breweries, seven grocers' shops, three smithies, two banks, eight gents' clothiers, three hotels, a chemist, a Freemasons' lodge and an Oddfellows' lodge.

Today little remains of all that, even though Dutch Flat is not a ghost town in the true sense of the word. Nevertheless, thanks to the commitment of the village council, something of the original charm has been preserved; today men still search for gold in the nearby rivers with some success; a small museum has been set up in the village; at present, the only hotel still standing, albeit empty, is being renovated; the old chemists' shop has been changed into an antique shop, and the Freemasons' and Oddfellows' lodges still exist – the latter in a house built in 1854 by the Hanoverian J. K. Hüdepohl.

The town today

Places like this are seldom found in California today. The authentic features of Dutch Flat have been preserved mainly because here, unlike so many other gold-mining towns, there has never been a major fire.

Not far from Dutch Flat, on the US 80, lies a town called Weimar which got its name not from the German town of the same name, but from the Indian chief Weimah who lived nearby. In 1886, some 30 years later and for no obvious reason, it was changed to Weimar.

El Camino Real

H–T 0–4

Literally translated, "El Camino Real" means "The Royal Road". The name came into being in the 18th c. and describes the road which begins in Baja California (see entry) and continues into Alta California and along which most of the mission stations (see entry) grew up. In what is now California, it began in San Diego and ran past the mission stations of San Luis Rey de Francia, San Juan Capistrano and San Gabriel, then westwards via Los Angeles, Ventura, Santa Barbara, San Luis Obispo, Morro Bay, through the Salinas Valley, Monterey and San Francisco. The route taken by the Camino Real essentially corresponds to the present-day Highway 101 on which most of the mission stations are situated.

Eureka

B/C 1

Humboldt County
Altitude: 43 ft/13 m
Population: 24,500

This town on Humboldt and Arcata Bay was founded in 1850 as a port, and is today still the only port of any size between San Francisco and the mouth of the Columbia River in Oregon. It was given the Greek name "Eureka" ("I have found it"), which also appears in the coat-of-arms of the US Federal State of California. The importance of Eureka today lies in the shipping of wood, especially redwood, from the surrounding forests.

Location and importance

The town's early history has a few black spots; Here in 1853 Fort Humboldt was built on lands which belonged to the Wiyot Indians. In 1860 American troops carried out a fearful massacre of the Indian wives and children when most of the menfolk were out hunting. The exact number of dead has never been ascertained. 25 years later, as in so many other Californian towns, the Chinese were expelled by force. They were victims of the xenophobia emerging again and again in the United States.

Indian massacre

◀ *Carson Mansion (Queen Anne style) in Eureka*

Ferndale

<table>
<tr><td>* Carson Mansion</td><td>From the same year (1885) dates what must surely be the most notable building in the town, Carson Mansion (143 M. Street), now a club. William Carson, a timber wholesaler and one of the richest citizens of Eureka, had this Victorian house built, mainly of redwood; its numerous pre-fabricated, almost Gothic-looking wood carvings and painted windows, together with its many interlocked sections, give it a unique appearance. Carson House stands on a raised plot and can be seen from afar when you approach it along 2nd Street (a visit is possible; see Culture and Art: Architecture).</td></tr>
<tr><td>Places of interest</td><td>Fort Humboldt State Historic Park (3431 Fort Avenue) is the site of the former Fort Humboldt, partially restored and displaying early logging techniques.
Also worth seeing is Sequoia National Park (see entry) situated within the precincts of the town, with its little zoo in the middle of a redwood grove (Glatt and W. Street). The zoo is open every day except Monday (tel. (707) 442-6552). A bank building, designed like an earlier palace, in the centre of the partly-restored old town, houses the Clarke Museum which is particularly rich in Indian basketwork and other artefacts, as well as documents on the history of Eureka and Humboldt County (3rd and E. Street). (Open: Tue.–Sat. noon–4 p.m.; admission free; tel. (707) 443-1947.)</td></tr>
<tr><td>Boat trips</td><td>One-hour boat trips on Humboldt Bay from the pier at the bottom of C. Street daily from the middle of June to the middle of Sept. Information: Chamber of Commerce, 2112 Broadway; tel. (707) 442-3738 or from Humboldt Bay Harbor Cruise (707) 445-1910.</td></tr>
</table>

Ferndale

Humboldt County
Altitude: 98 ft/30 m
Population: 2500

<table>
<tr><td>Location and urban features</td><td>Ferndale was founded by Danish farmers in the year 1860. It lies about 15 miles/24 km south-west of Eureka, and can be reached from there on the US 101 (5 miles/8 km the other side of the Fernbridge intersection). Worth seeing are the numerous old houses built in the Victorian style – Queen Anne, Eastlake and Gothic revival styles – with an unusual number of art galleries and craft shops. In addition to the three parish churches the main places worth seeing are Shaw House (703 Main Street), today a small boarding house (tel. 786-9958), and Berding House (455 Ocean Avenue), both built in about 1854. More captivating than any of the individual highlights, however, is the overall impression made by this magical little town.</td></tr>
</table>

Fort Bragg

Mendocino County
Altitude: 75 ft/23 m
Population: 5500

<table>
<tr><td>Location and origin</td><td>This town, founded in the year 1884 and situated on the US 1, is on the site of a fort built in 1857 to suppress the Indians. The fort was given up only ten years later and most of the land sold to woodcutters. The reason for the low population density of the coastal region is made clear when you realise that in spite of having only 5500 inhabitants it is actually the largest town between San Francisco and Eureka (see entry). The timber industry continues to be of importance. One of the many saw-mills, Georgia Pacific Mill, is open to visitors on weekdays.</td></tr>
<tr><td>Skunk Railroad</td><td>The biggest tourist attraction is undoubtedly "Skunk Railroad", as the</td></tr>
</table>

Wooden houses and well in Fort Ross

40 mile/64 km long railway line of the California Western Railroad to Willits is called. Pulled by an old diesel locomotive, it travels through redwood forests along the Noyo. The journey to Willits takes about two hours. There are two round trips each day from the end of June to the middle of Sept.; in the remaining months there is only one, to Northspur (tel. (707) 964-6371).

Two miles south of Fort Bragg on the US 1 you come to Mendocino Coast Botanical Garden, about 20 acres of rhododendrums, fuchsias, native plants and trees. Restaurant and picnic sites nearby (tel. (707) 964-4352).

Botanical Garden

Fort Ross State Historic Park

F 0/1

Some 50 miles/80 km north of San Francisco, on the US 1, lies Fort Ross State Historic Park. From 1812 to 1841 the Russians who built the fort settled here in the hope of being better able to provide Alaska with wheat and other foodstuffs than they could from Russia itself. 95 Russians, as well as Aleutians and Kodiaks, built their village and the fort. Then they began to fish for otters and finally to trade with Spanish California. It is open to debate whether they would have tried later to have taken over more Californian land but the Spaniards had decided in 1769 to occupy Alta California, in order to prevent a possible Russian penetration into the almost uninhabited areas in the west of the American continent. However, in 1812 the Spaniards had still not got past San Francisco Bay towards the north. They first learned of the arrival of the Russians when Fort Ross had already been built.

Location and importance

Inside the wooden fort were the commandant's house, the chapel and two log-cabins – all carefully reconstructed in latter years. Two to three dozen cannons were kept in the cabins.

Fresno

Russian Orthodox Chapel	The most interesting building is perhaps the Russian Orthodox Chapel, originally built in 1824 and which remained standing after the Russians withdrew until it collapsed in the great earthquake of 1906. It was rebuilt in 1916/1917 and again four years later, but burned down in 1970. After having been destroyed three times, it was given its present appearance in 1974. The Russian bell, which had melted in the fire, was re-cast.
Changing owners	Although they were never attacked, the Russians were ordered back from Fort Ross by their Czar; the hopes they had had for the colony were not fulfilled; the agricultural production was not sufficient for the needs of the Russians in Alaska, and the otter population was almost completely wiped out. The area was to have been sold to the Mexican government, but when negotiations foundered the rich John A. Sutter from Sacramento (see entry) jumped in and bought the land from the Russians for 30,000 dollars. Including the soldiers, the maximum Russian population must have been 700. In the period that followed Fort Ross changed owners several times, until in 1903 it passed to the state, who began to restore it.
Information	A new Visitor Center, through which you gain access to the complex, was completed in 1985. You can obtain all further information there. Fort Ross is open daily 10 a.m.–4.30 p.m.; tel. (707) 865-2391 or (707) 847-3286.

Fresno K 3

Fresno County
Altitude: 300 ft/90 m
Population: 294,000

Location and general information	Fresno, the eighth largest town in California, lies 213 miles/341 km north of Los Angeles and 184 miles/294 km south of San Francisco, on the CA 99, roughly in the centre of the state. In the vicinity can be found the National Parks of King's Canyon (see entry; 56 miles/90 km), Sequoia (84 miles/134 km) and Yosemite (see entry; 91 miles/146 km). Fresno enjoys a mediterranean climate, with average annual temperatures of 20°C, and has 300 days of sunshine in the year. The town's name comes from the Spanish word "fresno" (ash-tree).
Economy	As it did at the start of its existence, the town's economy still depends largely on its agricultural products, especially grapes, nectarines, plums, tomatoes and peaches. As Fresno lies in the unusually fertile San Joaquin Valley the total value of its agricultural production can exceed 2 billion dollars per year. In addition, one of the largest wine-producers in the country (Guild) and the world's biggest dried fruit firm (Sun Maid) are based here.
Colleges	32,500 students in all are registered at the two colleges of California State University and City College. There are also 35 specialist colleges. Probably Fresno's most famous son is the writer William Saroyan (see Famous Personalities).
Population	When it received its municipal charter in 1885, Fresno had exactly 3464 inhabitants, mainly Armenians, Volga Germans, Danes, Swedes, Irish, Scots, English and Portuguese, who had decided, on the basis of newspaper advertisements, to settle in Fresno. In the first decade of this century the town still had no more than 12,000 inhabitants; since then it has expanded rapidly; in the last decade alone the town has grown by over a third.
Places of interest	However, cultural development has not been able to keep pace with this population explosion. In Fresno you will find only one philharmonic

One of the numerous Pacific beaches on Highway 1 ▶

Glen Ellen: ruins of Jack London's house

orchestra, an opera company which performs only occasionally, several theatre groups and the Metropolitan Museum of Art History and Science (1555 Van Ness), better described as an extended museum of local history. (Open daily 10 a.m.–5 p.m., except public holidays; tel. 441-1444.) Also worth visiting are some parks on the edge of the beach, such as Roeding Park, with a variety of alpine and tropical plants. There is also a zoo, and Woodward Park with its Japanese garden open only at weekends.

Garberville   D 1

Humboldt County
Altitude: 530 ft/162 m
Population: 800

Location and
surroundings

Garberville lies near the exit from Highway 101, by the first redwood forest to be found south of Eureka (see entry), Richardson Grove State Park. It is only a few miles from the southern end of the Avenue of the Giants, the old motorway to Eureka. This runs parallel to the US 101, and crosses a 33-mile/52-km-long redwood area, including, for example, Humboldt Redwoods State Park, 15 miles/25 km north of Garberville. Thanks to its location and its variety of hotels, motels and restaurants, Garberville is an ideal base for trips into the surrounding redwood groves.

Geyserville   F 1

Sonoma County
Altitude: 206 ft/63 m
Population: 1000

Geyserville lies directly on Highway 101, about 21 miles/33 km north of Santa Rosa (see entry), in the north-east of Sonoma County. For the Indians who lived in this geothermal region Geyserville was a holy place. When the whites discovered it in 1847 they recognised the healing properties of these hot springs. Four years later they established the town and made it into a spa.

Throughout the whole area you can come upon geysers, which from time to time shoot up some 100 ft/30 metres into the air. Since about 1960 these geysers have served as a source of energy for the geothermic power station Pacific Gas and Electric Company which produces almost 1.2 million kilowatt hours.

Glen Ellen

Sonoma County
Altitude: 230 ft/70 m
Population: 1000

Situated in the heart of the vine-growing region, Glen Ellen is the head-quarters of numerous well-known wine producers. It lies on the CA 12, between Santa Rosa (see entry) and Schellville.

Location and importance

Only one mile/1.6 km away stretches Jack London State Historic Park, where the writer, who committed suicide is buried, and where the ruins of the house he built, Wolf House, are to be found; shortly before it was completed on August 22nd 1913 it was destroyed by fire, the cause of which was never discovered.

In his novel "The Valley of the Moon", published in the same year, London provided a literary memorial to the region around Glen Ellen, and at the same time revived the old Indian legends, according to which the name Sonoma means "many moons" in the Indian language.

In 1919 London's widow had the "House of Happy Walls" built, and today this is the Jack London Museum, with many documents relating to the life of the author, his collection of south sea island artefacts, some of the furniture saved from Wolf House, as well as all the contents of his intended workroom (one of the 26 rooms in the destroyed house), tel. (707) 938-5216.

Glen Ellen State Historic Park

Grass Valley

Nevada County
Altitude: 2412 ft/735 m
Population: 7000

Grass Valley, some 26 miles/42 km north of Auburn (see entry) on the CA 49, gets its name from the time it was founded in 1849 by the first settlers, who unexpectedly found plenty of fodder here for their cattle. They could not have suspected that under the meadows lay the biggest gold deposits in all California. The Empire gold-mine is today the centre of Empire Mine Historic Park and is open to visitors. In the 107 years of its existence nearly 6 million ounces of gold have been mined.

In Grass Valley also lived Lola Montez, the lover of King Louis I of Bavaria. The house in which she stayed for a time is to be converted into a museum.

Location and origin

Walking tours in the Empire Mine give the visitor a good impression of the working conditions in a gold-mine. You can go some 40 ft/13 m down into the shafts, which are lit for a length of 150 ft/45 m, but which are 367 miles/587 km long altogether. On a model you can see the direction and depth of the individual veins.

Walking tours

Bourn Villa, the villa which belonged to the former owner of the mine, can

Bourn Villa

also be visited. (10791 East Empire Street; open April–Nov. 9 a.m.–6 p.m.; in the remaining months until 5 p.m.; tel. 273-8522 or 273-7714.)

Healdsburg   F/G 1

Sonoma County
Altitude: 105 ft/32 m
Population: 7600

Location and importance

Healdsburg, on the Russian River and the US 101, 14 miles/23 km north of Santa Rosa (see entry), lies in the middle of one of the fertile vineyard areas of Sonoma County. The best known wine-cellars in and around Healdsburg, all of which are open to visitors, are: Simi Winery, 16275 Healdsburg Avenue; Chateau Souverain, 3 miles/ 5 km north on the US 101; Geyser Peak Winery, 8 miles/ 13 km north on the US 101, exit Canyon Road. The last has been in existence since 1880, and is thus one of the oldest wine businesses in California.
There are around 50 further wine-cellars along the Russian River. Details available from the Healdsburg Chamber of Commerce; tel. (707) 433-6935.

Canoe trips

Healdsburg is also a convenient starting point for a canoe trip lasting several days along the American, Sacramento and Russian rivers (Apr.–Oct.) as well as on the Colorado River (throughout the year). Information: tel. (707) 433-7249.

Hearst San Simeon Historic Park

See San Simeon

Indio   R 5/6

Riverside County
Altitude: 13 ft/4 m
Population: 25,500

Location and origin

Indio lies in the centre of the fertile Coachella Valley on the US 10, about equidistant from Los Angeles and San Diego (100 miles/160 km). Originally it was a work camp when the Southern Pacific Railroad was under construction in 1876, and it was initially named Indian Wells. Not until later did it receive its present name ("indio" is Spanish for Indian); Indians had in fact inhabited the valley since the 11th c.

Date capital

C. P. Huntington, president of the Southern Pacific Railroad, brought back with him from a trip to Algeria some date-palm seedlings; these formed the basic stock for the many trees which gave Indio the reputation of being the "Date Capital" of the United States. The "Date Festival" has been held here every year since 1921, the highlights of which are camel and ostrich races. 95% of all American dates are harvested in Coachella Valley, which is well irrigated by the distant Colorado, thanks to the All American Canal. You may obtain information regarding the history and cultivation of dates from a 25-minute slide show in Shields Date Gardens (80–225 Highway 111; open daily 8 a.m.–6 p.m.; tel. 347-0996).

Inyo National Forest   J/L 5/6

Location and importance

This National Forest, extending along the US 395 and US 6 as far as Nevada, covers an area of 1,900,000 acres/763,000 hectares, and is divided into several wilderness regions, John Muir, Golden Trout, Anselm Adams and Hoover. Within the whole area there are hundreds of lakes and rivers, as well as Mount Whitney (14,500 ft/4418 m), the highest mountain in the United States apart from Alaska. Moreover, it is only some 75 miles/120 km as the crow flies from the lowest point, Badwater in Death Valley (see entry for Death Valley National Monument), which lies 280 ft/86 m below sea level. The Palisade Glacier on the border of Inyo National Forest and Kings Canyon National Park is the most southerly glacier in the United States.

For all walks in the forest region during the period from June 1st to September you must obtain permits, either in Lone Pine (tel. (619) 876-5542), Mammoth Lakes (tel. (619) 934-2505), Bishop (tel. (619) 873-4207) (see entries) or in Lee Vining (tel. (619) 647-6525). | Walks

The National Forest is barred to visitors during the remaining months of the year. There is a visitors' centre for Inyo National Forest to be found south of Lone Pine, at the junction of the US 395 and CA 136 roads. (Open: daily in summer 8 a.m.–6 p.m., and during the rest of the year Mon.– Thur. 9 a.m.–5 p.m.; tel. (619) 876-4252.)

Irvine

Q 3

Orange County
Altitude: 207 ft/63 m
Population: 80,000

Irvine, situated on the US 1 south of Newport Beach (see entry), can claim to be the biggest community in the United States based on a "master plan". First established in 1971, in an area of 75,000 acres/30,000 hectares, it underwent rapid development. In Irvine there are extensive industrial complexes and a campus of the University of California, with some 17,000 students, and living quarters occupied almost exclusively by whites (88%). | Location and origin

Of interest is the Lion Country Safari (8800 Irvine Center), an area of 300 acres/120 hectares, through which you can drive your car (only with closed windows!) and view wild animals in their natural environment (open daily in summer 9.45 a.m.–5 p.m., during the rest of the year 9.45 a.m.– 3.30 p.m.; tel. (714) 837-1200). In the grounds of the safari park you will find the Irvine Meadows Amphitheater in which concerts are held from June to the end of September on Fridays, Saturdays and Sundays. The amphitheatre holds 10,000 people. (Information; tel. (714) 855-6111.) | Lion County Safari

Joshua Tree National Monument

Q/R 5–7

The Joshua Tree, which grows only in the Mojave desert, got its name from Mormons who saw in its branches the upstretched arms of the praying prophet. The area, which covers 850 sq. miles/2200 sq. m, has only two entrances: in the north (on the CA 62) in Twenty Nine Palms, and in the south (on the US 10) in Cottenwood Springs, 25 miles/40 km east of Indio (see entry). Both entrances have visitors' centres, where you can obtain maps of this national monument and other information, before setting out to explore this beautiful desert landscape at an altitude of 1000 to 6000 ft/300 to 1800 m. | Location and *importance

The Joshua trees reach a height of up to 60 ft/18 m, and belong to the Yucca family, a type of lily bearing white flowers in April and May. Many of these trees are said to be several hundred years old.

As almost everywhere in the Californian wastelands you will find here a variety of plant and animal life, even though only a few animals are to be seen during the day. In this extremely dry climate the ground actually | Flora and fauna

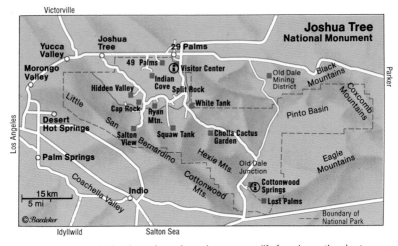

obtains the moisture it needs to support life from heavy thunderstorms during the summer months. However, the flora and fauna have adapted to these inhospitable conditions. Thus the plants either spread their roots wide under the soil, in order to trap the water before it seeps away, or else they penetrate deeply down to the ground water. The leaves of some plants are coated with wax to prevent water loss. In the few oases grow palms, especially the famous fan palm or Washingtonia filifera. This was named after Colonel Henry Washington, to whom is attributed the discovery of the area in 1855. By day the visitor will come across only a few species of animals, such as squirrels, dwarf antelopes and occasionally a coyote, the so-called prairie dog. Poisonous spiders and five different types of rattle-snake are native here; when it is very hot one must take great care in shady places, especially under rocks and bushes. When the temperatures are lower the snakes crawl out of their hiding-places to sun themselves.

"Wonderland of Rocks"

Anyone whose main interest lies in Joshua trees should follow a course to the west, where the thickest clumps of trees are to be found in the "Wonderland of Rocks". The interesting rock formations were shaped by the huge pressure and high temperatures under which the gneiss was forced up out of the earth many millions of years ago. There are also rocks of whitish and reddish quartz which, as magma, i.e. in a molten state, forced itself into the metamorphic rock and solidified.

Rules to be followed

Several roads run through the territory – the two entrance points at opposite sides are only 37 miles/60 km from one another so deciding which to take is no great problem for the tourist. Only in summer must you be equipped for the heat, which often exceeds 40°C. Apart from the two entrances, there is water only in Indian Cove Ranger Station west of Twenty Nine Palms, and in Blackrock Campground not far from Yucca Valley in the extreme west of the park. There are no filling stations in the whole of the Joshua Tree National Monument, but you can obtain fuel in the surrounding towns – Twenty Nine Palms, Joshua Tree, Yucca Valley and Indio.

In contrast to the rest of the park area, there are some motels and restaurants in these towns. However, as a precautionary measure you should take a supply of water with you.

Walks

In mild temperatures walks along the numerous trails and paths can be enjoyed. Especially worthwhile are walks in Hidden Valley, along the Cap

The Joshua tree calls to mind the prophet's outstretched arms

Rock Natural Trail, and the 2 mile/3 km long path on Mount Ryan (beautiful view).

The two Visitor Centers are open daily 8 a.m.–5 p.m.; tel. 619/367-7511.   Information

---

Laguna Beach   Q 3

Orange County
Altitude: 40 ft/12 m
Population: 18,450

Laguna Beach, situated on the US 1 below Newport Beach (see entry), stretches for more than 5 miles/8 km along the Pacific Ocean and must be one of the most beautiful places in California. There are bays, both small and large, lovely beaches, parks on the cliffs overlooking the sea, and a charming town centre with numerous boutiques, craft shops and interesting inns. In the sixties the hippies settled in Laguna Beach but soon disappeared from the scene.   Location and general information

Many events are held here throughout the year, such as the six-week-long Festival of Arts and Pageant of the Masters in July and August (tel. (714) 494-1145), and the Sawdust Festival at about the same time (sale of objets d'art and craft items; tel. (714) 494-3030).

The regional museum, the Laguna Beach Museum of Art (307 Cliff Drive) houses a considerable variety of exhibits and paintings and sculptures by Orange County artists. (Open: Tue.–Sun. 11.30 a.m.– 4.30 p.m.; tel. 494-6531.)   Places of interest

The Laguna Moulton Playhouse theatre, 606 Laguna Canyon Drive, stages plays for almost the whole year (tel. (714) 494-8021).

113

Lake Tahoe, the Marina

La Jolla

See San Diego

Lake Tahoe

G/H 5

Location and
*importance

Lake Tahoe, the larger part of which lies in eastern California and the smaller part in the US federal state of Nevada, is considered to be one of the most beautiful of mountain lakes and thanks to its immediate surroundings is one of the favourite winter sports regions. It covers an area of 200 sq. miles/518 sq. km, lies about 6200 ft/1900 m above sea level and is up to 1600 ft/490 m deep. With a length of 21 miles/34½ km, and a width of up to 12 miles/19 km, it is one of the largest lakes in California. Situated about 200 miles/320 km from San Francisco, and 100 miles/160 km from Sacramento, you can reach it by taking the US 80 as far as Truckee (see entry), where you change to the CA 89 or 267 southbound, and in about 15 miles/24 km you come to the bank of the lake. The CA 28 leads around the north of the lake, and the US 50 around the south. From time to time, both roads offer splendid views of the lake. Lake Tahoe is completely surrounded by mountains, from the Sierra Nevada in the west to the Carson mountains in the east. Many peaks are more than 10,000 ft/3000 m high; thousands of mountain streams empty into the lake. The best known is Eagle Creek, which plunges over the waterfall of the same name into Emerald Bay, 1500 ft/460 m below in the south-west of the lake. A dozen public beaches as well as sailing and motor boats (to be seen in great numbers at weekends in particular) provide the visitor with many opportunities for recreation.

Lake Tahoe in winter

The first white people to set eyes on Lake Tahoe in 1844 were Charles Frémont, later a Civil War general, and his German cartographer Charles Preuss. Frémont named it Lake Bonpland (in honour of a French botanist who had accompanied Alexander von Humboldt on his Latin-American expeditions). A decade later the name of the lake was changed to Lake Bigler; after a further decade it was changed yet again to Lake Tahoe. This comes from the word "da'au", which means "water" or "lake" in the language of the Washoe Indians. This change of name was not officially recognised until 1945, when a decree to that effect was issued by the Californian parliament.

Discovery

The climate at Lake Tahoe is moderately warm in summer but extremely cold in the winter months. Average temperatures for the four seasons are: spring 3°C., summer 16°, autumn and winter 7°. While the annual rainfall amounts to about 1 in/25 mm, the average annual depth of snow is some 16 ft/5 m.

Climate

On the north bank of the lake (in the townships of King's Beach, North Tahoe, Crystal Bay and Incline) no high-rise dwellings may be built; North Tahoe possesses an amphitheatre, where concerts are held and Shakespeare dramas performed every year in the second half of August; (tel. 583-7625).
On the west bank lie the townships of Tahoe City, Sunnyside and Home-wood, whilst the south bank is taken up completely by South Lake Tahoe. This thickly populated district has the most motels, hotels and restaurants of all the lake-side places; it is only a stone's throw from here to Nevada. The town of Stateline, which almost imperceptibly joins South Lake Tahoe, is the site of numerous hotels with 24-hour casinos (Caesar's, Harrah's and Harvey's). Here every day thousands of people throng round the gaming

Banks of the lake

Squaw Valley: a celebrated skiing area

machines, colloquially known as "one-armed bandits". Watching is almost as much fun as actually playing.

Trips round the lake

Trips can be made round the lake on the "Tahoe Queen" from South Lake Tahoe (tel. 541-3364), the "Dixie" from Zephyr Cove, Nevada (tel. 702/588-3508); half-day trips in the big motor boats from Sand Harbor (tel. 702/831-7631), and North Tahoe Cruises from North Tahoe (tel. (916) 583-0141). Cable-car trips from Heavenly Valley also start at South Lake Tahoe (from the US 50, turn into Ski Run Boulevard and look for the sign "Top of the Tram" (tel. 541-7544). From a height of 8300 ft/2540 m you can enjoy a panoramic view of the lake, although the viewing platform is very small.

Winter sports region

Heavenly Valley is only one of the many ski-resorts near Lake Tahoe. The others are: Squaw Valley, 7 miles/11 km north-west of Tahoe City on the CA 89, from the middle of November to April (tel. 583-6955); Alpine Meadows, 6 miles/9½ km north-west of Tahoe City on the CA 89, from the middle of November to June (tel. 583-8914 or 583-4232); Homewood, 6 miles/9½ km south of Tahoe City, on the CA 89, from November to April (tel. 525-7256); Echo Summit, 8 miles/13 km west of South Lake Tahoe on the US 50, from mid November to mid April (tel. 659-7154 or 659-SNOW). Somewhat further away lie Kirkwood, 30 miles/48 km south-west of South Lake Tahoe on the US 50, CA 89 and CA 88 roads, from November to May (tel. 209/258-6000) and Sierra Ranch, 12 miles/19 km south of South Lake Tahoe on the CA 89, from November to April (tel. 659-7475 or 659-7519). There are further winter-sports centres north-west of Lake Tahoe at Truckee (see entry).

Museum

Also in South Lake Tahoe you will find the Lake Tahoe Historical Society Museum (3058 US 50), with displays of artefacts, photos and documents reflecting the history of the area from early times onwards.

Seething mud in the Lassen National Park

Lassen Volcanic National Park   D/E 4

This national park, situated in the extreme south of the mountains with their waterfalls, and 165 sq. miles/427 sq. m in area, was founded in 1916 in order to protect Lassen Peak (10,460 ft/3187 m), one of the few volcanoes in the USA which have become active in recent years (others being Mount St Helens in Washington State, and some in Alaska and Hawaii). As the southernmost link in a chain of mighty volcanoes, including Mount Baker, Mount Rainier, Mount Hood, the former Mount Mazama (Crater Lake) and Mount Shasta, it forms the impressive remains of the once higher, but now collapsed Mount Tehama, the cauldron of which has been filled by subsequent eruptions. Lassen Peak is named after its discoverer, the Danish pioneer and district governor Peter Lassen.

Location and importance

Mount Lassen became active in May 1914, and continued to erupt sporadically until 1921. The biggest eruption occurred in 1915, when a mighty mushroom-shaped cloud rose to a height of 7 miles/11 km. Lava spread to the south-west and north-east. On the south-west side of the mountain it flowed to a width of 1000 ft/300 m, cooled off and hardened. To the north-east, the lava flowed in great rivers and caused a lot of snow to melt. The flow, together with the remains of earlier eruptions, became an avalanche of mud, which rushed faster and faster down the valley. Fertile fields were buried under a blanket of mud up to 20 ft/6 m deep. Three days later there was a fresh explosion, which blew a new crater in the mountain. The lava poured in the direction of the avalanche of mud as it surged downhill. On its way it uprooted and crushed dozens of trees.

History

The most extensive and interesting geothermal area within the National Park is, without doubt, Bumpass Hell, below Lake Helen and reached by a footpath 1 mile/1.6 km in length. By means of easily negotiable wooden planks along a length of 0.6 miles/1 km, you can observe from close

Geothermal areas

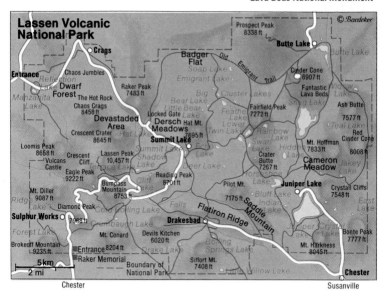

Chester   Susanville

quarters the land strewn with hot springs, volcanic gas-clouds (fumaroles) and bubbling whitish-grey mud-pots, over which an extremely intensive smell of sulphur pervades, and you can also feel it, for the high temperatures of some 100°C. heat up the whole area of Bumpass Hell. It got its name from its discoverer Kendall V. Bumpass, who walked into a thermal spring by mistake, and suffered such serious burns that he had to pay for his error with the loss of a leg.

Walks

You can obtain information about the numerous tracks inside the park from the literature available in the Visitor Center. A favourite walk leads up to the peak of Mount Lassen, an easy route, but one completely lacking in shade, off the CA 89 near Lake Helen, with a climb of some 8500 to 10,500 ft/2600 to 3187 m. It will take about four hours to climb up and down. From the top of the mountain on a clear day you can see the 14,168-ft/4317 m-high Mount Shasta to the north-west.

Information

The entrance to the park, with a Visitor Center, is on the west side, not far from the junction of roads 44 and 89, and is about 44 miles/70 km from Redding (see entry). At the Visitor Center you can obtain plenty of literature and information about the places to visit.
The park is open only from the middle of June to the middle of October. The south entrance, which has no visitor centre, is open in the remaining months only for the winter-sports area in the park; telephone information: 916/595-4444.

Lava Beds National Monument   C 5

In the extreme north-east of California in a thinly populated region seldom visited by tourists, extends the Lava Beds National Monument, founded in

Location and importance

◀ *Volcanic gases rising in the Lassen National Park*

1925 and covering an area of 72 sq. miles/186 sq. km, with strange lava formations dating back thousands of years. It is only a few miles from the Oregon border and lies between the CA 139 and US 97. Barren heaps of ash, some more than 330 ft/100 m high with steep craters, leave their mark on the landscape.

Caves

There are also more than 200 caves here, which provided hiding-places and also acted as small fortresses for the Modoc Indians in their last battles against the American army in the years 1872/1873. In spite of the far superior US forces, the Indians were able to hold out for six months. Some of the best-known caves bear descriptive names, such as Sentinel Cave, Catacombs Cave, Skull Cave (because so many skulls of mountain sheep were found there).

Note

There is a camp-site in Indian Wells but no filling station inside the park. The Visitor Center is on the south side; slide-shows are given here during the summer months. Further information: tel. 916/667-2283. Unmade-up roads lead into the area.

Lompoc

Santa Barbara County
Altitude: 105 ft/32 m
Population: 29,000

Location and importance

Lompoc, not far from the mission station known as La Purissima Concepcion (see entry for Mission Stations), lies in the valley of the same name, which has its origin in the language of the Chumash Indians who once lived there and, roughly translated, means "mussel mountain". Lompoc is only 10 miles/16 km from the Pacific coast, and can be reached via the US 101. Until a few years ago Lompoc was one of the important flower-growing districts of California. Today the area used for horticulture has shrunk to only 1600 acres/646 hectares, as many individual houses have been built here to accommodate the families of those employed at the Vandenberg airfield only a few miles away. The flower festival is held in June every year.

Lone Pine

Inyo County
Altitude: 3740 ft/1138 m
Population: 1700

Location and importance

This little township, situated on the CA 395, lies between Death Valley Monument (see entry) 90 miles/144 km distant and the foot of Mount Whitney, the highest mountain in North America, 13 miles/21 km away, from where you can travel through the Alabama Hills (red sandstone mountains of varying size). From Lone Pine – especially at sunrise – there is a beautiful view of Mount Whitney and the neighbouring tall peak of the western Sierra Nevada.

In the previous century Lone Pine provided a living for the farmers who had settled here, and later became the setting-off point for mountain tours. Conquering Mount Whitney, which was first climbed in 1873, is a strenuous undertaking and takes at least three days, as the difference in level between Lone Pine and the Whitney peak is nearly 6500 ft/2000 m.

The Alabama Hills were the scene of fierce battles between Paiute Indians, who were well able to hide out there, and the American troops. Because of their colourful appearance these hills have provided the setting for many films.

View of Long Beach from the "Queen Mary"

The Eastern California Museum, in which can be seen Indian artefacts and those from Lone Pine's pioneering period, is to be found in Independence, the county town of Inyo County, some 16 miles/26 km north on the CA 395 (open only Thur.–Sun.). Also in Independence can be seen the so-called Commander's House, a beautiful Victorian building, built for the commandant of Fort Independence (which no longer stands), and was moved to its present site in 1889. It can be visited on Sundays only from April to October, on other days by prior appointment (tel. (619) 878-2411, ext. 2259 or 2010, also for the Eastern California Museum).

Museums

Long Beach

P/Q 3

Los Angeles County
Altitude: 30 ft/9 m
Population: 373,000

Bordering on Los Angeles to the south, Long Beach extends along San Pedro Bay. The town was founded in 1881 under the name of Willmore City by the Englishman W. E. Willmore as a summer resort for the inhabitants of Los Angeles. Its name was changed before the end of the nineteenth century to Long Beach, thus showing by its name that here there exists a beach averaging 490 ft/150 m in width and over 5½ miles/9 km long.

With the construction of the harbour and the discovery of oil at the beginning of the 20th c., Long Beach became visibly urbanised, and today is the second largest town in Los Angeles County. Numerous important branches of industry have also become established here; particularly notable is the firm of aircraft manufacturers McDonnell-Douglas. A serious earthquake in 1933, which cost the lives of 120 people and caused damage amounting to 50 million dollars, slowed down development temporarily, but not for long.

Location and origin

In addition to a large congress hall and museums, Long Beach has the famous liner "Queen Mary" lying at anchor and converted into a hotel and museum, also the biggest aircraft in the world, "Spruce Goose", built by Howard Hughes.

* "Queen Mary"

The "Queen Mary" can be visited daily in summer 10 a.m.–4.30 p.m., in the other months until 3.30 p.m., and 4.30 p.m. at weekends. You will be shown all twelve decks of the ship and also the maritime museum equipped by Jacques Cousteau (tel. 435-3511). From Downtown Long Beach a double-decker bus leaves every half-hour for Pier J where the liner lies at anchor.

"Spruce Goose"

Near the "Queen", in a dome-shaped hall on Pier J, is housed the "Spruce Goose", a flying boat built of wood, which flew only a mile at a height of 65 ft/20 m (1947). Hughes designed the flying boat, which has a wing span of 295 ft/90 m and is as high as a normal seven-storey block of flats, as a troop-transporter to carry 750 soldiers with armoured cars.

Further places of interest

Also of interest is the Rancho Los Alamitos, dating from the year 1806 (6400 Bixby Hill Road), one of the oldest adobe-built houses in California. The furniture, however, is from a later date. (Open: Wed.–Sun. 1 p.m.–5 p.m.; admission free; tel. (213) 431-3541.)

Trips round the harbour lasting 1½ hours leave daily from Pier J at 11.15 a.m., 1.15 p.m. and 4 p.m. in the summer months; departure times in the remaining months are irregular (tel. 547-0802).

In Downtown Long Beach, at the bottom of Pine Street south of the Convention Center, a harbour village has been built along the coast in the style of the eighties of the previous century, with some 40 shops and restaurants.

By the Pacific Ocean can be found the Long Beach Museum of Art (2300 Ocean Avenue Boulevard) with an impressive collection. (Open: Wed.–Sun. noon–5 p.m., admission free; tel. 439-2119.)

Los Angeles

Los Angeles County.
Altitude: 30–5020 ft/9–1530 m. Population: 3,140,000; (Greater Los Angeles 8,400,000)

General

Location and
** importance

Los Angeles is the largest city in the federal state of California, and since 1984 the second largest in the United States, when it ousted Chicago from that position. It is situated in the southern part of California and some suburbs are directly on the coast of the Pacific Ocean between the port of San Pedro and the San Gabriel mountain range on the landward side.

Expanse

The city, which covered an area of 20 sq. miles/53 sq. km when it was legally constituted in 1850, has grown to 460 sq. miles/1200 sq. km in the course of 140 years, and thus in area is one of the largest cities in the world.

Conurbation: see special plan on the map at the end of the book

Greater Los Angeles incorporates more than 80 independent towns within the administrative district of Los Angeles County, ranging from the Santa Monica Hills in the west to Pomona in the east, and from the Tehachapi Mountains in the north to Long Beach in the south.

Megalopolis Los Angeles

Megalopolis Los Angeles also includes Orange County in the south, Ventura County in the north as well as parts of Riverside County and San Bernardino County in the east. This socio-economic region is growing ever closer as a result of the continuous urbanisation of former agricultural districts.

Los Angeles: Downtown architecture ▶

Los Angeles

Administration

The administration of this huge region is extremely complicated. In addition to the city corporation with a mayor elected every four years directly by the populace, and the assembly of city councillors, there is also the Board of Los Angeles County. This consists of five Supervisors, often called "five little kings", who are similarly elected every four years by an electoral district numbering 1.5 million inhabitants. They are responsible for public health, welfare institutions, building planning, fire brigade (but not the police), prisons and streets of the city as well as for the other 81 towns and the county's rural population numbering around one million.

City School District

Moreover, there is the largely autonomous Los Angeles City School District whose authority extends beyond the city precincts. Its members are directly elected and are independent of the other two administrative structures. Carrying out the decisions of the Board of Supervisors is the responsibility of a chief administrative officer nominated by this body.

Tom Bradley

Such a complicated bureaucratic structure pre-supposes a high measure of co-operation between those holding office, but conflicts are inevitable. One man who has succeeded for years in heading this multi-layered conglomerate is the mayor Tom Bradley, a former Los Angeles police chief. He was appointed mayor in 1976, and has been re-elected three times. In 1990 he stands as candidate for the fifth time.

Population

Development

Like most Californian towns Los Angeles developed only slowly at the outset. In the year 1785, four years after it was founded, it had a total 139 inhabitants, and even in 1890 there were only 50,000 compared with 300,000 in San Francisco. The number doubled by 1900 and again by 1905, when the census showed 200,000 people. In the following eight decades the population increased more than thirteenfold.

Growth

In contrast to most other large towns and cities in the USA, the population of Los Angeles has continued to increase, mainly due to the influx of people into the suburbs, especially the San Fernando Valley. However, the decline in population in the inner city (Downtown Los Angeles) has been halted in recent years.

The city has received an influx of US citizens from other parts of the United States, attracted by the sun, the economic boom and the increasing prosperity.

Ethnic variety

Immigrants from neighbouring Mexico, from other Latin-American countries and Asia have also contributed to the population explosion. So today in Los Angeles you will find Buddhist temples and Chinese supermarkets, Korean billiard halls and Armenian mamoul bakeries, Mexican clinicas and yerbarias (fruit and vegetable shops), Vietnamese acupuncture clinics and Guatemalan love-potions.

Religion

In line with the multiplicity of races, all religions are represented in Los Angeles. The city is the seat of a Catholic archbishop; the principal church in his diocese is the St Vibiani Cathedral (south Main Street, corner of 2nd Street). There are also several Greek and Russian Orthodox communities, the second largest Jewish community in the United States after New York, one of the biggest Mormon temples, with a 256 ft/78 m high tower crowned by a gilded sculpture of an angel almost 16 ft/5 m high (10777 Santa Monica Boulevard), as well as churches of all the Protestant sects represented in the USA.

Transport and Communications

San Pedro harbour

Los Angeles has no natural harbour. However, in San Pedro, 25 miles/ 40 km from Downtown Los Angeles, there was already a little harbour in the 1850s, providing an anchorage for sailing-ships. No start was made in extending it until the turn of the century, when a rail connection between Los Angeles and San Pedro came into being. When, following the merging of various districts, a land corridor developed between the harbour and Los Angeles, San Pedro was officially declared the port of Los Angeles in 1909. With neighbouring Wilmington and Terminal Island (where there was feverish ship-building during the Second World War) it developed into one of the five largest ports in the United States. Today it is the biggest fishing-port in the whole country.

The International Airport at Inglewood, known as "LAX", is one of the largest in the country, used by more than 45 million passengers each year. Around 56 airlines, including British Airways, LTU and most American lines operate services to the airport (airport information; tel. 646-5252).

International Airport (LAX)

Transport from the airport:
The municipal bus company Rapid Transit District (RTD) runs a number of buses to various parts of the Los Angeles conurbation (for information tel. (213) 626-4455 or (213) 973-1222).

Because of the distance from the airport to the city, a taxi is very expensive. The hotels near the airport offer a free pick-up service with minibuses running all the time (from the hotel/motel – telephones available near the luggage reclaim).

All the major car-rental chains, such as Hertz, Avis, Budget, Alamo have a branch office at the airport (see Practical Information: Car Rental).

In addition to the main LAX airport, there are a further six regional airports in the Greater Los Angeles area, namely in Burbank, Newport Beach (see entry: John Wayne Orange County Airport), Long Beach (see entry), Ontario, Santa Monica (see entry: Municipal Airport) and Van Nuys.

As almost everywhere in the United States of America, railway traffic has lost much of its importance in Los Angeles. Apart from the daily rush-hour traffic from the suburbs into the city centre, the only line of any importance is to San Diego (see entry) and Oakland/San Francisco (see entry).

Long-distance services are available from two coach stations, i.e. Greyhound (the company also has stopping places in other parts of the city) and Trailways.

As the city does not as yet have an underground system, coaches compete for all the public transport which, in view of the size of Los Angeles, is not ideal. At the latest count there were no less than 141 routes, running from Downtown to all the distant parts of the metropolitan district. The system of the RTD (Rapid Transit District) bus company is so complicated that

Los Angeles International Airport *LAX*

the tourist is unlikely to spend long enough in the city to become familiar with it.

Under the heading "Sights from A to Z" details are given of the buses which run to some of the attractions in Los Angeles. However, there are problems if the tourist is not setting out from the city centre because the buses all start in Downtown. In such a case you should obtain the time-tables of the most important routes from, for example, the Greater Los Angeles Visitors and Convention Bureau (685 S. Figueroa Street; tel. (213) 689-8822 or 6541 Hollywood Boulevard, Hollywood; tel. (213) 461-4213). If in doubt telephone RTD direct (tel. (213) 626-4455), where you can obtain the information you require throughout the day and night.

The fare on the regular buses is 85 cents, plus 25 cents for a transfer ticket. You must have the right money ready, because the drivers cannot give change.

"Dash" minibuses

The "Dash" minibuses which ply within the city centre can be recommended without reservation. These little grey buses run at ten-minute intervals to places of interest, such as the Music Center, Little Tokyo, Chinatown, the Pueblo de Los Angeles State historic park and a number of hotels. The fare is only 25 cents. One disadvantage is that the minibuses run only on Monday to Friday until about 7 p.m.

Taxis

Because of the distances involved, taxis are expensive and often difficult to find outside the Downtown area, so it is necessary to order one by telephone. There are plenty of taxis to be found at all places where there are a lot of people (airports, big hotels downtown, railway stations), as well as in Hollywood and Beverly Hills.

Freeways (motorways)

The motorways, known as "freeways" in the USA, because there are no tolls to pay, are used by almost 4½ million people (not cars) in the course of 24 hours, and cover a total distance of approximately 580 miles/925 km. Although traffic is extremely heavy in the rush-hours (7 a.m.–9 a.m. and 4 p.m.–7 p.m.), without the freeways it would be almost impossible to get around.

Downtown Los Angeles is surrounded by four freeways: the Santa Monica Freeway, which then becomes the San Bernardino Freeway and links Santa Monica in the west with San Bernardino in the east (US 10);

the Pasadena and Harbor Freeway, linking Pasadena in the north-east with San Pedro in the south (CA 11);

the Golden Gate and Santa Ana Freeway, which runs from Sacramento in the north to San Diego in the south (US 5);

and the Hollywood Freeway, which is part of the great north–south coastal route, the US 101.

There are also the following freeways: Glendale (CA 2), Long Beach (CA 7), Ventura (CA 134), Foothill (US 210), Pomona (CA 60), Marina Del Rey (CA 90) and San Gabriel River (US 605).

Before you use a freeway you should consult a map to ascertain the correct exit to take.

Culture

General

At one time, the paucity of cultural life in the city gave rise to jokes, such as "What is the difference between Los Angeles and yoghourt?" Answer: "Yoghourt has an active culture!". This has now been rectified long since and after a late start Los Angeles has caught up with San Francisco, the traditional cultural capital of California, and is well on the way to overtaking it.

Music Center

Today, Los Angeles possesses a Music Center, with three large auditoria, one for opera, the other two for theatre. Several concert halls are to be added in the vicinity by 1991. There are also fifteen to twenty smaller theatres in all parts of the city.

Los Angeles: "The Stack", a highway intersection

The museums, although mainly of recent date, have achieved world ranking thanks to donations from a number of prosperous citizens. In addition to the museums in Los Angeles, there are others in the immediate vicinity: the J. Paul Getty Museum in Malibu (see entry: a larger museum complex is at present being built in Los Angeles), the Norton Simon Museum in Pasadena (see entry) and the Huntington Library and Gardens in San Marino (see entry for Pasadena).

Museums

Light entertainment is provided by a large number of cabarets, jazz and rock-bars. In addition, Los Angeles, together with Hollywood, is still the film capital of the world and numerous premières are screened here.

Other entertainment

Los Angeles has about 30 universities and colleges within the city precincts. There are at least twice as many more in the neighbouring towns. The best-known institutions of higher education include the biggest university of the state, the University of California in Los Angeles (UCLA), together with its School of Medicine. There are also the University of Southern California, Occidental College, Los Angeles City College and Yeshiva University.

Universities and colleges

Because of the risk of earthquakes, skyscrapers were not built until quite recently. For many years the City Hall, built in 1932 with 27 storeys, was the tallest building in the city. Only after it became possible to erect earthquake-proof buildings did a real building boom take place. Nevertheless, as far as the number and height of skyscrapers is concerned, Los Angeles cannot compare with San Francisco, perhaps not even with San Diego. The tallest buildings, all situated downtown, are:
First Interstate Bank, 707 Wilshire Blvd. (843 ft/257 m);
Security Pacific National Bank, 333 South Hope Street (730 ft/222 m);
Crocker Bank, 350 S. Hope Street (715 ft/218 m);

Skyscrapers

127

Atlantic Richfield Towers (ARCO), Flower Street, 5th/6th Street (690 ft/ 210 m).

Economy

Building

In contrast to San Francisco Los Angeles, thanks mainly to the discovery of oil and the development of the aircraft industry, has become since the Second World War more of an industrial than a commercial city. Admittedly the skyscrapers of the banks dominate the downtown skyline – the old-established banks of Wells Fargo, Bank of America, Bank of California and United California have been joined in recent years by US branches of Japanese banks – but the stock exchange is of secondary importance. Los Angeles has noticeably become a city of service industries, thus creating new jobs in that sector.

As a result of the continuing building boom the construction industry has also contributed to keeping the unemployment rate low in spite of the many new immigrants.

Film industry

The film industry, which employed about 100,000 people in 1950 and made Los Angeles – or, more exactly, Hollywood – the "film capital of the world", has lost out mainly to television. Today more television films than feature films are made in Hollywood, Burbank and Universal City. Nevertheless, there are still several hundred firms working in the field of producing and selling films.

History of the city

1542

On orders from the Mexican viceroy, the Portuguese Joan Rodriguez Cabrillo discovers California and lands in October at San Pedro, which today forms part of Los Angeles, and at Santa Monica.

1769

Gaspar de Portola, the first Spanish governor of California, names a river near where the city stands today El Rio de Nuestra Sênora La Reina de Los Angeles de Porciuncula.

1781

22 men, 11 women and 11 children are the first inhabitants of Los Angeles, founded on 4th September, or, as it was named at the time, El Pueblo de Nuestra Sênora La Reina de Los Angeles de Porciuncula.

1785

Los Angeles now has 185 inhabitants, mainly engaged in agriculture and cattle-raising.

1786

The population has grown to 500.

1795

Grapes and olives are planted for the first time, followed by hops ten years later.

1816

A start is made on building a church on the plaza. It is finished in 1822.

1821

Los Angeles has a population of around 1000 "gente de razon" (non-Indians, most of whom are mulattos and mestizos) as well as some 500 Indians.

1835

Los Angeles is raised by the Mexicans to the rank of ciudad (city) and in a short time becomes the capital of Alta California.

1836

On 13th August Governor Pio Pico surrenders in Los Angeles to the US forces under Robert F. Stockton and John Charles Frémont.
After both have left the city there is a revolt against the US military government, and the Americans are driven out.

Los Angeles is re-conquered; the capitulation in Cahuenga signals the defeat of the Californios and with it the ceding of Alta California to the United States. — 1847

The emergence of the state leads to the establishment of Los Angeles County. — 1850

"Los Angeles Star" is the first newspaper, appearing weekly. — 1851

The population has grown to 4485, and comprises 1% of the total population of the state. — 1860

The brothers Isaiah and Samuel Hellman from Bavaria found the first bank in Los Angeles (Hellman's First Bank). — 1865

Xenophobia leads to a massive attack on the Chinese; 15 Chinese are publicly hanged. — 1871

Introduction of obligatory elementary education.
Opening of the first high school (corner of Broadway and Temple Street). — 1873

The University of California is founded by the Episcopal Church on its present site.
The population is almost 12,000 (compared with 233,000 in San Francisco). — 1880

The "Los Angeles Times" appears for the first time. — 1881

The Santa Fe Railroad reaches Los Angeles. — 1885

The Occidental College is set up by Presbyterian clergy and laymen. The oldest and most respected club in California, the California Club, is founded. — 1887

Founding of Orange County, formerly a part of Los Angeles County. — 1889

50,395 people live in Los Angeles. — 1890

Edward L. Doheny discovers oil near Los Angeles, leading to an economic boom. — 1892

Stephen M. White from Los Angeles is the first white man born in California to become a federal senator. — 1893

Charles F. Lummis founds the Landmarks Club, with the aim of restoring the mission stations and other historic monuments. — 1895

The population has risen to 102,000.
Founding of the Automobile Club of Southern California. — 1900

The founding of the Pacific Railway Company makes it possible to have a tram network in the county, by constructing tramlines to Pasadena, Long Beach and other places. — 1901

Founding of Beverly Hills.
First film studio built.
First sailing-ship race (Los Angeles–Honolulu). — 1906

The number of oil-drilling derricks has increased to 109.
Through a merger of smaller firms, the Southern Californian Edison Co. is set up providing electric power to 14 counties. — 1909

The population, numbering 319,000, is only 100,000 below that of San Francisco. — 1910

Los Angeles

1911	Construction of the first film studio in Hollywood.
1912	One of the first museums, the Southwest Museum, is formed, dealing mainly with the history and culture of the Indians.
1917	The banker Hubert C. Eaton begins to lay out Forest Lawn Cemetery, the best known cemetery in California.
1919	Founding of the University of California in Los Angeles (UCLA) as a branch of the University of California.
1920	For the first time, the population of Los Angeles is higher than that of San Francisco (576,673 compared with 506,676).
1921	Simon Rodia begins to build the tower named after him in the Watts quarter of the city.
1922	Opening of the Hollywood Bowl. The building economy has a unprecedented boom creating sufficient living space for the population which is increasing by almost 100,000 people per annum.
1927	The "Los Angeles Open" golf tournament comes into being. Regular air services between Los Angeles and San Francisco.
1929	The Academy of Motion Picture Arts and Sciences awards the Oscar film prize for the first time.
1930	The population exceeds the million mark: 1,238,000 inhabitants are counted.
1932	Olympic Games in Los Angeles.
1933	A serious earthquake in Long Beach, which claims 120 lives and causes heavy damage, is also felt in Los Angeles.
1934	Heavy rainfall in one of the driest areas of North America causes serious flooding in Los Angeles and its surroundings.
1940	The first freeway comes into use (Pasadena Freeway); others follow in the next few years. The population growth is slowed down, but not stopped, by the economic slump felt throughout America.
1943	The number of workers employed in aircraft factories in and around Los Angeles increased twelvefold, from 20,000 to 243,000, in the years 1940–1943.
1946	The demobilisation of thousands of soldiers and sailors, who fought on the Pacific Front and are now living in Los Angeles, leads to an unprecedented housing shortage until the wartime economy is converted to a peacetime one.
1950	The number of inhabitants has increased to almost 2 million (1,970,000).
1956	The Brooklyn Dodgers baseball team moves to Los Angeles.
1960	The population reaches the 2½ million mark.
1962	The Cultural Heritage Board is set up. Its task is to protect city buildings of historical or cultural importance by making them listed buildings.
1964	The Music Center, with the three auditoria named Dorothy Chandler Pavilion, Ahmanson Theater and Mark Taper Forum, is opened.

Serious riots in the Watts quarter of the city; 34 dead, 1000 injured and almost as many arrests. Opening of the Los Angeles County Museum of Art.	1965
The population has increased to 2,809,000.	1970
A serious earthquake in the San Fernando Valley belonging to Los Angeles (6·6 on the Richter scale) claims lives and causes great damage.	1971
The second year without rain causes a very serious drought and leads to water rationing.	1977
Floods in and around Los Angeles and resultant landslides cause heavy damage.	1978
For the second time within a few years heavy rainfall in the months of January and February leads to floods.	1982
The Summer Olympics are held in Los Angeles for the second time.	1984
The population of Los Angeles is estimated at 3,144,800, its highest ever.	1985
Under the law all buildings within the area of the geological faults along the Pacific Coast must be made earthquake-proof by 1990.	1986
Opening of the first shopping centre in the inner city (Seventh Market Place, Figueroa Street, between 7th and 8th Avenue).	1987
Opening of the Gene Autry Western Heritage Museum in Griffin Park. Permission to build a new concert hall, Walt Disney Concert Hall, in the Music Center. Plans are drawn up for the complete restoration of the old town (Pueblo Historic Park).	1988
The US Environmental Protection Agency determines to make Los Angeles one of the cleanest cities in the world by 2008. The package includes 120 individual measures (including the planting of two million trees within the next few years) and will cost 2000 dollars per head of the population. The number of cars should be reduced and the release of emissions which contribute to global-warming should also be reduced.	1989

Places of interest from A to Z

Academy of Motion Picture Arts and Sciences

The Academy of Motion Picture Arts and Sciences (8949 Wilshire Boulevard) was founded in 1927. This institution became famous as a result of the Oscar film award-giving ceremonies held there. Since Emil Jannings received an Oscar for his star rôle in the film "The Way of All Flesh" it has been awarded annually in this building (see also Hollywood).
Temporary exhibitions are held continuously in the foyer. In addition, you can watch permanent showings of old films in one of the finest cinemas in the city; one of the most important film libraries is also available to the public. (Open: Mon., Tue., Thur. and Fri. 9 a.m.–5 p.m.)

ARCO Plaza

One of the few shopping centres within the city proper, and also one of the oldest, is to be found very close to some large hotels (505 S. Figueroa

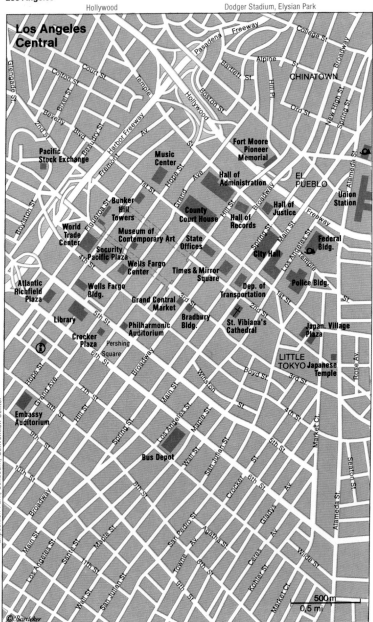

Hollywood   Dodger Stadium, Elysian Park

Los Angeles Central

Exposition Park, Coliseum, Convention Center

Street). In addition to dozens of shops and restaurants, the information office of the RTD (Rapid Transit District) is situated inside. The shops are open daily 9.30 a.m.–5.30 p.m., the restaurants in the evening as well. Worth seeing is the fountain sculpture, created by the Austrian architectural artist Herbert Bayer, which stands in front of the centre.

Barnsdall Park

Situated on a hill in eastern Hollywood surrounded by olive trees (488 Hollywood Boulevard), Barnsdall Park, measuring only 10 acres/4 hectares in area, offers some attractions such as the municipal art gallery and Barnsdall House, built in 1917 by the famous architect Frank Lloyd Wright for the oil heiress Aline Barnsdall, and typical of the building style of the period. Its ground plan resembles a flower. (Guided tours: Tue.–Thur. 10 a.m.–1 p.m. on the hour, Sat. 12 noon–3 p.m. also first three Sundays of each month.)

Bel Air

Lying north of Westwood and west of Beverly Hills, having grown up during the twenties, Bel Air is one of the most elegant of urban districts, with very beautiful and expensive villas. The steeply climbing and winding roads can be negotiated only by car. In Stone Canyon Road stands the most expensive luxury hotel in Los Angeles, Bel Air. It is spaciously built in the Spanish mission style and stands in the middle of an idyllic park surrounded by the scent of bougainvillea, magnolias and avocado wood. The private atmosphere of this hotel, which has the appearance of a picturesque village with its arcades and colonnades, appeals to such famous guests as the Rockefellers and the Kennedys.

Beverly Hills

Although an independent town with some 33,000 inhabitants, Beverly Hills is completely surrounded by the metropolitan area of the city of Los Angeles, and has grown so close to it that the tourist will scarcely get the feeling that he is in a different borough. Situated about 12 miles/19 km west of Downtown Los Angeles, Beverly Hills was first laid out in 1906 by a land speculator from Beverly Farms in Massachusetts (hence its name) in accordance with a plan whereby the streets would run at a 45° angle north from Wilshire Boulevard. However, the town developed only slowly, even after the Beverly Hills Hotel was built in 1912, and the census of 1920 showed the population to number only 674.

It was due entirely to the growing film industry that more and more film people settled in the wide tree-lined streets, and found it even more pleasing to possess plots of land in the hills at the foot of the Santa Monica mountains, where they built large villas. Pickfair (1143 Summit Drive), the house built by the husband and wife actors Douglas Fairbanks and Mary Pickford and where the actress lived in complete seclusion until her death in 1980, was from 1920 until 1935, when they separated, the social focal point of the film colony. Another particularly beautiful house is Greystone Mansion, which the oil millionaire Edward L. Doheny had built, and which for a time housed the America Film Institute.

Today, Beverly Hills is the richest town in America. 75 years ago the growing of beans brought it its first profits, then came the oil magnates and the film millionaires. The average annual income per family of £100,000 is four times more than the American average.

Beverly Hills is also the town of superlatives: here are the cleanest streets and the best-kept districts, the most modern fire-engines and most efficient

History of the town

Town of the rich

Los Angeles

waste disposal. 3000 private swimming pools, 250 private tennis courts, 140 jewellery shops, 214 first-class restaurants and a vast number of beauty salons, business and divorce lawyers and medical practices, mainly psychologists and psychiatrists, round off the picture of this town. The percentage of banks, saving banks and police is also higher than elsewhere in the United States.

Rodeo Drive

Apart from the villas in the canyons and hills, the City Hall built in 1932 in the Spanish-Baroque style (corner of 450 N. Crescent Drive and Santa Monica Boulevard) and the nearby Beverly Hills Civic Center which is nearing completion, nowhere can one observe better the ambience of this town which simply radiates affluence than on Rodeo Drive, between Wilshire and Santa Monica Boulevards. In this, the most expensive shopping mile in the world and the meeting point of the international jet-set, can be found 50 or 60 luxury shops and restaurants.

Legal peculiarities

Beverly Hills has its own laws, which sometimes seem a bit strange. People walking through the villa-lined streets tend not to be viewed with favour. For one thing there are no pavements and, for another, a pedestrian looks suspicious. You must provide proof of identity when asked by the police to do so, to avoid being arrested for vagrancy. As an alternative to walking, some business-minded entrepreneurs offer jogging tours through the attractions of "Billionaires' Hill". Since 1987 smoking has been prohibited in all restaurants (except hotel-restaurants), although you can still continue to enjoy a cigarette a few streets away in the restaurants of Los Angeles. The size of shop signs is also legally controlled, as everything which smacks of money – such as advertising posters which are usually so conspicuous everywhere else – is prohibited. There are also special regulations relating to car parking at night.

Panorama of Los Angeles

The world of Beverly Hills is a different world; you seem to be a long way from Los Angeles and yet you are close to it.

Biltmore Hotel

This hotel (506 S. Grand Avenue; tel. (213) 624-1011), built in 1923 and renovated several times since, the last time in 1986, is in the Renaissance style and has been a listed building since 1969. Although the immediate vicinity of the hotel, especially Pershing Square which is frequented mainly by the homeless, no longer retains its former elegance, this has not damaged the hotel's reputation, since in 1986 the main entrance was moved from S. Olive Street, directly on Pershing Square, to Grand Avenue at the back. The foyers preserved in the Spanish style are impressive as is the Biltmore Bowl banqueting hall, seating 1500.

Bradbury Building

This house (304 South Broadway), commissioned by the businessman Louis Bradbury in 1893 and today used as offices, has been a listed building since 1962. From the outside it appears quite plain, and stylistically is a glaring contrast to the first cinemas built in that century. The interior, however, is a surprise with its open staircases and an interior courtyard of four storeys lit from above, thus illuminating the richly decorated wrought-iron banisters and beautiful wood panelling. A lift, the oldest of its kind in Los Angeles, is still in use and takes visitors to the top.

Broadway

The original cinemas of previous decades, several of which still serve their original purpose, have become places of entertainment for the growing Hispanic population (known in Los Angeles as "latinos"), with mainly   General

135

Los Angeles: shop window on Rodeo Drive

Bunker Hill: modern residential quarter

Spanish and Mexican films. Today Broadway has become the main shopping street of the latinos. Consequently it is loud and lively here, especially on Sundays when all the shops are open.

On Broadway you will find the oldest, well-preserved office building, Bradbury Building (304 S.), the interesting and very reasonable Clifton Cafeteria (608 S.), as well as more cinemas, the oldest of which ae the Cameo (528 S.) and the Arcade (534 S.), both built in 1919. The Palace (611 S.) dates from 1913, the Rialto (810 S.) from 1917, and the richly decorated Million Dollar, in which Sid Graumann began his career, from 1918. All the others were built in the twenties and early thirties and are mainly typical of the American film palaces of the time both internally and externally. Examples are Loew's State (1921; 703 S. Broadway), the Orpheum (842 S.) and the United Artists (933 S.) both dating from 1926, and the Tower (1927; 802 S.), the Los Angeles (1931; 615 S.) and the Roxie (1932; 518 S. Broadway).
The whole cinema district is under a preservation order.

Places of interest

Bunker Hill

Bunker Hill, not far from the present Civic Center, was where the well-to-do Angelenos lived in their Victorian houses at the turn of the century. In 1901 an open cable-railway, modelled on that in San Francisco, was constructed to make it easier for the residents to climb the eastern part of its hill, and which during the brief period of its existence earned the name "Angel's Flight" (now the name of a restaurant in the Hyatt Regency Hotel). In the fifties and sixties all the Victorian houses were demolished to free the land for new development.
Since then several residential skyscrapers (the first in 1964) have been built on Bunker Hill near the Music Center and the Museum of Contemporary Art. The California Plaza is now being built on the last available site. Three multi-storey office blocks, the first of which was already occupied in 1988, a large block of flats and a shopping centre will line the square; they are expected to be completed during the nineties.
Dash minibuses run to Bunker Hill.

California Afro-American Museum

This very new museum in Exposition Park (600 State Drive, by the Harbor Freeway; tel (213) 744-7432) offers numerous exhibits of the history, culture and art of the Afro-Americans and negroes in North and South America. (Open: daily 10 a.m.–5 p.m.)

California State Museum of Sciences and Industry

This museum, which is also situated in Exposition Park (700 State Drive; tel. (213) 744-7400) houses a large number of exhibits which you can operate yourself – therefore a special favourite of children. Of particular interest is a newly installed earthquake exhibition which explains the causes and effects and the action to be taken. Films worth seeing are shown each day in the MAX Theater. (Open: daily 9 a.m.–5 p.m.)

Chinatown

There are neither as many Chinese living in Los Angeles as in San Francisco, nor is their quarter (in Block 800 of North Broadway, north of Downtown, and in the side streets) as interesting or as old as Grant Avenue in San Francisco. The Chinese, who could be found in Los Angeles as long ago as the fifties and sixties of the previous century, were initially domiciled in the

Los Angeles: pagoda in Chinatown

area where Union Station now stands. When construction of the station began the district forming the present-day Chinatown was made available to the community, Its 50-year jubilee was celebrated in September 1988. The centre of Chinatown is the Plaza (951 N. Broadway) with restaurants, banks and numerous shops, some of which are built in the pagoda style. Many Vietnamese also live in Chinatown today and Vietnamese shop-signs are to be seen in many shopping centres. The youth of both peoples, judging by clothes and appearance, seem to have become better assimilated into the community than those in San Francisco.

The prosperous Chinese from Taipei and Hongkong have turned their backs on Chinatown and moved to the suburbs, particularly to Monterey Park and Alhambra (both to the north of the city centre), where in the last few years Chinese enclaves, with typical supermarkets, restaurants, book-shops and newsagents, have grown up.

*City Hall

When it was built in 1926–1928, the City Hall (situated in the middle of the Civic Centre at 200 N. Spring Street) was the first building to exceed the maximum height of thirteen storeys which was permitted at that time. As this building regulation was not revoked until 1957, it required a special public referendum before the City Hall could be built to a height of 27 storeys. The eclectic-monumental building style can be attributed mainly to its pyramid-shaped tower and the Egyptian, Greek and Roman elements. From the veranda of the 27th floor, entry to which is free (open Mon.–Fri. 9 a.m.–4 p.m., there is a beautiful view over Los Angeles and the surrounding mountains, especially when the weather is clear and smog-free. Upon entering the City Hall you are greeted by a hologram portrait of the mayor Tom Bradley. Inside there is no lack of fine building materials. A tiled dome

Los Angeles: City Hall ▶

above the entrance rotunda and all kinds of marble pillars are examples of the luxurious way this building is furbished. (Open: Mon.–Fri. 9 a.m.–5 p.m.; tel. 485-2121.)

Civic Center

In the Civic Center near the City Hall can be found the following administrative buildings: Hall of Records (320 West Temple Street; tel.974-6616), built in 1961 by the Viennese Richard Neutra (open Mon.–Fri. 8 a.m.–5 p.m.); the Criminal Courts Building (210 West Temple Street; tel. 974-4017), built in 1925, the seat of several state and municipal courts (open Mon.,–Fri. 8 a.m.–4.30 p.m.); the Federal Courthouse building (312 N. Spring Street; tel. 894-3650), seat of the federal district court, built in 1940 in the New Functionalistic style of the period; the Parker Center (155 N. Los Angeles Street; tel. 485-2121), built in 1955, and the Los Angeles police headquarters, named after a former police chief.

*El Pueblo de Los Angeles State Historic Park

Location and origin

The park is bordered by Alameda Street in the south, Sunset Boulevard and N. Spring Street in the east and north, and by the Hollywood Freeway in the west. Somewhere in the gounds – exactly where nobody knows – Los Angeles was founded by a small group of settlers at the behest of the King of Spain. It was not until 1953 that an effort was made to restore the 27 historic buildings. Eleven of them are open to the public, five were turned into museums.

Avila Adobe

Avila Adobe, the house of the mayor (alcalde) at the time, was built in the Adobe style in 1818. After being in the possession of his family for 40 years, it had a chequered history. After an earthquake in 1971 it was fully restored and fitted out to reflect the life style of a prosperous Spanish family of around 1840. (Open: Mon.–Fri. 10 a.m.–3 p.m., weekends 10 a.m.–4.30 p.m.)

Church

The Church of Our Lady Queen of Angels (535 N. Main Street) on the Plaza was built between 1818 and 1822, and today belongs to the archbishopric of Los Angeles. Originally constructed in the Adobe style, it has been restored and extended several times. (Open: 24 hours a day.)

Masonic Hall

The Masonic Hall (416 N. Main Street, tel. 628-1274) is one of the oldest temples of Freemasonry in the city (1858) and is still the meeting room of lodge no. 42. Nearby is a small museum. The single-storey building with a wrought-iron balcony above is reminiscent of the Italian Renaissance. (Open: Tue.–Fri. 10 a.m.–3 p.m. admission free.)

Firehouse

The Old Plaza Firehouse (by the Plaza) is a brick building dating from 1884, and at the time was an inn, boarding-house and shop. Today it houses a museum, displaying fire-fighting equipment from the 19th c. as well as photos of other old fire-stations. (Open Tue.–Fri., 10 a.m.–3 p.m., 4.30 p.m. at weekends.)

Pico House

Pico House (430 Main Street) was built in 1869 by the last Mexican governor of California, Pio Pico, and is reminiscent in style of an Italian palazzo. For many years it was the prime hotel in Los Angeles. It is now a private house.

Pelanconi House

Pelanconi House(17 W. Olvera Street) is one of the city's first brick-built houses, and named after its second owner, the Italian Antonio Pelanconi. This is also now a private house.

Olvera Street

After the restoration of Old Los Angeles, Olvera Street was opened in 1930

El Pueblo de los Angeles Historic Monument

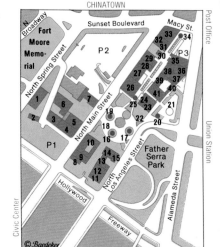

1 Brunswig Laboratory (1924)
2 Beauty Bldg.
3 Brunswig Annex (1897)
4 Vickrey/Brunswig Building (1883)
5 Plaza House (1883)
6 Brunswig Warehouse (about 1912; Juvenile Cours Building)
7 Plaza Catholic Church (1818 to 1822)
8 Masonic Hall (1858)
9 Merced Theatre (1870)
10 Pico House (1869/70)
11 Garnier Building (1890)
12 425 North Los Angeles Street (1898)
13 Turner Building (1960)
14 Hellman/Quon Building (1900)
15 Firehouse (1884)

16 Founder's Plaque
17 King Carlos III of Spain
18 Plaza (1825 to
19 Felipe de Neve
20 Indian Garden (1986)
21 Placita de Dolores (1979)
22 Leo Politi Mural (1978)
23 Biscailuz Building (1926)
24 Plaza Methodist Church (1925/1926)
25 Olvera Street Cross
26 Simpson/Jones Building (1894)
27 Jones Building (ca. 1880)
28 Machine Shop (1910 to 1920)
29 Sepulveda House (1887)
30 Pelanconi House (1855 to 1857))
31 Hammel Building (1909)
32 Siqueiros Mural (1932)

33 Italian Hall (1907/08)
34 Water Trough (1930)
35 Path of Zanja Madre
36 Old Winery (ca. 1870 to 1914)
37 El Pueblo Park Offices (1914)

38 Old Winery (ca. 1870 to 1914) ; El Paseo Inn)
39 Avila Adobe (ca. 1818)
40 Park Offices (Exhibits)
41 Plaza Substation (1904)
P Parking

as a Mexican market, but in latter years the range of goods on sale has lost much of its charm, so that recently plans have been lodged for a further re-modelling. In addition to market-stalls and shops, there are many restaurants in the houses. The road bears the name of the first judge in Los Angeles County, Agustin Olvera.

The Visitor Center is to be found in Sepulveda Building, which dates from the year 1887 (North Main Street; tel. (213) 628-1274). Here you can watch the film "Pueblo of Promise" about the early history of Pueblo. The Visitor Center is open Mon.–Fri. 10 a.m.–3 p.m., Sat. 10 a.m.–4.30 p.m.

Information

*Farmers Market

The origin of the Farmers Market (Hollywood Freeway, Silver Lake exit) goes back to the year 1934 when, at the height of the economic depression, eighteen farmers got together and set up stalls on a piece of open land near Wilshire Boulevard (6333 West 3rd Street, corner of Fairfax Avenue) in order to sell their produce direct to the consumer. This experiment was so successful that Farmers Market kept on expanding. Today, in addition to more than 60 fruit, vegetable and food traders, there are no fewer than 20 restaurants and countless other specialist shops, some first class. Some days up to 40,000 people visit Farmers Market. (Open: Mon.–Sat. 9 a.m.–6.30 p.m., Sun. 10 a.m.–5 p.m., closed on public holidays.)

Farmers Market Tower   *Forest Lawn Memorial Park: Sculpture of David*

Forest Lawn Memorial Park

Scarcely any other city has so many "famous" cemeteries, and none is more famous than Forest Lawn (1712 South Glendale Avenue, Glendale), which is said to have more than a million visitors every year – a number exceeded by no other cemetery. Its founder Hubert Eaton acquired a small cemetery in 1917 and over the years converted it into a last resting place with the atmosphere more of a park than a cemetery. Leonardo da Vinci's "Last Supper" represented in a church window, can be seen in the "Memorial Court of Honor"; American history is conjured up in the "Court of Freedom", and a 18 × 30 ft/5½ × 9 m mosaic reproduction of a famous painting shows the signing of the Declaration of Independence in 1776. You can see a copy of Michelangelo's larger than life sculpture of David, as well as a painting 95 ft/29 m long × 44 ft/13½ m wide of the "Crucifixion". The graves are allowed to have only a simple plaque or sculpture, which must be passed by an art committee created specially for that purpose. In the words of its founder, "I want to establish a large park, without ugly monuments and other signs of death, but filled with tall flowers, the greenest of lawns, bubbling fountains and fine memorials".

Well-known film actors are buried here, including Clark Gable, Alan Ladd, W. C. Fields, Charles Laughton, Carole Lombard, Jean Harlow, Errol Flynn, Humphrey Bogart, Spencer Tracy and Chico Marx, as well as numerous personalities from public life. (Open: daily 9 a.m.–5 p.m.; admission free.)

Gene Autry Western Heritage Museum

This museum, opened in November 1988 in Griffith Park (4700 Zoo Drive, Ventura Freeway, exit to Victory Blvd./Zoo or Golden State Freeway, exit to Griffith Park Blvd.; tel. 667-2000) contains over 14,000 artefacts on the history of the West or Wild West, and also has two galleries for temporary exhibitions. In seven galleries by means of rare old films such as westerns

Tar hollow outside the G. C. Page Museum of La Brea Discoveries

with Buffalo Bill, a reproduction of a Hollywood studio, and costumes and other exhibits dating from the time the wild west was discovered, you can see how Hollywood portrayed the wild west on film.

George C. Page Museum of La Brea Discoveries

This steel-roofed museum, opened in 1977 (5801 Wilshire Boulevard; tel. (213) 936-2230) shows reconstructed fossils of prehistoric animals found in the giant tar-craters of Rancho La Brea, such as mastodons and mammoths, for which tar proved to be an excellent preserving medium. Throughout the years, hundreds of thousands of bone sections from over 170 different mammals and birds have been dug up, from which a number of complete skeletons have been reconstructed. Some of the great tar-craters can be visited. Films and slide-shows explain the Ice Age fauna to the visitor. (Open: Tue.–Sun. 10 a.m.–5 p.m.)

Griffith Park

This park, situated in the eastern part of the Santa Monica Mountains, and covering an area of 4000 acres/1620 hectares, is the biggest state park in California. In the park is the Los Angeles Zoo, the Griffith Observatory and a planetarium, a Greek theatre with 4000 seats, a riding centre created for the 1984 Olympic Games, golf courses and tennis courts and lots more. Walks lasting several hours or drives into the mountains provide splendid views. The park bears the name of its founder Griffith J. Griffith who donated the greater part of the parkland to the city in 1896.
Location and general

Los Angeles Zoo (5333 Zoo Drive; tel. (213) 666-4090) has been in existence only since 1966, and thus is one of the newest zoological gardens in the USA. About 2000 animals, many grouped in their natural environment and
Los Angeles Zoo

143

The famous Hollywood sign

according to their native habitat, roam around on the 115 acres/46 hectares. Among other things there is a reptile house, a section for aquatic animals and one for birds. The new koala-bear house and the children's zoo are very popular. (Open: daily 10 a.m.–5 p.m., except Christmas Day.)

Observatory and planetarium

On a clear evening from 7 p.m.–10 p.m. the telescope of the observatory (2800 E. Observatory Road; tel. (213) 664-1191) gives a unique view of the star-lit sky. In the planetarium a big Zeiss projector shows natural manifestations such as eclipses of the sun and moon, the Northern Lights and star cycles.

In the Hall of Science astronomical phenomena are explained. In a "laserium" you will be completely surrounded by laser beams. (Open: summer Sun.–Fri. 12.30 p.m.–midnight, Sat. 11.30 a.m.–10 p.m.; remaining months Tue.–Fri. 2 p.m.–10 p.m., Sat. 11.30 a.m.–10 p.m. and Sun. 12.30–10 p.m.)

Greek Theater

In this open-air theatre (2700 North Vermont Avenue) jazz and rock concerts with very well-known soloists are held from May to October. The newspapers give details of the programme. (Information: tel. (213) 410-1021.)

*Hollywood

Location and history of the town

Although Hollywood has become known worldwide, it is no longer an independent township as it has formed part of Los Angeles since 1910. It lies about 8 miles/13 km north-west of downtown Los Angeles in the foothills of the Santa Monica Mountains, the so-called Hollywood Hills. Purchased more than 100 years ago (1887) by the Kansas real-estate broker Harvey Wilcox as cheap waste and arable land, Hollywood was named after the ranch of the same name and the holly trees which were to be found there in abundance at the time. From 1903 to 1910 it was an independent community of about 400 inhabitants. Business-minded film people, such

Star cult in a shop window . . .   *. . . and in the street*

as Samuel Goldfish (later Goldwyn) from Russia, Carl Laemmle from Baden-Württemberg and William Fox from New York, set up the first film studios in what had been horse-stables. At that moment was born the "film capital" of Hollywood, which offered ideal conditions – patent regulations, relating to Edison film cameras, could be more easily overcome here. From the daily treks of immigrants from the east of the USA – the novel "Grapes of Wrath" documents this trend – they could recruit cheap labour, including extras for the mammouth productions then becoming popular. In addition, there was the almost unbroken sunshine and the short escape route to Mexico – this latter possibility has to be borne in mind, for the venturesome film people did not enjoy a good reputation on account of their low moral standards. Signs such as "No dogs or actors admitted" (golf course) were not rare by any means.

On entering Hollywood you are welcomed by the famous name-sign in giant letters 50 ft/16 m high, which is brightly illuminated on festive occasions. These letters, reminiscent of pop-art, were erected in 1923 on wooded scaffolding by real-estate brokers as an advertising gimmick. Since then they have won cult status, so that splinters and pieces which broke off when the sign was renovated in 1977 were sold as relics.

"HOLLYWOOD"

Hollywood Boulevard, Hollywood's main east-west axis, has been compared with New York Broadway because of its night-life, but instead of theatres Hollywood has only extravagant cinemas, such as the Chinese and Egyptian Theatres (6925/6704 Hollywood Boulevard) built originally by Sid Grauman in the twenties. In the Hollywood Wax Museum (6767 Hollywood Boulevard) you can see wax figures of the stars. The elegant shops which once lined Hollywood Boulevard have long since disappeared, the film stars having moved to other districts, particularly Beverly Hills (see also Mann's Chinese Theater).

Hollywood Boulevard

Los Angeles

Hollywood legends

Thus Hollywood with its main streets – Hollywood Boulevard, Sunset Boulevard, Melrose Avenue and Vine Street – now exists solely on its former glitter and the Hollywood legends. Since the first film studio was set up followed by many others, Hollywood has become the very embodiment of films, even although no films have been made there for a long time, the large studios having moved to the Burbank and Universal City districts.

Oscar Film Award

On May 15th 1929 Douglas Fairbanks awarded the first of those gold dwarfs – later known as "Oscars" – in the "Flower Hall" of the Roosevelt Hotel (7000 Hollywood Boulevard). Since then at least 22 Oscars have been awarded every year by the Film Academy in Beverly Hills (see also Academy of Motion Picture Arts and Sciences) in Hollywood or Downtown Los Angeles, namely, two each for documentaries and short films and eighteen for the best artistic individual performances in full-length feature films (main and supporting rôles), production, script (original script and one based on a literary precedent), music (film song, original and adapted film music) and filming technique (camera work, decor and scenery, costumes, sound, film-cutting, special effects). There are also awards for the best foreign feature films and, above all, the title "Best Film of the Year", which can quadruple the award-winner's box-office takings.

Before the actual awards are made, when each member of the Academy gives his vote in every category, experts each nominate five individual performances. The sole condition is that the film concerned should have been shown in a cinema in Los Angeles during the course of the year. For all those employed in the film industry an Oscar is the crowning point of their careers, not least because the decisions are made by experts, not by critics or the public.

Tips

Only a few of Hollywood's beautiful Art Deco houses still remain; a present-day feature of the town is the number of good, some a lot too expensive, restaurants. Coach tours are arranged by Gray Lines (1207 West 3rd Street; tel. (213) 481-2121), Starline Sightseeing Tours (6845 Hollywood Boulevard; tel. (213) 463-3131) and other companies.

Hollywood Bowl

Location and importance

Hollywood Bowl, situated north of Hollywood Boulevard on Highland Avenue, is a natural amphitheatre which will accommodate up to 30,000 people (of whom 10,000 have to stand). From the beginning of July to the middle of September the Los Angeles Philharmonic Orchestra performs four times a week something which has become a permanent institution, namely, "Symphonies Under The Stars". These concerts enjoy great popularity and are directed by some of the world's leading conductors. The church service at sunrise on Easter Sunday is a long-standing tradition. (Open: daily July–Sept. 9. a.m.–sunset; tel. (213) 850-2000.)

Museum

In the grounds of the Hollywood Bowl, near the Patio Restaurant, you will find the Hollywood Bowl Museum (3201 Highland Avenue), which houses photographs and other exhibits relating to the history of the Bowl and its concerts, and where you can listen in small rooms to tape-recordings of some historic concerts. (Open: all the year 9.30 a.m.–4.30 p.m., on concert days to 8.30 p.m.; tel. (213) 850-2058.)

Koreatown

One of the newer ethnic quarters, which has expanded even more in the last few years, is Koreatown. Some 100,000 Koreans now live in a district west of Downtown Los Angeles in about 200 streets. So far, however, the Koreans have preferred to keep to themselves and have made little attempt to attract tourists in the way that Chinatown and Little Tokyo (see entries) have done. Their houses border on Vermont Avenue, Pico Boulevard, 8th

Stone sculpture by Isamo Noguchi on the plaza in Little Tokyo

Street and Western Avenue. The Angelenos say that the district is scarcely recognisable any more; the old houses have all been freshly painted and some converted, and everywhere there are Korean shops with signs only in Korean. There are acupuncture clinics, shops selling medical herbs, roast algae, kimchee (fermented white cabbage) and beautiful imported Korean articles such as porcelain musical-boxes. A Buddhist temple, Thal Mah Sah, stands in one of the main streets (3505 W. Olympic Boulevard). Not far away is the Sin Sae Kae department store (3150 W. Olympic). Korean restaurants are also to be found in abundance; however, the sharply spiced food is an acquired taste.

*Little Tokyo

Little Tokyo, the Japanese enclave in Los Angeles, with its numerous new buildings is a clear indication of a thoroughly prosperous ethnic group. Situated around 1st Street between Main and Alameda Streets, within walking distance of the City Hall, the Japanese Village Plaza quarter has developed, with a culture centre, dozens of Japanese shops and restaurants and a large shopping centre. The few 19th c. houses still remaining fit into the picture well. Today, more than 100,000 Japanese live in Los Angeles and the surrounding county; after the Japanese community had been decimated by internment after the war started in 1942, it is now bigger and probably richer than ever. Little Tokyo can easily be explored on foot.

Location and general

Mention must be made of the Japanese American Cultural and Community Center, with a theatre in which from time to time Japanese Kabuki and Noh groups appear, as well as the Bunraku, puppet theatre, a gallery with temporary exhibitions of Japanese art, and a Japanese library, which includes books on Japanese-American relations. (Open: Tue.–Fri. noon–5 p.m., Sat. 10 a.m.–4 p.m., Sun. noon–4 p.m.; gallery: Tue.–Sun. noon–5 p.m.; theatre booking-office: Mon.–Fri. 10 a.m.–6 p.m., Sat. and Sun. noon–5 p.m.; Center: tel. (213) 628-2725; theatre: tel. (213) 680-2000.)

Japanese American Cultural and Community Center

147

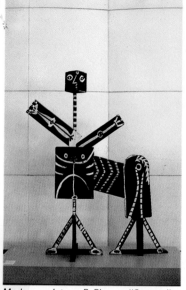

Modern sculpture: P. Picasso "Centaur"...　　　　　*... and old: Indian sculptures*

Plaza	The Plaza in front of the Center was designed by the American-Japanese sculptor Isamu Noguchi, with a big rock sculpture dedicated to the "Issei", the generation of the Japanese immigrants (their descendants born in America are called "Nisei". Near the Center is a symbolic garden, half Japanese and half American, which is an oasis in the middle of the downtown concrete jungle (entrance through the basement of the Center).
Temple	Also worthy of note is the Higashi Hongwanji Temple, a Buddhist house of prayer dating from 1925 , built in traditional Japanese style.
Guided tours	The Little Tokyo Business Association arranges tours to the main places of interest. (Information: tel. 620-0570.)

Los Angeles Central Library

The main library (600 West 5th Street; tel. (213) 612-3200), which has 65 branches in Los Angeles, has not re-opened following a serious fire in April 1986. At that time the whole patent collection was destroyed, as well as 400,000 of the 2.3 million volumes. Only 400,000 books remained undamaged.

The building, at present surrounded by scaffolding, was erected in the years 1922–1926 and, with its pyramidal tower, it represents a mixture of Beaux Arts and various oriental styles. The interestingly arranged internal rooms, some with murals depicting the history of California, cannot be visited at present. The repairs and modernisation planned will be completed in 1991 at the earliest.

Los Angeles Children's Museum

In this museum, designed specially for children (310 Main Street; tel. 687-8800), young people are able to handle many of the things on display

Los Angeles County Museum of Art

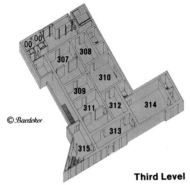

© Baedeker

Third Level

THIRD LEVEL
Parisian Cubism, German Expressionism, Russian Avant-garde, Bauhaus, DeStijl, Dada, Surrealism, Abstract Expressionism

Rooms 307–311 European art from 1900–1950
Rooms 312–314 Abstract Expressionism
Room 315 Contemporary art

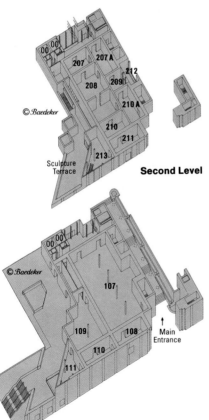

© Baedeker

Sculpture Terrace

Second Level

SECOND LEVEL
American and European painting and sculpture since the Second World War, art from South California since the 50s, contemporary ceramics and glassware, Robert Graham, retrospective column

© Baedeker

Main Entrance

Plaza Level

PLAZA LEVEL (FIRST LEVEL)
Temporary exhibitions of modern and contemporary art, Avant-garde, 'Machine Age', Gemini-(G.E.L.) prints, German Expressionism, works by David Hockney, Robert Longo and Frank Stella

Room 107 W. M. Keck Foundation Gallery

149

Los Angeles

and even play with them. Active participation is expected of the young visitors, whether it involves the "City streets" department, the children's television station, the way an airline functions or trying to live in the world of the disabled. (Open: Wed. and Thur. 2 p.m.–4 p.m., Sat. and Sun. 10 a.m.–5 p.m.; additional opening times during the school holidays.)

Los Angeles County Museum of Art

Location and origin

Although this museum (5905 Wilshire Boulevard, tel. (213) 937-2590) first opened in 1965, its history goes back to the year 1913 when the Los Angeles County Museum of History Science and Art was dedicated. In addition to individual bequests, it possessed several collections which had been given to the museum over the years. As a result, it came near to bursting at the seams.

However, it was not until 1954 that there was a real call for an arts museum on its own. Four years later the county gave its agreement, and after a further four years building work started and took three years to complete. The three original buildings cost twelve million dollars; the opening in 1965 was a huge success.

Importance

Although the museum is scarcely a quarter of a century old it has, as a result of a large number of gifts donated in the interim, gained a worldwide reputation and should not be missed by any visitor to Los Angeles who is interested in art. It now consists of four separate buildings, connected with each other underground, and ranged around a large courtyard.

New exhibition building

The Robert O. Anderson Building, erected as recently as 1986, has a new façade in the Babylonian style and provides adequate room for its important 20th c. art collection, including works from Europe and the USA. Not until September 1988 was an unusual pavilion opened for the large stocks of Japanese art; from an architectural point of view this is without doubt the boldest undertaking this continually expanding museum has made. Its creator was the architect Bruce Goff, who died while the building work was going on.

Subsidy

The museum is maintained by the county, not by the city; the individual buildings were financed by donations from private patrons. The cost of the Anderson Building, for example, amounted to 35 million dollars, and that of the Japanese Pavilion 12½ million. The other buildings which date from the beginnings of the museum bear the names of their chief sponsors: Howard Ahmanson, Armand Hammer and Leo S. Bing.

Anderson Building

Art from the 20th c. is housed in the two upper floors of the Anderson Building, whilst the ground floor is used for temporary exhibitions. European works of art from 1900 to 1950 are displayed in galleries 307–311, including works belonging to such art schools as expressionism, cubism, Russian avant-garde, German expressionism, dadaism and surrealism. The German expressionists are well represented: Nolde, Meidner, Barlach, Schmidt-Rottluff, Kollwitz, Pechstein, Kirchner and Heckel. Schwitters holds a special place among the dadaists. Of those Americans who pay homage to abstract expressionism, works by Stuart Davis, Hans Hofmann, Mark Rothko, Morris Louis, Willem de Kooning, James Pollock and Frank Stella, to mention only the most important, are represented (galleries 312–314).

More recent American art

On the second floor you can follow the development of American – especially South Californian – art of the last three decades; pop art and minimalism are particularly well represented. Also displayed here are works by contemporary potters and glass-blowers, as well as sculptures and new modern acquisitions. Works by retrospective contemporary artists such as Frank Stella, David Hockney, Robert Longo as well as other special exhibi-

150

Japanese pavilion

tions are to be found in the five galleries on the ground floor. In the basement of this building are the offices and workshops of the museum's custodians.

Also with two floors, the Ahmanson Building has the most space for exhibits, having galleries placed around an atrium. Many art forms are represented – from the antiquarian to the 19th c. – and require maximum concentration from the visitor. Chinese and Korean art and Asiatic lacquer-work are to be found in the basement. On the ground floor you will find British decorative art (gallery 102A), British painting and sculpture (105), the unique Gilbert collections of Italian late Renaissance mosaics and large silver items (103 and 104), American painting, sculpture and decorative art from the 18th and 19th c. (106–113), African and South Sea art (114) and pre-Columbian art (115).

Ahmanson Building

On the first floor the tour begins with Egyptian art (201) and then continues with ancient western Asiatic art, including five reliefs from the second millenium B.C. from the palace of King Ashurnasir II in Nimrod, Assyria (201A). Then follows a newly-installed gallery of Iranian art, two 16th c. carpets being outstanding. Antique glass from various countries and civilisations is on show in galleries 203 and 219, Greek and Roman sculptures in gallery 205. Medieval and Renaissance art (205–208) and European paintings and sculptures from later epochs (210–217) are without doubt the main sections of the museum. Outstanding examples from this collection are pictures by Rembrandt ("The Raising of Lazarus" and "Man in a Black Hat"), Rubens ("Adoration of the Shepherds"), Frans Hals ("Portrait of a Man"), Fra Bartolommeo ("The Holy Family"), Canaletto, Georges de la Tour ("Magdalene with the Smoking Flame", one of the four representations of Mary Magdalene by the French master) and one of St Andreas by El Greco. Of the German masters, Dürer, Hans Baldung (known as Grien), Lucas Cranach the elder, Riemenschneider and Schongauer are represented. There is also a good collection of works by French impressionists.

First floor

151

Los Angeles

Second floor

The second floor is devoted exclusively to Asiatic and Near Eastern art. The tour begins with Indian sculptures from the first millenium, mainly of sandstone, bronze and gilded bronze, and a representation of the dancing god Shiva dating from the 10th c. (301). Works of art from south-east Asia, Sri Lanka, Nepal and Tibet are to be found in galleries 302 and 303; many – including 15th c. Indian water-colours (304) – come from the collection by Frau Nasil Heeremaneck, who supported the museum in the seventies.
Islamic art – mainly textiles – from Iraq, Iran and Turkey can be seen in galleries 305 and 306. Costumes and textiles from various countries and epochs (307) complete this tour.

Hammer Building

In the two-storey Hammer Building only the upper floor is devoted to art. It contains a part of the important collection by the oil-industrialist Armand Hammer. Originally intended as a gift, it is today actually on loan, as Hammer fell out with the museum and is now thinking of building his own museum to house his whole art collection. On this floor, in addition to the Hammer Collection, are sketches, prints and photographs in three galleries. On the ground floor are offices and in the basement the museum shop and a gallery for special exhibitions.

Bing Center

The Bing Center houses a large auditorium, the Plaza Café and libraries which are accessible to the public only by prior arrangement.

Japanese Pavilion

The building of the Japanese Pavilion resulted from a gift. A collector was prepared to give the museum 300 screens and scrolls from the Edo period (17th c.) and as the museum did not have sufficient space for its now extended Japanese exhibits it was decided to build a special room for them. The collector Joe. D. Price had originally chosen the architect Goff to build the pavilion on his land in Oklahoma. However, Goff subsequently favoured housing the collection in a museum. His design was amended by another architect only to the extent that the building had to conform to the earthquake requirements and other building regulations laid down by Los Angeles. The roofs were supported by cables fixed to the curved beams, reminding one of Japanese gateways. The transparent walls are obviously meant to imitate Japanese shoji (paper screens). The curved interior of the pavilion contains cascades and pools.
The building consists of two parts: in one can be found prints, a Netsuke collection, ceramics, kimonos and sculptures, which were already in the museum's possession but only a part of which could be displayed. The second wing is fitted with ramps; this is where the screens and scrolls from the Price collection are displayed. As there is not sufficient room for everything, it is planned to alternate the exhibits.

Building plans

Extensions to the museum are still not complete. The next projects are a library, a small lecture hall, and possibly a home for the decorative arts. In Hancock Park in which the museum stands there is sufficient space for such developments.

Opening times

The museum is open Tue.–Fri. 10 a.m.–5 p.m., Sat. and Sun. 10 a.m.–6 p.m. Admission free on the second Tuesday of the month.

Los Angeles County Museum of Natural History

Location and general

When this museum, built in the Spanish Renaissance style (900 Exposition Boulevard, Exposition Park; tel. (213) 744-3414), was opened in 1913 it housed the collections of the Los Angeles County Museum of Art, but in time this grew to such an extent that a special museum had to be built for the works of art. Since 1965 the 35 rooms and galleries have been available for natural history exhibits. The material on display includes sections for aquatic animals, birds, reptiles, fossils of mammals – including those of three dinosaurs – and also an extensive section for minerals, semi-precious and precious stones. (Open: Tue.–Sun. 10 a.m.–5 p.m., in summer until 6 p.m.).

Mann's Chinese Theater

Autographs on the forecourt of Mann's Chinese Theater

153

Stone figures on the façade of the Mayan Theater

Mann's Chinese Theater

Location and furnishings

Very often hundreds of people are to be found in front of Mann's Chinese Theater (6925 Hollywood Boulevard) – still the great sensation of Hollywood. This cinema was built in 1927 and opened with Cecil B. De Mille's film "King of Kings". Like the Egyptian Theater on Hollywood Boulevard and the Million Dollar on Los Angeles' Broadway, the Chinese Theater is also a creation of Sid Grauman, who had a predeliction for exotic cinema palaces. Now it is run by Ted Mann, who named it after himself. Both the inside and the outside incorporate numerous Chinese features. The entrance is guarded by two giant Chinese heavenly dogs, to keep away evil spirits. The foyer is fitted with thick oriental carpets; large vases and urns, the statue of a Chinese philosopher and the three wax figures in the corner, clothed in exotic Chinese robes, emphasise the Chinese character of this room.

"Autograph collection"

In the forecourt you can see the largest "autograph collection" in the world: foot and hand-prints of more than 150 film personalities, together with their signatures. It is said that it was the silent-film actress Constance Talmadge who first – by mistake – walked on the wet cement and inspired Grauman to this original undertaking. There is still enough space left for the foot and hand-prints of actors, directors and producers to last for another thirty years.

Other cinemas

Two less attractive cinemas, Chinese 2 and 3, are built nearby. In the years to come the whole cinema complex will probably be surrounded by a giant new building, the Hollywood Promenade, with flats, offices and shops.

Mayan Theater

Location and origin

The Mayan Theater (1040 Hill Street, near 11th Street) opened in 1927 with George Gershwin's musical "Oh, Kay!" reflects the pre-Columbian

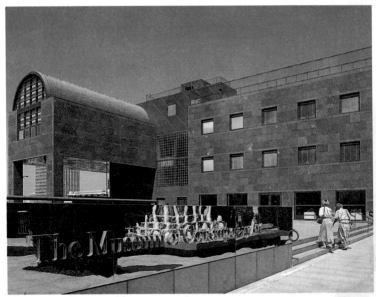

Exterior of the Museum of Contemporary Art

"Temporary Contemporary": Picture Gallery

Maya style. It was commissioned by the oil millionaire Ed Doheny.

The façade is covered with well-preserved stone figures – including the mighty Maya god Huitzilopochtli – and geometric mosaics, copies of those found in the Yucatan cities of Uxmal and Chichen Itza.

The glazed tiles in the foyer were made specially for the Mayan Theatre by a Mexican artist, and are reproductions of tiles found in a sun-temple in Guatemala.

"Dark-room"

As the Mayan Theatre is situated in a run-down area (1040 Hill Street, near 11th Street) and for years has been used only to show pornographic films, the auditorium is nearly always kept dark, so you can see very little of what is described as a very beautiful room. It is said that the lights are not even switched on during the intervals between performances.

Belasco Theatre

As a second theatre building, the Belasco Theatre, stands in the immediate vicinity of the Mayan Theatre, one gets the impression that the otherwise unattractive Hill Street was once part of a theatre district. However, the Belasco Theatre, named after the actor, producer, theatre director and playwright David Belasco, who was born in San Francisco, has been a church for years.

Mural painting

On the side-wall of the house opposite the Mayan Theatre (1031 S. Hill Street; best seen from the car-park) is a painting, over 65 ft/20 m long, by the well-known mural artist Kent Twitchell. It depicts the painter Ed Ruscha.

*Museum of Contemporary Art (MOCA)

Location and origin

This, the newest museum in Los Angeles (250 South Grand Avenue), was founded in 1979 as "a private museum with a public conscience", but the main building on Bunker Hill, designed by the Japanese Arata Osozaki, which was expected to be opened in time for the Olympic Games in Los Angeles in 1984, was in fact not ready for occupation until December 1986. In the meantime the administrators used a storeroom provided by the city, which was very skilfully converted into a number of galleries by the well-known architect Frank Gehry.

"Temporary Contemporary"

It became known as the Temporary Contemporary (152 North Central Avenue) and was so well received that it has continued in use as a kind of permanent branch of the main museum.

General

Until this museum was founded Los Angeles was without a collective home for art which is exclusively contemporary, not just modern. The main building was erected on the last piece of vacant land on the California Plaza, a giant complex of offices and apartment buildings, shopping centres and restaurants, between the City Hall and the actual city centre. Pontus Hulten, former manager of the Centre Georges Pompidou in Paris, was chosen as the first director of the museum, but he withdrew from the post before the two buildings were inaugurated, and his deputy Richard Koshalek was appointed in his place.

The museum was set up so that there would be a home in Los Angeles for contemporary art, and the many native collectors could be catered for. It is hoped that one day it will acquire what is probably the most important private collection of contemporary art, that of the industrialist Frederic R. Weisman, before – as already mentioned – he builds his own museum.

Stock of exhibits

In the meantime two important collections have been donated to the museum: 80 works that were in the possession of the Italian Count Giuseppe Panza di Biumo (mainly of abstract impressionism and pop-art), as

Sculpture by Lipchitz outside the Dorothy Chandler Pavilion

well as 64 from the estate of the collector Barry Lowen (minimalists from the sixties and seventies, neo-expressionists, post-minimalists from the eighties.).

Together with gifts of individual works, the museum has a stock of 425 paintings, sculptures, prints, sketches, photos, installations and other works, and it is still in the building-up phase.

The natural lighting conditions of the Isozakis Museum, built of red sandstone, are extremely advantageous, thanks to its pyramidal superstructures, cubes and cylinders which give the low building the appearance of being at the same time higher and yet firmly anchored to the ground. The division of the old storeroom into small and large galleries, with ramps and staircases, provides many possible arrangements for exhibitions.

Lighting conditions

It is not possible to give details about the exhibition rooms, because the relatively meagre stocks are constantly being changed, and also because many temporary exhibitions are held. During a visit to the two museums it was found that there were nine exhibitions being held at the same time – five in the new museum (including a large-scale one by the German painter Anselm Kiefer) and four in Temporary Contemporary.

Both museums are open on Tue., Wed., Sat. and Sun. 11 a.m.–6 p.m., Thur. and Fri. until 8 p.m. (admission free on Thursday evening; information: tel. (213) 626-6222).

Opening times

Music Center

The Music Center (135 N. Grand Avenue), situated on the summit of Bunker Hill, was built from sandstone in the years 1964–1967, and is similar in many ways to the Lincoln Center in New York, dating from about the same period. At the time, the total cost of the three buildings amounted to 34 million dollars, half of which came from public collections made by Mrs

Location and general

Mark Taper Forum (in background)

Dorothy Chandler, the mother of the publisher of the "Los Angeles Times". A plaza links the three buildings which, were it not for the giant sculpture by Jacques Lipchitz, would have a somewhat desolate appearance.

Dorothy Chandler Pavilion

In the Dorothy Chandler Pavilion concerts (Los Angeles Philharmonic Orchestra), operas (Los Angeles Music Center Opera) as well as musicals and solo performances take place. The 3200 seats are filled almost every evening. The opera company, performances by which are held in the months of October, December, February, April and May, has a modern repertoire by American standards: in the 1988/1989 season, for example, the company performed "Tales of Hoffmann" and "Orpheus in the Underworld", both by Offenbach, Janáček's "Katja Kabanowa", Rossini's "Tancredi", Verdi's "Othello" and "Salome" by Richard Strauss. The Joffrey Ballet also appears here, mainly in the spring.

Ahmanson Theater

Four musicals and stage plays are presented each season in the Ahmanson Theater, as well as guest performances by the New Yorker Broadway Theater, and also some of their own productions by the Center Theater Group (2100 seats).

Mark Taper Forum

In the semi-circular Mark Taper Forum (740 seats) the Center Theater Group presents contemporary plays, including premières, large numbers of which have found their way to Broadway. Thus it has become one of the most successful regional theatres in the United States.

Walt Disney Music Hall

The Walt Disney Music Hall is at present under construction, and will be built in accordance with plans drawn up by the Californian architect Frank Gehry. It is to be the permanent home of the Los Angeles Philharmonic, and is to be used exclusively for concerts given by it and other orchestras. The hall is not expected to be completed before 1992.

General information: tel. 972-7211
L.A. Opera: tel. (213) 972-7211
Joffrey Ballet: tel. (213) 972-7642
Ahmanson and Taper: tel. (213) 410-1062.

Pacific Palisades

This district, part of Los Angeles, lies north-west of the city, high above the Pacific Ocean. It was founded in 1921 by the Southern Conference of the Methodist Episcopal Church, and thought of as a kind of spiritual centre of the sect. Since then Pacific Palisades has developed into an elite part of the city, the inhabitants of which have the highest average income in Los Angeles. It has also been the exile home of some prosperous German writers, such as Thomas Mann (he had a house built here at 1550 San Remo Drive), Emil Ludwig and Lion Feuchtwanger, whose house went to the University of Southern California after the death of his widow in 1987.

Pacific Coast Exchange

The stock exchange known as Pacific Coast Exchange (233 S. Beaudry Avenue; tel. (213) 977-4500) came into being in 1957 as a result of the merger of the previously independent Los Angeles and San Francisco exchanges, and today is the second largest in the country after that of New York. The Los Angeles Stock Exchange was founded in 1889, and that in San Francisco in 1882. Only about 10% of the shares traded here are issued by Californian companies, the rest are also handled on the New York Exchange or the American Stock Exchange (also in New York and some other American cities).
From a gallery, where there are some historic artefacts, you can watch what is going on in the stock exchange. (Open: Mon.–Fri. 6.30 a.m.–1.30 p.m.)

San Pedro

San Pedro, 25 miles/40 km from the city centre, is indeed a part of Los Angeles, but is often regarded as an independent district. A start was made on developing this natural harbour in the 1880s. It was completed towards the end of the century, but not until 1909 did it form a part of Los Angeles with which it is linked by a narrow corridor.

Location and general

In San Pedro can be found the Cabrillo Marine Museum (3720 Stephen White Drive; tel. (213) 548-7562), housed in the enclosed 70-year-old public-baths and in several small houses in which the aquaria are situated. (Open: Tue.–Sun. 10 a.m.–5 p.m.; admission free.)

Cabrillo Marine Museum

The Los Angeles Maritime Museum (pier 84, bottom of 6th Street; tel. (213) 548-7618), houses items and photographs relating to the history of the port. It displays ship models – including an 18 ft Titanic re-creation and the liner model used to film the Poseidon Adventure. (Open: Tue.–Fri. 9 a.m.–4 p.m., Sat. and Sun. 10 a.m.–5 p.m.; admission free.)

Maritime Museum

The Villages at Ports O'Call complex is laid out like a port of New England on the east coast of the United States. Here you will find no fewer than 75 shops, some with an international flavour, and 15 restaurants. From here, too, you can watch the activity in one of the world's biggest harbours, Worldport LA (Los Angeles). (Open: 11 a.m.–9 p.m., restaurants until 10 p.m.)
From San Pedro you can go by boat or helicopter to Santa Catalina Island (see entry). The helicopter flies every day if there is sufficient demand. Information: tel. 800/262-1472 (departure from pier 95).
Information on boat trips: tel. 514-3838 (leaving from piers 95 and 96).

The Villages at Ports O'Call

Bus no. 446 (Fermin/San Pedro), change to bus no. 147.
By car: Harbour Freeway in a southerly direction, take Harbor Boulevard exit.

*Simon Rodia (Watts) Tower

Location and
history of the
building

The tower, named after its builder Simon Rodia, stands in East 107th Street No. 1765, and you can reach it via the Harbor Freeway, exit 14, Gage Avenue.

In 1921 Simon Rodia, an immigrant builder and carpenter from Naples, began to build "his" four towers from cement, steel poles and wire-netting, clad with something like 70,000 mussel-shells and glass, tile and mirror fragments. In 33 years of work he completed four towers, two of which are 112 ft/34 m high, and represent perhaps the most complete example of folk-art today.

Simon Rodia

Simon Rodia was certainly no trained architect, but – scorning all help – created buildings with an almost Gothic effect, which can best be compared with the architecture of the Spaniard Antonio Gaudi. When the towers were completed in 1954 he made a present of them to a neighbour, moved to Martinez, a town near San Francisco, and never returned to Watts.

Cultural
monument

In 1959 the towers were bought by two young people. Their efforts to prevent their demolition were crowned with success when after four years the sculptured complex was declared a cultural monument. However, this did not prevent the towers from being damaged by vandals. Restoration has been in progress for some years now, so that access is limited. The interior can be visited on only four days in the year.

Southwest Museum

Founded in the year 1907 by the Southwest Society, the Southwest Museum opened on its present site in 1914. Situated at 234 Museum Drive, it is reached via the Pasadena Freeway, exit 43rd Avenue. This building in the mission-house style lies in the Highland Park area of the city, high above the Pasadena Freeway, north-east of the city centre. Today, the museum owns one of the best collections of Indian art and culture; exhibits come from as far apart as Alaska and Tierra del Fuego on the southernmost tip of South America. Its founding was attributable to the initiative of Charles F. Lummis, who applied himself at an early stage to preserving Indian culture, and set up the Southwest Society for that purpose. Over the years the stock of North American Indian artefacts increased, mainly as a result of the acquisition of the Poole Collection, including among other things Navaho carpets and basket-work. The building contains a well-stocked museum shop, as well as a library with works on Indian culture. A festival of Indian art is held in October each year.

Museum and library open: Tue.–Sat. 11 a.m.–5 p.m.; the museum also Sun. 1 p.m.–5 p.m.

Union Station

This station, built in the Spanish mission-house style between 1934–1939 (800 North Alameda Street), proved to be one of the last large city railway stations of its kind in the United States. It was a communal project by three private railway companies, Southern Pacific, Santa Fe and Union Pacific. Particularly worth noting are the waiting-room, over 50 ft/15 m high and with a ceiling of wooden beams, the marble floors and the numerous arcades. The Union Passenger Terminal became less important with the

Union Station, one of the oldest in the USA

Universal Studios: general view

Universal Studios: in action

decline in long-distance travel. At the present time it is being converted to a regional transport junction of Greater Los Angeles (see Facts and Figures: Transport).

**Universal Studios

Location and origin	One of Los Angeles' most important sights, the Universal Studios (Hollywood Freeway, exit Linkershim Blvd.), was created in 1915 by the German-American film pioneer Carl Laemmle on the site of a chicken farm. At that time the part of town now known as Universal City was still wild, hilly countryside. Initially Laemmle built only two sets, on which the first silent films were made in the open air.
Tours of inspection	As an advertisement for the new film industry he arranged tours of inspection for 25 cents, when he explained to the visitors how films were made.

Today, such trips are considerably more expensive (about 17 US dollars) and last a lot longer, but are every bit as good as the Disneyland Pleasure Park (see under Anaheim). Since the new tours were introduced exactly a quarter of a century ago 55 million people have been taken around the 40 acre/16 hectare film studio, the biggest in the world, for a glimpse behind the scenes of film making. You can see King Kong, almost 33 ft/10 m tall, as well as the shark from the film "Jaws", fitted with internal mechanism. You also pass by sets where special effects conjure up, for example, the skills of Fred Astaire dancing on the ceiling, or the secrets of making a bicycle appear to fly through the air.

Natural catastrophes take place before the onlooker's very eyes: avalanches in the Alps and (since the autumn of 1988) an earthquake in Los Angeles (8.3 on the Richter scale). You can experience the Battle of Galactica portrayed with laser beams, pass by Alfred Hitchcock's "Psycho House", and witness films actually at the production stage. After the two-hour tour you can also pay a visit to the show in the Entertainment Center. You can walk through a whole row of buildings made for films.

The Universal Studios are open every day in the summer months 9 a.m.–5 p.m., the rest of the year 10 a.m.–3.30 p.m., weekends 9.30 a.m.–3.30 p.m.; the Entertainment Center stays open longer. For information tel. 818/508-9600, to arrange group visits (more than 20 persons) tel. 818/777-3771.

Opening times, information

University of California, Los Angeles (UCLA)

With almost 35,000 students, this high college (405 Hilgard Avenue, Westwood) is the largest constituent of the University of California. Having originated from a so-called Normal School founded in 1882, it began to expand when it acquired its present campus site in the Westwood area of the city. In the year 1929 the college institute, laid out in the form of a rectangle, was re-opened. To these four buildings, based on an Italian model, have been added 80 more in the last six decades. The 400 acre/160 hectare campus is today one of the most beautiful in California.

Location and origin

Its numerous gardens are noted for their exotic plants. A botanical garden situated in a canyon, 3¾ acres/1½ hectares in area (open: weekdays 8 a.m.–5 p.m., weekends 8 a.m.–4 p.m.), is laid out like an unusual woodland landscape. Royse Hall, one of the four original buildings, has a large auditorium in which numerous concerts take place. The adjoining Haines Hall houses the Museum of Cultural History, with temporary exhibitions. In Schoenberg Hall (named after the composer Arnold Schoenberg who worked at the UCLA for a number of years) unusual concerts are often given. There is a large gallery in the Dickson Art Centre.

Sights

Cars are allowed only on the main roads of the campus, so you must find the places of interest on foot. Guided walks are available on Mondays to Fridays 8 a.m.–5 p.m., starting from the Visitor Center, Ueberroth Building, corner of Le Conte & Broxton Avenue. For more detailed information tel. (213) 206-8147.

Tips and information

University of Southern California

This private university was established on its present site (3551 University Avenue, Harbor Freeway, exit 9th Exposition Avenue) two years before the UCLA, and in the interim has grown to have 32,000 students (53 students registered in its first year). The present campus covers an area of some 150 acres/60 hectares, on which stand nearly 90 university buildings. The better known include the Schoenberg Institute, housing the works bequeathed by the composer (open: Mon.–Fri. 10 a.m.–4 p.m.; information about exhibitions tel. 743-5362), the Hancock Memorial Museum (with the furniture from the 19th c. house, since pulled down), the Fisher Gallery (in which temporary exhibitions are held of items from the estimated 250 million dollar collection of the oil magnate Armand Hammer), the Norris cinema and the Bing Theater, in which public performances are given. (Guided tours of the campus: Mon.–Fri. 10 a.m.–2 p.m.; most buildings are open 9 a.m.–5 p.m.; information tel. (213) 743-2983 and (213) 743-2311.)

Location and general

Watts

Watts, one of the smallest parts of Los Angeles, lies south-west of the centre of the city and is inhabited mainly by negroes and Mexicans. One week in August 1965 the tension prevailing there exploded, 34 people met their death, over 1000 were wounded and enormous damage was caused.

Unemployment, poor living conditions, friction with the police and a general feeling of frustration were the root causes of the riots. They were triggered off by the arrest of a negro by a white police officer for allegedly being drunk in charge of a vehicle. Shops owned by whites were plundered, cars set on fire and occasional shots fired. As the police were unable to control the situation the armed National Guard was called in, but even it could not restore order until the sixth day. Since then Watts has calmed down again, but tensions remain and bands of youths still make trouble there. You should therefore take due care when visiting Watts (see also Simon Rodia Towers).

Wells Fargo History Museum

Like the museum of the same name at the big Californian bank in San Francisco, this museum (333 South Grand Street) also describes, by means of artefacts and photos, the bank's history and its contribution to the development of the West and of California in particular. Slides and videos are shown in a small projection-room. (Open: all banking days 9 a.m.–5 p.m.; admission free; tel. (213) 253-7166.)

Westin Bonaventure Hotel

This Downtown hotel, near the freeways (400 South Figueroa Street, with a second entrance on Flower Street), is one of the most unconventional buildings designed by the hotel architect John Portman of Atlanta. The five free-standing round towers, with lifts going up and down on the outside, dominate the skyscraper scene of Downtown Los Angeles like no other building. Around the inner atrium, in the building of which much concrete was used, are numerous shops and restaurants. The hotel, built in 1978, has 1500 rooms (tel. (213) 624-1000).

Los Gatos   I 1

Santa Clara County
Altitude: 384 ft/117 m
Population: 27,000

Location and origin

Los Gatos, established about 1850, is protected by two mountain peaks: El Sombroso (the Shady One) and El Sereno (the Nightwatchman). It lies south of San Francisco Bay, at an intersection of the CA 17, and owes its name to the wild cats which once roamed the area (los gatos = the cats). Until the start of the Second World War it was a small community, the inhabitants of which made a living mainly by growing fruit. Today, Los Gatos forms part of the catchment area of Santa Clara and Santa José (see entries).

Places of interest

Los Gatos offers the tourist a museum of history and natural history (Main & Tait Street; open: daily except Mon. 1 p.m.–4 p.m.; admission free) and an old town district with restored houses of Spanish and Victorian origin, shops, restaurants and workshops (50 University Avenue; open: Mon.–Wed. and Sat. 10 a.m.–6 p.m., Thur. and Fri. 10 a.m.–9 p.m., Sun., noon–5 p.m.; tel. 354-2646).

Los Padres National Forest   M/N 1/2

Location and general

Los Padres National Forest, lying west and east of the CA 33 and US 5 highways and east of Santa Barbara (see entry), covers a total area of

J. Paul Getty Museum · Malibu

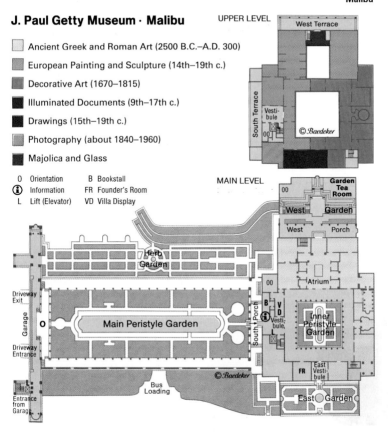

Ancient Greek and Roman Art (2500 B.C.–A.D. 300)

European Painting and Sculpture (14th–19th c.)

Decorative Art (1670–1815)

Illuminated Documents (9th–17th c.)

Drawings (15th–19th c.)

Photography (about 1840–1960)

Majolica and Glass

O Orientation	B Bookstall
(i) Information	FR Founder's Room
L Lift (Elevator)	VD Villa Display

1,875,000 acres/750,000 hectares, and rises in places to a height of 8860 ft/ 2700 m. Within its boundaries are several wild parks, such as Ventana, San Rafael and Santa Lucia, as well as two areas where the condor is a protected species. This largely unspoiled wilderness admittedly with few trails suitable for walks, is served mainly by unmade-up roads, and possesses no visitor centre or information offices of any kind. Originally created as long ago as 1903, the area has been extended several times, finally reaching its present official boundaries in 1936. In that same year it received its name, in memory of the Franciscan monk who set up eight mission stations in the immediate surroundings.

Malibu

P 3

This community, which still belongs to Los Angeles, lies between the Santa Monica Mountains and the Pacific coast, along the CA 1, and possesses some of the most beautiful Pacific beaches in Los Angeles. Like the neighbouring Pacific Palisades, Malibu, with a population of some 10,000, is one

Location and general

J. Paul Getty Museum: Cypriot figure

Picture of an Egyptian woman

Statue of Hercules (Herakles) . . .

. . . and of a successful athlete

of the most well-to-do parts of the city. Scholars differ regarding the meaning of its name; although it is certain that "Malibu" can be traced back to the Umalibo ranch belonging to the native Chumash Indians, the actual meaning of the word is uncertain, although it could well be the name of a person.

Warning

In the interests of the residents, parking is prohibited on the streets of Malibu and Pacific Palisades.

Beaches

Worthy of mention are the beaches running from south to north, seven of which are maintained by the city of Los Angeles: Topanga Beach, originally a private beach; Las Tunas Beach, quite narrow even at low tide; Malibu Pier, used mainly by anglers; Surfrider Beach, chiefly the domain of surf-riders; Corral Beach, 1 mile/1½ km long, inaccessible at high tide; Paradise Cove, particularly good for swimming; Pirate's Cove, barely 650 ft/200 m long; Zuma Beach, where you should watch out for giant waves, and Nicholas Beach. Further north lies Leo Carrillo State Park, which also has an especially beautiful beach.

**J. Paul Getty Museum

Location and importance

The main place to visit in Malibu is the J. Paul Getty Museum (17985 Pacific Coast Highway). It was opened in 1954 in the oil-magnate's villa in Pacific Palisades, and moved to Malibu in 1973. The style of building is reminis-cent of the Roman villa buried when Vesuvius erupted in the year A.D. 79. Initially only Greek and Roman sculptures, decorative art, mainly French furniture and 15th to 18th c. European art was collected. After Getty's death in 1976, and after his heirs had settled their differences, the museum – with assets of 2.2 billion dollars – became the richest in the world, scarcely able to make use of the interest earned on its capital.

Layout

First, the building itself: it stands on a wooded hill above Santa Monica Bay, about 440 yds/400 m from the Pacific Coast Highway. The narrow road up to the museum is lined with tall eucalyptus trees and leads directly to the underground garage. From the garage a lift goes up to a loggia with Corinthian pillars, from where you have your first view of a 330 ft/100 m long garden around a elongated pond. On both sides of the garden area there is a colonnade. Only after walking along this 330 ft/100 m stretch do you come to the villa, an exact copy of a building from Pompeii almost 2000 years old has been perfectly achieved.

Plans for enlargement

A few years ago 107 acres/43 hectares of land on a hill in the Santa Monica Mountains above Brentwood, not far from Westwood and the campus of the University of California in Los Angeles (UCLA), were acquired. Here it is intended to build a large museum with a research institute and an art library. The museum complex as drawn up by the architect Richard Meier is – judging from its huge dimensions of 0.75 sq. miles/1.9 sq. km and the astronomical building costs – a truly American project, and is expected to be completed in 1994. Then, the present museum in Malibu will display only sculptures but, in anticipation of developments to come, has already extended its collecting activities to other spheres, such as photographs and illuminated manuscripts.

What will the visitor find inside? Getty's own collection, added to since his death, necessitating a continuous re-arrangement of the 38 galleries – 13 on the ground floor and 25 on the upper floor. Within the limited space of this guide we can mention only the most important highlights of the extensive collection. The brochures issued by the tourist office in Los Angeles, according to which it takes two hours to visit the museum, are somewhat optimistic, as in that time you can see only a fraction of the exhibits.

Malibu

Antiquarian art

The sculptures on the ground floor still form the most important part of the museum. One of the oldest pieces is a 16 in/40 cm tall female figure from Cyprus which is almost 4500 years old, the stylised form of which has a compelling effect. There are a large number of Greek and Roman sculptures, the latter partly in terracotta but mainly in marble, such as the seated man playing the lyre, surrounded by two sirens.

One of the outstanding pieces in the Getty Collection is the marble figure of Hercules, standing almost 6½ ft/2 metres tall, and dating from the second century A.D. This larger than life figure of the hero is holding in its left hand the club with which they were – according to legend – Hercules slew the Nemean lion, and in its right the lion's hide. If you compare this Hercules with the sculpture of the "Victorious Athlete" dating from the early period of the Olympic Games (4th or 3rd c. B.C.), you will see that the athlete's left arm is hanging down, while his right points to his laurel wreath.

Only a few bronzes of this kind are still preserved. There are also several portrait statues and statuettes from the Roman period. Some well-preserved Greek terracotta vessels, some still gloriously colourful (vases, amphora and so-called craters), are to be found in one gallery.

There are scarcely any paintings remaining from ancient times, because the material on which they were painted wasted away over thousands of years. In the dry air of the Egyptian desert, however, portraits of mummies painted on wood have been preserved, as they were placed in the linen wrappings of the mummy. One example is the true to nature portrait of a woman (Romo-Egyptian). Other less impressive paintings can be seen on the shrines and sarcophagi. A further gallery houses antique silver and gold work.

Manuscripts

It was not until 1983 that the Getty Museum first began to collect illuminated manuscripts from the time before the art of printing books had been developed. Nevertheless, it has already amassed a considerable collection, as witness the German, French, Italian and British exhibits on the upper floor. Almost all the manuscripts emanate from the purchase of the Louis Collection from Aachen.

Paintings

Even though Getty never showed any particular interest in buying paintings, he nevertheless purchased in the thirties a whole range of important works by Rembrandt (including the "Old Man in Armour"), Jan Steen, Jacob Ruysdael, one of the forty remaining paintings by Georges de la Tour, a Goya, a Gainsborough, two paintings from the Rogier van der Weyden school (including a "Descent from the Cross"), two Corots and works by the French impressionists Pissarro, Monet and Degas; there are also works by the post-impressionists Gauguin and the forerunner of the Art Nouveau style, Toulouse-Lautrec.

Drawings, decorative art.

Also worthy of attention are the sketches displayed on the upper floor, including works by Dürer and Hans Baldung (known as Grien), Raphael, del Sarto, Veronese, Rembrandt, Rubens, Poussin and Watteau. Most of the examples of decorative art come from France; of the richly-decorated furniture, that which stands out is a cabinet, probably made for King Louis XIV, above the door of which is a bronze medallion of the monarch surrounded by military trophies. Of the porcelain items, special mention should be made of a basket from the Sèvres porcelain factory.

Photographic collection

The photographic collection is distinguished by the numerous original prints from the 1840s. The two oldest photographs in this collection, some of which are by unknown photographers, date back to 1841. In addition to others from the 19th c., there are also numerous examples of work by photographers from the present day such as Man Ray, Imogene Cunningham, Walker Evans and the German August Sander.

Admission to the Getty Museum is free. Open: Tue.–Sun. 10 a.m.–5 p.m., closed on main public holidays.

Notes:
Opening times and
how to get there.

If you wish to go there in your own car, you must book in advance by telephone, as visitors will be admitted only if there are parking places available. If you intend to go at weekends or during the busy season, it has been found most advisable to book one or two weeks in advance. The booking-office is available every day 9 a.m.–5 p.m.; tel. (213) 458-2003.

Another option is to travel by taxi; this can take you to the museum entrance but must then leave at once. Taxis can be ordered by phone from the entrance hall in the basement for the return journey.

From Santa Monica you can travel to the museum by bus no. 434. It stops in front of the museum entrance on the Pacific Coast Highway. It is about another 880 yds/800 m to the actual entrance. You can get an entry ticket from the bus driver which must be handed over at the desk. However, as this bus does not run very often, it is best to phone the Rapid Transit District (RTD) bus company (tel. (213) 626-4455) to find out the exact departure and arrival times and the fare. You should have the right money available, as the bus driver cannot give change.

Mammoth Lakes   J 5

Mono County
Altitude: 7800 ft/2377 m
Population: 4000

Mammoth Lakes is more than 370 miles/600 km from Los Angeles (approached via the US 10, US 15, CA 395 and CA 203 highways) and almost 310 miles/500 km from San Francisco (via the US 80, US 50, CA 395 and CA 203). Although Mammoth Lakes and the surrounding countryside, including the 12,080 ft/3680 m high Mammoth Mountain 4 miles/6 km away, can be enjoyed at any time of the year, it is one of the best winter sports resorts in the country, where you can ski from the end of November until the beginning of July. With 17,000 skiers finding their way here on one working day – there are correspondingly more at weekends and on public holidays – Mammoth Lakes, although perhaps less well-known than Vail (Colorado) and Squaw Valley, is the busiest ski resort in the United States. This region, south-east of Yosemite National Park, lies within the Inyo National Forest (see entries), not far from such places of interest as Devils Postpile National Monument and the John Muir Wilderness Area (many trails for walks). In the snow-free months a visit to the Mammoth Lakes region can be combined with one to Yosemite National Park, Mono Lake and Bodie (Bodie State Historic Park) (see entries).

Location and
importance

There are flight connections to Los Angeles, Oakland and San José; for information about flights tel. 800/824-2610.
Local buses run in Mammoth Lakes and to the ski-slopes.

Transport

Marina Del Ray

See Santa Monica

Mendocino   E 1

Mendocino County
Altitude: 125 ft/38 m
Population: 2000

Façades in Mendocino

Window of an antique shop in Mendocino

Mendocino lies on the CA 1 running parallel to the Pacific coast, and is some 150 miles/240 km from San Francisco (US 80, CA 116, CA 1). Originally known as a port for shipping timber, some of its early houses have been well preserved and lend a colourful appearance to this little coastal town. Many artists settled here after the Second World War. Today Mendocino boasts a number of galleries, the best known of which is the Mendocino Art Center (45200 Little Lake Street), where exhibitions, concerts and theatrical productions are held, and instruction is also given in various branches of art.

An unusually large number of boutiques in Main Street and in the side streets complete the shopping facilities. Of the many pubs built for the lumberjacks and port workers – Mendocino is said to have had no fewer than 22 in the second half of the 19th c. – only a few remain, such as Dick's Place near the Mendocino Hotel on Main Street (built in 1878 and worth seeing). One of the oldest houses, Ford House on the side of Main Street facing the sea, dates from 1854; it is now an information bureau; tel. (707) 937-5397. Also worth a visit are Kelly House, built 1861 (45006 Albion Street), now a local museum and library, and MacCallum House, dated 1882 (45020 Albion Street). In spite of a tendency to modernise, Mendocino has succeeded in retaining its village character. It shows no signs of urbanisation in the way that Carmel (see entry) does. An interesting stroll is along the cliffs high above the sea.

Merced

Merced County
Altitude: 170 ft/52 m
Population: 42,000

Merced lies in the fertile agricultural region of the San Joaquin Valley where in addition to rearing cattle, peaches, tomatoes, almonds and alfalfa are grown; it is well-known because of its location on the approach road to the western entrance to Yosemite National Park (see entry) which is scarcely 60 miles/100 km away.

Only some 7 miles/12 km north-east of Merced lies the charming Lake Yosemite State Park (boats for hire, fishing and water-sports facilities).

Mission stations

In accordance with normal American practice, the simple term "Mission" is used in the text. This actually means the particular mission station concerned.

When the Spanish King Carlos III had cause to fear that either the Russians or the British (the latter had just annexed Canada) would attempt to seize the as yet unexploited lands in Alta California, he managed to forestall them; he instructed the Franciscan monks coming from Mexico to build mission stations in Alta California, as he believed that in this way it would be easier to control the surrounding land. The Fathers were to convert the native Indians to Christianity and also initiate them into the secrets of husbandry. However, he clearly overestimated his abilities, and this ambitious undertaking, to acquire land on the one hand and save souls on the other, was doomed to failure from the start.

Mission stations

Entrance front of the Carmel Mission

El Camino Real

Living witnesses to this period are the 21 mission stations which were built in the course of 54 years (1769–1821) along the Pacific coast from San Diego to Sonoma. This almost 600 mile/960 km stretch of the California Highway No. 1 has been called "El Camino Real" (see entry) since Mexican times. The Spanish word "real" has two meanings: "really, actually" and "royal, splendid". So it is up to you how you wish to interpret the roadsign: "Road to Reality" or "The Royal Road".

Their condition today

After their secularisation under Mexican rule only a few mission stations remained in their original condition, as fire, earthquake and malicious damage led to their destruction. Almost all have been restored and are accessible to visitors, but only a few still serve their true, religious purpose.

Tourism

The peace to be enjoyed in the well-kept gardens will provide the visitor with a welcome change from the busy Californian towns and cities. All mission stations can be visited. They are listed below in order of the date when they were built.

Mission of San Diego de Alcala (1769)   S 2

Location

Mission Valley, 6 miles/10 km from the San Diego catchment area; a well-signed diversion off Highway 8 leads to it. (Open: daily 9 a.m.–5 p.m.; tel. 619/281-8449.)

History

The Spanish military governor Gaspar de Portolo took possession of the land near San Diego Bay on behalf of Spain. In 1769 the Spanish Franciscan Father from Majorca, Junipero Serra, founded the mission stations, the first of which was built in San Diego. A few years after it was founded, however, it was moved 6 miles/10 km inland, because disputes had arisen between the Spanish troops and the Indians. In 1775 the Indians set fire to the new mission; the Fathers sought refuge with the army and it was 1777 before they built a new mission station with the help of the Indians. However, it quickly became dilapidated following secularisation. All that remains is a church with a bell-tower, declared a basilica in the seventies, a beautiful garden and a small museum.

*Mission of San Carlos Borromeo de Carmelo (1170)   J 1

3080 Rio Road, Carmel. Situated about 5 miles/8 km from Monterey, on the southern edge of Carmel. (Open: weekdays 9 a.m.–5 p.m., Sun. 10.30 a.m.–5 p.m.; tel. (408) 624-3600.)   Location

Because of its architecture and its location on Monterey Bay, the Carmel Mission, as it is generally known, is one of the most beautiful of the mission stations. When it was founded it formed the northernmost point of Spanish dominance. Here, too, soldiers and priests soon separated; Serra moved the mission station some 5 miles/8 km into a valley by the Carmel river. It remained Serra's headquarters until his death, by which time there were already nine mission stations. Here you can still see the spartanly simple room with its wooden bed and writing table, from which Serra supervised the mission stations and watched over the baptism of more than 5000 Indians.   History

From 1934 onwards the mission and the church, built in 1797 in the Moorish style by a Mexican stone-mason, were restored in their old form. It is one of the few mission stations to retain its square inner courtyard. Here, too, lies the tomb of Serra, who was canonized by Pope John Paul II on September 25th 1988.

Mission of San Antonio de Padua (1771)   K 1

Situated near the village of Jolon, about 40 miles/66 km south of Soledad and 36 miles/58 km north of San Miquel; turn off the 101 Jolon Road or Fort Hunter Ligett Military Reservation. (Open: weekdays 9.30 a.m.–4.30 p.m., Sun. 11 a.m.–5 p.m.)   Location

This mission fell into decay so quickly after being secularised in 1834 that no buyer could be found for it when it was advertised for sale eleven years later. Everything that was not nailed or screwed down was stolen, and the interior demolished. It was 1907 before a start was made on restoration, especially of the church and the inner courtyard, and this was not completed until the fifties. A small museum houses some interesting artefacts from long ago. The rural character of the isolated valley gives the mission its special charm.   History

Mission of San Gabriel Arcangel (1771)   P 3/4

537 West Mission Drive, San Gabriel, reached via turn-offs from San Bernardino Freeway (1–10), exits Atlantic or Rosemary Ave. (Open: daily 9.30 a.m.–4.15 p.m.; tel. (818) 282-5191.)   Location

This mission's church, which still serves as such today, was built by the Franciscan Antonio Cruzado in 1806, using as a model the Moorish cathedral at Cordoba, with some notable modifications. The bell-tower fell victim to an earthquake in 1812 but the church remained standing. North America's first grape-vines were cultivated on its land and, although others followed its example, San Gabriel's area of cultivation remained the biggest and its mission the most prosperous. Serra had brought some cuttings from Spanish vines with him in 1769 so as not to be dependent on imports from Spain for his communion wine. At the beginning of the 19th c. up to 11,000 gallons/50,000 litres of wine were produced here each year.   History

Exterior of the Dolores Mission

At the San Gabriel mission, where some 1000 Indians – called Neophytes – lived and worked, soap, leather and tallow were produced as well as barley, maize, beans, peas and lentils. More than 2000 orange, lemon, fig, apple, peach and pear trees were planted.

Places of interest The museum with its parchment scrolls and old and valuable books going back to the 15th c. is well worth a visit. On the mission land is a cemetery where more than 6000 Indians are buried, mainly victims of epidemics. At the beginning of the 19th c. about 100,000 of North America's 900,000 Indians must have lived in California.

Mission of San Luis Obispo de Tolosa (1772)   M 1

Location At the corner of Monterey and Chorro Street, San Luis Obispo, about halfway between Monterey and Los Angeles; tel. (805) 543-6850.

History Little remains of this mission station, once a flourishing cattle centre. Today its ruins lie in the town centre of San Luis Obispo. After secularisation the mission was stated to be the property of the Indians; cattle could be taken away unhindered; the church and other buildings quickly fell into decay. At a public auction in 1845 the mission station was sold for only 510 dollars. A hotel sprung up directly opposite. More than 100 years ago the church was "modernised" in the New England style, when the bell-tower was given a totally unsuitable spire.

Mission of San Francisco de Asis (Mission Dolores: 1776)   H I

Location 16th and Dolores Street, near Market Street. (Open: daily 9a.m.–4.30 p.m. in summer, 10 a.m.–4 p.m. in winter; tel. 415/621-8203.)

Romantic ruins of the San Juan Capistrano Mission

The mission, situated in the southern part of Downtown San Francisco, still displays its former size and importance. It was built near the Dolores Stream which flowed into a lake no longer there (it reached from 16th to 23rd Street). The outside of the church is less notable than the Baroque altar inside, which came from Mexico. The patio (inner courtyard), common to almost all mission stations, has also long since disappeared and a basilica erected in its place.

In a cemetery lie the remains of 5500 Indian victims of an epidemic, as Indians in this region showed themselves to be particularly prone to disease.

History

*Mission of San Juan Capistrano (1776)

Q 3/4

This mission station lies near Junction 1–5/Pacific Highway, about 4 miles/6 km from Dana Point. Los Angeles is 60 miles/100 km away. (Open: daily 7.30 a.m.–5 p.m.; tel. 714/493-1111.)

Location

The San Juan Capistrano mission, shrouded in romance, is a favourite with tourists; its church is also worthy of attention. Its construction was not started until 20 years after the founding and took until 1806 to complete. Its name goes back to the Italian jurist and later Franciscan crusading priest John of Capistrano (14th/15th c.), who was canonised at the end of the 17th c. This mission, dedicated by Serra, is the only one in Orange County, south of Los Angeles. The church with its twelve domes was badly damaged by earthquakes in 1812 and 1918 and, like other buildings forming part of the mission, only partially repaired. Since the church could not be used as a result of the earthquake a mere six years after completion – 40 Indians had been buried in the ruins – services were held in a little adobe-built church.

This mission station is one of the few remaining which are fully preserved.

History

Santa Barbara Mission: remains of an irrigation system

Legends

There is a romantic legend concerning these ruins. It is said that the swallows which nest in the stonework set off each year on their migration south on October 23rd (the day on which John of Capistrano died in 1456), and return on St. Joseph's Day, March 19th. This legend is immortalised in a 50-year-old hit tune "When the Swallows Come Back to Capistrano", and still lives on – even though the dates do not exactly agree.

Mission of Santa Clara de Asis (1777)

I 1

Location

This mission is scarcely 3 miles/5 km from Pueblo San José, on the CA 82, between Franklin and Bellamy Streets. It has the same opening times as the university, i.e. until 8 p.m. in the summer months and until 11 p.m. in the remaining months.

History

After the founding of the Santa Clara de Asis mission almost half a century passed before the church was built, and today we see only a 1929 copy – four earlier churches were destroyed by earthquake or fire. This one is the most successful as far as fulfilling the aims of the missions is concerned; more Indians – 8536 to be precise – were baptised here than in any other mission station.
After secularisation in 1834 it was handed over to the Jesuits, and formed the nucleus of the first of California's colleges, the University of Santa Clara. Today the mission forms part of the campus.

Mission of San Buenaventra (1782)

O 2

Location

211 E. Main Street, Ventura, from Highway 101 turn into Main Street via California Street. (Open: weekdays 10 a.m.–5 p.m., Sun. 10 a.m.–4 p.m.; tel. (805) 643-4318.)

◀ *Fountain outside the Mission Church of San Buenaventura*

Mission stations

La Purisma Concepcion Mission

History

One of the last of the mission stations to be founded by Father Serra, little now remains of San Buenaventura except the church which, like so many others, suffered damage in the 1812 earthquake. The gardens which once surrounded the church have long since given way to buildings of all kinds, principally because of their location in the centre of the present-day town. At the time when the mission stations were built this region was inhabited by Chumash Indians, said to have been the most highly developed tribe in California.

*Mission of Santa Barbara (1786)   O 2

Location

2201 Laguna Street, corner of Oliveros Street, Santa Barbara. Approached from Downtown via the well-signed Santa Barbara Street. (Open: weekdays, 9 a.m.–5 p.m., Sun. 1 p.m.–5 p.m.; tel. 805/682-4713.)

History

The "Queen of the Mission Stations", as Santa Barbara is generally called, was the only one to remain with the Franciscans after being secularised and to be preserved by them in its original condition to the present day. However, this applies only to the buildings, for the large estates which once belonged to the mission were lost after 1834.

Places of interest:
Church

The church, completed in 1829 after the original had been destroyed by earthquake in 1812, is the work of Father Antonio Ripoli. It has a Roman temple façade and was built by the obviously extremely skilled Chumash Indians. In the library Ripoli discovered the Spanish translation of a work by the Roman engineer and military technician Vitruvius Pollio, dating from the year 27 A.D. The drawings by Vitruvius of Doric columns and Roman temples inspired Ripoli's design; a French visitor said of the church that "he had not expected to find such luxury in this country, so far away from all the beauties of Europe". It is the only mission with two towers, and had to be rebuilt in earthquake-proof construction after the 1925 eruption which laid waste the whole of Santa Barbara. Today it serves as a parish church.

In the buildings of the mission station you will find a museum with objets d'art from the colonial period and many interesting artefacts, as well as the archives of the Californian Franciscans. Until 1968 the seminar of the Franciscan Province of California was also held here. Especially worth seeing are the garden, and the cemetery in which many prominent early Spaniards as well as 4000 Chumash Indians found their last resting-place.

Museum, archives, garden

Near the mission you can see the remains of the extensive irrigation system, part of which is still in use today.

Irrigation system

*Mission of La Purisma Concepcion (1787)   N 1

The best route to the mission, the ruins of which are still be be seen and which forms part of the town of Lompoc, is via the US 101 and CA 246 (Buellton exit) (Open: daily 9 a.m.–5 p.m.; tel. 805/733-3713.)

Location

This mission station is the only one situated in the State Historic Park and is located in a charming valley surrounded by the Santa Ynez Mountains. After the first mission building had been completely destroyed in the 1812 earthquake, the Fathers moved their mission somewhat further north, but there too, not far from the old Camino Real, they were still pursued by misfortune. A disastrous drought, a fire and finally in 1824 an Indian rising crushed by Spanish troops did not allow the original building plans to come to fruition. La Purisma is the only mission without an inner courtyard. Secularisation further affected it, until finally there was little left but ruins.

History

In the 1930s La Purisma was restored from the ground up by the Civilian Conservation Corps, a body formed by the Roosevelt government, with the result that no other mission gives such a good insight into life in the mission stations. In addition to the church, a monastery, military barracks, a tannery, a soap factory, various workshops and the water-reservoir have been rebuilt in their old authentic form, so that visiting them is essential for a real understanding of days gone by.

Places of interest

Mission of Santa Cruz (1791)   I 1

Corner of Emmet and High Streets, Santa Cruz. The reproduction stands on Mission Hill; tel. (408) 426-5686.

Location

Practically nothing is left of this mission, and no attempt has been made to restore it. In 1825 an earthquake demolished the building, and scarcely had makeshift repairs been carried out when the foundations were weakened by the spring tide of the Santa Cruz river. In 1857 another earthquake destroyed what was left and looting added to the devastation. Near the original site can be seen a smaller reproduction of the church, and a little museum in a wing of the monastery is open to visitors.

History

Mission of Nuestra Señora de la Soledad (1791)   K 1

Ft. Romie Road, about 3 miles/5 km north-west of Soledad, the site of a state prison, not far from the US 101. (Open: Tue.–Sun. 10 a.m.–4 p.m.; tel. (408) 678-2586.)

Location

Little remains of the Nuestra Señora de la Soledad mission. Its Spanish name means "Our Lady of Solitude". The Franciscan Fathers thought they recognised the Spanish "soledad" in the name the Indians had given it. One is still haunted today by this feeling of solitude, and can well understand why the Fathers tried to flee from this oppressive isolation. In scarcely four and a half decades 30 Fathers took on the leadership.

History

Epidemics and floods occurred frequently; in 1831 the church collapsed, and a storehouse had to be converted quickly into a chapel. Secularisation did the rest. Only this chapel and a wing of the inner courtyard have been restored.

Mission of San José de Guadalupe (1797)   I 1

Location   Fremont, 43300 Mission Boulevard, at the junction of the CA 238 and Washington Boulevard. (Open: daily 10 a.m.–5 p.m.; tel. (415) 657-1797.)

History   This mission was set up about 14 miles/23 km from the present town of San José, on a slope of the Diablo Mountains (the town was not established until 1851) and was intended as a base for expeditions against hostile Indians and also as a place for baptisms. Only one wing of the inner courtyard has been restored, and this houses a museum with artefacts from the mission period and some Mexican sculptures. Shortly after it was secularised the mission leader of many years' standing, Father Narciso Duran, founded an orchestra made up of Indians who had been taught to play western stringed instruments. After secularisation the church served initially as a parish church. It was finally destroyed by a serious earthquake in 1868. There are plans for the old mission church to be restored.

Mission of San Juan Bautista (1797)   J 1

Location   2nd and Mariposa Street, San Juan Bautista, 3 miles/5 km south of the US 101 on the CA 156. (Open: daily 9.30 a.m.–5.30 p.m., Mar.–Oct. 9.30 a.m.–4.30 p.m. rest of year; tel. (408) 623-4528.)

History   Like the Santa Barbara mission, that of San Juan Bautista – situated in the centre of the town of the same name, in the middle of a state park – was used only occasionally, and today serves as a parish church for the predominantly Mexico-American population. The damage caused by the 1906 earthquake was not put right until 70 years later. As it lies directly on the San Andreas Fault the mission was particularly at risk from earthquakes. However, during the 1906 earthquake it stayed more or less on its foundations. As in the San José de Guadalupe mission, music received special attention; Father Esteban Tapis formed a choir and an orchestra. He also drew up a notation system based on colours, which made it easier for the Indians to read the notes.

Items of interest The church stands on the west side of the square and is the only mission church to have three aisles. The painted altar is by Thomas Doaks, a sea-farer from New England stranded in Monterey, and apparently one of the first "Yankees" to come east. He undertook to do the painting work in return for board and lodging.

Mission of San Miguel Arcangel (1797)   L 1

Location   The mission lies on the US 101, about 9 miles/15 km north of Paso Robles and 33 miles/53 km north of San Luis Obispo. (Open: daily 10 a.m.–5 p.m., the museum 10 a.m.–4 p.m.; tel. 805/467-3256.)

History   This mission, situated in the extreme north-east of San Luis Obispo County, over 37 miles/60 km north of the town of the same name, has – in contrast to most of the others – a church (the third one, and completed in 1821) which has withstood the rigours of time rather better, so that in 1901 and 1928 it had to be merely renovated, not rebuilt. As a result of secularisation the mission lost its estates, which extended as far as the Pacific Ocean 30 miles/50 km away, and during the 1850 gold-rush it was a favourite place for fortune-seekers to stay. By the end of the 19th c. there was a bar in the monastery!

The church, however, was not adversely affected; it remains intact and is one of the best-preserved examples of mission architecture. The interior is richly painted; Indians worked under the artist Estevan Munras from Monterey and succeeded in producing some interesting "trompe l'œil effects" (French for "deceiving the eye"). Above a statue of its founder is an all-seeing Eye of God, supposed to exert a hypnotic effect upon believers. In the nearby museum you can see interesting items from the mission period.

Items of interest

Mission of San Fernando Rey de Espana (1797)

P 3

15151 Mission Boulevard, San Fernando, at the junction of the Golden State (1–5) and San Diego Freeway (1–405), easy to reach from Pasadena and Downtown Los Angeles. You can also take bus no. 24 from 11th and Main Street in Los Angeles. (Open: weekdays 9 a.m.–5 p.m., Sun. 10 a.m.–5 p.m.; tel. 818/361-0186.)

Location

Although this mission bears the name of a secular ruler, that of King Ferdinand III of Castille, he was nevertheless canonized after his death. He founded the University of Salamanca, and he also fought successful wars against the Moors. The mission lies west of the town of the same name, about half-way between the San Buenaventura and San Gabriel mission stations. The largest of the buildings fell victim to the 1812 earthquake; only one monastery wing about 260 ft/80 m long remains standing. The symptoms of decline which followed secularisation were rectified between 1879 and the 1930s, so that now not only the monastery but also the church, the bell-tower, and various workshops have been restored to their original condition. Eight years after secularisation the mission had to endure a kind of gold-rush itself because some of the precious metal was discovered on one of its properties. This was still seven years before the actual gold-rush at the Sacramento River, but the finds were so unimportant that interest soon waned.

History

In the restored monastery made of adobe – one of the longest of its kind – can be found the workshops, where the handiwork of the time is documented. Here, too, pilgrims walking along the Camino Real could rest. Particularly beautiful, being stocked with exotic plants of all kinds, is the cemetery, where thousands of Shoshone Indians, as well as many Franciscans, are buried. This mission was the last of four to be built in twelve months; never before had so many new missions been established within a single year.

Places of interest

*Mission of San Luis Rey de Francia (1798)

R 4

4050 Mission Avenue, Oceanside, from which place it is 5 miles/8 km away on the CA 76. From San Diego the distance is 33 miles/53 km. (Open: weekdays 10 a.m.–4 p.m., Sun. noon–4 p.m.; no admission during mass; tel. 619/757-3651.)

Location

This mission is also named after a canonized monarch, Louis IX of France, who was admitted into the band of the saints because of his crusades against the heathens in 1297. It is the last of ten mission stations built by Father Fermin Francisco de Lasuen and lies in the far south between the San Diego and San Juan Capistrano missions, some 5 miles/8 km east of the present town of Oceanside. It was Father Antonio Peyri who in the years 1811–1815 supervised the building of this mission church which holds 1000 people. The Moorish style and the tower with its red-painted window-sills,

History

Church of the San Francisco Solano Mission

gables and pilasters give this church its very unusual appearance. Adjoining the church is the interior courtyard with a monastery; on one side of the church was the Indian village, on the other stood a military barracks which were found in every mission station. Below these buildings were a garden and a laundry.

After the usual neglect of the secularised buildings, a start was made in 1893 on restoring the mission, which had meanwhile become the property of the Catholic church. Today it serves as a seminary.

Items of interest	This, the largest and most beautiful mission station, possesses an interesting museum in the former monastery and in the workshops, where some paintings and wood sculptures from Mexico are well worth seeing. In the magnificent garden with its cloister is the first mastix tree (also known as the pepper tree, from Peru) to be planted in North America, as well as an Indian cemetery. The French visitor who had admired the Santa Barbara mission in 1840, considered that from an architectural point of view the mission of San Luis Rey de Francia was the most impressive and symmetrical in the whole of California.

Mission of Santa Ines (1804)　　　　　　　　　　　　　　　N 1

Location	1760 Mission Drive, Solvang, via the CA 154 about 33 miles/53 km north of Santa Barbara or via the US 101 about 43 miles/70 km. (Open: weekdays 9.30 a.m.–4 p.m., in summer until 5 p.m.; Sun. noon–5 p.m.; tel. 805/688-4815.)
History	Only after a long pause in what had been a hectic period of building activity did the 19th mission appear, roughly on the site where the Danish township of Solvang is today. The name comes from St Agnes (Spanish Santa Inés), and appears in its Spanish form in the naming of the Santa Ynez mountain chain and of the valley of the same name. The original building was a victim

of the 1812 earthquake. Subsequently, a second building went up in the years 1813–1817, but was damaged in the Indian uprising kindled in the mission of La Purisma Concepcion 25 miles/40 km away. Restoration started in 1904 but was restricted to the church, bell-tower and a part of the inner courtyard. Santa Ines is one of the smallest mission stations; perhaps this is where its special charm lies.

Mission of San Rafael Arcangel (1817)

H 1

1104 Fifth Avenue South, corner of Court Street, San Rafael, only three blocks from the US 101 (Central San Rafael exit), 19 miles/30 km north of San Francisco. (Open: daily 11 a.m.–4 p.m. except Sun. 10 a.m.–4 p.m.; tel. (415) 454 6141.)

Location

This mission was originally intended as a hospital for the Dolores mission, as there was a desire to keep away from the latter the many Indians suffering from epidemic illnesses. The actual reason for building the 20th mission, some 13 years after the 19th, was in fact quite different: the Russians had set up in Fort Ross a base for otter-catching, and the Spaniards wanted at all costs to prevent a further Russian advance southwards. Basically the mission was never more than a kind of sanatorium and monastery; it was pulled down in 1870 but was rebuilt in the same style in 1949.

History

Mission of San Francisco Solano (1823)

G 1

Near the plaza in Sonoma. From San Francisco, 38 miles/60 km away, it is easily reached via the US 101, CA 121 and 12. It is part of the Sonoma State Historic Park and houses the Jorgensen collection of watercolours of Missions of California; tel. (707) 938-1578.

Location

The last of the mission stations and the only one to be built during the period of Mexican rule, it bears the name of one of the Spanish missionaries in Peru. After secularisation General Mariano Guadalupe Vallejo went to the trouble of nominating the governor Figueroa commandant of North California as a precautionary measure against the Russian advance. At the same time Figueroa became administrator of the mission and was to maintain it as a buffer against the Russians. For reasons which are not known the church collapsed. In its place was built a parish church, which was also destroyed but was rebuilt in the years 1911–1913. The nearby monastery built in 1825 survived, and is thus the oldest building in Sonoma. It houses a museum. The annual celebrations held by the wine-producers begin here.

History

Modesto

I 2

Stanislaus County
Altitude: 88 ft/27 m
Population: 126,000

Situated on the Tuolumne River, in the north-east of the San Joaquin Valley, Modesto has made a name for itself through its processing industry: conserve factories, dairies, slaughter-houses and wine-producing form the most important industries of the town, which has more than doubled its population since 1970. Its name can be traced back to a San Francisco banker, who "modestly" (Spanish "modesto") declined the suggestion that the town be named after him.

Location and origin

Modesto, established in 1870, possesses a row of Victorian houses dating from that time, a natural history museum (1100 Stoddard Avenue), a post-

Places of interest

office decorated with murals from the depression years (1125 I Street), a museum of local history (1402 I Street) and a railway station built in the Spanish mission style, now used only for freight (J & 9th Street). A two-day balloon festival is held in the middle of September. In the immediate vicinity of Modesto are numerous lakes, offering extensive facilities for water-sports (Modest Reservoir, Turlock Lake, Lake Don Pedro). The town was also the scene of the well-known film "American Graffiti", the director of which, George Lucas, hails from Modesto. (Information: Convention and Visitors Bureau, 1114 J Street; tel. 577-5200.)

Mojave Desert
J–R 3–8

Location and general

The Mojave Desert (pronounced "mohárvee") is a barren stretch of land running south of the Sierra Nevada and north of the San Bernardino and San Gabriel mountains, covering an area of 15,000 sq. miles/38,850 sq. km, its eastern boundary being formed by the states of Nevada and Arizona. Although the main parts of the desert are very hot and dry, attempts at agricultural cultivation in the extreme west, Antelope Valley (Los Angeles County), have been crowned with success. Originally, the Chemehuevi and Mojave Indians lived here.

Solar technology

As the sun pours down on many days of the year (over 3000 hours), the average air-humidity is very low (thus protecting the steel in the modern industrial plant from rust) and vast land-areas are for the most part unused, the Mojave Desert offers ideal conditions for the production of regenerative energy. In this region of America most energy is consumed around midday, for the Californians switch on their air-conditioning punctually at twelve o'clock. In all, there are seven solar power stations at three sites, the main one being that of Dagget on Highway No. 1; the eighth solar power station is nearing completion.

Solar fields

In Dagget they are experimenting with different systems: the economically unprofitable solar-tower power station and the "solar-dish", standing on a single foot and made up of several individual mirrors. The latest technology is based on solar fields: with so-called "low-tech", the sun's energy is trapped by means of parabolic mirror channels, up to 330 ft/100 m long and over 16 ft/5 m wide. Using conventional power-station techniques, steam and resultant energy is produced by means of oil which is heated in the channels.

Edwards Air Force Base

In the south-western part of the Mojave Desert is the Edwards Air Force Base with a concrete landing-strip for NASA space-shuttle flights.

Mono Lake State Reserve
J 5

Location and *importance

Lake Mono, situated close to the CA 395, is about 14 miles/23 km south-east of the eastern entrance to Yosemite National Park (see entry) and about the same distance south of Bodie (see entry for Bodie State Historic Park). This salt-water lake, 6240 ft/1900 m above sea level, is 13 miles/21 km wide and 8 miles/13 km long. Although several rivers flow into Lake Mono, it has no outlets, and is one of the oldest lakes in the world, having been formed perhaps 700,000 years ago. In the water, which has a higher salt content than most lakes, only a few life forms can exist, mainly single-cell algae; these provide food for the salt-water flies and crabs, which in turn are eaten by 70 kinds of migratory birds which reside on Lake Mono in spring and summer. These are mainly phalaropes (wading birds), grebes and

Sinter turrets in the Mono Lake ▶

Californian gulls. It is estimated that each year a million of these three species alone nest by Lake Mono at various times. About 90% of all Californian gulls are hatched on Lake Mono – especially on its volcanic island of Paoha and the Negit peninsula, which is linked to the mainland by a dam.

Limestone turrets

Phenomena of a special kind are the limestone turrets, most of which are to be found on the south bank. They are formed when the chalky spring water from the bed of the lake mixes with the very alkaline lake water. This forms limestone, and over the course of centuries curiously shaped turrets are formed where the springs enter the salt-water. This chemical process takes place only in the lake itself; when the water level falls and the turrets poke out of the water they cease to grow. Limestone turrets can be seen high above the present bank, and their age has been estimated at up to 13,000 years.

Fall in water-level

In the last 50 years the water-level of the lake has fallen by over 40 ft/12 m since Los Angeles began to tap four of the seven rivers which flow into Lake Mono. At the same time the salt content has doubled. In order to put a stop to any further danger of emptying the lake and completely changing the ecological system, legal steps have been taken after the city of Los Angeles had refused to listen to all compromise proposals. The effects of the struggle for water here in California can be seen at first hand.
The Visitor Center of the committee which is active in preserving the lake is in the neighbouring town of Lee Vining (tel. 619/647-6386).

Monterey   J 1

Monterey County
Altitude: 40 ft/12 m
Population: 29,000

*Location and history

As well as being beautifully situated on Monterey Bay, on the peninsula of the same name, Monterey has an interesting past. From 1770–1822 it was the capital of Spanish California (Los Angeles, San Francisco and the present capital Sacramento did not exist at that time) and, after Mexico had broken free from Spain, it remained the provincial capital for a further 24 years. Thereafter it quickly lost its political importance.

Importance

The tourist trade now constitutes the main source of income as the fishing industry declined following the disappearance of sardines from the Monterey waters.

Places of interest

Places of interest include houses from the Spanish and Mexican periods, a fishing-port, which is not as busy as it once was, as well as Cannery Row, made famous by John Steinbeck's novel of the same name (1945). This once industrial street was converted some years ago into a complex of restaurants, shops, cafés and art-galleries, so that only the walls of the buildings remain as a reminder of that which Steinbeck described in his novel. For instance, the unique Monterey Bay Aquarium has been opened on the site of an old canning factory.

Monterey State Historic Park

In Monterey State Historic Park the following houses are worth a visit: (open: daily 10 a.m.–5 p.m. (Summer), 10 a.m.–4 p.m. (Winter); tel. (408) 649-2836.)
Casa del Oro, a restored grocery shop dating from 1845, at the corner of Scott and Oliver Streets (closed Mon. and Tue.).
Casa Soberanes, an adobe-built house with walls 3 ft/1 m thick, dating from 1842, now a museum of the history of Monterey 1830–1970. (Corner of Pacific and Del Monte Streets.)
Custom House, built in the adobe style in 1827 at the time of Mexican dominance, now houses an historical exhibition covering the period 1830–

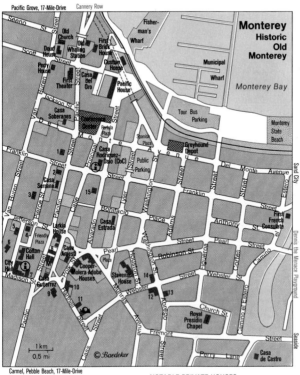

Monterey Historic Old Monterey

NOTABLE PRIVATE HOUSES

M = Museum of Art & Maritime Museum

ⓘ Visitor Information

1 Merritt House	7 Brown Underwood Adobe House	11 General Freemont's Quarters
2 Capitular House	8 Sherman	12 Casa Pacheco
3 Casa de Soto	Headquarters	13 Casa Madariaga
4 Casa de la Torre	9 Stokes Adobe House	14 Casa Abrego
5 Casa Alvarado	10 First Federal Court	15 Casa Sanchez
6 Casa Vasquez		

1850. Two of the famous Monterey cypress trees are growing in a garden in front of the house.

First Theater on Custom House Plaza is California's oldest theatre and was originally a boarding-house and inn (also built in the adobe style). Theatrical performances have been regularly held here since 1847; now on Wednesday to Saturday in July and August and on Friday and Saturday in the remaining months. (Information tel. (408) 375-4916; Corner of Pacific and Scott Streets.)

Larkin House, dating from the 1830s, served Thomas Larkin as the American Consulate Bureau in Mexico (510 Calle Principal, Main Street; closed Tues.).

Pacific House, dating from 1847, today a museum of Californian history, with an Indian exhibition (Custom House Plaza).

Robert Louis Stevenson House, where the English poet lived for four months, when visiting his future wife. Numerous Stevenson artefacts (530 Houston Street; closed Wed.).

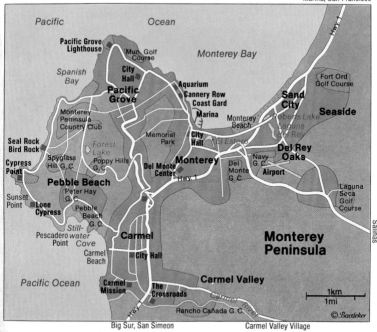

Marina, San Francisco

Pacific   Ocean

Pacific Grove
Lighthouse

*Spanish
Bay*

Mun. Golf
Course

Monterey Bay

City
Hall

**Pacific
Grove**

Aquarium
Cannery Row
Coast Gard
Marina

Monterey
Peninsula
Country Club

*Forest
Lake*

Memorial
Park

City
Hall

Monterey
Beach

Fort Ord
Golf Course

**Sand
City**

Seaside

Roberts Lake

Laguna
Del Rey

**Seal Rock
Bird Rock**

**Cypress
Point**

Spyglass
Hill G. C.

Poppy Hills
G. C.

Del Monte
Center

Monterey

El Estero

Del
Monte
G. C.

Navy
G. C.

**Del Rey
Oaks**

**Sunset
Point**

**Lone
Cypress**

Peter Hay
G. C.

Pebble
Beach
G. C.

Pebble Beach

Hwy 1

Airport

Laguna
Seca
Golf
Course

*Still-
Pescadero water
Point   Cove*

Carmel

**Monterey
Peninsula**

Salinas

Carmel
Beach

City Hall

Pacific Ocean

**Carmel
Mission**

**The
Crossroads**

Carmel Valley

Carmel River

1km
1mi

© Baedeker

Big Sur, San Simeon   Carmel Valley Village

Presidio	Presidio of Monterey, now the home of the Defense Language Institute, has artefacts and dioramas on the history of Presidio Hill from the times of the Indians, Mexicans, Spaniards and Americans. (Pacific Street, near Scott Street; admission free.) The Royal Presidio Chapel is the only one still in existence in California, and in continuous use since 1795. Note the richly-decorated façade. (San Carlos Cathedral, 550 Church Street; admission free.)
Museums	Monterey possesses two museums, the Monterey Peninsula Museum of Art, with Californian, Indian and Asiatic art as well as temporary exhibitions of photographs (559 Pacific Street; tel. (408) 372-7591), and the Allen Knight Maritime Museum, displaying material relating to the history of ships in the region. (550 Calle Principal; tel. (408) 375-2553.)
** **Bay Aquarium**	The most important place to visit in Cannery Row (No. 886) is the Monterey Bay Aquarium at the end of the road. It is the biggest marine aquarium in the USA, with the emphasis on displaying more than 6000 living things (from otters to sharks, octopuses and wolf-eels) and their biosphere in Monterey Bay, an extraordinarily rich marine biotope. The visitor is offered many opportunities of viewing coastal formations, marine plants, fish and other aquatic animals, as well as coastal and sea birds, through glass-walled pools, telescopes, macroscopes and micro-scopes and also underwater video cameras which you can operate yourself by remote control. Also to be seen on three floors are algae forests, marine mammals, coastal bird-life and much more. (Open daily except Christmas Day 10 a.m.–6 p.m.)

Seal in the Monterey Bay Aquarium, the largest in the USA ▶

Former warehouse of the Monterey Canning Company

Sections

On the main floor a "Habitat Path" leads to the many sections of the aquarium. The most impressive are called "Monterey Bay Habitats" (a 90 ft/27.5 m long cross-section through the bay), "Kelp Forest" (a giant pool 28 ft/8.5 m high containing 277,000 galls/1.26 million litres of water), or "Great Tide Pool".

In the "Marine Mammals Gallery" are models of numerous marine mammals native to the bay, especially whales, dolphins, sea-lions and seals. In a two-storied special aquarium frolic sea-otters, threatened with extinction and being bred here.

In "Mexico's Secret Sea", a new section opened in 1989, you can wonder at the colourful underwater world of the Gulf of California, with over 300 strange life-forms, such as eels and scorpion-fish.

Also opened in the same year, the "Jewels of the Pacific" section shows a spectrum of marine animals and underwater formations from the Pacific Coast.

Cannery Row

Other buildings in Cannery Row which are worth seeing are:

No. 851: Kalisa's Lak Ida Café built in 1929, a brothel from 1936 (immortalised by Steinbeck), a coffee-house since the mid-fifties.

No. 835: opened in 1918 as a Chinese Wing Chong grocery shop (Won Yee, who lives on the top floor, appears as Lee Chong in Steinbeck's "Cannery Row"; the novel begins with a description of the shop). Today keepsakes of the author are to be found here.

No. 800: The Pacific Biological Laboratory, near Steinbeck Western Biological Laboratory, where the author spent much time from 1930–1935.

No. 799: Here stands Flora Wood's "Lone Star Café", which Steinbeck called Dora Flood's "Lone Star Café/Bear Flag Restaurant", another brothel from 1923–1941. The present concrete building houses an antiques warehouse.

No. 711: Once this was the storehouse for the Monterey Canning Co.; now there are shops and a fish restaurant.

Nos. 650 and 654: On this site were situated Monterey's second Chinese

The "lone cypress" on 17 Mile Drive

restaurant and the hotels of Messrs. Wu and Sam, replaced years ago by the elegant Spindrift Inn.

No. 400: Where once stood a magnificent villa, almost completely destroyed by fire in 1924, and later a fish-canning factory, there now stands the luxury hotel Monterey Plaza.

No. 242: Here too, where the Enterprise Canning Factory once packed sardines, stands one of Monterey's many luxury hotels, the Monterey Bay Inn.

Nearby Pacific Grove, a town with almost 15,000 inhabitants, boasts numerous Victorian houses, a natural history museum and the Asilomar Conference Center. There is also Ocean View Boulevard, 4 miles/6 km long and very suitable for walkers, offering views of the rocky coast. South of Monterey lie Pebble Beach and Del Monte, both with almost palace-like villas and golf-courses which are among the finest on the Monterey peninsula.

Surroundings

As far as weather is concerned, the months of September to June are the best time to visit the peninsula; (however, rain can be expected in January and February), but the three summer months often mean fog and low clouds.

Tips

Only a few miles from Monterey, on the south side of the Monterey peninsula, lies Carmel (see entry). The many charms of the countryside make it worthwhile going the long way round, the "Seventeen Mile Drive". This begins at Pacific Grove Gate and then goes along the Pacific coast and for part of the way through the Del Monte Forest, where there is a number of large villas. The forest is impressive by reason of its rich abundance of cypress trees and the Monterey pines. You will also drive past picturesque beaches, isolated cliffs, the "Lone Cypress", the Pebble Beach Golf Course and the "Lodge at Pebble Beach" Hotel, where rooms cost 300 US dollars. Many kinds of gulls live in the Seal and Bird Rocks. Often you can spot

17 Mile Drive

Sunset over Morro Bay

Gold-washing house in Mother Lode County (Columbia)

sea-lions and seals there too. Cypress Lookout offers a particularly beautiful view north and south along the Pacific coast.
You have to pay a toll to use this private road. (Further information; tel. 800/654-9300.)

Morro Bay

San Luis Obispo County
Altitude: 200 ft/61 m
Population: 9000

This peaceful bay, about halfway between Los Angeles and San Francisco, was discovered in 1769 by the same Spanish expedition under Father Juan Crespi which had earlier founded the first mission in San Diego (see entry). It is dominated by the 560-ft/170-m-high volcanic rock known as Morro Rock ("morro" is Spanish for a rock rounded at the top). The township itself did not come into being until the second half of the 19th c. A large fishing fleet is based here.

Location and general

South of the town, on the CA 1, lies the Morro Bay State Park (tel. (805) 772-2694), an area of almost 1500 acres/600 hectares, with a golf course, picnic and camping sites, as well as an important natural history museum (tel. (805) 528-0513) and a small aquarium with about 300 aquatic animals (595 Embarcadero; information tel. (805) 772-7647). Short trips round the harbour start from house no. 1205 Embarcadero, and on Saturdays and Sundays during the season there are evening trips with refreshments available (tel. (805) 772-2257).

Morro Bay State Park

Mother Lode County

Mother Lode County describes the region from Mariposa in the south, near the western entrance to Yosemite National Park (see entry), as far as Georgetown, some 10 miles/16 km north of Coloma (see entry), where the first gold was discovered in 1848. It is about 120 miles/192 km long and its width varies from a few hundred metres up to 2 miles/3.2 km. Mother Lode County probably did not receive its name until 20 years after the discovery of rich deposits of gold-quartz. It was wrongly assumed that there were only a few quartz veins containing gold. In fact, however, there were other important mines north of so-called Mother Lode. You can drive to that area along the CA 49, passing uninhabited ghost-towns, once flourishing gold-mining townships.

Location and importance

Mount Shasta

Siskiyou County
Altitude: 3550 ft/1083 m
Population: 2900

Situated not far from Redding (see entry) in the Shasta Trinity National Forest on the US 5, this little town is the starting point for water-sport trips to Siskiyou Lake, 2½ miles/4 km away, and for climbing the 14,168-ft/4317-m-high mountain of the same name, Mount Shasta. For a time the peak was called Shatasia or Sastise. These are variations of the spelling of the name of the Shasta Indians who originally lived there. A somewhat lower peak stands west of Mount Shasta and bears a similar name, Mount Shastina.
Mount Shasta was first climbed in 1854.

Location and general

Muir Woods National Monument   H 1

Location and general	The tallest trees in the world are the so-called redwoods or mammoth trees (see entry for Redwood Highway, Redwoods), which thrive only in California and South Oregon, including those in Muir Woods National Monument some 15 miles/24 km north of San Francisco. Since 1908 the park has been controlled by the National Park Service, which has a Visitor Center (tel. (415) 388-2595) at the entrance where detailed information can be obtained.
Age of the trees	This 550 acre/223 hectare area of forest, named after the famous naturalist and founder of the Sierra Club, John Muir, contains large numbers of redwoods, the botanical name of which is sequoia sempervirens. The tallest trees in Muir Woods reach a height of 240 ft/73 m. In the first 100 years they grow 12 ins/30 cm each year, then the rate of growth slows down. The oldest mammoth tree (now dead) was 2200 years old; the average age is 400–800 years. The trees' root systems spread out sideways to about 150 ft/46 m, but the depth never exceeds 6½ ft/2 m.
Trails for walking	In Muir Woods there are about 6 miles/10 km of well-signed trails. As it is often cool and damp even in summer, you should take warm clothing.
How to get there	From San Francisco, take Highway 101 via the Golden Gate Bridge as far as the CA 1 turn-off, which takes you direct to Muir Woods. At the weekend it is also possible to take the ferry from San Francisco (Ferry Building) to Larkspur.

Napa   G 1

Napa County
Altitude: 16 ft/5 m
Population: 53,000

Location and importance	Situated at the southern end of the valley of the same name, some 52 miles/85 km from San Francisco, Napa is one of the largest Californian towns north of San Francisco. It was founded in 1848 and bears the name of the long extinct Napa Indians. Today it is the main despatching point for the wines produced in the Napa Valley as far as Calistoga (see entry). In addition, there are a number of tanneries and other light industries and electronic firms. The western boundary is formed by the Napa Mountains; further to the west lies the other famous wine-valley, Sonoma (see entry), in Sonoma County. The Howell Mountains form the eastern boundary of Napa County and they also protect the valley from storms.
Wine production	The most important wine production takes place along the stretch from Yountville to St Helena (see entry), near Oakville and Rutherford: names such as Mondavi, Beaulieu, Inglenook, Heitz and Louis Martini have a good reputation in America. North of St Helena, on the CA 128, you pass the wine lodges belonging to the Beringer Brothers, Christian Brothers and Charles Krug (the latter is one of the oldest in the valley), and still further north are those of Hans Kornell and Schramsberg, one of the few American champagne producers. In recent years some 50 Californian wine-producing concerns have passed into the hands of overseas owners, or share-holdings in them have been acquired by foreign firms. These include Inglenook and Beaulieu (British) and Beringer (Swiss). In the last 20 years the number of wine-producers in the Napa Valley alone has grown from 30 to 200. As the bigger firms in particular offer guided tours, the valley is becoming more and more tourist-orientated (about 2.5 million tourists each year).

Wine-cellars in the Napa Valley

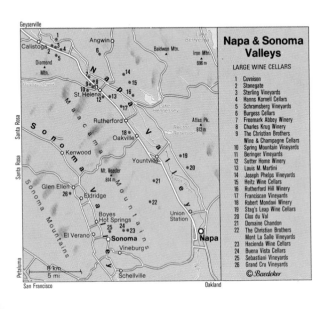

Napa & Sonoma Valleys

LARGE WINE CELLARS

1 Cuvaison
2 Stonegate
3 Sterling Vineyards
4 Hanns Kornell Cellars
5 Schramsberg Vineyards
6 Burgess Cellars
7 Freemark Abbey Winery
8 Charles Krug Winery
9 The Christian Brothers
   Wine & Champagne Cellars
10 Spring Mountain Vineyards
11 Beringer Vineyards
12 Sutter Home Winery
13 Louis M. Martini
14 Joseph Phelps Vineyards
15 Heitz Wine Cellars
16 Rutherford Hill Winery
17 Franciscan Vineyards
18 Robert Mondavi Winery
19 Stag's Leap Wine Cellars
20 Clos du Val
21 Domaine Chandon
22 The Christian Brothers
   Mont La Salle Vineyards
23 Hacienda Wine Cellars
24 Buena Vista Cellars
25 Sebastiani Vineyards
26 Grand Cru Vineyards

© *Baedeker*

Napa

Wine trains

Since 1989 it has been possible to become acquainted with the Napa Valley wine-producing district by travelling in authentic Pullman saloon coaches (George Mortimer Pullman built the first luxury saloon and sleeping-cars in Chicago in 1858), visiting vineyards and taking part in wine-tastings. On the 36 mile/58 km round trip from Napa to St Helena gourmet dishes are served in the elegant dining-car.

Newport Beach   Q 3

Orange County
Altitude; 26 ft/8 m
Population: 65,000

Location and
urban features

Newport Beach, often likened to Cannes on the French Riviera, does indeed have a beautiful sandy beach over 5½ miles/8 km long, but it is extensively urbanised. Newport Beach includes Balboa, Balboa Island, Corona Del Mar, Newport Heights, Lido Isle, Harbor Island, Bay Shores and Linda Isles. There are luxury hotels with hundreds of rooms, as well as magnificent villas, elegant shops and first-class restaurants. Sunning themselves in Newport Beach will be found the rich from Orange County and Los Angeles, which is less than 37 miles/60 km away on the CA 1 coast road. Not far from Newport Beach lies the campus of the University of California of Irvine – the whole region once formed part of the Irvine Ranch, the rural character of which has long been lost.

Places of interest

Newport Beach possesses an excellent museum with temporary exhibitions as well as its own permanent exhibits (850 San Clemente Drive; open: daily except Mon.; tel. (714) 759-1122). About 5 miles/8 km to the south, near the coast road, you will find the Sherman Library and Gardens, also a charming garden with exotic flora (open: daily; tel. (714) 673-2261). The marina, with berths for 9000 sailing craft and motor boats, is one of the largest on the Pacific coast. The Marina Village and eight other shopping centres can meet the needs of every customer. There is a pleasure park called "Fun Zone" on Balboa Boulevard, above Balboa Pier, from which there are boat trips of various kinds. (Information: tel. (714) 644-3017.)

Oakland   H 1

Alameda County
Altitude: 43 ft/13 m
Population: 347,000

Location and
origin

Oakland, connected with San Francisco by the San Francisco–Oakland Bay Bridge, and situated only 8 miles/12 km east of the metropolis on the west bank of the great bay, was where the lumberjacks lived who discovered the big oak-forests near the bay and the beautiful redwood stands in the nearby hills, very little of which remain today. Then came the gold-diggers, and in 1852 the town named after its oak trees was founded. Oakland grew in importance in 1869 when it was made the terminus of the transcontinental railway; in the same year the mayor of the day laid out in the centre of town the Merritt salt-water lake which bears his name. The construction of piers and a ship-canal confirmed the important role which Oakland was to play as a traffic junction.

Economy

After the devastating earthquake of 1906 which left Oakland relatively unscathed, the town received such an influx of people from San Francisco

Exterior of the Oakland Museum . . .

. . . and the Department of Californian History

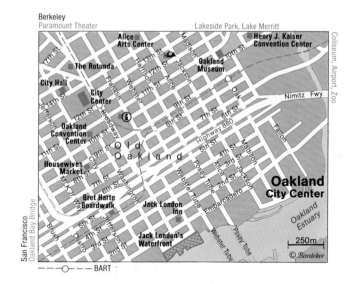

that its population doubled between 1900 and 1910. In the twenties industry gained a foothold and larger office buildings appeared. The Second World War brought additional changes: the port facilities were improved, and in the fifties Oakland, more farseeing than San Francisco in that respect, was reorganised to take container freight traffic and soon overtook San Francisco to become the biggest container port on the west coast. This, in turn, resulted in more than 1000 road-transport companies setting up their headquarters in Oakland.

Bret Harte Boardwalk, Jack London Square

Of the writers who lived in Oakland in their youth, Bret Harte and Jack London (see Famous Personalities) are the best-known. Bret Harte Boardwalk got its name from the former, and the latter gave his name to Jack London Square at the end of Broadway, where a bust of the author stands, as well as to the "First and Last Chance Saloon", a bar where Jack London not only drank his whiskey but also wrote many of his short stories. Adjoining Jack London Square at the bottom of Alice Street is Jack London Village, with shops, restaurants and a marina.

Gertrude Stein

The authoress Gertrude Stein, born in neighbouring San Francisco, also spent a part of her youth in Oakland. In the early 1880s she lived on a farm with her parents. Her famous saying, "When you get there, there's no there there", now often used to refer to Los Angeles, was said to have expressed her disappointment at the fact that, after forty years' absence in Europe, the house of her youth in Oakland was no longer standing.

Lake Merritt

In the centre of town lies Lake Merritt, a 160 acre/64 hectare salt-water lake, on which you can take boat trips.
Not far from the lake, which is surrounded by Lakeside Park, a fairytale park and a Japanese garden have been laid out. There are also a botanical garden, picnic-sites and footpaths. At the south-west end of the lake stands the Oakland Museum, with its large open-air exhibition grounds.

J. Miller Park

Another park, Joaquin Miller Park, is also named after a Californian writer who lived in Oakland.

7 miles/11 km south of the town centre is a zoo which you can reach by the US 580 road (open: daily; tel. (415) 632-9523).

Oakland Zoo

Anyone who happens to be in Oakland on the first or third Saturday in the month should not fail to visit the Paramount Theater of Arts, one of the last of the Art Deco cinema palaces remaining in the USA, where at 10 a.m. there are guided tours through the building which was designed by the architect Timothy L. Pflueger. The Oakland Symphony Orchestra now performs here (tel. (415) 893-2300).

Paramount Theater of Arts

Oakland Museum, situated at the south-west corner of Lake Merritt (1000 Oak Street) contains interesting collections of the natural history, history and folk-art of California (extensive grounds). It is the only museum devoted to California's history and culture as well as exclusively to works by Californian artists.
The origins of this museum go back to the year 1910 when the Oakland Public Museum was built, followed a few years later by the Oakland Art Gallery. The present museum, a largely subterranean building, was designed by the well-known architect Kevin Roche.
This limitation to one theme was dictated largely by economic necessity, for Oakland was unable to compete with other museums for more expensive paintings.

* **Oakland Museum**

The top floor – through which you enter the museum – is devoted to the works of Californian painters.
Below that you will find a large exhibition room on the history of California. On the bottom floor (the word floor is not quite right, because the levels are arranged terrace-wise one below the other) the theme is the state's natural history. There is also an auditorium.
In addition to Californian painters, photographers are also well represented, including Anselm Adams, Dorothea Lange, Edward Weston and Edward Muybridge. (Open: Wed.–Sat. 10 a.m.–5 p.m., Sun. noon–7 p.m.; tel. (415) 273-3401.)

Exhibits

Ojai

Ventura County
Altitude: 650 ft/227 m
Population: 7300

Ojai (pronounced "oohigh"), founded in 1874, lies in the valley of the same name where cattle are reared and citrus fruits cultivated. Originally named after the Californian writer Charles Nordhoff, it received in 1916 the name of the valley which had been taken from the language of the Chumash Indians (meaning "moon"). The town impresses the visitor because of its remoteness (take the US 101 and turn off onto the CA 150 south of Carpentaria), and the harmony of the architecture, unusual in Californian townships of this size.

Location and origin

Countless artists, musicians and writers have lived here, either permanently or temporarily, including the conductor Leopold Stokowski and the Indian mystic Krishnamurti. Each year a music festival is held at the end of May/beginning of June, and a Shakespeare festival at the end of June. At the end of April Ojai is the venue for a tennis tournament which claims to have been the first held anywhere in America. In 1937 Frank Capra filmed "Lost Horizon" in Ojai, based on the novel by James Hilton; not too far away from Hollywood, it seemed to him to be the most fitting arena, his "Shangri-La" (perhaps also because the name sounded somewhat similar).

Artists' town

Oroville

Butte County
Altitude: 175 ft/53 m
Population: 9900

Location and origin	This town, 62 miles/100 km from Sacramento and 154 miles/245 km from San Francisco (via the US 80 and CA 70), was established at the time of the gold-rush around 1850, and amongst its first settlers it must have had some gold-diggers who were well versed in the Bible and who named it Ophir City (after the legendary Old Testament land from which Solomon's fleet brought back gold and other precious items). Only six years later it was re-named Oroville by its inhabitants who were obviously Latin scholars.
The last of the Yahi Indians	At that time the region was still inhabited by the Yahi Indians, who were to be wiped out by the whites in the decades which followed; the last member of this tribe was discovered, half-starved, in a slaughter-house near Oroville, and spent the last five years of his life in the Museum of Anthropology of the University of California in Berkeley (see entry), where he, as the last surviving wild Indian, was transplanted from stone-age culture into the 20th c. His biography appeared under the title of "Ishi", and contains interesting pointers to earlier Indian culture.
Gold-rush	Oroville, situated on the northern and central arm of Feather River, today offers few clues to its former gold-rush period. Only Miner's Alley and a Chinese temple dating from 1863 (open: Mon.–Thur.; tel. (916) 533-1646) remain, even though Oroville's Chinese quarter is California's second largest after San Francisco's Chinatown. It is maintained that, with the aid of gold-pans, gold can still be found today in Feather River north of Thermalito Bridge, and in its tributaries. Today, however, citrus and other fruits and olives are cultivated here; there are also several canning factories.
Oroville Dam	Some 10 miles/16 km north-east of Oroville (CA 162 and Canyon Drive) the 775-ft/235-m-high Oroville Dam has been constructed, forming the lake of the same name; with banks totalling 170 miles/269 km in length it is an important part of the California State Water Project, which was begun in the sixties to bring water from the north of the state down to the central regions and the south.

Oxnard

Ventura County
Altitude: 50 ft/16 m
Population: 120,000

Location and origin	Oxnard, on the CA 1 south-west of its junction with the US 101, first came into being towards the end of the 19th c., but developed quickly, thanks to its agricultural hinterland and two fleet installations to the south, Port Hueneme and Point Mugu. It owes its name to the owner of a sugar-beet refinery, one of the first pioneers to come here. From Channel Islands Harbor, at the end of Peninsula Road near Channel Islands Boulevard, there are direct connections to Channel Islands National Park (see entry), the offices of which, however, are to be found in Ventura (see entry). From Oxnard it is only 11 miles/17 km to the nearest island, Anacapa.
Carnegie Cultural Arts Center	The Carnegie Cultural Arts Center (424 South C. Street) owns works of art, an important archaeological collection and artefacts on local history (open: Tue.–Sat.; admission free; tel. 984-4649). Previously the building served as a library and town-hall.

Pacific Grove

See Monterey

Pacific Palisades

See Los Angeles

Palm Desert

See Palm Springs

Palm Springs   Q 5

Riverside County
Altitude: 470 ft/142 m
Population: 36,000

Palm Springs is less than 113 miles/180 km from Los Angeles, via the US 10 and CA 111 roads. Together with its sister towns of Palm Desert, Rancho Mirage, Cathedral City, Desert Hot Springs, Idyllwild and Indian Wells it has grown together into what is really one single holiday haunt and winter resort for the richest Americans. Although it lies in the Colorado Desert there are, as the name suggests, springs and numerous palm trees. Palm Springs was discovered as long ago as 1774 by Spaniards, who named it Agua Caliente (hot water), after the hot springs frequently found in this tectonic region. Cahuilla Indians lived there, and today they own a reservation covering almost 31,000 acres/12,500 hectares, nearly one-fifth of which lies within the town of Palm Springs, so that the 150 members of the Agua Caliente Group of the Cahuilla are the biggest land-owners in Palm Springs.

Location and origin

One hundred years later, Palm Springs was still just a sleepy railway town with a few shops and several hut-like houses. Not until the thirties of this century was it "discovered" for a second time, this time by important figures from Hollywood, including Frank Sinatra, Bob Hope and, somewhat later, Elvis Presley and Liberace. They were followed by politicians: Presidents Eisenhower, Kennedy, Johnson and Nixon spent holidays here; President Reagan was a frequent guest at the house of the publisher Walter Annenberg; President Ford lived here. Prosperous retired people from the north-east of the country as well as from Californian towns and cities settled in Palm Springs and the surrounding districts, primarily to escape the cold winters and also because in addition to holidays they could spend pleasant week-end breaks here.

Town of VIPs.

In order to beautify the barren wasteland, some 50,000 palm trees were planted and irrigation channels laid, thus making it possible to establish gardens and build swimming pools, which none of the houses lack. Since the Second World War giant palace-like hotels have been built, the biggest of which, Marriott's Desert Springs Resort and Spa, has almost 900 rooms, 16 tennis courts, a golf course and a big open-air swimming pool on a 350 acre/140 hectare site (opened in 1987). In the season from the middle of December to the end of May the prices reach dizzy heights, such as 1400 dollars for a suite for one night.

Out of season, when it gets very hot in Palm Springs and the surrounding country (up to 45°C in the summer months) but remains quite dry, most of the prices are halved when the temperatures double.

Palm Springs

Palm Springs: an oasis in the desert

Cacti in the Living Desert Reserve

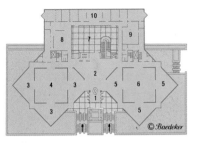

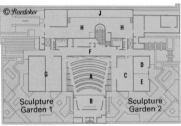

Palm Springs Desert Museum

1 Entrance area
2 Orienteering centre
3 Art gallery
4 Gallery for temporary exhibitions
5 Natural History gallery
6 Gallery for temporary exhibitions
7 Sculpture courtyard
8 Members' room and loan gallery
9 Offices
10 Library and Administration

A Communications centre (auditorium))
B Stage
C Green Room
D Art classroom
E Classroom for Natural History
F Foyer
G Store
H Sales kiosks
J Store

However, the months of June, September and October are quite bearable in Palm Springs (particularly in view of the lower prices!), while in November it often rains.

Golf and tennis are the order of the day; there are no fewer than 70 golf courses in the vicinity, and in many of the hotels you can relax after physical exertions in fresh, bubbling spring water. — The town for golf

Further places of interest

In addition to touring the town and seeing the houses of the VIPs, anyone spending several days in this domain of the rich and super-rich can book a whole series of other excursions. — Note

Palm Canyon, about 6 miles/10 km south of the centre of Palm Springs at the end of South Palm Canyon Drive, is a 15 mile/25 km long canyon wilderness belonging to the Agua Caliente Indians; it is covered with some 3000 fan-palms and there are fantastic views of the canyon, to which an easy footpath leads. You can also view the neighbouring Andreas and Murray Canyons. (Open: daily Sept.–May 9 a.m.–4 p.m.) — Palm Canyon

The Desert Museum (101 Museum Drive) houses beautiful displays of western art and Indian artefacts, as well as natural history exhibits. Worth visiting are the sculpture gardens. (Open: mid-Sept.–end June Tue.–Fri. 10 a.m.–4 p.m., Sat. and Sun. until 5 p.m.; tel. (619) 325-7186.) — Desert Museum

Moorten Botanical Garden (1701 South Palm Canyon Drive) contains countless species of desert flora, placed in order according to where they were found and with detailed descriptions on the signposted pathways. (Open: daily 9 a.m.–5 p.m.; tel. (619) 327-6555.) — Moorten Botanical Garden

Living Desert Wild Animal Park and Botanical Gardens is a 1200 acre/ 480 hectare open space with birds, birds of prey, mammals and reptiles in their natural surroundings, as well as desert plants, a palm-oasis, tracks — Living Desert Reserve

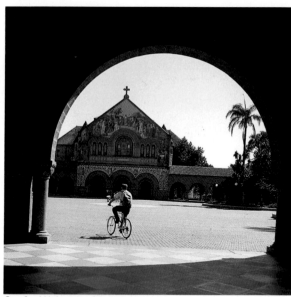

Stanford University: Memorial Church

leading into the hills and canyons. (Open: Sept.–May daily 9 a.m.–5 p.m.; address: 47-900 Portola Avenue, 2 miles/3 km south of the 111 road, in Palm Desert; tel. (619) 346-5694.)

Mount San Jacinto

A special experience is offered in the form of a ride by cable-car up the 8600-ft/2600-m Mount San Jacinto. The valley station is on the northern edge of Palm Springs. The railway, built in Switzerland in the early sixties, winds its way up the difference in altitude in fourteen minutes, during which time you pass through several climatic zones. Even if it is a hot day in the valley it is cool on the peak.

(Trips at least every half hour Mon.–Fri. 10 a.m.–8 p.m., weekends and public holidays 8 a.m.–8 p.m.; last trip down to the valley 11.45 p.m.; tel. (619) 325-1391. How to get there: 111th Street, turn into Tramway Road, then uphill for 3 miles/5 km.)

Shopping streets

It goes without saying that there are very many high-class shops in every part of Palm Springs, such as in the new Desert Fashion Plaza, Palm Springs Mall, Palm Desert Town Center and on El Paseo Drive.

Palo Alto

I 1

Santa Clara County
Altitude: 23 ft/7 m
Population: 56,000

Location and origin

The town of Palo Alto lies 29 miles/47 km south of San Francisco on the US 101. The Spanish name means "tall tree" and can be traced back to a centuries-old redwood tree (the Spaniards named it "palo colorade"), under which the Spanish governor camped with his expedition when they were searching for San Francisco Bay. The trunk of the tree is still there, by

Palo Alto: Entrance front of the University Museum of Art

the San Francisquito brook, at the junction of Palo Alto Avenue and Camino Real. A century later Governor Leland Stanford revived the name by calling his ranch (where Stanford University now stands) Palo Alto. This name was also used when the town was founded in 1892. A year later a railway station of the Southern Pacific Railroad was built here; by absorbing other districts the town then extended as far as the bay of San Francisco. The part which reached as far as the Santa Cruz Mountains, however, was intentionally not built on.

Thanks especially to the university, Palo Alto has become an important home of the American electronics industry, with numerous small firms having been set up by university graduates. The biggest company established here is Hewlett-Packard. Its premises cover such a large area that it is as big as a town, with 25 car-parks, a large swimming-pool and a municipal golf-course (see entry for Silicon Valley).

Hewlett-Packard

However, Palo Alto owes its fame mainly to the fact that in 1891 the college, originally called Leland Stanford Junior University, came into being with 559 students (one being the future president Herbert Hoover). Stanford established the college in memory of his precocious son who, before he died in Rome at the age of 16, had undertaken archaeological expeditions on his own.

* Stanford University

The original site covered an area of 8250 acres/3300 hectares, the driveway lined with palms and the rest of the parkland being the creation of Frederick Law Olmsted (known especially as the designer of Central Park in New York). By way of Palm Drive you come to the inner courtyard, bordered on one side by arcades and on the other by the Memorial Church; its stylistic forbears are to be found in the Romanesque and the Californian mission style.

Although the 1906 earthquake caused considerable damage to the slowly developing campus, including the collapse of the Memorial Church, this could not stop the growth of the university which, in its relatively short

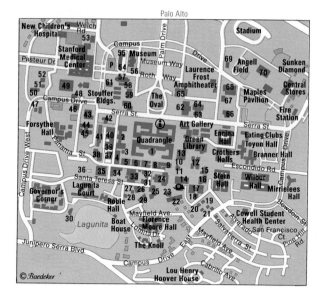

Palo Alto

Stanford University
Palo Alto

1 Memorial Church
2 Physics Lecture Hall
3 Skilling
4 Durand
5 Mitchell
6 Building 550
7 Building 530 – 540
8 Building 520
9 Building 500
10 Clock
11 Placement Center
12 Meyer Library
13 School of Education
14 Bookstore
15 Sweet Hall
16 Center for Educational Reserach (CERAS)
17 School of Law
18 Kresge Auditorium
19 Rogers
20 Muriposa
21 The Bridge
22 Braun Music Center
23 Dinkelspiel Auditorium
24 The Nitery (Bldg. 590)
25 Tresidder Mem. Union
26 Bowman Alumni House
27 Black House
28 Harmony House
29 Faculty Club
30 Elliott Program Center
31 Old Fire House
32 Building 570
33 Press Bldg., Storke Bldg.
34 Terman Engineering Center
35 Roble Gym
36 Roble Pool
37 Noble
38 Hepl End Station

39 Salvatori Applied Electronics
40 Electronics
41 Hansen Labs
42 Sequoia Hall
43 Center for Integrated Systems
44 Applied Physics
45 Ginzton Lab
46 Cogen Facility
47 Ventura Hall
48 Fairchild Center
49 Center for Molecular & Genetic Medicine
50 Medical School Office Building
51 Mayer Cancer Research Laboratory
52 Psychiatry Building
53 Falk CVR Building
54 Anatomy
55 Health Research & Policy Building
56 Rodin Sculpture Garden
57 Keck Science Building
58 Organic Chemistry
59 Old Chemistry Building
60 Herrin Hall & Labs
61 Mudd Chemistry Building
62 Graduate School of Business
63 Memorial Hall
64 Little Theater
65 Littlefield Center
66 Old Pavilion
67 Department of Athletics
68 Encina Gym
69 Track House
70 De Guerre Pools & Courts

period of existence, showed itself equal to those eastern universities which were centuries older (especially Harvard and Yale), and in some disciplines, such as medicine, engineering and English literature, it even outstripped them.

After the First World War the university became the home of the library now known as the Hoover Institution, the nucleus of which was formed by the Hoover Collection and which is devoted mainly to the themes of war, revolution and peace. It is housed in the 280 ft/85 m tall Hoover Tower. Another landmark of the university is the library tower (Green Library).

The students, numbering some 15,000, attend lectures by 1200 professors. These include or have included no less than ten Nobel Prize winners and 75 members of the National Academy of Science.

The campus includes the Stanford University Museum of Art, also built in memory of the young Leland Stanford and opened three years after the university was established. The building, based on the National Museum in Athens, was not completed until 1905. Of outstanding importance are the oriental department (which has now grown to 7000 exhibits, only a fraction of which can actually be displayed), and the Egyptian department. An important collection of Indian funerary objects, many examples of Cypriot sculpture and, more recently, numerous European works of art from the last two centuries, form the highlights of this important university museum. Also worth seeing is the sculpture garden, laid out only in recent years on the south side of the museum, devoted exclusively to bronzes by the French sculptor Auguste Rodin – 20 works in all – including the "Gates of Hell", the group-sculpture "Adam and Eve", "The Spirit of Eternal Rest" and several male figures.
Stanford University Museum of Art

The museum (tel. (415) 723-3404) is open Tuesday to Friday 10 a.m. to 4 p.m., at weekends 1 p.m. to 4.45 p.m.; admission free. It is closed during the university holidays, approximately from the beginning of July to the end of August. Guided tours lasting one hour, covering the whole campus, start from the arcades at 11 a.m. and from the Visitor Center (tel. (415) 723-2300) at 2 p.m. On these tours you will also see the Hoover Institution (the library is open 8 a.m.–5 p.m.). By booking in advance it is possible on Thursday afternoons to have a free visit to the Stanford Medical Center (tel. (415) 723-4000).
Opening times, guided tours

Pasadena

Los Angeles County
Altitude: 866 ft/264 m
Population: 123,000

Founded in 1875, the town can be reached from Downtown Los Angeles in less than 20 minutes, along the Pasadena Freeway (exit Orange Grove/Arroyo), or by bus no. 434; the town's melodic name is not in fact of Spanish origin, but comes from a Chippewa Indian word meaning roughly "crown of the valley".
Location and origin

In its early days Pasadena was a kind of winter spa resort, mainly for visitors from the Middle West of the United States; the first hotels appeared in the 1880s, but only the Huntington Sheraton, originally named the Wentworth, still remains. It opened its doors again in 1989 following a complete refit.

Increasing numbers of well-to-do Americans from other parts of the country settled in Pasadena in order to spend their retirement years in the agreeable climate. Particular mention should be made of the houses built by the brothers Charles and Henry Greene in an interesting mixture of Oriental and Art Deco styles, which dominate whole streets in Pasadena to this day.

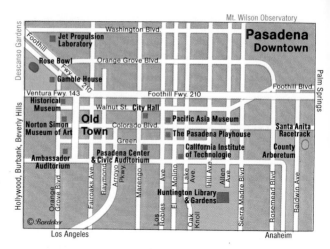

California Institute of Technology

The Throop Polytechnic Institute was founded in 1891. In 1920 it was given its present name, California Institute of Technology. This private college employs 780 teachers for its 1800 students. It also runs the almost 6600 ft/2000 m high observatory on Mount Palomar in the north of San Diego County, while the scarcely less well-known observatory 5600 ft/1700 m up on Mount Wilson near Pasadena is directed by the Carnegie Institution. One department of the California Institute of Technology is the Jet Propulsion Laboratory, which has made important technological contributions to the scientific expeditions to the moon and other planets.

The Old Town

Worth seeing is Pasadena's Old Town, reached by turning into Raymond Avenue off the main street Colorado Boulevard. On the way you will pass single or two-storied houses not more than 25–50 ft/8–16 m wide, the ground floors of which are now occupied mainly by shops.

Museums

Many tourists come to Pasadena to visit two museums, the Norton Simon Museum in Pasadena and the Huntington Library and Art Gallery in neighbouring San Marino.

* Norton Simon Museum of Art

Foundation

The Norton Simon Museum of Art (open: Thur.–Sun. noon–6 p.m.; tel. (818) 449-6840) was founded in 1924 as the Pasadena Museum of Modern Art, and erected on its present site in 1969. In 1974 it was reorganised under the supervision of the industrialist Norton Simon, rebuilt and re-opened a year later as somewhere to display his own impressive collection. Larger works of contemporary art for which there is no room in Pasadena are on permanent loan to Los Angeles County Museum of Art (see entry under Los Angeles).

Exhibits

The museum contains important works from almost all periods. The Italian masters represented include Filippino Lippi, Raphael ("Madonna and Child with Book") and Tiepolo ("Victory of Virtue and Steadfastness"), to name only some of the more important. From the Dutch and Flemish masters you will find Rembrandt (a "Titus" painting, a self-portrait and the "Bearded Man with the Broad-brimmed Hat"), as well as numerous etchings; there is also a Rubens, a particularly beautiful Mernling ("Jesus Blessing") and a portrait by Franz Hals. The Spaniards are represented by the painters

Vincent Van Gogh: "Portrait of a Peasant"

MAIN LEVEL

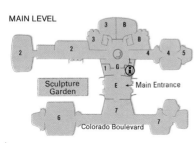

Pasadena
Norton Simon Museum

MAIN LEVEL
1 Rodin
2 European painting
3 20th c. art
4 European Renaissance
5 Early Italian art
6 Art from India and
   south-east Asia
7 19th and 20th c. art

B Bookstalls
E Entrance area
G Cloakroom

LOWER LEVEL

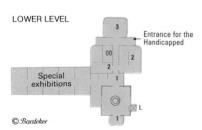

LOWER LEVEL
1 Degas
2 Dutch and Flemish painting
3 Art from India and
   south-east Asia

L Lift (elevator)

00 Toilets

© Baedeker

209

Norton Simon Museum of Art: exterior

Henry E. Huntington Library: exterior

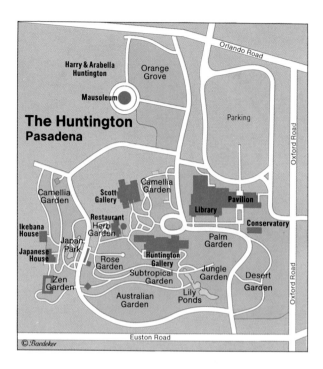

Murillo, Zurbaran and Goya; you will also find a number of graphic works by Goya.

~~The widest display is devoted to the various periods of French art~~; ranging from Rigaud, Poussin, Chardin and Watteau (17th and 18th c.) to Degas, Monet, Manet, Rousseau, Seurat, Cézanne, Renoir, Gauguin and Matisse (19th and 20th c.). The collection could be described as an almost panoramic vista of French art. The "Portrait of a Farmer" by van Gogh hangs in this department. In a special gallery in the basement you will find 88 examples of the work of this Impressionist, including countless models for his little bronze figures. Cubist works by Picasso, Braque and Juan Gris lead on to painters who worked in Germany, including the American Lyonel Feiniger, the Russians Jawlensky and Kandinsky and the Swiss Paul Klee.

French art: van Gogh

19th and 20th c. sculptures can be seen both inside the museum as well as outside in the gardens; these include Rodin's "Burghers of Calais", a Henry Moore, a Henri Laurens and an interesting artistic presentation by the contemporary American John Mason of an oven for baking bricks. Particularly worthy of note, however, are bronzes of the Indian Chola period (10th c.) as well as stone-sculptures from India, Tibet and Nepal.

Sculptures

**Henry E. Huntington Library and Art Gallery

From Los Angeles the way to this museum complex (1151 Oxford Road, San Marino; tel. (818) 405-2100) is via the Pasadena Freeway (exit for

Location and history

Huntington Gallery

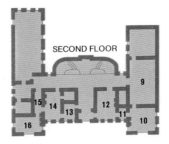

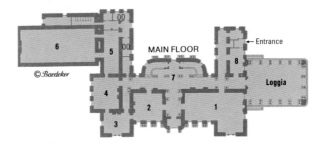

© *Baedeker*

MAIN FLOOR

Room 1: Gobelins (including sketches by François Boucher, 17th c. tapestries)

Room 2: Paintings by Gainsborough, Reynolds, Romney and Turner; French furniture

Room 3: Paintings by Constable; English and French applied art

Room 4: Paintings (including portraits) by William Hogarth, Geoffrey Kneller, and Gilbert Stuart (portrait of Washington)

Room 5: English miniatures (17th & 18th c.)

Room 6: Paintings by Thomas Gainsborough (including the "Blue Boy") and Thomas Lawrence ("Pinkie")

Room 7: Sculpture by J. A. Houdon, Roubillac, and P. Warren; 18th c. Chelsea porcelain

Room 8: Bronze statuettes (Renaissance)

SECOND FLOOR

Rooms 11–15: Temporary exhibitions (including English watercolours and drawings, European prints, etchings by Dürer and Rembrandt; English silverwork)

Room 16: Artistic representations of sport, hunting scenes and life in the country, including paintings by Ben Marshall, George Morland and George Stubbs

Altadena/Arroyo), or by taking bus no. 432, but this service is not very frequent.

As unusual as the museum itself is its history. Like so many others, Collis Huntington, a small shopkeeper in Oneonta in New York State, left the town of his birth in 1849 to go in search of gold in distant California. However, it was not gold which made him a very rich man, but the fact that he went into railway construction at the right time. A large part of his fortune went directly to his nephew Henry, who also inherited the rest through marriage – he married Arabella, his uncle's widow. With this money Henry bought a 500 acre/200 hectare ranch in San Marino – today it is a township of elegant villas with about 13,000 inhabitants – and in the years 1909 to 1911 he built his palace-like villa with its huge garden. While Arabella concerned herself

The Huntington: Japanese Garden

mainly with the acquisition of European, especially English, works of art, Henry devoted himself completely to the library, which today boasts one of the most important manuscript collections of English and American history in the world, and to laying out the garden. Henry Huntington was no idler; he founded the Pacific Electric Railway Co., which ran the whole tramway network in Los Angeles and the county and as the result of clever purchases he became the biggest landowner in southern California. By the time of his death in 1929 he had considerably increased the fortune he had inherited. In 1919 he donated the whole of his land and estates in San Marino to the library, gallery and garden. At the same time he founded an ancillary research institute with an initial capital of 10½ million dollars.

The treasures, such as the Ellesmere Manuscript from Chaucer's "Canterbury Tales" dating from 1410, and, in the same display cabinet, numerous superbly illuminated books of hours dating from the Middle Ages, are unique. You can then admire a two-volume Johannes Gutenberg bible, printed on parchment in 1455. Not far away can be seen some manuscript pages from Benjamin Franklin's autobiography, which he wrote between 1771 and 1790, leaving a half of each page empty for later amendments and corrections. Also displayed are the completely illegible "Forests" manuscript by Henry Thoreaus, letters by George Washington and Mark Twain, the Shakespeare Folio Edition, a copy of the large-format original edition of Audobon's "Birds of America" and much more. There are reading and work rooms available to academics, who have the choice of nearly four million items.

Literary art treasures

The works of art are no longer housed solely in the villa, but also in a new building erected specially for the purpose, the Virginia Steele Scott Gallery. The superb collection is devoted mainly to American art, but also includes important English works of art of the 18th and 19th c., including "Blue Boy", Thomas Gainsborough's most famous painting, and the scarcely less famous "Pinkie" by Thomas Lawrence. Sir Joshua Reynolds, George

Virginia Steele Scott Gallery

213

Romney, Sir Henry Raeburn are all represented, as well as works by the French artists Fragonard, Houdon, Baptiste Greuze and François Hubert Drouais; particular mention should be made of the pictures of children which were obviously Arabella's favourite.

Memorial Collection	The Arabella Huntington Memorial Collection, containing predominantly French sculptures from the 18th c., tapestries, porcelain and furniture from the same period, is housed in the west wing of the library.
Gardens	If the treasures in the museum and gallery were the only things to see, they would be quite sufficient to fill the three and a half hours allowed to visitors each day. However, the beauties of nature displayed in the gardens easily match the aesthetic pleasures experienced inside the building. Each of the gardens, here blended into a whole, will attract its own admirers. Most visitors, however, make for the Japanese garden which, with its red bridge, traditional Japanese five-roomed house, the Ikebana house, traditional Bonsai trees and little Zen Garden, inspires them just to sit and meditate. Other parts of the grounds are: the Herb Garden, the Shakespeare Garden with plants such as existed in the poet's time, the Desert Garden and – in direct contrast – the Jungle Garden, the Rose Garden and two Camellia Gardens, the Palm Garden and the Subtropical Garden and finally, just behind the mausoleum where the Huntingtons lie buried, the Orange Grove.
Opening times	**Tue.–Sun. 1 p.m.–4.30 p.m.** You are recommended to arrange Sunday visits by telephone because the crush is particularly heavy on that day; tel. (805) 405-2141. There is a guided tour through the Botanical Gardens every day at 1 p.m.

Petaluma   G 1

Sonoma County
Altitude: 13 ft/4 m
Population: 36,000

Location and general	This town, situated on the US 101 about 37 miles/60 km north of San Francisco, was founded in 1852, and even before that it was already providing the rapidly growing metropolis with agricultural products. To an immigrant Canadian, Petaluma – the Miwok Indian word for "flat back" – appeared to be an ideal place for chicken farming; he imported white Leghorn chickens, and in 1878 invented the incubator. Chicken farming reached its peak in 1920 when Petaluma, often called the egg-capital of the world, despatched 22 million eggs.
	Today there is nothing left of the chicken farms, even though the buildings of historic Petaluma have been amazingly well preserved, and its earlier importance as a river port for trade with San Francisco is still clear to see. Petaluma also possesses a shopping centre with 30 shops and two restaurants.

Pinnacles National Monument   K 1

Location and origin	This national monument, created by the federal government in 1908, lies in the Gabilan Mountains on the CA 25, south-east of Salinas (see entry). It is an area of 3 sq. miles/8 sq. km of volcanic origin, which has been eroded by wind, rain, frost, heat and chemical reactions of various kinds, producing interesting rock formations with cliffs and pinnacles. It is assumed that a volcano was formed as the result of earth eruptions 23 million years ago; its remains can be seen in Pinnacles Monument. Beyond the actual peak district (4 miles/6 km wide and 7 miles/11 km long), the National Monument includes a further area of 20 sq. miles/52 sq. km, as well as numerous caves.

Hangman's Tree in Placerville

Cliff arch near Point Lobos

It is possible to walk through the whole area, but some of the paths are difficult. The west entrance leads via Soledad to the US 101 and the east entrance via the CA 25. You can telephone the Visitor Center on 408/389-4578.

Note

Pismo Beach

M 1

San Luis Obispo County
Altitude: 33 ft/10 m
Population: 4700

This little town, right by the Pacific Ocean south of San Luis Obispo (see entry) on the US 101, stands out because of its 22 miles/35 km of beach, where several kinds of edible mussels can be dug up at any time of the year, and all kinds of water sports can be pursued.
Pismo Beach – the name comes from the language of the Chumash Indians and means "tar" – is also known for being (at the time of going to press) the last place close to the sea to allow cars to drive on ramps right on to the beach. Known for its extensive sand dunes, vehicles are prohibited in the Dunes reserve.

Location and general

Placerville

H 4

El Dorado County
Altitude: 1880 ft/570 m
Population: 7000

Placerville, only a few miles from where the first gold was found in Coloma (see entry), still lies in the gold-region, at the junction of Mother Lode Street

Location and origin

Cove in Point Lobos State Reserve

Point Reyes National Seashore

(now the CA 49) and the main highway from Sacramento to the Comstock silver mine in Nevada (now the US 50). Originally the town was named Dry Diggins; this was later changed to Hangtown, because so many unruly gold-diggers were hanged in order to maintain law and order. On a house in Main Street where the gallows stood, a life-sized figure of a "hanged man" can still be seen today. Little of its wild past remains in Placerville. Today it lies in the middle of a fruit-growing area, where a big "Cherry Carnival" is held in the middle of June, and where the apple harvest is celebrated from September to December, during which period 45 farmers welcome visitors.

Three famous Americans began life in Placerville: Mark Hopkins, a grocer who became a railway magnate and one of San Francisco's richest men (a hotel bears his name), the butcher Philip Armour, founder of one of the largest meat processing companies still in existence, and the coach-builder John Studebaker, one of the first important motor-car manufacturers in Detroit.

"From rags to riches"

Placerville can be used as a base for trips through Mother Lode County (see entry; information from the Chamber of Commerce, 542 Main Street; tel. (916) 621-5885). Anyone who feels like looking for gold in one of the streams or rivers in the neighbourhood can do so under the expert guidance of a gold-digger (tel. (916) 622-2484).

Note

Point Lobos State Reserve

J 0

This unusual coastal region in the south of Carmel Bay lies only a few miles from Carmel (see entry), and the harshness of its granite cliffs and caves forms a stark contrast to the civilised township. As a result of the constant movements of the waves over many millions of years a gradual erosion of the rock has taken place, producing some strange formations. Along sign-posted trails through this 1250-acre/500-hectare-tract, declared a nature reserve since 1933, (more than half of which lies under water), you can admire its beauty from close quarters: the numerous rocks lying off the coast, the caves, the rock-enclosed ponds which continually re-form, the fish in the clear waters and – with luck – sea-otters and sea-lions.

Location and °importance

Point Lobos is also a good point from which to observe the whales swimming not too far from the coast, on their way north or south, depending on the time of year. You can cover the whole area, but this rather difficult stretch, almost 6 miles/10 km long, starts at the entrance to Point Lobos on the CA 1 and will take some three to five hours. If you have less time to spare you should at least walk along the Cypress Grove Trail (many Monterey cypresses) and the North Shore Trail.

Walks

Point Lobos State Reserve is open daily, 9 a.m.–5 p.m., often longer in the summer months. Information: tel. 408/624-4909.

Opening times

Point Loma

See San Diego

Point Reyes National Seashore

G/H 0/1

Only 30 miles/48 km north of San Francisco on the CA 1 you will find Point Reyes, declared a "National Seashore" in 1962 and now forming part of the Golden Gate National Recreation Area which starts in San Francisco. The

°Location and origin

British landed on this peninsula 41 years before the Pilgrim Fathers at Plymouth. In 1579 Sir Francis Drake dropped anchor here and took possession of the land for the British Crown, but his homeland did not concern itself unduly with the west of the newly-discovered continent. 24 years later, on January 6th 1603, the Spanish seafarer Don Sebastian Vizcaino landed on the peninsula and – as it was the Feast of the Epiphany – named it La Punta de los Reyes (the Point of the Kings).

"Earthquake Way"

Point Reyes lies at the end of the San Andreas Fault, which was responsible for the devastating earthquake of 1906 and others (the last being in October 1989) which have struck San Francisco. From the Bear Valley Visitor Center starts a so-called "Earthquake Way", about 1100 yds/1 km in length, along which can be found seismographic evidence of earthquake movements, such as parts of a fence which formed one unit prior to the earthquake and which are now five metres apart.

Nature reserve

Numerous sea-birds spend the winter in this protected coastal terrain; several species of deer live in the forests, as well as foxes. Recent attempts have been made to re-introduce the elk.

Grey whales

In the months of December and January the Californian grey whale can be observed on its migration from the north to Baja California. As there is more fog in Point Reyes than at any other point along the Californian coast, a lighthouse was built in 1870. From here you get a splendid view of the whales as they swim past. They can be seen again in the months of April and May when they return to the Arctic.

Trails for walking and riding.

From the Bear Valley Visitor Center more than 75 miles/120 km of trails suitable for walking and riding lead into all parts of this coastal nature reserve. Information regarding the length and condition of these trails, as well as maps, can be obtained from the Visitor Center. Nearby can be found a reproduction of a Miwok Indian village (the Miwoks were the original inhabitants of the region). The Visitor Center is open only Thur.–Mon. Further information: tel. 415/663-1092.

Red Bluff   D/E 3

Tehama County
Altitude: 310 ft/94 m. Population: 10,500

Location and origin

The town gets its name from the red sandstone and gravel cliffs in the surrounding countryside. Situated on the upper reaches of the Sacramento River, at the junction of the US 5, CA 99 and CA 36, Red Bluff, in the middle of the 19th c. was mainly a stopping-off place for gold-diggers who often went back there when they realised that the soil was favourable for growing wheat and fruit. Its position on the Sacramento River made Red Bluff a centre for private and commercial shipping. Timber and agriculture remain the chief sources of revenue even today.

W. A. Ide Adobe State Historic Park

Only 2 miles/3 km to the north-east on the US 5 (Wilcox Road exit), you will find the William A. Ide Adobe State Historic Park, with the restored adobe residence (built 1846; tel. 895-4303) of the only president of the short-lived Republic of California. In the town itself stands a beautiful Victorian house with its original furnishings. In the Kelly Griggs House Museum (311 Washington Street) you can see a collection of Chinese and Indian artefacts. (Open: Thur.–Sun.; tel. 527-1129.)

Redding   D 3

Shasta County
Altitude: 560 ft/170 m. Population: 45,000

Redwood sculptures

This town, founded in 1872 and situated on the upper reaches of the Sacramento River and on the edge of the Sierra Nevada, is particularly important because of its favourable position as a starting point for numerous excursions into nearby districts: Lake Shasta (its famous caves are only 16 miles/25 km away), the 14,170 ft/4317 m high Mount Shasta (about 6 miles/10 km away), Whiskeytown Shasta Historic Park with its gold-digging past (6 miles/10 km) and Shasta Trinity National Forest. Redding is also well-placed traffic-wise being at the junction of several highways: the US 5, which runs south to San Diego via the county capital of Sacramento, the CA 299 to the Pacific coast via Eureka and the CA 44 to Lassen Volcanic National Park (see entries).

Location and importance

The town's main place of interest is the Museum & Art Center (19111 Rio Drive) with Indian and pre-Columbian artefacts as well as documentation on the history of Shasta County (open: June 1st–Aug. 31st, Tue.–Sun. 10 a.m.–5 p.m.; remaining months Tue.–Fri. and Sun. noon–5 p.m.; tel. (916) 225-4155). The museum stands on the northern edge of the town in beautiful Caldwell Park, right on the shores of the Sacramento River (various water-sports).

Museum & Art Center

To cater for the tourists who stream into the charming countryside to the west, north and east of the town, Redding possesses more than 20 hotels and motels.

Note

Redwood Highway

A–D 1/2

Redwood Highway is the name given to that 300 mile/480 km stretch of the US 101 which passes through the terrain where about 97% of all Californian Redwoods grow, most of them between Leggett and the Oregon border. Humboldt Redwoods State Park runs along both sides of the high-

*Location and ** importance*

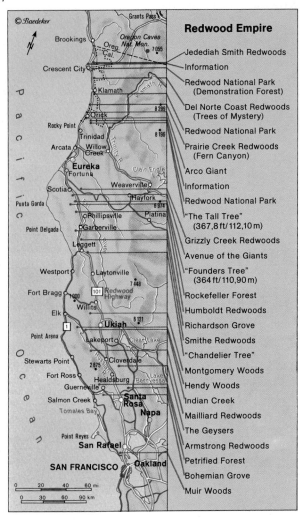

© Baedeker

Redwood Empire

Jedediah Smith Redwoods

Information

Redwood National Park (Demonstration Forest)

Del Norte Coast Redwoods (Trees of Mystery)

Redwood National Park

Prairie Creek Redwoods (Fern Canyon)

Arco Giant

Information

Redwood National Park

"The Tall Tree" (367,8 ft / 112,10 m)

Grizzly Creek Redwoods

Avenue of the Giants

"Founders Tree" (364 ft / 110,90 m)

Rockefeller Forest

Humboldt Redwoods

Richardson Grove

Smithe Redwoods

"Chandelier Tree"

Montgomery Woods

Hendy Woods

Indian Creek

Mailliard Redwoods

The Geysers

Armstrong Redwoods

Petrified Forest

Bohemian Grove

Muir Woods

way. Before this road was built the Avenue of the Giants – parallel to it – was the main route from Philipsville in the south to Pepperwood in the north. Redwoods also grow in Grizzly Creek Redwoods State Park, a few miles east of the US 101 on the CA 36 south of Carlotta, and in Redwood National Park between Orick and Crescent City (see entry), on the Oregon border, to which the Del Norte Coast Redwoods State Park belongs. Almost everywhere where Redwoods grow you will come across stalls selling wood-carvings, ranging from little boxes to larger-than-life legendary figures.

Redwood Empire: Avenue of the Giants ▶

| North Coast Daylight | Part of the Redwoods and many other natural beauty spots along the north Californian coast which are difficult to get to can also be enjoyed by taking a ten-hour train ride on the North Coast Daylight from Willits to Eureka (see entry). On this journey you will pass through no fewer than 25 tunnels and over 29 bridges. (Information: North Coast Daylight, Box 3666, Eureka CA 95502; tel. 707/442-7705.) |
| Information | All the information and brochures you require on the rather extravagantly named "Redwood Empire" can be obtained from the Redwood Empire Association, 1 Market Plaza, Spear Street Tower, San Francisco CA 94105; tel. 415/543-8334. |

Redwoods

Extent and general	Redwoods grow along the coast from Monterey (see entry) northwards inland as far as Oregon, and also in a small part of the Sierra Nevada. The botanical name of the former is sequoia sempervirens and that of the latter sequoia gigantea. It is not generally known that it was the Austrian botanist Stephan Endlicher who first described these trees in 1847 and chose for them the name sequoia in honour of Sequoyah, the author of the Cherokee alphabet.
Age and size	The Sierra sequoias (found mainly in the Yosemite and Sequoia National Parks) live longer (maximum age 3200 years) than the coastal sequoias, which are far more prevalent but reach an age of only 220 years at the most. Both are exceeded age-wise by the less imposing Bristlecone Pine of the Sierra, the oldest specimen of which is said to be 4600 years old. The tallest tree that has been measured was a coastal sequoia which reached 360 ft/110 m. The Sierra sequoias, however, have a larger girth and are broader. Many have met an early end as the result of storms, particularly through being struck by lightning. Tree-fellers have also reduced their volume considerably. Now these trees are a protected species, only a limited degree of felling being allowed.
Propagation	Propagation of Redwoods takes place in a manner which is somewhat different from that of other conifers. The cones, sometimes containing as many as 1000 seeds (a normal tree has about 600 cones), do not fall to the ground of their own accord, but are pulled off by squirrels who do not in fact eat the seeds. For some time now the authorities have adopted the practice of setting fire deliberately to sections of the forest, something which previously occurred naturally. This dries out the cones lying on the forest floor and they then open up within a few days. The seeds fall on the ashes, which have cooled in the meantime, and young trees shoot up within a few months; most die, admittedly, but sufficient survive. These biological links were not appreciated until a comparatively short time ago.
Distribution	Only a few sequoias thrive outside California and Oregon. The Russians, who settled in Fort Ross (see entry for Fort Ross State Historic Park) in the first half of the 19th c., were the first to plant sequoia seeds and saplings in Europe.

Riverside

Riverside County
Altitude: 860 ft/262 m
Population: 176,000

| Location and general | Riverside is the capital of the county of the same name, and is to be found south-east of Los Angeles on the CA 60 and 91 close to the US 10. Established about 1870, it was initially a silkworm-breeding centre, but within a |

few years had developed into an important agricultural area, concentrating mainly on growing navel oranges which had been cultivated by mutation in Brazil in 1873. Most navel oranges still come from here today, although Riverside has experienced rapid growth since 1950 and is now an important commercial and industrial town.

A citrus experimental station was the nucleus of the University of California in Riverside. With some 7500 students, the campus is the smallest of the nine university sites.

March Airport lies near the town.

Riverside has the following places which are worth a visit:

The municipal museum (37220 Orange Street), exhibiting historical, anthropological and natural history items. (Open: daily except Mon.; admission free; tel. (714) 782-5273.)

The California Museum of Photography, which has been in existence for over 15 years, and is to be found in a new building at 3824 Main Street. (Open: Tue.–Sat. 10 a.m.–5 p.m., Sun noon–5 p.m.; tel. (717) 784-FOTO.)

The historical Mission (3649 7th Street), where Spanish antiques, paintings, 900 bells, etc. are on exhibition. (Guided tours daily at 11.30 a.m. and 2.30 p.m.; tel. (714) 784-0300.)

Mount Rubidoux Memorial Park, at a height of 1300 ft/400 m on the western edge of town, with the Serra Cross in honour of the founder of the mission, and the Tower of World Peace. (Tel. (714) 787-7301.)

Places of interest

Sacramento

G/H 2/3

Sacramento County
Altitude: 27 ft/8 m
Population: 293,000

Sacramento lies about 93 miles/150 km north-east of San Francisco on the US 80, and has been the capital of the federal state of California since 1854. John A. Sutter (see Famous Personalities) founded the town in 1839, and named it after the nearby river. The old fortification known as Sutter's Fort has been restored and is now a tourist attraction.

Location and history

In the early fifties the town suffered from several floods as well as frequent fires. The old town (Old Sacramento), cheek by jowl with the Sacramento River, with plenty of shops and restaurants, was restored around 1980. In 1856 the first Californian railway was opened between Sacramento and Folsom, and was later connected to the Transcontinental Railway line running between the east and west coasts.

Conurbation: see separate plan on the map at the end of the book

Places of interest

The Big Four Building is named after the four most influential men in the Californian railway industry. They all lived in Sacramento before moving to the larger and more important San Francisco: they were Charles Crocker, Mark Hopkins, Collis B. Huntington and Leland Stanford. (Address: I Street, between Front and Second Street.)

Big Four Building

Comprehensive exhibition of documents on the history of Sacramento and California. (Address: 1020 O Street; open: Mon.–Fri. 8 a.m.–5 p.m.)

California State Archives

The old neo-classical Capitol, with its 234-ft/70-m-high dome, was built between 1861 and 1869; extensions were added later. A complete

*California State Capitol

223

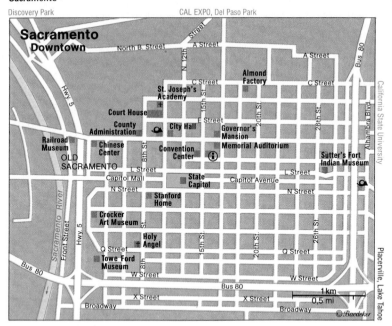

Sacramento
Downtown

Discovery Park

CAL EXPO, Del Paso Park

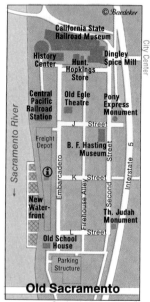

Old Sacramento

Crocker Art Gallery

restoration of the old Capitol (cost: 68 million dollars) was completed in 1982. Since then the marble mosaic floors and many chandeliers again shine as they did in the old days, and make the Governor's official seat and the parliamentary chambers (which can also be visited when parliament is not sitting) interesting and attractive to tourists. (Address: 10th Street and Capitol Mall; open: daily 9 a.m.–5 p.m.; admission free; information about daily guided tours tel. (916) 324-0333.)

The colourful gardens, extending over several blocks and with tall palms and numerous other species of trees and plants, make the building the most beautiful Capitol in the United States.

Since December 1988 a bronze group sculpture, the Vietnam War Memorial, has stood in the north-east part of Capitol Park (L and 15th Street); its construction was entirely funded by donations, and it commemorates those who sacrificed their lives in the longest war involving the United States of America.

Sacramento: Californian State Capitol

Seven historic rooms in the old Capitol, with furniture and other accoutrements from the beginning of the 20th c., provide the visitor with a glimpse of the past. Films are also shown. (Open: daily 9 a.m.–5 p.m.; in winter only at weekends 10 a.m.–5 p.m. Information available in the Capitol Building, Room 124; tel. (916) 324-0333.)

California State Capitol Museum

With a floor area for exhibits of over 100,000 sq. ft./10,000 sq. m., the California State Railroad Museum is the world's largest railway museum. It houses 21 restored locomotives and railway coaches of all ages, as well as 46 other items. Almost all the wagons can be viewed inside. With the same admission ticket you can also visit the old "Pacific" railway station. (Address: 125 I Street, in Old Sacramento State Historic Park; tel. (916) 448-4466 recording or (916) 445-4209.)

California State Railroad Museum

Sacramento's oldest railway station, Central Pacific Railroad Station, dates from the 19th c., and has been opened up to visitors as a branch of the Californian State Railroad Museum.

Central Pacific Railroad Station Museum

In the completely restored station building you will find the Central Pacific Passenger Depot, where you will be transported back to the second half of the 19th c. In the summer months you can travel to Miller Park in historic trains. (Address: Front Street, near the Railroad Museum; tel. (916) 445-4209.)

Central Pacific Passenger Depot

A reconstructed Victorian building, originating from 1873, houses the oldest art museum in the western United States. It has been extended several times. In addition to paintings and drawings by Californian artists (from Sacramento in particular), the exhibits include European, East Asian and recently also some contemporary works of art and photographs.

Crocker Art Museum

Old Sacramento: reminders of the past

Rafting on the Sacramento River

Sutter's Fort: first outpost of the white man in California

(Address: 216 O Street; open: Tue. 1 p.m.–9 p.m., Wed.–Sun., 10 a.m.–5 p.m.; tel. (916) 449-5423.)

The Hastings Building, dating from 1853, was originally a bank; today it is a museum where you will find a reproduction of California's first Supreme Court, as well as the Pony Express Museum and the Wells Fargo Museum. (Address: 2nd and J Street; tel. (916) 324-0539; open: Tue.–Sun. 10 a.m.–5 p.m.; admission free.) **Hastings Building**

This magnificent Victorian villa, built in 1878, served as a residence for thirteen Californian Governors, the last being Ronald Reagan, who lived there from 1966 to 1975. (Address: 16th and H Street; tel. (916) 324-0539.; open: daily 10 a.m.–5 p.m.; guided tours on the hour every hour 10 a.m.–4 p.m.) **Historic Governor's House**

About 26 acres/10.5 hectares of Sacramento's old town, between I and M Street and also 2nd and Front Street, have been restored in the style of the years 1849–1870, including the cobbled streets (buggy rides available). At weekends, at 11.30 a.m. and 1.30 p.m., guided walks through the old town are organised starting from the Central Pacific Passenger Depot (tel. (916) 445-4209). **Old Sacramento**

In the old town stands the Eagle Theater, built in 1849; performances on Friday and Saturday evenings. (Address: 25 Front Street; tel. (916) 446-6761.) Eagle Theater

The Old Sacramento Schoolhouse is a reproduction of a school of 1880. (Address: corner of Front and L Streets; tel. (916) 443-8818; open: Mon.–Fri. 9.30 a.m.–4 p.m., weekends noon–4 p.m. Schoolhouse

Sacramento is carrying out a project to restore the old harbour district to what it looked like in days gone by. A start has been made on the east Old harbour district

bank of Sacramento River, between I Street Bridge and Tower Bridge. Since 1989 "Delta King", the ship which used to ply between Sacramento and San Francisco from 1920 to 1941, has been laid up; it could hold 1000 passengers and 2000 tonnes of freight. In the Second World War it served as a hospital ship, and has now been converted to a floating hotel, with 44 single cabins, 12 restaurants, function rooms for a total of 200 people, as well as a museum and theatre.

History Center

The Sacramento History Center is a modern museum with four galleries: The information centre introduces the visitor, by means of a 9-minute film and a computer system, to the way the gallery has been built up (ground floor).
The Topomorphology Gallery describes the changing environment and the interaction of man and geology in the Sacramento Valley (first floor).
The Community Gallery presents the sometimes conflicting social forces in the community known as Great Sacramento (first floor).
On the ground floor also there is a gallery of agricultural technology and one for exhibitions held on a rota basis. (Address: 101 I Street; tel. (916) 449-2057; open: daily 10 a.m.–5 p.m.)

*Sutter's Fort

Where Sutter's Fort Museum stands today was once the site of the first outpost of the white man in California, set up by the German-Swiss immigrant Johann August Sutter in 1839. The adobe house built in the same year has been restored in the original style, and today houses relics of the pioneering and gold-rush period; there are also items on show to remind us of the town's founder, whose estates reached as far as the other side of the American River near Coloma (see entry). After gold was discovered Sutter was literally overrun by gold-seekers, so that he was forced to flee. (Address: 27th & L Street; tel. (916) 324-0539; open: daily, 10 a.m.–5 p.m.; last guided tour begins at 4.15 p.m.)

Indian Museum

The Indian Museum nearby offers an insight into the life-style of California's original inhabitants. (Address: 2618 K Street; tel. (916) 324-0539; open: daily, 10 a.m.–5 p.m.)

Tower Ford Museum

The Tower Ford Museum was first set up in 1987 and contains a collection of 150 Ford cars, with an example from each year of manufacture and at least one model from each of the years 1903–1953. (Address: 2200 Front Street; tel. (916) 442-6802; open: daily, 10 a.m.–5 p.m.)

St Helena   G 1

Napa County
Altitude: 256 ft/78 m
Population: 5000

Location and general

Some 37 miles/60 km north of San Francisco lies St Helena, one of the important wine-producing towns in the Napa Valley, with six big wine firms operating in the town or nearby: Beaulieu, Beringer, Inglenook, Hans Kornell, Charles Krug and Louis M. Martini. Not far away the 4300-ft/1300-m-high Mount St Helena looks down over the Napa Valley. It forms part of the Mayacamas Mountains (named after the old Indian village of Miyakmah, near Calistoga – see entry).

Silverado Museum

The English author Robert Louis Stevenson spent his honeymoon in a house on the mountainside where there was once a silver mine. The Silverado Museum (1490 Library Lane) in memory of Stevenson contains first editions of his works, manuscripts, photographs and letters from the author. (Open: Tue.–Fri. noon–4 p.m.; admission free; tel. (707) 963-3757.)

Lake Beryessa

About 4 miles/6 km south of St Helena, by the CA 29, you will find the

John Steinbeck's birthplace in Salinas

artificial Lake Beryessa, formed as a result of the building of the Monticello Dam; its banks are 165 miles/265 km in length, and there are numerous opportunities for water sports.

Salinas

J 1

Monterey County
Altitude: 53 ft/16 m
Population: 84,500

Salinas is to be found some 50 miles/80 km south of San José, in the middle of a fertile agricultural region, where mainly lettuce, sugar-beet and fruit and vegetables of all kinds are grown, and some canning is done as well. Founded in 1856, its name comes from the salt-marshes at the mouth of the river of the same name; it became well-known as the birthplace of John Steinbeck (see Famous Personalities).

Location and importance

Several of Steinbeck's works are set in Salinas or the Salinas Valley, for example, "Tortilla Flat" (1935), "East of Eden" (1952) and "Of Mice and Men" (1937). The house in which Steinbeck was born (132 Central Avenue, corner of Stone Street) is an imposing building, which now houses a restaurant on the ground floor. The house is not open to visitors. However, you can see some Steinbeck memorabilia in the John Steinbeck Library (110 W. San Luis Street; open: Mon.–Thur. 10 a.m.–9 p.m., Fri. and Sat. 10 a.m.–6 p.m.; tel. 758-7311.)

John Steinbeck

Salton Sea

R/S 6

An ancient dried-up bed of a lake became an actual "sea" again in 1905. Having broken through an irrigation canal in Imperial Valley, the Colorado

Location and how to get there

229

River flooded over into the old bed and filled it to a depth of 82 ft/25 m and a diameter of almost 250 ft/75 m. The river continued to flood until 1907; the resultant lake (now 30 miles/48 km long and 8–14 miles/13–23 km wide, with a surface of 235 ft/74 m and lying below sea-level) has no outlets, apart from some ditches dug to lead water away.

Recreation Area

The Salton Sea State Recreation Area has been created on the northern bank. This area, covering 16,680 acres/6672 hectares, provides 175 well-equipped camping sites, which are especially popular with fishermen and water-sport enthusiasts (water-skiing, boats) and naturalists (walks, bird-watching).

San Bernardino   P/Q 4

San Bernardino County
Altitude: 1050 ft/320 m
Population: 129,000

Location and general

San Bernardino, the capital of the largest county in the USA, lies on the Barstow Freeway (US 215) and on the CA 66, some 56 miles/90 km east of Los Angeles, 106 miles/170 km north-east of San Diego and 450 miles/725 km south-east of San Francisco; it is 25 minutes by car from Ontario International Airport. The town occupies a position surrounded by mountains, fertile valleys and deserts, and is one of the fastest growing parts of California.

Development

The Franciscan Fathers of the San Gabriel mission (see entry for Mission Stations) founded an "asistencia" (hospital) here in 1810, but it was pillaged several times by the Paiute Indians. As it was founded on the name day of San Bernardino of Siena it was named after that saint. Four decades later Mormons settled here, and laid the town out in the manner of Salt Lake City. However, the Mormon leader Brigham Young recalled them after only six years. Nevertheless, the town developed without further hindrance, and today is one of California's orange-growing centres.

Rim of the World Drive

The CA 18, also called "Rim of the World", is a very famous highway. It leads to Lake Arrowhead (water-sports), Big Bear Lake, Baldwin Lake and other popular destinations. The 38-mile/62-km-long road, which winds and twists its way up to a height of 7220 ft/2200 m, provides plenty of picturesque views. The most beautiful panoramic view, however, is from the highest point, known as Lakeview Point.

San Buenaventura

See Mission Stations

San Carlos Borromeo de Carmelo

See Mission Stations and also Carmel

San Diego   R/S 3/4

San Diego County
Altitude: 43 ft/13 m
Population: 925,000

General

San Diego is situated some 120 miles/200 km south of Los Angeles. The town's southern boundary is also the border with Mexico. Being on two protected bays, San Diego Bay, which is separated from the sea by Point Loma and by Coronado Island/North Island, and the multi-lobed Mission Bay, San Diego has become an important port. It is the biggest American naval base after Norfolk. The equitable warm and dry climate and the beautiful and fertile surrounding countryside (oranges, tomatoes, avocados, fruit and vegetables) make San Diego a popular place in which to live.

The town is a favourite centre for seminars and conventions, as well as being important in the research sphere (space travel, oceanography, electronics, three universities). This is where the "Atlas" rockets used in space flights were developed.

San Diego is the oldest town in California and – from its foundation in 1769 – the one where development was the slowest. Early in the Second World War (about 1940) San Diego had barely 150,000 inhabitants. Since then its attractions have increased to such an extent that it has become the second town in California, after Los Angeles, to have a million people.

The 1988 population was estimated at 1,003,000, after having totalled 925,000 in 1983 and only 875,000 three years before.
Since 1980 the number of people living in San Diego has increased by 20%. With the exception of Houston in Texas and Phoenix, the capital of Arizona, no other large American town has experienced such a high percentage increase. It is worth mentioning that in 1979 a plan was put forward by the town council limiting the town's growth, and estimating a population by 1996 of 1,050,000 – a figure which will certainly be exceeded.

San Diego offers the visitor an enchanting natural beauty and a climate with plenty of sunshine: the 1410-acre/565-hectare Balboa Park, with perhaps the world's finest zoo; more than 68 miles/110 km of beaches in town and county; countless opportunities for water sports (including sailing and motor-boats); excursions into the nearby wastelands or – by tram – to Mexico. It has more public and private golf courses than any other American town. There are also several stud-farms.

The weather is exceptional. The sun is nearly always shining, and the drop in temperature extremely small, certainly smaller than anywhere else in California. Average temperatures are 16°C in spring, 21°C in summer, 19°C in autumn and 14°C in winter. Fluctuations from these are rare; very hot summer temperatures occur only now and again, and temperatures below freezing point are unknown. Like everywhere else on the Pacific coast, in the summer months there are sometimes early morning mists and low cloud, and the sun often does not get through before 10 a.m. or noon. There are occasional showers only between November and February.

History

As long ago as 1542 a Spanish expedition under Juan Rodriguez Cabrillo had sailed into San Diego Bay and discovered what was later to be known as California. On his voyage along the Californian coast 60 years later Sebastian Vizcaino entered the bay and gave it the name of his flagship, St Didacus de Alcala. Didicus (Diego in Spanish) was a 15th c. Franciscan monk who was canonized after his death as a reward for his fantastically strict regime of penitence. In 1769 an expedition came from the governor of Baja California, Don Gaspar de Portola, to Alta California with some Franciscan monks on board, including Father Junipero Serra, beatified in 1988, who started to build the first of 21 mission stations (see entry) on 16th July 1769 which is also the date when San Diego really came into being. The

Location and importance

Conurbation: see separate plan on the map at the end of the book

Population

Development

Making use of leisure time

Climate

Origin

231

San Diego

present-day Mission of San Diego de Alcala is to be found some 6 miles/ 10 km inland from its original site.

19th century

It was not until 1820 that a plaza was built, surrounded for the next 20 years by about 40 adobe houses. At that time, no more than 200 Mexicans and Spaniards lived there. The first North Americans came around 1803. However, when in 1846 during the Americo-Mexican war the town was occupied by American marines, there was merely a handful of white men living in the Old Town. San Diego changed owners several times in the following five months; only after the Battle of San Pasqual, east of the present Escondido, did it finally fall into American hands.

With the acceptance of the federal state of California into the Union in 1850 San Diego County came into being, and the town was given its charter. At first this did not speed up its development in any way. Only when, in 1885, the Santa Fe Railroad arranged for San Diego to be connected to the transcontinental railway network was there a noticeable upswing. Shortly after the population had increased to 40,000, however, the first crisis occurred and the hoped-for economic boom failed to materialise.

Furthermore, the extension of the harbour which was now underway proved insufficient to break the predominance of San Francisco and the new San Pedro Harbor of Los Angeles.

First half of the 20th century

The town's real upswing began to take place after three major events: first the completion of the Panama Canal in the autumn of 1914; secondly, the Panama-Californian Exhibition held in Balboa Park in 1915/1916, which directed the world's attention towards San Diego; and thirdly, the moving of an army and, in particular, a naval base to San Diego during the First World War.

When the town was redeveloped in 1868, Balboa Park was saved – thanks to a far-sighted city father – and this extensive green area still exists today.

Present-day expansion

The town is expanding on all sides, and now covers an area of 310 sq. miles/800 sq. km; in the south it reaches as far as Point Loma and nearly to the Mexican border in the suburb of Chula Vista, in the north to La Jolla, and

▼ Skyline of San Diego at twilight

in the west to La Mesa and El Cajon. Whether, in view of the many facilities offered to residents in the suburbs, the authorities will succeed in breathing life back into the town centre and avoid what has happened in Los Angeles, remains a fateful question for San Diego.

Economy and culture

After the Japanese attack on the Pacific naval base in Honolulu in December 1941 when the United States were considering a new base, the choice fell on San Diego. Since then the 11th Naval Squadron has been stationed here; it is also the headquarters of the Pacific Fleet. This military presence is of the greatest importance to San Diego's economy. The second most important economic factor is the aircraft industry (the Convair works are the biggest employers), and the third is tourism. The building of space-rockets, oceanic and bio-medical research, electronics and higher education (especially the University of California at San Diego in La Jolla) also play a decisive rôle in the town's economy.

Economy

Unfortunately San Diego's cultural development has lagged behind its economic progress. One of the main reasons is that potential patrons of the arts were somewhat late in deciding to settle in the town. As public subsidies are rare, the town's cultural pursuits depend mainly upon private sponsorship. As a result, San Diego has no adequate museum and is outclassed by San Francisco and Los Angeles in the musical sphere as well. Only the theatre has recently gained in importance.

Culture

Transport

San Diego can be the beginning or the end of a trip through California. Its airport, only a few miles from the centre of town (Lindbergh Field), is to be moved further out into the county in the foreseeable future. It serves thirteen airlines, including American, American West, Continental, Delta, TWA and United Airlines, with direct flights from the east coast. (Airport information: tel. (619) 231-5220.)

Airport

Balboa Park: lily pond outside Botanical Building

Routes
When coming from the north by car along the US 5 or 15 and the CA 163 turn-off past the Miramar Naval Air Force Base, you drive straight into town. Another road which leads through the town from north to south is the US 805. You approach from the east along the US 8, CA 125 (east of La Mesa) and CA 94, which then merges with the US 5. Greyhound and Trailway buses operate a service to downtown San Diego.

It is worth taking the two and a half hour train ride from Los Angeles to San Diego or vice-versa; Amtrak Station in San Diego is situated on Broadway and Kettner Boulevard. (Information: tel. 800/872-7245.)

Tips for the car driver
In San Diego – like Los Angeles – the car is the best form of transport. Most of the places of interest described in this book will be found quite near to the freeways, and there is generally adequate parking space. If you come by car you should, whenever possible, choose a motel or hotel with an underground garage. You should also note that most streets in the town centre are one-way.

The speed limit on the freeways is 55 m.p.h. (80 km.p.h.) and 35 m.p.h. (55 km.p.h.) in town, unless the signs show otherwise.

Public Transport
Public transport (buses and trams) are normally time-consuming for the tourist because they go all round the town, do not use the freeways and stop frequently. (Time-table information from the San Diego Transit Company; tel. (619) 233-3004.)

Places of interest from A to Z

*Balboa Park

General
Most of the town's museums are to be found on this 1412 acre/565 hectare site. It is therefore advisable to park your car on the big car-park in front of

the zoo and visit the places of interest on foot. The time required to see the park depends on where your interests lie. Experience suggests setting aside one full day for the museums and another for the remaining sights. Apart from a few modern buildings, most of those on Balboa Park were erected for the Panama California Exhibition of 1915/1916, and are therefore mainly in the Spanish-Mexican style.

What served as a swimming pool for patients in the US naval hospital in the Second World War is today a pond with sea-lilies and goldfish, and with the Botanical Building nearby; the latter also reminds one of days gone by, for the steel framework was actually made for a station belonging to the Santa Fe Railroad but was purchased by the managers of the exhibition. Inside there are more than 500 species of tropical and sub-tropical plants to be seen. (Open: daily except Fri. 10 a.m.–4 p.m.; tel. (619) 236-5717.)

Botanical Building

The fifteen bungalows of the House of Pacific Relations, reminiscent of the Mexican colonial period, were each intended for one of the Latin-American countries participating in the exhibition. They have retained their purpose to this day. (Open: only on Sundays, April to Oct. 2 p.m. to 5 p.m.; admission free. During these months folk-concerts and dances are also held.)

House of Pacific Relations

The exhibits in the Museum of Man were collected by the Smithsonian Institute in Washington from the Indian Pueblos in the south-west of the United States; further excavations were made at the ruins of the Aztec and Maya settlements in Latin America. Among other things, they illustrate the early history of the human race by portraying prehistoric man. Today thousands of artefacts make up the exhibits displayed in this ever-expanding museum, which also mounts exhibitions alternating on a rota basis. (Open: daily except on important public holidays 10 a.m.–4.30 p.m.; tel. (619) 239-2001.)

Museum of Man

The relatively new Museum of Photographic Arts is housed in the arcades of the Casa de Balboa and presents exhibitions of black and white, and colour, photographs on specific themes or by well-known photographers, as well as video and film programmes from its own archives. (Open: daily 10 a.m.–5 p.m., Thur. 10 a.m.–9 p.m.; tel. (619) 239-5262.)

Museum of Photographic Arts

This theatre, also built in 1935/1936 for the California Pacific International Exposition and based on Shakespeare's Globe Theatre in London in the style of the 15th c., was destroyed by fire in 1978, but was re-built and is now the home of the San Diego Repertory Company.
Directly next to it are to be found two further units of the Simon Edison Center for the Performing Arts: a theatre for contemporary plays (225 seats), named after the famous 19th c. Shakespeare director Cassius Clay, and the Lowell Davies Festival Theater, an open-air stage with over 600 seats, where the Shakespeare Festival is held in summer. For information on times of performances and prices of admission for all three theatres: tel. (619) 239-2255.

Old Globe Theater

The Reuben H. Fleet Space Theater is a planetarium and cinema combined which, by means of a 75 ft/23 m long, hemispherical dome-projector, gives you the impression that you are floating in space. In the adjoining Science Center you may handle as well as look at the items on display. The demonstrations in the Space Theater (55 mins) take place eight times a day in the summer months and seven times in winter (Sun.–Thur. 9.45 a.m.–9.30 p.m., Fri. and Sat. 9.45 a.m.–10.30 p.m.; tel. (619) 238-1168).

Reuben H. Fleet Space Theater and Science Center

In this museum, a round building dating from 1930, aircraft from the earliest days right up to NASA missiles are displayed, including a replica of the "Spirit of St Louis", the aeroplane in which Charles A. Lindbergh made the first solo transatlantic flight (the original is in the National Aerospace Museum in Washington). The International Aerospace Hall of Fame in the same building shows photographs and memorabilia of the pioneers of

San Diego Aerospace Museum

San Diego

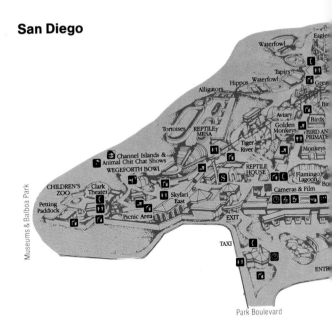

Waterfowl
Eagles
Tapirs
Waterfowl
Hippos
Alligators
Great
Bir
Aviary
Golden
Monkeys
Birds
BIRD AN
PRIMATE
Tortoises
REPTILE
MESA
Tiger
River
Monkeys
Channel Islands &
Animal Chit Chat Shows
WEGEFORTH BOWL
REPTILE
HOUSE
Flamingo
Lagoon
Bo
CHILDREN'S
ZOO
Clark
Theater
Cameras & Film
Petting
Paddock
Skyfari
East
Picnic Area
EXIT
TAXI
ENTR
Park Boulevard

Museums & Balboa Park

San Diego Zoo

Zoo

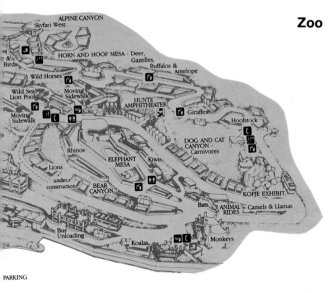

Skyfari West
ALPINE CANYON
HORN AND HOOF MESA - Deer, Gazelles,
Buffalos & Antelope
& Birds
Wild Horses
Zebra
Wild Sea Lion Pool
Moving Sidewalk
st.
HUNTE AMPHITHEATER
Moving Sidewalk
Giraffes
Hoofstock
Rhinos
DOG AND CAT CANYON - Carnivores
ELEPHANT MESA
Kiwis
Lions
under construction
BEAR CANYON
KOPJE EXHIBIT
Bats
ANIMAL RIDES - Camels & Llamas
Bus Unloading
Koalas
Monkeys

PARKING

© *Baedeker*

flight. (Open: daily 10 a.m.–4.30 p.m.; tel. Museum: (619) 234-8291, Hall of Fame: (619) 232-8322.)

The San Diego Museum of Art, originally called the Fine Arts Building, is a copy of the 17th c. University of Salamanca in the so-called Platero style (i.e. finely-chiselled terracotta and silversmith work). Busts of Spanish painters adorn the façade, and their works hang in the museum's collection. The main interest lies, perhaps, in the pre-Renaissance paintings and those by Flemish masters, as well as 19th and 20th c. art, and a large department housing American, Chinese, Japanese and other oriental works of art, including Indian and Persian miniatures. There are also some contemporary sculptures.

San Diego Museum of Art

Next to the museum a sculpture-garden has been constructed which, although small, boasts some exquisite works by contemporary sculptors, including Alexander Calder, Barbara Hepworth, Juan Miró, Henry Moore and Louise Nevelson. The museum also presents exhibitions on a rota basis. (Open: Tue.–Sun. 10 a.m.–4.30 p.m. Guided tours on the hour, 10 a.m.–2 p.m., Tue., Wed. and Thur., on other days at 1 p.m. and 2 p.m.; tel. (619) 232-7931.)

The Natural History Museum, established more than 100 years ago, has been housed in its present building since 1932, and displays southern Californian fossils, birds, reptiles, mammals, insects, plants and marine animals. Several life-size dioramas are dedicated to the fauna and flora of the Californian coast. (Open: daily 10 a.m.–4.30 p.m., in summer 10 a.m.–5 p.m.; tel. (619) 232-3821.)

San Diego Museum of Natural History

More than a quarter of Balboa Park is taken up by the San Diego Zoo, one of the largest in the world and certainly one of the most beautiful.

**San Diego Zoo

Spanish Village: artist at work

Its reputation as a unique place of interest has grown with the years. Its beginnings go back to the Panama Pacific Exhibition, when animals were put on show in San Diego for the first time; it has occupied its present site since the early twenties but is continually being extended, for example by the 2½ acre/1 hectare rain forest environment which was first laid out in 1988, complete with lush vegetation, waterfalls and artificially-produced mist. Here you can see more than 500 exotic plants and 100 animals in their natural surroundings, including majestic tigers from Sumatra, mysterious tapirs from Malaysia, water-dragons and other Asiatic animals. The sub-tropical climate here is not very different from that in San Diego.

Collection

Because of the gradient of the canyon, the visitor must be prepared to face some steep winding climbs, but will be rewarded by impressive sights which will stay in the memory. Immediately after passing through the turnstile you will be greeted by rose-pink flamingos, succeeded by giant tortoises which are native to the Galapagos Islands; then come the koala bears, which cling to branches of eucalyptus trees in their native Australia, and the golden monkeys. You can also go into the bird-houses with their hundreds of birds, some of which are very rare.

The zoo is laid out rather like a botanical garden, in which many exotic plants grow and multi-coloured flowers bloom the whole year through.

A Children's Zoo is a special attraction for the youngsters, who can admire the young animals and also stroke some of them.

Tips

Those who find walking difficult can take a 3 mile/5 km bus trip through the canyons and over the hills. By this means they will be able to see a great many of the animals and have the benefit of expert commentaries. There is also a cable-railway which travels over the tree-tops at a height of about 115 ft/50 m, from which you can have a bird's-eye view of the zoo. The zoo is open from 9 a.m. to 5 p.m. in July, August and the first week in September, and from 9 a.m. until 4 p.m. in the remaining months of the year. (Information: tel. (619) 234-3153 or (619) 231-1515.)

San Diego: Hotel del Coronado

From the direction of San Diego, take the CA 163 and the US 15 as far as the junction with the CA 178, and follow this eastwards as far as the exit to Via Rancho Parkway.

Wild Animal Park

The Zoological Society of San Diego, which manages the zoo and over 500 animals, opened up a 1750 acre/700 hectare game reserve some years ago situated about 30 miles/50 km north of San Diego. Here you can go on a safari lasting almost an hour, and watch some 2500 animals, native to Africa and Asia, in their natural environment. Also new is the biggest planted area of bonsai trees in the US American West. It is also planned to extend the Kupanda Botanical Center into a so-called Baja Garden, with succulents and cacti native to Baja California.

(The Wild Animal Park is open 9 a.m.–4 p.m.; in July, Aug. and beginning of Sept. 9 a.m.–6 p.m.; tel. (619) 234-6541 or 480-0100.)

This, the world's biggest open-air organ, was a gift made to the town in 1915 by the sons of Adolph Spreckels, an immigrant from Hanover in Germany, who became a multi-millionaire in America. Since then, except during the Second World War, a concert has been held every Sunday afternoon at 2.30 p.m. The organ has some 3500 pipes, the smallest being 1½ in/4 cm and the largest almost 33 ft/10 m in length. When the organ is not being used it is protected by a metal curtain weighing 12 tonnes.

Spreckels Organ

The Timken Art Gallery, built in 1965 on the Panama Plaza, houses an important collection of Russian icons from the 16th to the 19th c., works by Italian, French, Spanish and Dutch painters, as well as American art from several centuries. (Open: Tue.–Sat. 10 a.m.–4.30 p.m., Sun. 1.30 p.m.–4.30 p.m.; admission free; tel. (619) 239-5548.)

Timken Art Gallery

In a number of low-built houses in the Spanish Village and Arts Center artists and craftsmen (potters, painters, sculptors, gold and silversmiths, photographers and weavers) can be seen at work. The articles and works of art they produce are on sale. Sometimes artists erect their easels in the

Spanish Village Arts and Crafts Center

239

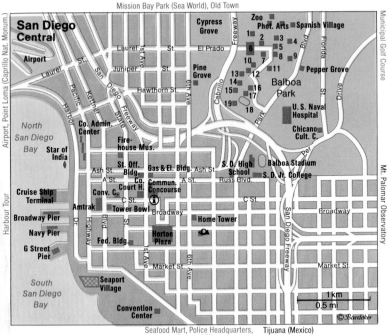

Mission Bay Park (Sea World), Old Town

Seafood Mart, Police Headquarters, Tijuana (Mexico)
Seaport Village

1 Old Globe Theatre
2 Museum of Arts
3 Botanical Building
4 Natural History
 Museum
5 Timken Art Gallery
6 Museum of Man

7 Hall of Champions
8 House of Hospitality
9 Space Theater
10 House of Pacific Relations
11 Organ Pavillion
12 Federal Building
13 Balboa Park Club

14 Palisades Building
15 Conference Building
16 Federal Building
17 Municipal Gym
18 Balboa Park Bowl
19 Aerospace
 Historical Center

courtyard where you can also watch them at work. (Open: daily 11 a.m.–4 p.m., except on Jan. 1st; admission free; tel. (619) 239-8812.)

Coronado

How to get there

From downtown you can reach Coronado in a few minutes by crossing the Coronado Bridge off the US 5. If you are in no hurry you can go on the ferry which starts from Broadway Pier in San Diego. (Information about times of departure: tel. (619) 234-4111.)

Location and general

The garden town of Coronado (pop. 20,000) is situated on a peninsula. Whilst it has its own town council, it is nevertheless regarded as a suburb of San Diego, to which it is linked by the bridge over San Diego Bay and by the ferry. It was named after the islands of Los Coronados which lie off the shores of Baja California (see entry). Because of its majestic beauty it is also known as Crown City, although when he named the islands in 1602, the seafarer Viczaino wished to honour the three Romans who were crowned as martyrs.

San Diego – Horton Plaza, downtown shopping centre

Coronado's only building of interest, but one which is well worth seeing, is the Hotel del Coronado, built in 1888. Its mixture of Spanish and Mexican styles is unique in America today since, in spite of its wooden construction, it is still used as a luxury hotel (almost 700 rooms including those added on).

*Hotel del Coronado

Predominantly Chinese workers with no previous knowledge of building techniques completed the hotel in less than eleven months. The main four-storey building, over 100 years old, has had no structural alterations of any kind during that period, although the guest-rooms have been renovated several times. It was the largest building outside New York to be fully served by electricity at that time. Thomas Edison himself supervised the electrical installation.

No fewer than twelve American presidents, film actors, Charles Lindbergh, and many other VIPs have been guests in this famous hotel. Numerous films have also been made here, including "Some Like it Hot" with Marilyn Monroe, Jack Lemmon and Tony Curtis.

Perhaps the most interesting room in the hotel is the 30-ft/9-m-high dining-room, in the construction of which not a single nail or any kind of supporting beam was used; the pine ceiling is held together by wooden dowels.

Gaslamp Quarter

Gaslamp Quarter lies in the centre of the inner town between Broadway and San Diego Bay. The sixteen or so blocks of houses built between 1880 and 1910 comprise most of the Victorian houses still preserved in San Diego, as a result of which it has been declared an historic (listed) district. As the restoration work in the 35 acre/14 hectare quarter is not yet complete, only a few streets are worth a visit; the main one being Fifth Avenue, between E and F Streets, where houses nos. 832 and 840 are particularly worthy of attention. Some of the streets have already been re-surfaced in

Historic district

La Jolla Cove

red brick; however, it will be some time before the work, estimated to cost 12 million dollars in all, is finished.

Villa Montezuma

Not very far from Gaslamp Quarter stands Villa Montezuma (1925 K Street), built in 1887, an unusually luxurious Victorian house constructed when San Diego was enjoying its first brief economic boom between 1886 and 1888. Well worth seeing are the stained-glass windows (more than 20), some rooms restored in their original style, as well as alternating exhibitions in the house which now functions as a museum. (Open: Tue.–Fri. and Sun. 1 p.m.–4.30 p.m.; tel. (619) 239-2211.)

Horton Plaza

Horton Plaza also lies downtown between Broadway and G Street, 1st and 4th Avenue. From an architectural point of view it is one of California's most interesting shopping centres. The name is derived from one of San Diego's pioneers, Alonzo Horton, who in 1867 bought for only 265 US dollars some 1000 acres/400 hectares of land in what was then a village. This included practically the whole of the downtown district of today. Horton Plaza boasts some 140 shops, including four department stores (Nordstrom, Robinson's, The Broadway and Mervins), numerous restaurants, a cinema and a theatre. The bright colours and avant-garde architecture, together with the open-air displays, make it all most attractive.

**La Jolla

Location and general

La Jolla (pronounced "la hoya") extends along a 7-mile/11-km curved strip of coastline, 14 miles/22 km north of Downtown San Diego (take the US 5 and then the Ardath Road exit). It has rich vegetation and enjoys mild weather all the year round, but, like all places on the coast, it is plagued with mists in summer.

Although the name translates as "jewel", the original name of La Hoya (as still recognisable from the pronunciation) comes from a geographical word for "cave".

Today La Jolla has about 30,000 inhabitants, the numbers having increased appreciably during the last decade.

Even though La Jolla forms part of San Diego and is the seat of the University of California at San Diego, it functions quite independently, so that most visitors consider it more of a village enclave than a suburb of San Diego. It has in fact been able to preserve its idyllic atmosphere. Mail posted there is stamped "La Jolla", not "San Diego". The abundance of elegant shops in Girard Avenue is a distinguishing feature.

As a result of the university and other research institutes being here, many academics, budding artists and writers have made their homes here. This intellectually active life has produced numerous galleries and, in particular, a museum of contemporary art.

Autonomy

The heart of La Jolla is best explored on foot, especially Girard Avenue, mentioned above, and the main street, Prospect Street, with the town's finest hotel, Hotel Valencia. You should also take a stroll along the coast road, the north-eastern extension of Prospect Street, beginning at the junction of Park Row and Prospect Place. You will pass the famous La Jolla Cove (small bay) and Ellen Browning Scripps Park, some 100 ft/30 m below Prospect Street, with shallow steps leading down to it.

Another somewhat longer walk will take you to the scientific institutes and past many modern houses. The following are the most important places to look out for:

A tour of the town

The University of California at San Diego came into being in the year 1912. This branch of the central Californian university, with some 14,000 students, has made a name for itself in a number of spheres, especially in that of medicine. The campus is well worth a visit, mainly because of the interesting architecture of some of the newer buildings, such as the library. There are many modern sculptures to be seen on the campus. (Address: La Jolla Village Drive and North Torrey Pines Road, not far from the US 5; guided tours: tel. (619) 534-4831.)

University of California

The Scripps Aquarium belongs to the Institute of Oceanography founded in 1903 and an integral part of the University of California since 1912. This oldest and biggest American marine institute employs a staff of 1000 scientists and other personnel. Its library is one of the most important of its kind. The aquarium, which has 300,000 visitors every year, portrays marine life in the coastal waters. Progress made in oceanography is displayed in 22 tanks. (Address: 8602, La Jolla Shores Drive; tel. (619) 534-6933; open: daily 9 a.m.–5 p.m.)

Scripps Aquarium

The Salk Institute lies north of the university campus, on a canyon overlooking the Pacific. It was founded in 1960 by Dr Jonas Salk, the discoverer of the polio vaccine, and is devoted exclusively to bio-medical research. The 500 people who work there include four Nobel Prizewinners who are aiming at a better understanding of cancer illnessess, birth defects, alcoholism and brain functions. The building, designed by the well-known architect Louis Kahn, must be one of the most unconventional in La Jolla. (Address: 10010 North Torrey Pines Road, on Torrey Pines Scenic Drive; visits to the institute: tel. (619) 453-4100.)

Salk Institute

On the boundary between La Jolla and Del Mar you will find Torrey Pines State Park, where one of the rarest species of pine in the world grows on the rocky subsoil of the cliffs and canyons by the Pacific. Apart from La Jolla, the Torrey pine (pinus torreyana) thrives only on the island of Santa Rosa,

Torrey Pines State Park

Old Town, San Diego – Casa de Estudillo

30 miles/50 km south-west of Santa Barbara (see entry). It was identified as long ago as 1850 and bears the name of a famous contemporary American botanist.

The park covers almost 1000 acres/400 hectares of land: canyons, mesas (plateaux), many footpaths and a sandy beach almost 3 miles/5 km long. Here you can also watch sail-planes and glider. (Information: tel. (619) 755-2063.)

Museum of Contemporary Art

Originally built as a villa for Ellen Browning Scripps, who contributed much to La Jolla's development, the Museum of Contemporary Art was first changed into a centre for local artists in 1941, and then converted into a museum. Its extensive collections include southern Californian works of art, minimalist, pop-art, installations and other forms of modern art; there is also a department dedicated to the development of the modern chair. Temporary exhibitions are also arranged. (Address: 7000 Prospect Street; tel. (619) 454-3541 or (619) 454-0267; open: Tue.–Fri. 10 a.m.–5 p.m., Sat. and Sun. 12.30 p.m.–5 p.m.)

Mission Bay

Location and general

The Mission Bay section of the town lies north-west of Downtown and south of La Jolla. With its many small coves Mission Bay, covering some 4500 acres/1800 hectares, is a convenient and beautiful holiday resort for the citizens of San Diego. Every conceivable kind of water sport is practised here and thanks to the constantly warm climate can be enjoyed practically all the year round. The beaches are almost 27 miles/43 km long; there is also a yacht club, a marina from which you can take steamer trips round the bay, half a dozen luxury hotels for permanent guests, as well as several golf-courses, one of which is even floodlit at night.

If you drive west along the US 5 as far as the exit to East Mission Bay Drive

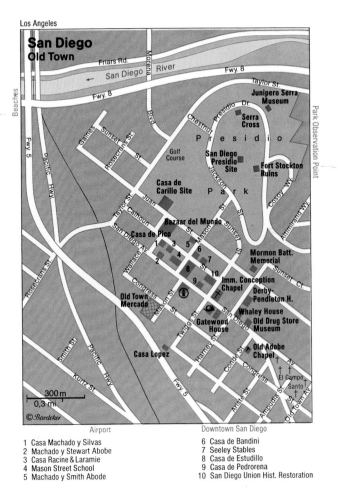

Los Angeles

San Diego
Old Town

1 Casa Machado y Silvas
2 Machado y Stewart Abobe
3 Casa Racine & Laramie
4 Mason Street School
5 Machado y Smith Abode

6 Casa de Bandini
7 Seeley Stables
8 Casa de Estudillo
9 Casa de Pedrorena
10 San Diego Union Hist. Restoration

you will find an information counter where you can get all the details you require: tel. 276-8200.

Mission San Diego de Alcala

See Mission Stations

Old Town

To get to San Diego's Old Town take the US 5 and the Old Town Avenue exit, or the US 8 and the Morena Boulevard exit.
The Old Town San Diego State Historic Park, the very core of the old part of town, takes the visitor through the town's Mexican and early American

State Historic Park

Whaley House, the oldest brick house in California

history. It was probably founded in 1820 by demobilised Mexican soldiers who had done their military service at the Presidio or in the fort on Presidio Hill (both part of the old town today). Many of the historic buildings, including numerous adobe houses, have been repaired in recent years; the Historic Park was not laid out until 1868. The houses, which are now open to visitors, date from 1827 to 1869, roughly comparable as regards building date with the houses in El Pueblo de Los Angeles State Historic Park (see entry for Los Angeles).

In the Old Town State Historic Park you will find:

Casa de Estudillo (1829)

This fairly large restored adobe dwelling, Casa de Estudillo, today houses Spanish-Mexican and early American relics and furniture. (Address: 2645 San Diego Avenue; tel. (619) 237-6770; open: daily 10 a.m.–5 p.m.)

Pendleton House (1854)

Pendleton House, situated behind Whaley House, is fitted out with authentic furniture from the period at which it was built. (Open: Wed.–Sun. 10 a.m.–4.30 p.m.)

San Diego Union Museum (1868)

The "San Diego Union" newspaper first saw the light of day in this house. The interior still retains the appearance of a newspaper office of more than 100 years ago. (Address: 2626 San Diego Avenue; tel. 297-2119; open: Tue.–Sun. 10 a.m.–5 p.m.; admission free.)

Seeley Stables (1869)

The Seeley Stables originally served the American mail; today you can see various horse-drawn wagons, including the covered wagons in which the first settlers came to California. (Address: 2648 Calhoun Street; tel. (619) 237-6770; open daily, 10 a.m.–5 p.m.)

Casa de Lopez (1834)

Casa de Lopez, once a candle-maker's workshop, is today a museum with candles from all over the world. (Address: 3890 Twiggs Street; admission free.)

Cabrillo National Monument – lighthouse

Junipero Serra Museum stands on the site of the first mission to be built in Alta California. Today it contains artefacts connected with the mission's history and the origin of San Diego. (Address: 2727 Presidio Drive; tel. (619) 297-3258; open: Mon.–Sat. 9 a.m.–4.45 p.m., Sun. noon–4.45 p.m.)

Junipero Serra Museum

Whaley House, the oldest brick-built house in southern California, was once a private residence, then the home of a theatrical troupe, and the court-house for San Diego County until 1871. It has been restored to its original condition and equipped with furniture from the middle of the last century. A reproduction of the old village apothecary's shop has been built in the grounds. (Address: 2482 San Diego Avenue; tel. 298-2482; open: Wed.–Sun. 10 a.m.–4.30 p.m.; closed Nov. 14th–Dec. 14th.)

Whaley House (1856)

Adjoining the plaza, the hub of community life in old Pueblo and now at weekends the scene of frequent dances and concerts, stands the modern Bazaar de Mundo with many shops and restaurants in an arcade with an interior courtyard. Here there is music and dancing. (Tel. (619) 296-3161.)

Bazaar del Mundo

There are guided tours every day at 2 p.m.; for information tel. (619) 237-6770. Maps, etc. are available from the Old Town Chamber of Commerce, tel. (619) 291-4903.

Guided tours through the Old Town

Point Loma

On this peninsula south of Downtown San Diego, stretching from San Diego Bay to the Pacific Ocean, will be found the Cabrillo National Monument, erected to commemorate the discovery of California by the Portuguese seafarer Juan Rodriguez Cabrillo in September 1542, only three months before he died.
Linked to the peninsula by causeways are Shelter Island and Harbor Island, from where you get a fine view of the skyscrapers of San Diego.

Location and general

On Point Loma peninsula there is also a station for naval exercises, as well as one of the country's largest naval cemeteries (Rosecrans National Cemetery).

The best way to get to the Cabrillo National Monument–situated right at the end of Point Loma, 10 miles/16 km from San Diego – is to go via North Harbor to Rosecrans Street, then turn into Cannon Street, Catalina Boulevard and Cabrillo Memorial Drive.

When visibility is good, the National Monument provides a panoramic view as far as La Jolla to the north, the Pacific to the west, Mexico to the south and San Diego County to the east. In the months of December, January and February it is also a good point from which to observe the whales on their migration south.

A brief visit to the well-equipped Visitor Center with its little museum will provide by means of brochures and a slide-show information about the origins of the National Monument and the history of the discovery of California. Not far away stands the Cabrillo Monument, erected by a compatriot of Cabrillo, the Portuguese Alvaro de Bree.

A short walk takes you to the old lighthouse which was in use from 1855 to 1891. It was then replaced by a new lighthouse with stronger lights, which still serves shipping to this day. The old lighthouse has meanwhile been restored. Numerous footpaths lead down to the shore of the peninsula. On the Bayside Trail and Sylvester Road you will find a strange mixture of desert and coastal vegetation. All the animals and plants are protected species.

The Cabrillo National Monument is open daily 9 a.m.–5.15 p.m.; in the summer months 9 a.m.–7.45 p.m.; tel. (619) 557-5450.

*San Diego Maritime Museum

The San Diego Maritime Museum, established in 1948, consists of three ships which have been restored to their original condition and are lying alongside Harbor Drive, between Ash and Laurel Streets.

The three-masted "Star of India" is a sailing ship which was built in the Isle of Man in 1863 and sailed round the world several times. It plied between England and New Zealand as a passenger and cargo ship, and often had on board as many as 400 British passengers who were emigrating to New Zealand. From 1901 to 1923 it was in service for America on the Alaska route before coming to San Diego. The ship, which is still seaworthy, last went to sea on the occasion of the celebrations to mark the bi-centenary of American Independence on July 4th 1976.

The others are the ferry-ship "Berkeley", built in 1898 and which plied between San Francisco and Oakland, and the luxurious 1904 motor-yacht "Medea", which still occasionally makes trips round the bay.

The San Diego Maritime Museum in open daily 9 a.m.–8 p.m.; tel. (619) 234-9153.

*Seaport Village

Seaport Village leisure resort is, like that in San Pedro, Los Angeles (see entry), a shopping and restaurant centre in the form of a large village. On a 12½ acre/5 hectare site close by San Diego bay 28 houses have been built, now occupied by 50 shops and several restaurants. (Address: 849 West Harbor Drive; tel. (619) 235-4013.)

The built-up area as well as the park section of Seaport Village are constantly being extended; for example a 2½ acre/1 hectare pleasure and shopping village to be known as "Seaport Village – A Water Odyssey".

◀ *San Diego Maritime Museum – luxury yacht "Medea"*

San Diego Sea World: dolphins performing . . .

. . . and enjoying a well-earned rest!

There is also to be the "Night Court" with jazz and blues clubs, restaurants and piano-bar in the courtyard of a former police station, built in the mission style. (Open: daily 9 a.m. to sunset; admission charge; information: tel. (619) 226-3901.)

**Sea World

Near Mission Bay will be found a counterpart to Disneyland (see entry Anaheim), the Sea World Pleasure Park (1720 South Shores Road). From San Diego take the US 5 (exit for Sea World Drive). Penguins in their hundreds, dolphins, sea-lions, otters and whales have been trained here to show off their newly-learned skills in more than 30 different performances. Water fantasies, hydrofoil boat trips, cable railways and much more are features of this maritime leisure park. There are similar parks in Orlando (Florida), San Antonio (Texas), Aurora (Illinois). Until they were sold at the beginning of 1989 they represented the most profitable branch of the Harcourt Brace Iovanovich publishing firm. Since two of the four-toothed whales (orcinus orva) seriously injured two of their trainers in 1987 the whale programme has been somewhat curtailed.

Excursions from San Diego

There are plenty of tours available from San Diego, including some to Tijuana (see entry) and other places in Mexico by bus or boat, into the Anza Borrego Desert (see entry), along the 52 mile/84 km "Scenic Drive" from within San Diego to as far as La Jolla, and trips round the harbour. The following are some of the companies which offer such trips:
Big T's Desert Tours, 4605 32nd Street; tel. 280-3819
El Paseo Tours, Chula Vista, CA; tel. 585-7495
Ensenada Express, B Street Pier; tel. 232-2109
Five Star Tours, Amtrak Station; tel. 232-5049
San Diego Harbor Excursions, 1050 N. Harbor Drive; tel. 234-4111
San Diego Mini Tours; tel. 234-9044

Note

San Francisco

H 1

San Francisco County
Altitude: 62 ft/19 m
Population: 705,000

San Francisco is the third largest city – after Los Angeles and San Diego – in the state of California, and lies at the north end of a hilly peninsula, 30 miles/48 km long and 6 miles/10 km wide, which separates the Pacific Ocean from San Francisco Bay, one of the world's best natural harbours. On its north side it is bounded by the Golden Gate, the 1-mile/1½-km-wide and 380-ft/116-m-deep entrance into San Francisco Bay. Artificial earth-banks, especially on the east side of the peninsula, have extended the area of the city.

**Location and origin

The metropolitan area of the city incorporates the surrounding counties of Marin (north), San Mateo (south), Alameda and Contra Costa (both east).

Conurbation: see separate plan on map at end of book

The city has a central administration which is headed by a Mayor who comes up for selection every four years.
The Mayor is aided by a Chief Executive Administrator, the counterpart, albeit with lesser powers, of the City Managers found in many other American cities. The Board of Supervisors, the equivalent of a single chamber for local government, consists of eleven elected members.
The city's current constitution dates from 1931 but has been subject to over 400 amendments which makes it some 110,000 words long.

Administration

A particular feature of San Francisco are the mists which form along the coast in summer; the heat from the hinterland then forces them through the Golden Gate into the bay. Warm outer garments are advisable, especially in the afternoons when a strong sea-wind blows.

Climate

Its situation on a tectonically unstable section of the earth's crust around the Pacific Ocean (the San Andreas fault) means that, after the serious earthquakes of 1906 and 1989, there is always the possibility of further seismic movements (often followed by "microquakes"). The three penultimate earthquakes occurred on August 8th 1989 (5.2, 4.2 and 4.5 on the Richter Scale), and were felt as far away as San Luis Obispo to the south (222 miles/358 km) and Sonoma to the north (60 miles/96 km). The last microquakes occurred after the serious earthquake of October 1989.

San Francisco is one of the most popular destinations in the United States, indeed in the whole world, because of its unique rural position, its cosmopolitan atmosphere and endearing reminders of days gone by, including the cable-cars along the ultra-steep streets. Unconventional modern high-rise buildings such as the pyramid-shaped Transamerica Building and the skyscraper of the Bank of America, the biggest bank in the United States, give the city a new and unfamiliar silhouette.

Tourism

Population

The population of San Francisco originally grew very slowly and in 1846, which saw the end of Mexican rule, amounted to barely a thousand. This dropped to a few hundred in the years that followed – in 1847 the count was actually 459.

Development

The 1849 Gold Rush sparked off a population explosion; only one year later the total was estimated at 25,000. After reaching 342,000 in 1900 the figure fell back after the 1906 earthquake, to 175,000. The numbers peaked at 775,000 in 1950, then fell to 679,000 in 1980 as a result of people moving to the surrounding rural areas. The subsequent upward trend – 714,000 were counted in 1985 – is due mainly to the influx of coloured people, as the number of Whites plummeted from 700,000 in 1950 to less than 450,000.

San Francisco has an Asiatic population whose share of the total is larger than in any other American city: 85,000 Chinese, 30,000 Filipinos, 14,000 Japanese, as well as Koreans, Vietnamese, Samoans, Malays and others.

Ethnic variety

Apart from the many Asians in their number, the people of San Francisco hail from a host of different ethnic backgrounds. When figures on the national origins of San Franciscans were compiled more than ten years ago it emerged that 42% of the city's children did not speak English in their homes: 9% spoke Spanish at home, 4.2% Italian, 3.7% German and 1.8% French. The number of Spanish-speaking families is likely to have increased considerably since then.

Gays form one of San Francisco's most prominent and militant minorities. They are well organised and also politically very active. When in 1978 the mayor of the time and the city's first homosexual Supervisor were gunned down by a disgruntled ex-colleague who then got off with a relatively light sentence, the city erupted in days of civil clashes. The new Mayor, Dianne Feinstein, was obliged to nominate another gay to take the murdered Supervisor's place. A public enquiry at the end of 1984 established that 40% of all single men are homosexual. Since the immune-deficient illness Aids has taken a hold the homosexual scene has fundamentally changed. The climate has become more and more governed by a fear of infection, with political demands for more money to fight the disease, and to avoid discrimination against the ill and infected. In 1987 about 70% of San Francisco's gays were infected.

Gays

◀ *View of San Francisco – in foreground the yacht harbour and Pier 39*

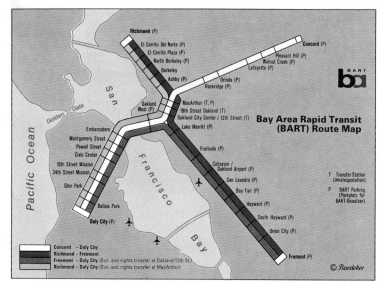

Richmond (P)
El Cerrito Del Norte (P)
El Cerrito Plaza (P)
North Berkeley (P)
Berkeley
Ashby (P)
Concord (P)
Pleasant Hill (P)
Walnut Creek (P)
Lafayette (P)
Orinda (P)
Rockridge (P)
Oakland West (P)
MacArthur (T, P)
19th Street Oakland (T)
Oakland City Center / 12th Street (T)
Lake Merritt (P)
San Francisco Bay
Golden Gate
Embarcadero
Montgomery Street
Powell Street
Civic Center
16th Street Mission
24th Street Mission
Glen Park
Balboa Park
Daly City (P)
Fruitvale (P)
Coliseum / Oakland Airport (P)
San Leandro (P)
Bay Fair (P)
Hayward (P)
South Hayward (P)
Union City (P)
Fremont (P)
Pacific Ocean

Bay Area Rapid Transit (BART) Route Map

T   Transfer Station (Umsteigestation)
P   BART Parking (Parkplatz für BART-Benutzer)

Concord – Daly City
Richmond – Freemont
Freemont – Daly City (Sun. and nights transfer at Oakland/12th St.)
Richmond – Daly City (Sun. and nights transfer at MacArthur)

© Baedeker

Religion	In the city of multifarious ethnic backgrounds there are churches for almost all the religions practised in the USA (including two Russian Orthodox cathedrals). The largest Lutheran congregation is that of St Mark's near St Mary's Cathedral. The city is also the seat of a Catholic Archbishop and of the Episcopalian Bishop for the whole of Northern California.

In the city of multifarious ethnic backgrounds there are churches for almost all the religions practised in the USA (including two Russian Orthodox cathedrals). The largest Lutheran congregation is that of St Mark's near St Mary's Cathedral. The city is also the seat of a Catholic Archbishop and of the Episcopalian Bishop for the whole of Northern California.

The city has long been a hotbed for religious sects, of which the most famous was the People's Temple under Jim Jones. In the early 1970s Zen Buddhism gained its first foothold in the States in San Francisco, mainly through the books of Alan Watts, a former Anglican priest.

Transport

Port

San Francisco's natural harbour, once America's principal port for trade with the Far East, has in recent years lost much of its importance.

Nowadays many of the 46 piers stand empty or out of commission. Container traffic has drastically declined, having been taken over as long ago as 1969 by Oakland on the opposite side of the bay. The San Francisco fishing industry has also declined considerably.

Airport

The airport, 14 miles/23 km south of the city, was opened in 1927 as Mills Field which, with expansion, changed its name to San Francisco Airport and finally to San Francisco International Airport. Today it is one of the largest in the United States and serves over 28 airlines. There is another large airport at Oakland on the east side of San Francisco Bay.

Railways

Like many American cities, rail transport in San Francisco has become almost insignificant, with only one station handling the commuter traffic of the Southern Pacific Railroad. The Amtrak trains that run along the Pacific Coast leave from Oakland and passengers get there by shuttle bus from the Transbay Transit Terminal.

A cable car – the first means of public transport

San Francisco is served by a large number of local and long-distance bus lines and has two main bus stations, the Greyhound Terminal and the Transbay Transit Terminal.

Bus services

The bus network serving virtually every part of town is San Francisco's most important form of public transportation. There are 57 routes altogether and the fixed fare includes transfers between the different forms of transportation in the Municipal Railway Company (MUNI) system, which also covers the streetcars (trams) and cable cars.

MUNI

San Francisco does not have an underground system as such, but in 1981 the four streetcar lines that ran along Market Street were moved underground. In 1972 the first line of the Bay Area Rapid Transit (BART) of California was opened, connecting the centre of San Francisco with the surrounding counties.
There are 31 stations on the 75 mile/120 km network, eight of them in San Francisco itself. The 3 mile/5.5 km stretch that runs under the waters of the bay between San Francisco and Oakland is the longest of its kind in the world.

Except for New Orleans and Sacramento, the capital of California, San Francisco is the only city in the USA to have retained its trams, or streetcars as they are called in the States. It has five streetcar lines, part of them underground, as well as three cable car lines, a service that dates back over 100 years.

Streetcars, Cable Cars

The ferries that were needed to cross the bay before the bridges were built have by now almost all gone out of business, but passenger ferries still operate to the bay communities of Sausalito and Larkspur as well as to Tiburon (from Ferry Building) and to Angel Island and Alcatraz (from Fisherman's Wharf).

Ferries

University of San Francisco, with the Church of St Ignatius

Victorian houses, a contrast to the skyscrapers of San Francisco

From San Francisco Highway 101 is the fastest route to Southern California and the other main roads are Interstate 180 and State Highway 1 along the coast.

Going northwards, Highway 101 crosses the Golden Gate Bridge to Northern California, the north-west of the United States, and Canada, with Coastal Highway 1 branching off to follow the Pacific coast.

Interstate Highway 80 runs east over the San Francisco-Oakland Bay Bridge to State Highway 17 and Interstate 680 to the south; State Highway 24 and Interstate Highway 680 also lead north and Interstate 580 proceeds east.

Culture

Until 1960 San Francisco was the undisputed cultural centre of California but has since had to share this distinction with Los Angeles, which is five times its size.

Today San Francisco has four large theatres and a number of "little" theatres. It has its own opera company, the San Francisco Ballet (America's oldest ballet company), a symphony orchestra and some first-class art museums – the M. H. de Young Memorial Museum, the Asian Art Museum, the San Francisco Museum of Modern Art and the Palace of the Legion of Honor, as well as the important natural science museum of the California Academy of Sciences and others.

At the end of March and in early April each year a Film Festival is held in the Palace of Arts and Science and the Castro Theater. Started in 1927, it was the first of its kind to be held in America.

Three large universities – the Catholic University of San Francisco founded in 1855 (7000 students), the state University of California in Berkeley (30,000 students) and Stanford University (12,000 students) in Palo Alto – make San Francisco an important academic and research centre. The University of California Medical Center in San Francisco, incorporating the University Hospital, is also of considerable importance. Other important colleges are the San Francisco State University, the Hastings College of Law, Lincoln University and the San Francisco Art Institute.

Architecture

San Francisco's architectural face is characterized by the skyscrapers in the city and the mainly 19th c. wooden houses in the residential quarters which are described as Victorian houses because of the period when they were built.

Although the finest of the houses built between 1879 and 1906, especially those on Nob Hill and in Van Ness Avenue, were destroyed in the earthquake, there are still over 13,000 such houses in the Bernal Heights, Duboce Triangle, Eureka, Glen Park, Haight-Ashbury, Mission District, Noe Valley, Potrero Hill and Western Addition areas of the city.

Between 1870 and 1880 many houses with blind windows were built in the Italian style, so called because much of the detail was based on Roman ornamentation.

In the 1880s the vertical style known as the San Francisco Stick was in vogue; it was so called to distinguish it from the simple "stick" buildings along the East Coast and in the Middle West. The architecture emphasises the vertical structure, with the outside decoration resembling a bundle of sticks.

In the 1890s the Queen Anne style was developed. These were expensive, mainly detached houses adorned with towers and cone-shaped caps, high gables and massed-produced ornaments. All these houses were built with

Old and new buildings of the Bank of California

redwood which was abundant around San Francisco, and which is cheap, weather-resistant and resists fire and termites

Cast-iron houses

San Francisco does not have many so-called cast-iron houses, the distinguishing features of which are the stanchions on the outside as well as the inside. The best known is the 1907 Columbus Tower, the green colour of which makes it stand out against the surrounding low buildings. Because of the contrasting styles, people like to photograph it with the Transamerica Pyramid in the background.

Skyscrapers

San Francisco's ten tallest buildings are all to be found in the financial quarter. No skyscrapers may now be built outside that area of the city, and it is questionable whether council planning consent will in future be granted even in the financial quarter for a building taller than Transamerica Pyramid. The three tallest building are:
Transamerica Pyramid, 600 Montgomery Square (860 ft/260 m)
Bank of America, 555 California Street (765 ft/232 m)
California Center, 345 California Street (715 ft/217 m)

Economy

Banks

Unlike Los Angeles, with its oil industry and high industrialisation, and other parts of Southern California, San Francisco has never been in the forefront of industrial cities.
It owes its importance much more to services and tourism. Foremost among its service industries are its banks, which include America's biggest bank, the Bank of America, as well as the Bank of California, the Wells Fargo Bank and the Crocker Bank.

The city is also noted for its insurance companies, to the largest of which it owes its latest landmark, the Transamerica Pyramid. In the Pacific Stock Exchange San Francisco also has the most important trading exchange in the American West.

Its many hotels and restaurants are of incalculable value to the city's economy. The city is such a magnet that every year it attracts five times as many visitors as the resident population, with almost a third of these three million visitors coming to San Francisco for conventions.

Industry centred on the port, once the most important sector of San Francisco's economy, has been declining for many years and will probably never recover its earlier importance – the same is true of the city's fisheries and canneries.
Many industrial corporations have their headquarters in San Francisco but their factories in other parts of California; chief among these is Crown Zellerbach.

History of the city

Juan Rodriguez Cabrillo sails into the waters of what is now known as San Diego Bay and six weeks later sights in San Francisco Bay and Farallon Islands which have been part of the city since 1872.

Sir Francis Drake is the first European to land on the coast of Northern California, probably on the opposite side of the bay from San Francisco in what is now Marin County. He names the land "Nova Albion" and claims it in the name of Queen Elizabeth I.

Sebastian Rodriguez Cermenho lands in a bay on the Marin coast which he calls La Bahia de San Francisco (now Drake's Bay). This is the first use of the name which was given to the city.

The present San Francisco Bay is discovered by Gaspar de Portola and his troops approaching from the landward side. Portola, later to be the first Governor of Spanish California, is leading a "Holy Expedition" northwards from Sonora in Mexico in conjunction with Father Junipero Serra, founder of the mission.

A group of 250 Spanish soldiers and civilians, led by Juan Bautista de Anza, decide on the site for the San Francisco Presidio.
Consecration of the first "Mission Dolores", originally San Francisco de Assisi.

President Andrew Jackson offers the Mexicans, who had cast off Spanish rule in 1821, 500,000 dollars for the bay of San Francisco. In the same year William Richardson, an English whaling captain (married to a Mexican, and a convert to Catholicism) founds the village of Pueblo Yerba Buena.

Yerba Buena now numbers some 350 souls – Americans, Indians, Dutch and Spanish.

On July 9th Yerba Buena becomes part of the United States when 70 marines from the US frigate "Portsmouth" land there and hoist the Stars and Stripes in the village square. Three weeks later a ship arrives bringing 238 Mormons in search of their promised Zion; they find themselves back in a different part of the United States, the country from which they were trying to flee.

Yerba Buena's first American "alcade" or mayor, Lieutenant Washington A. Bartlett, announces on January 30th that henceforth the town is to be

San Francisco in 1852 (contemporary engraving)

called San Francisco. At this time it has a resident population (Americans, Indians, Dutch and Spanish), excluding military and naval personnel, of 459.

1848   While building a windmill for John Augustus Sutter, James Marshall discovers gold on January 24th at Coloma in the foothills of the Sierra Nevada. His discovery sets the seal on the future of San Francisco. When news reaches the outside world, prospectors set out in their thousands for San Francisco which serves as the setting-off point for the gold fields on the Sacramento River.

1850   San Francisco's population has grown to 25,000 and it becomes a city. A few months later California becomes the 31st State of the Union.

1862   Opening of the telegraph line direct to New York.

1865   Following smaller earth tremors, San Francisco suffers its first major earthquake on October 9th, followed by a second quake on October 23rd which causes considerable damage to the city.

1869   The Central Pacific Railroad completes the building of the railroad from the East Coast to San Francisco, an event that is enthusiastically celebrated in the city.

1870   The City Government decides to build the Golden Gate Park.

1873   On August 2nd the cable-car, Andrew Hallidie's brainchild, makes its first trip over the 100-yard-stretch of Clay Street between Kearny and Jones Streets.

1875   Opening of the Pacific Stock Exchange.

1876   The Southern Pacific Railroad completes construction of the line from San Francisco to Los Angeles.

1877   July sees the first serious rioting against the Chinese. A Citizen's Safety Committee restores law and order.

1887   February 5th goes down in history because it was the only day on which snow covered the whole of San Francisco.

Fifteen new banks are opened within a month; the following year sees the founding of the Bank of America, now the USA's biggest bank.	1903
A serious earthquake on April 18th destroys four-fifths of the city. Even worse than the force of the earthquake (8.25 on the Richter Scale) is the raging fire which follows and which the fire-fighters cannot quell because the water-mains burst. Some 28,000 houses are destroyed and 500 people killed. During the rapid reconstruction many buildings are designed in the neo-classical style, influenced by the Chicago Exhibition of 1893.	1906
A plague epidemic is successfully brought under control after several months.	1907
James Rolph begins 19 years in office, thereby becoming the city's longest-serving Mayor. The city's first streetcar line commences operations in Geary Street.	1912
The great Panama-Pacific International Exposition is opened in Lincoln Park a few months after the first ship to take the new route through the Panama Canal docks in San Francisco. Dedication of the present City Hall.	1915
Opening of the M. H. de Young Memorial Museum in Golden Gate Park.	1921
The island of Alcatraz off San Francisco becomes a Federal Penitentiary.	1933
A general strike paralyses San Francisco for weeks.	1934
November 12th: The San Francisco-Oakland Bay Bridge is opened to traffic.	1936
May 27th: Dedication of the Golden Gate Bridge constructed by Joseph B. Strauss.	1937
April 24th: Opening of the inaugural assembly of UNO in the War Memorial Opera House, followed by the signing there two months later of the original charter.	1945
September 18th: Yoshida, the Japanese Prime Minister, signs the Treaty marking the ending of hostilities between Japan and the USA in the War Memorial Opera House.	1951
March 23rd: The penitentiary on Alcatraz is closed down. A year later the island is occupied by Sioux Indians who lay claim to Alcatraz, but they are forced out in 1971.	1963
April 15th: One of the first big peace marches protesting against the Vietnam War takes place in Market Street. Others follow at regular intervals.	1967
Mayor George Moscone and Harvey Milk, one of the eleven Supervisors, are gunned down in City Hall by an ex-colleague who had been fired by Milk and whose sentence to seven years in jail had resulted in protest demonstrations. A week later Dianne Feinstein, Chairman of the Board of Supervisors, is named as Moscone's successor. She is the city's first woman Mayor.	1978
Dianne Feinstein is re-elected Mayor with an overwhelming majority.	1983
After two years' closure the cable cars come back into service on June 21st.	1984

Alcatraz Island, with the marina in the foreground

1986
The Nobel Peace Prizewinner, Mother Teresa, builds a convent in San Fancisco.
At the seventh attempt the electorate votes for the restriction on building in downtown San Francisco. In future not more than 475,000 sq. ft/4.4 hectares of building can be started annually.

1987
Whereas the townscape was changed in the early eighties by several new skyscrapers, there are now more than half a dozen new hotels which have changed the appearance of the district around Union Square. Some 16% of available office space is empty; rents are falling for the first time.

1988
After ten years as Mayor, Dianne Feinstein is replaced in office by Art Agnos.
When digging foundations for a new bank building at the corner of Kearny and Sacramento Streets artefacts are discovered which point to Chinese having settled in San Francisco prior to 1850.

1989
For reasons of economy, the Pentagon decides to close the Presidio. This infuriates the citizens and results in protests.
On October 17th at 5.04 p.m. (during the rush-hour) San Francisco is struck by the worst earthquake (6.9 points on the Richter Scale) since that of 1906. The Marina quarter is the worst affected: a lot of houses are set on fire as the result of gas leaking from burst mains. A 1¼ mile/2 km section of the San Francisco-Oakland Bay Bridge collapses, burying numerous cars.

1990
June: Serious fires, some started deliberately, cause widespread devastation in southern California.

San Francisco from A to Z

Alcatraz Island

The former penitentiary of Alcatraz, located 1½ miles/2.4 km north-east in San Francisco Bay, is one of the most fascinating places to visit. The first Spaniard to land there, Ayala, named it Isla de los Alcatraces ("Island of the Pelicans"), because he found vast numbers of these birds nesting on the sandstone island.

General

As this rocky island, covering an area of some 12 acres/5 hectares and rising to a height of 135 ft/41 m, has no springs, it remained uninhabited for years. In 1853, during the Californian gold-rush when the number of ships visiting the foggy bay increased considerably, a lighthouse was erected. Soon afterwards the island was fortified and became a military prison during the Civil War (1861–1865). From 1933 to 1963 it became the most infamous and feared of all federal prisons in the USA. Even the most incorrigible jail-breakers hardly ever succeeded in escaping.
In the course of its 30-year existence the penitentiary received a total of 1576 convicts. There were never more than 250 at any one time, even though there were 450 cells measuring about 10 x 4 ft/3 x 1.5 m. At times the number of guards, etc. was greater than that of the convicts.
After the prison was closed the island was virtually forgotten for six years until it was taken over by Indians who squatted there for seven years. Although the island has been open to visitors since 1973 only emergency repairs have been made to the run-down buildings.

History

Ship departures: Pier 43 (Fisherman's Wharf). It is necessary to book in advance; tel. (415) 546-2810. Ferry services: in summer daily 9 a.m.–5 p.m. autumn to spring daily 9 a.m.–3 p.m., with 1½ hour guided tours.
As the island is frequently shrouded in mist and the wind is almost always strong, visitors are recommended to wear warm clothes.

Tips

The Anchorage

Situated in Leavenworth Street, this shopping and leisure centre is one of San Francisco's latest attractions. There are nearly 50 shops and restaurants on various levels, as well as an hotel in a delightful architectural setting.
The centre of the complex is an inner courtyard, where buskers from all parts of the city perform in a mini-amphitheatre.

Angel Island State Park

Angel Island lies north of the city in San Francisco Bay. It has an area of 750 acres/300 hectares. In the course of the last hundred years it has been used as a quarantine station for Asian immigrants and also as a coastguard station, becoming a prisoner-of-war camp and anti-aircraft site during the Second World War. The uninhabited island is now a municipal park where some 200 red deer are allowed to roam free.

General

Motor vehicles are banned from the island but it is a favourite spot for excursions from the city as there are pleasant cycle tracks and paths for pedestrians as well as large picnic sites.
Moorings: Pier 43½ (Fisherman's Wharf). Ferry services: in summer daily; autumn to spring Fri.–Sun. to Ayala Cove.

Note

Bank of America

The marble skyscraper belonging to the Bank of America, between Pine Street and California Street, is 52 storeys high and rises 778 ft/237 m. Built

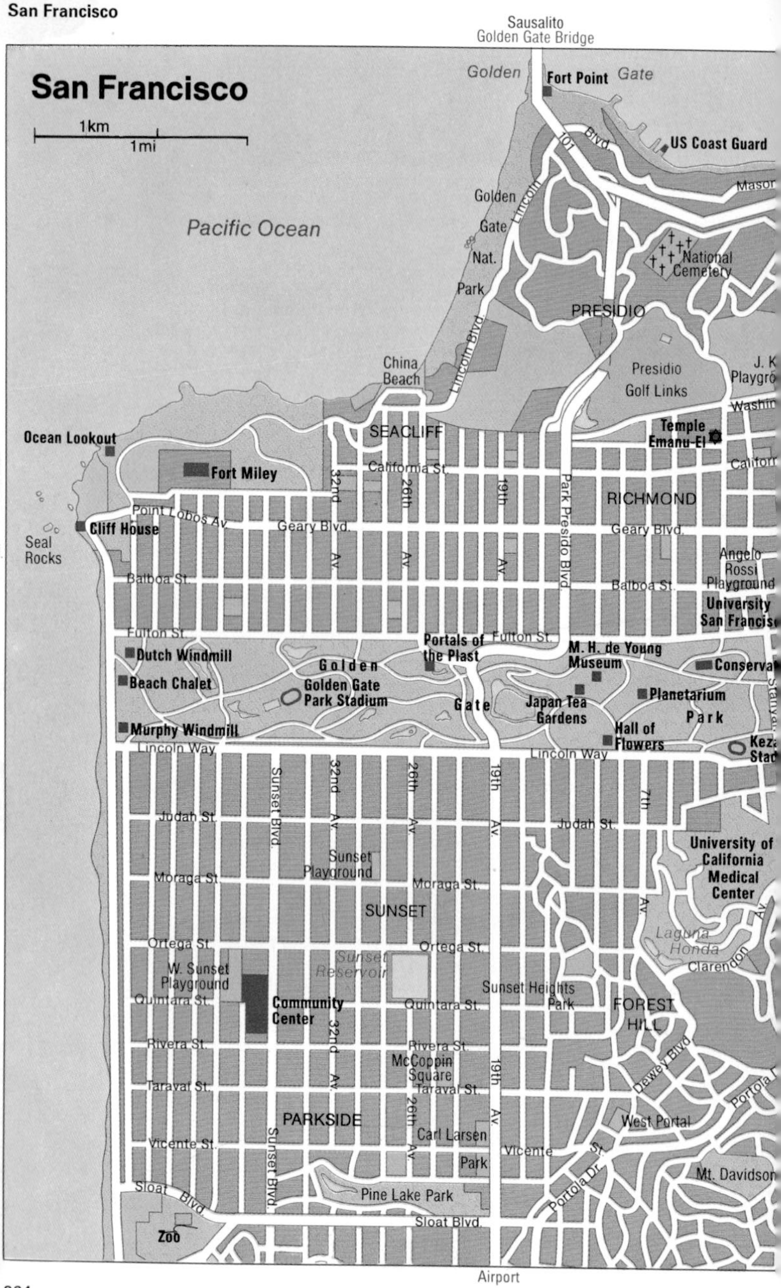

San Francisco

1km
1mi

Sausalito
Golden Gate Bridge

Golden   Fort Point   Gate

US Coast Guard

Mason

Pacific Ocean

Golden
Gate
Nat.
Park

PRESIDIO

National
Cemetery

China
Beach

Presidio
Golf Links

J. K.
Playgro

Washin

SEACLIFF

Ocean Lookout

Temple
Emanu-El

Fort Miley

California St.

Cliff House

Point Lobos Av

Geary Blvd.

RICHMOND

Geary Blvd.

Seal
Rocks

Balboa St.

Balboa St.

Angelo
Rossi
Playground

University
San Francisc

Fulton St.

Fulton St.

Portals of
the Plast

M. H. de Young
Museum

Conserva

Dutch Windmill

Golden

Beach Chalet

Golden Gate
Park Stadium

Gate

Japan Tea
Gardens

Planetarium

Park

Murphy Windmill

Hall of
Flowers

Kez
Stad

Lincoln Way

Lincoln Way

Judah St.

Judah St.

Sunset Blvd

Sunset
Playground

University of
California
Medical
Center

Moraga St.

Moraga St.

SUNSET

Laguna
Honda

Ortega St.

W. Sunset
Playground

Sunset
Reservoir

Ortega St.

Clarendon

Quintara St.

Community
Center

Quintara St.

Sunset Heights
Park

FOREST
HILL

Rivera St.

Rivera St.

McCoppin
Square

Taraval St.

Taraval St.

Dewey Blvd

Portola

PARKSIDE

Carl Larsen
Park

Vicente St.

Vicente

West Portal

Sloat Blvd

Pine Lake Park

Mt. Davidson

Zoo

Sloat Blvd

Portola Dr

Airport

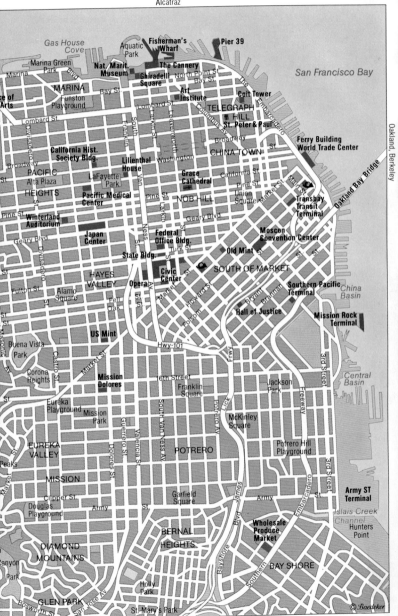

Alcatraz

Gas House Cove

Fisherman's Wharf

Aquatic Park

Pier 39

San Francisco Bay

Marina Green Park

Nat. Marit. Museum

The Cannery

North Point St

Bay St

The Embarcadero

MARINA

Ghiradelli Square

Art Institute

Coit Tower

ce of Arts

Funston Playground

Bay St.

Columbus Av.

TELEGRAPH HILL

Ferry Building World Trade Center

Lombard St.

Lombard St.

Washington

Broadway

St. Peter & Paul

Oakland, Berkeley

California Hist. Society Bldg.

Lilienthal House

CHINA TOWN

PACIFIC

Alta Plaza

LaFayette Park

Grace Cathedral

California St.

Oakland Bay Bridge

HEIGHTS

Broadway

St

Pacific Medical Center

Pine St.

Pine St.

NOB HILL

Union Square

Pine St.

Market St.

Transbay Transit Terminal

Winterland Auditorium

Pine St.

Ness

Larkin St

Geary Blvd.

Moscon Convention Center

Geary Blvd

Japan Center

Federal Office Bldg.

Turk St.

Old Mint

State Bldg.

HAYES VALLEY

Civic Center

SOUTH OF MARKET

Southern Pacific Terminal

China Basin

Alamo Square

Opera

Fell

Oak

Howard St.

Bryant

Brannan

Mission Rock Terminal

Fulton St.

St

St

St

St

Hall of Justice

Folsom

Buena Vista Park

US Mint

Hwy-101

Fwy

Central Basin

Corona Heights

Castro St

16th Street

Franklin Square

Jackson Park

3rd Street

Eureka Playground

Mission Dolores

Mission Park

South Van Ness Av

Potrero Av

Kansas St

McKinley Square

Freeway

EUREKA VALLEY

Guerrero St.

Dolores St.

Valencia St.

POTRERO

Potrero Hill Playground

3rd Street

Army ST Terminal

Peaks

MISSION

Clipper St.

Garfield Square

Army

Bayshore Blvd.

James

Islais Creek Channel

Douglas Playground

Army

St

Embarcadero

Hunters Point

DIAMOND

MOUNTAINS

BERNAL HEIGHTS

Wholesale Produce Market

Canyon Park

Holly Park

Southern

BAY SHORE

© Baedeker

GLEN PARK

Bosworth St.

San Jose Av

St. Mary's Park

in 1969, it is the headquarters of the biggest private bank in the world, with assets of about 30 billion dollars. The building was designed by two eminent firms of architects, Wurster, Bernardi & Emmons and Skidmore, Owings & Merrill, with Pietro Belluschi as consultant. The material used is reddish South Dakota granite.

In the topmost storey there is a restaurant with a magnificent view. (Table reservations: tel. (415) 433-7500.)

Bank of California

Bank building

The Bank of California (400 California Street) is the oldest bank on the West Coast. The first bank building, which was erected here in 1867 on the site occupied by the present Banking Temple, was in the Neo-Renaissance style. It was pulled down just before the earthquake of 1906. The second head office, at the corner of Sansome Street, takes the form of a granite temple with pillars on two sides.

Museum of Money of the American West

The Museum of Money of the American West in the basement is not very large but is an important source of information about the history of the American West. Here may be seen gold quartz from the time of the Gold Rush, and nuggets of gold and silver. There is also a collection of gold coins and banknotes from the second half of the 19th c.

The interesting collections of the museum also include weapons which are historically important, some of them having been used in duels by famous personalities of the past.

**Cable Cars

Cable Car Barn

This red-brick building at the corner of Washington Street and Mason Street was erected in 1887 as the control centre for the three cable car lines still in existence. From an observation gallery it is possible to see just how the cable cars work. (Open: Apr.–Oct. daily 10 a.m.–6 p.m., Nov.–Mar. daily 10 a.m.–5 p.m.; admission free.)

Museum

The little museum shows three of the first vehicles which plied in Clay Street, equipment such as gripping and braking mechanisms, cables 1½ ins/3½ cm in diameter, gas lanterns and warning-bells, photographs and models of all the types of cable car ever put into service. There is continuous screening of a film lasting a quarter of an hour about the cable cars and how they operate. (Admission free.)

History and method of operation

Inventor and manufacturer of the cable cars was Andrew Hallidie, an engineer born in London. He conceived the idea of replacing the horse trams, which found the steep streets of San Francisco difficult to negotiate safely, with a more modern transport system. Without any power of its own, the cable car is suspended with the aid of a "grip" on an endless cable housed in a trench under the street and is thus pulled up the steep slope (gradient up to 21%). When the cable cars stop or the lines cross over, the "gripman" releases the cable, clamping it on again when the car moves off. Four powerful braking systems ensure safety when going downhill (the speed of the cars, which always have right of way, is a steady 9½ m.p.h./15 km.p.h.). At the termini the "gripman" and "conductor" together – often with the help of the passengers – turn the car round on a turntable.

The first stretch was opened in 1873. By 1880 there were eight lines in operation covering a total network of 110 miles/180 km. Today only 11 miles/17 km remain. Since 1964 the system has been declared an historic monument.

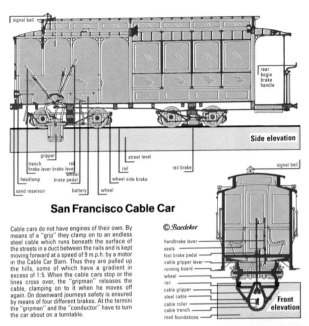

signal bell

rear bogie brake handle

Side elevation

gripper

trench brake lever
rail brake lever
street level

rail
rail brake
signal bell

headlamp
rail wheel
brake pedal
rail
wheel side brake

sand reservoir
battery
wheel

© Baedeker

handbrake lever
seats
foot brake pedal
cable gripper lever
running board
wheel
rail
cable gripper
steel cable
cable roller
cable trench
road foundations

Front elevation

San Francisco Cable Car

Cable cars do not have engines of their own. By means of a "grip" they clamp on to an endless steel cable which runs beneath the surface of the streets in a duct between the rails and is kept moving forward at a speed of 9 m.p.h. by a motor in the Cable Car Barn. Thus they are pulled up the hills, some of which have a gradient in excess of 1:5. When the cable cars stop or the lines cross over, the "gripman" releases the cable, clamping on to it when he moves off again. On downward journeys safety is ensured by means of four different brakes. At the termini the "gripman" and the "conductor" have to turn the car about on a turntable.

Cable Car Barn – the control centre

California Palace of the Legion of Honor

California Palace of the Legion of Honor

General

On the extreme north-west outskirts of San Francisco, in a most picturesque situation on a hillock in Lincoln Park, stands the Neo-Classical
museum building known as the California Palace of the Legion of Honor, a
copy of the Palais de la Légion d'Honneur in Paris. It was built in 1915 as the
French pavilion for the Panama-Pacific Exposition, and is unique among
American museums in being devoted exclusively to French art. (Open:
Wed.–Sun. 10 a.m.–4.45 p.m.)

Works of art

Thanks to numerous gifts, especially from the Spreckels family (for
example, one of the five original castings of Rodin's "The Thinker" which
stands in the Court of Honor), Mr & Mrs A. B. Huntington and Mr & Mrs H. K.
S. Williams, the museum has the most comprehensive collection of French
art outside France. After a reorganisation of the galleries in 1979–1980
there has been a permanent exhibition called "The French Legacy", in
which the most important works in the museum have been brought
together.

Achenbach
Foundation for
Graphic Arts

In the south wing is an exhibition by the Achenbach Foundation for Graphic
Arts, the largest collection of graphic works in the West of the USA, including those which Mr Moore Achenbach and his wife Sadie presented to
the city.

*The Cannery

General

On the south side of Fisherman's Wharf (see entry) an interesting complex
with fashion houses, food shops, boutiques, art galleries, restaurants and
leisure facilities has developed since 1968 on the premises, now nearly 90
years old, of the redundant Del Monte fruit canning factory. Open-air
concerts, poetry readings and other shows are put on here. Musicians and

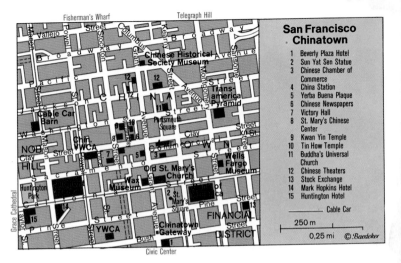

San Francisco
Chinatown

1 Beverly Plaza Hotel
2 Sun Yat Sen Statue
3 Chinese Chamber of Commerce
4 China Station
5 Yerba Buena Plaque
6 Chinese Newspapers
7 Victory Hall
8 St. Mary's Chinese Center
9 Kwan Yin Temple
10 Tin How Temple
11 Buddha's Universal Church
12 Chinese Theaters
13 Stock Exchange
14 Mark Hopkins Hotel
15 Huntington Hotel

------- Cable Car

250 m

0,25 mi   © Baedeker

actors perform in an inner courtyard among the old olive trees. In Cannery Casuals there is a Byzantine mosaic ceiling.

*Chinatown

The largest Chinese city outside Asia is in San Francisco on Grant Avenue between Bush Street and Columbus Avenue. The people are the descendants of Asians, mainly railway workers, who settled here from 1850 onwards, just after the Gold Rush. With ever-increasing immigration from Asia in the last 30 years, Chinatown has experienced its greatest period of population growth. Since 1950 the Chinese population has increased from 30,000 to 85,000.

General

Almost completely destroyed in the 1906 earthquake, Chinatown was rebuilt entirely in the Chinese style and was soon even more attractive than before the disaster. Now with its temples, theatres, workshops, small businesses, stores, antique and souvenir shops, teahouses and pharmacies with their odd nostrums, Chinatown has become one of the major sights of San Francisco.

The headquarters of the Chinese Six Companies (843 Stockton Street) is perhaps the most important institution in Chinatown. In the 19th c. it recruited Chinese labourers, the so-called "coolies" – the word means roughly "hard labour" – to build the Transcontinental Railway. Later it functioned as a sort of arbitrator to sort out quarrels between the Chinese. Today it has lost something of its former prestige but is still of considerable social significance.

Chinese Six Companies

The Fidelity Savings Bank at 845 Grant Avenue near Washington Street was built in 1971 in the most extravagant Chinese style. The roof is covered with gilded tiles.

Fidelity Savings Bank

This building was erected in 1977 on the corner of Clay Street and Stockton Street. It is the head office of the oldest Chinese friendly society in America, the Kong Chow Benevolent Association. Visiting times for the temple which bears the same name are posted on its doors.
The central post office for Chinatown is housed two floors up.

Kong Chow Benevolent Association and Temple

A cable car passes Old St Mary's Church

Temple of the Buddhist goddess Tin How

This museum devoted to the history of the Chinese in America can be found in Adler Place branching off near 1140 Grant Avenue. The collections are primarily of objects, photographs and documents relative to the role of the Chinese during the Californian Gold Rush. The museum also has important material about later periods. Every exhibit is labelled in Chinese and English. (Open: Tue.–Sat. 1 p.m.–5 p.m.; closed on public holidays.)

Chinese Historical Society Museum

Chinatown Gateway stands on the corner of Grant Avenue and California Street. It is a gate of characteristic Oriental construction, decorated with dragons and other beasts.

Chinatown Gateway

Old St Mary's Church, on the corner of Grant Avenue and California Street, is the oldest Catholic church in San Francisco. It was built in 1845 and badly damaged in the 1906 earthquake and again by a serious fire 60 years later. It has been restored in its original style. Originally a cathedral, it is now simply a parish church.

Old St Mary's Church

From Old St Mary's Church there is a view of St Mary's Square. On the square stands Rafael Bufano's statue of Dr Sun Yat-Sen, the first president of the Republic of China (January 1st 1912–February 14th 1912). Early in the 20th c. he spent several years of political asylum in San Francisco.

St Mary's Square

On the spot where Dick Young House now stands (823 Grant Street) the first human habitation of Yerba Buena, as San Francisco was originally called, was erected on June 25th 1835. In fact it was a tent which was replaced by the first timber house a few months later. A plaque has been fixed to the wall of Dick Young House to commemorate the event.

Dick Young House

Tin How Temple is on the top floor of 125 Waverly Street (between Washington and Clay Streets). It is relatively easy for non-Buddhists to visit the temple. It was founded in 1852 on another site, and bears the name of Tin How, the Buddhist Queen of Heaven. (Open: daily 9 a.m.–5 p.m. and 7 p.m.–9 p.m.)

Tin How Temple

This pagoda-like building on the corner of Grant Avenue and Washington Street is at present occupied by the Bank of Canton. It was originally built in 1909 as the Chinatown telephone office.

Bank of Canton

Buddha's Universal Church, the largest Buddhist temple in America, was built in 1961 on the corner of Washington Street and Kearny Street by members of the Pristine Orthodox Dharma, a strongly Americanised modern offshoot of Buddhism. On the roof may be seen, in addition to a lotus pool, a Bodhi tree, said to be a shoot from the tree under which more than 2500 years ago the Buddha arrived at enlightment (Bodhi). Visits are allowed only if notified in advance by telephone (982-6166).

Buddha's Universal Church

In and around John Street there are three Chinese theatres. A visit is particularly interesting because of the simple style of staging, the dissonant music, the exotic audience, the wonderful costumes and the apparent lack of event in the plots of the plays, the performance of which used to go on for days and weeks on end, and in which even the women's roles were formerly taken by men.

Chinese Theater

* Civic Center

The Civic Center is located in the south-west part of the city centre, surrounded by Market Street, Van Ness Avenue, and McAllister Street. No other city in America has such a magnificent official and administrative centre as San Francisco. Its focal point is Civic Center Plaza, a square around which the following buildings are grouped:

General

City Hall in the Civic Center

City Hall

On the west side of the square stands the City Hall, built between 1912 and 1915, and the fifth that San Francisco has had. The Californian architects John Bakewell and Arthur Brown jnr. conceived a building on the lines of a French Renaissance château. It is nearly 400 ft/120 m long and 300 ft/90 m wide. Its offices are round an enclosed courtyard over which a dome has been built. The latter is 300 ft/93 m high, appreciably higher than the Capitol in Washington.

Main Public Library

The Main Public Library, the headquarters of the city's library services, stands on the east side of the square, opposite the City Hall. The building was constructed in 1917 by George Kelham in Beaux-Arts style; the steel magnate George Carnegie provided financial support. The library has a stock of some 1.8 million books, not to mention a considerable collection of newspapers and manuscripts, and also houses temporary exhibitions on the 2nd and 3rd floors.

Civic Auditorium

The Civic Auditorium, the oldest building in the Civic Center, is on the south side of Civic Center Plaza. It was designed in 1915 by the architect Arthur Brown jnr. for the great Panama-Pacific Exhibition and now, together with Brooks Hall, built alongside it in 1958, it serves as the city's conference centre.

*Museum of Modern Art

The San Francisco Museum of Modern Art is housed in the War Memorial Veterans Building on the west side of Civic Center Plaza. It is a private institution, unlike the three other major art museums in San Francisco, the Asian Art Museum, the M. H. de Young Memorial Museum (both in Golden Gate Park) and the California Palace of the Legion of Honor (see entries). Its origins go back to the 1890s, but it was set on a firm footing only in 1916, thanks to the efforts of the San Francsico Art Association. The San Francisco Museum of Modern Art was the only museum of its type on the West

San Francisco Museum of Modern Art

Coast until a museum of modern art was opened in Los Angeles in 1986. It is only recently that it has been obvious even from the outside that this is a museum devoted exclusively to the art of the 20th c. As part of a modernisation programme, works by the American sculptors Tony Smith and Peter Voulkos have been placed in front of the Art Deco façade, and in the entrance hall the statue of George Washington has been replaced by a geometric object made of steel by the Californian sculptor Bruce Nauman.

Understandably, Californian artists are singled out for attention, followed by American painters and sculptors who have made the West Coast their cultural home, such as Mark Rothko, Jackson Pollock, Clyfford Still, Robert Motherwell and Philip Guston.

Permanent collections

The collections of the museum now contain works by nearly every important modern European or American artist. These include French artists (Henri Matisse and Georges Braque in particular, but also Paul Cézanne, Fernand Léger, Camille Pissaro, Jean Dubuffet, Pierre Bonnard and Georges Rouault), German (Max Ernst, Max Pechstein, Hans Purrmann, Kurt Schwitters, Hans Hartung, Karl Hofer, Georges Grosz, Ernst Ludwig Kirchner, Franz Marc and Fritz Winter), and Russian (Alexej Jawlensky and Wassily Kandinsky). There are also works by the Spanish artists Joan Miró and Pablo Picasso.

The museum also possesses works by the following sculptors: Hans Arp, Constantin Brâncuşi, Henry Moore, Alexander Archipenko, Jacob Epstein, Henri Laurens, Jacques Lipchitz and Marino Marini.

As well as the American artists mentioned above, the museum exhibits works by others who have aroused public interest during recent years, including Stuart Davis, William de Kooning, Frank Stella, Jim Dine, Helen Frankenthaler, Arshile Gorky, Adolph Gottlieb, Robert Indiana, Elsworth Kelly, Kenneth Noland, Georgia O'Keefe, Claes Oldenburg, Ad Reinhardt and Mark Tobey.

The museum also has a large collection of photographs, including original prints by Ansel Adam, a photographer who died in 1984.

"Khurusan Gate" by Frank Stella (1969)

Sculptures by Jackson Pollock, Robert Hudson and Manuel Neri

Octagon House

Vedanta Temple

The War Memorial Opera House stands just south of the Museum of Modern Art. It was built in 1932 by Arthur Brown jnr. together with the Veterans Building opposite the City Hall.

War Memorial Opera House

The United Nations was inaugurated in the War Memorial Opera House and the Veterans Building. The Charter founding the world organisation was signed by the representatives of 43 nations on the stage of the Opera House on June 26th 1945. This event is commemorated by the square known as United Nations Plaza.

Until 1980 performances were given here by both the San Francisco Opera (founded in 1923) and the San Francisco Symphony. Now, however, the Symphony Orchestra is able to use the recently built Louise M. Davies Symphony Hall.

The opening of this concert hall in September 1980 was the fulfilment of a long-cherished ambition of music-lovers in San Francisco; at last the Symphony Orchestra had a home of its own. The building was designed by the New York firm of architects Skidmore, Owings & Merrill, with the collaboration of Pietro Belluschi. It represents a successful compromise between tradition and modernity and fits in well with the Art Deco style of the other buildings.

*Louise M. Davies Symphony Hall

Cow Hollow

In the years following the Gold Rush the part of present-day Union Street west of Van Ness Avenue was a green valley. People used to call it "Cow Hollow" and the name has remained.

General

The area began to be developed about a century ago, and there has been a genuine example of urban renewal here in the last 25 years. The numerous Victorian houses have been restored, some being converted for commercial purposes. Now there are fashion boutiques, antique shops, galleries, restaurants and some of the best-known singles bars and cafés.

275

Embarcadero Center

Octagon House

The long section of Union Street between Van Ness Avenue and Steiner Street, incorporating eight blocks of houses, is worth a visit to see the large number of Victorian dwellings. An undoubted curiosity is Octagon House (2645 Gough Street, corner of Union Street), built as the result of a short-lived vogue for octagonal houses in the late 1850s. It serves now as the headquarters of the National Society of Colonial Dames of America. The house is also a museum, and the exhibits date from the American colonial period. (Admission free; guided tours on the second Sunday and the second and fourth Thursdays of each month, noon–3 p.m.)

Vedanta Temple

At 2963 Webster Street, on the corner of Filbert Street not far from Union Street, stands the striking Vedanta Temple. It was built in 1905 by the architect J. A. Leonard in collaboration with Swami Trigunatitananda, the founder of the Vedanta Society of North California which is still in existence.

With its grotesque mixture of various styles – Queen Anne, Colonial, Oriental, Moorish and mediaeval – the building is supposed to symbolise the Vedanta concept that all religions are but ways of approaching the one God. Vedanta is the highest of the six systems in the Hindu philosophy of religion.

*Embarcadero Center

General

Situated between Embarcadero, Battery and Clay Streets, this shopping and leisure centre must be regarded as one of the most interesting and original examples of urban renewal. The six buildings – five skyscrapers with between 32 and 43 storeys and the 20-storey Hyatt Regency Hotel – are the work of the Atlanta architect John Portman. Four skyscrapers are linked by means of footbridges which give access to more than 175 shops and restaurants. The plazas between the buildings are on different levels; in several places sculptures by various artists are exhibited.

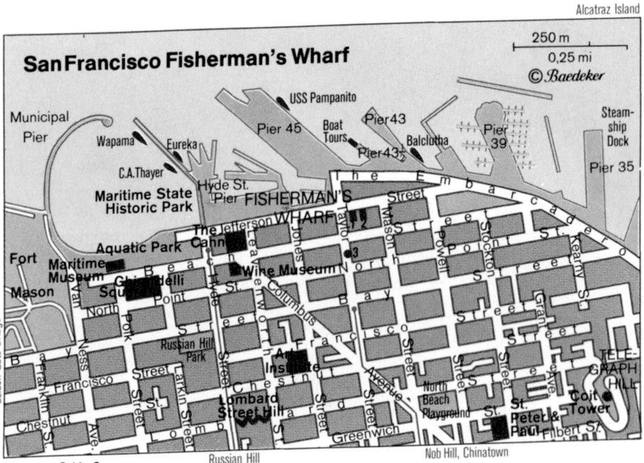

San Francisco Fisherman's Wharf

—— Cable Car

1 Ripley's "Believe it or Not" Museum   2 Wax Museum   3 St. Francis Statue

The ground-plan of this hotel is virtually a triangle, and the building leans out to the north at an angle of 45°.
Even more sensational is the hotel's foyer. It is 330 ft/100 m long and 190 ft/57 m high, reaching up to the 17th floor. Restaurants, shops and bars are grouped around it. The centre piece of this unique hall is a four-storey-high ball made of gilded aluminium piping, a work by the sculptor Charles Perry.

Hyatt Regency Hotel

Ferry Building

At the foot of Market Street, east of Embarcadero Plaza, stands Ferry Building, built between 1986 and 1903 and once the real symbol of San Francisco with its Neo-Romanesque façade and its 230-ft/70-m-high tower, modelled on the campanile of Seville Cathedral.
Until the building of the San Francisco–Oakland Bridge and the Golden Gate Bridge the area around Ferry Building was the place where all roads met.
Every day 170 ferries kept up a shuttle service to the other side of the bay. Now there are just a few boats serving Sausalito, Larkspur and Tiburon.

General

The building now houses both the Port Authority and the California State Division of Mines Museum containing a valuable collection of stones and minerals, as well as the World Trade Center with its exhibition of products from all parts of the globe. (Open: Mon.–Fri. 9 a.m.–3 p.m.; admission free.)

Museums

*Fisherman's Wharf

The Embarcadero ends near Fisherman's Wharf, a picturesque harbour on the North Waterfront with some 200 fishing boats. At one time there were Genoese feluccas (two-masted sailing ships), then came Chinese junks, to be followed by boats owned by Neapolitans and others from southern Italy, who gave this quarter its Italian atmosphere.
Now the harbour is more like a fairground with many shops and restaurants. However, there are still some fishermen who will take tourists out with them for a fee; their boats are moored near the block between Jones

General

277

Fisherman's Wharf: boating harbour

Golden Gate Bridge (in the foreground Fort Point)

Street and Leavenworth Street. Most of their daily catch, including crayfish and crabs, is delivered to the many local restaurants.

The "Believe it or not" Museum (175 Jefferson Street) has some 2000 curiosities from all corners of the globe. (Open: every day 9 or 10 a.m.– 10, 11 p.m. or midnight.)

Museums

To the east is the Wax Museum at Fisherman's Wharf, with over 200 wax figures imported from England on show. (Open: 9 or 10 a.m.–10 p.m. or midnight.)

In the latest earthquake in October 1989 gas escaped from burst mains and ignited, burning down large parts of the marine quarter. Following prompt renovation, however, the damage will soon be repaired.

Note

Ghirardelli Square

Ghirardelli Square was inaugurated in 1964. It was the first of a number of projects designed to give new life to abandoned factory complexes. (Others that have been completed as shopping and leisure centres are The Cannery, Pier 39 and The Anchorage; see entries.) The Italian Domenico Ghirardelli's old red-brick chocolate factory has been turned into a centre for shoppers, art-lovers and those in search of entertainment or a good meal. Its belfry (built in 1916) is modelled on that of the Château of Blois in France. Later additions are rose gardens decorated with fountains (for example, Rose Court with its concrete fountain by Lawrence Halpin, the garden-designer of Ghirardelli Square) and terraces with fine views.

**Golden Gate Bridge

The Golden Gate Bridge passes over the Golden Gate, the strait between the San Francisco Peninsula and Marin Peninsula. As well as being one of the largest bridges in the world, the splendid scenery all around makes it undoubtedly the most beautiful. The bridge was inaugurated on May 28th 1937. It had taken four years to build (1933–1937), and the director of the project was Joseph B. Strauss. Construction proved very difficult on account of the strong cross-currents, and there were some fatal accidents. At the date of its completion it was the longest suspension bridge in the world. For years it was the symbol of San Francisco, though this distinction is now claimed by the Transamerica Pyramid.

General

The bridge, which is illuminated in the evening, is nearly 2 miles/2.7 km long and 90 ft/27.5 m wide; it stands 220 ft/67 m above normal water level. The supporting towers are 740 ft/227 m high.

Every week 25 painters use about two tons of red-lead paint ("International Orange") to keep the paintwork in good condition. This remarkable fact is another reason why the Golden Gate Bridge is known all round the world. A toll is payable only when travelling from north to south.

In spite of the heavy traffic, the superb views make a walk across the bridge well worthwhile. There is a wire-netting screen to deter potential suicides who contemplate leaping over into the water – there have already been 600. At the end of the bridge stands a monument to its builder, J. B. Strauss from Cincinnati. He constructed more than 400 major steel bridges all over the world including one in Lengingrad.

Sightseeing

Fort Point lies below the bridge and was built between 1853 and 1861 to protect San Francisco from attack. It is one of the earliest military buildings in the American West. For the most part it was never used, but served as a construction base while the Golden Gate Bridge was being built. In 1970 it was declared an historical monument.

Fort Point

This large leisure park in San Francisco and Marin County, covering an area of some 620 sq. miles/1600 sq. km, was created in 1972 in order to prevent the coastal area from being used for industrial purposes or being built up.

Golden Gate National Recreation Area

Golden Gate Park

Importance

Golden Gate Park, in north-west San Francisco, is 3 miles/5 km long and ½ mile/800 m wide. Originally there were just arid dunes here; in 1887 the Scottish botanist and landscape gardener John McLaren planted over 5000 different kinds of flowers and trees (originally mainly eucalyptus, acacia, spruce and oak) to make it one of the most splendid parks in the USA, with reserves for several species of deer, including Wapiti, and bison.

*California Academy of Sciences

The California Academy of Sciences was founded in 1853 with its museum (open daily, 10 a.m.–5 p.m.; admission free on the first Wed. of each month) built in 1916, lies in the east of the park.

Its collections are mainly devoted to natural history. In the west wing are displays of minerals, fossils, mammals and birds of North America. The east wing has an African department and rooms for space travel, anthropology, natural history and botany.

The Morrison Auditorium is here, as well as the Morrison Planetarium, the first "Theatre of Stars" that was not imported from Germany but constructed in the United States in 1951–2. 3800 star patterns are projected on to a dome 65 ft/20 m in diameter.

The Steinhart Museum at the end of the courtyard, with the great fountain, has a vast collection of aquatic creatures. In its 243 tanks are over 10,000 fish, dolphins and reptiles (including alligators).

M. H. de Young Memorial Museum

The M. H. de Young Memorial Museum is located in a building erected on the initiative of the newspaper publisher Michael H. de Young at the time of the California Midwinter Exposition in 1894. In some 40 galleries you will find works (some donated by William R. Hearst, Samuel H. Kress and Roscoe and Margaret Oakes) from Egypt, Greece and Rome, from the Middle Ages and the Renaissance, from North America and Europe. Folk art from Africa, the South Seas and America is represented by first-rate pieces. There are many paintings by Rembrandt (including two portraits), Rubens, El Greco (John the Baptist), van Dyck, Frans Hals, Fra Angelico, Titian, Verrochio, Cellini, Tiepolo, Goya, Gainsborough, Watteau and Monet. The interior has rooms fitted out in period style from Spain, France, England and Germany which are well worth seeing. (Open 10 a.m.–5 p.m.; closed on Mon. and Tue.; the admission ticket also entitles you to visit the Asian Art Museum and the California Palace of the Legion of Honor.)

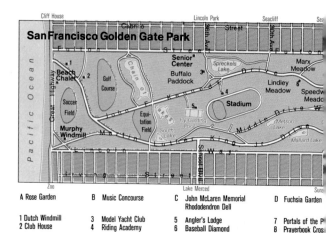

San Francisco Golden Gate Park

A Rose Garden	B Music Concourse	C John McLaren Memorial Rhododendron Dell	D Fuchsia Garden
1 Dutch Windmill	3 Model Yacht Club	5 Angler's Lodge	7 Portals of the P
2 Club House	4 Riding Academy	6 Baseball Diamond	8 Prayerbook Cros

Occupying the two-storied west wing of the M. H. de Young Memorial Museum is the Asian Art Museum (Avery Brundage Collection). Its exhibits are mainly the private collection, donated in 1966, of Avery Brundage, president from 1952 to 1972 of the International Olympic Committee. There are now nearly 10,000 sculptures, paintings, bronzes, jade-carvings, ceramic objects and architectural pieces from Japan, Korea, China, India, Iran and other Asiatic cultures.

Asian Art Museum

The examples of Chinese lacquerwork and ebony carving are exceptional, as are the Chinese scrolls and bark paintings. The chief attraction of the museum is the Jade Room. With about 1200 works of art in jade it is the largest collection in any western country. It covers virtually all the Chinese periods, but the emphasis is mainly on the Ming and Ching periods (about A.D. 1400–1900). There are also a Japanese Department and a library with 12,000 volumes on art in the Near and Far East.

As special exhibitions are often held, only some 10 percent of the total collections can be displayed at any one time.

South-west of the museum lies the charming Japanese Tea Garden, with its curved bridges (the Moon Bridge is a special attraction), little waterfalls, a gaily coloured pagoda and a tea-house. It is particularly beautiful in early April when the cherry-blossom is out (about 200 trees).

* Japanese Tea Garden

At the side of the road opposite the Japanese Tea Garden lies the Strybing Arboretum. It is a botanical garden occupying some 65 acres/26 hectares, with 6000 species mainly bushes and trees from Asia, grouped according to their region of origin.

Strybing Arboretum

North-east of the Academy of Sciences is the Conservatory of Flowers, a large hot-house containing palms, chiefly from South America and the islands of the South Pacific. This is the oldest building in the park and one of the best examples of Victorian architecture. It was brought by freighter from England to San Francisco and re-erected here in 1879. It is now a protected building.

Conservatory of Flowers

In the conservatory may be seen, as well as a tropical garden, orchids, ferns and other plants, and displays of various varieties of flowers – arum lilies, begonias, chrysanthemums and many others – according to the season.

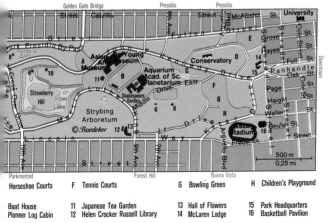

Horseshoe Courts	F	Tennis Courts	G	Bowling Green	H	Children's Playground

Boat House	11	Japanese Tea Garden	13	Hall of Flowers	15	Park Headquarters
Pioneer Log Cabin	12	Helen Crocker Russell Library	14	McLaren Lodge	16	Basketball Pavilion

M. H. de Young Museum: Indian art . . .

. . . and Eskimo art

12th c. Japanese figures of guards

Jackson Square

To the north behind the Transamerica Pyramid lies Jackson Square, one of the most interesting parts of San Francisco from an historical point of view. Contrary to what the name suggests it is not a square, but just a few streets. In 1972 it was the first part of San Francisco to be declared an area of historical interest; a considerable number of the 19th c. business establishments largely survived the 1906 earthquake and, following restoration, have been listed as protected buildings. These include No. 472, one of the oldest and, in its simplicity, most handsome office buildings in San Francisco of the years 1850–1852; between 1865 and 1875 it housed the French Consulate.

Today Jackson Square is a shopping and wholesale centre for interior design materials and arts and crafts.

Location and general

Japantown

The Japantown district lies between Geary Boulevard and Post Street and between Filmore Street and Laguna Street. It is the cultural and social centre for the 12,000 or more Japanese ("Nisei") living in San Francisco. Their name for the city is Soko. The first Japanese came to San Francisco 120 years ago, but it was only after the 1906 earthquake that they began to settle in what is now called Japantown. In Japanese the district is called Nihonmachi.

During the Second World War most of the Japanese and Japanese-Americans ("Nisei") were forcibly interned. On being set free most of the former returned to their distant homeland, and it was only slowly that the others moved back to the district in which they had formerly resided.

Location and general

The opening of the Japan Center in 1968 gave the district a great stimulus. Now there are the 14-storey Miyako Hotel (on the third floor there is a room with Japanese furnishings and a sunken bath), a theatre, a temple and a

Places of interest

283

M.H. de Young Memorial Museum

San Francisco

| A Cloakroom | B Telephone | C Bookshop | D Café | 00 Toilets |

Rooms 1 & 2	Old World
Room 3	Medieval and Renaissance (Spain)
Room 4	El Greco
Room 5	Renaissance of the North
Room 6	17th c. (North Italy)
Rooms 7, 9, 10 & 11	Renaissance (Italy)
Room 8	18th c. (Germany)
Rooms 12, 13 & 15	Kress Galleries (Rembrandt era)
Rooms 14 & 16	Kress Galleries (Rubens, Van Dyck and contemporaries)
Room 17	Gainsborough, Reynolds and other British artists

Room 18	18th c. (England)
Room 19	18th & 19th c. (Great Britain)
Room 20	17th c. (Great Britain)
Room 21	British art
Rooms 22 & 25	Temporary Exhibitions
Room 23	18th c. (French)
Rooms 33 & 34	Oakes Galleries 17th & 18th c. (Italian)
Room 35	18th c. (Europe)
Rooms 36–38	Temporary exhibitions
Rooms 39–48	American Galleries
Room 49	Africa, Oceania and America

Rooms not listed (e.g. 24, 26–32) are at present closed

shrine, several restaurants and tea-houses, art exhibitions, many shops selling goods imported from Japan, and also the Japanese General Consulate.

Peace Plaza, entered through a gate ("romon") designed by Yoshiro Taniguchi, is noted for its Japanese garden and the five-storey Peace Pagoda. In spring there is a cherry blossom festival (Sakura Matsuri; see also Golden Gate Park, Japanese Tea Garden).

Peace Plaza

*Lombard Street

A short section of this street on Russian Hill has become one of San Francisco's great tourist attractions. It is called the "crookedest street". It has a fall of one in two and a half and ten Z-bends.

Market Street

Impressive Market Street, one of the few thoroughfares cutting diagonally across the grid-iron street pattern of San Francisco, forms the boundary between the run-down south of the city with its wide roads and the up-and-coming north with narrow streets.

General

When there was a danger that the inhabitants of the slums might swamp the northern districts it was thought that the only way to reverse the trend was by a thorough redevelopment of Market Street. Accordingly, between 1964 and 1979, the street was transformed in appearance; trees were planted, the

◀ Lombard Street, the most winding street in San Francisco

National Maritime Museum

sidewalks repaved with red stone and numerous skyscrapers built.

Surroundings
Market Street leads south-west to Twin Peaks, north-east to Embarcadero Plaza and to the Ferry Building on San Francisco Bay. On the left where Powell Street leads into Market Street is the southern turntable for the cable cars. Behind it rise the 46-storey Hilton Hotel, which was completed in 1971, and the Ramada Renaissance Hotel opened in 1986.

Mexican Museum

Location and general
The Mexican Museum (open: Wed.–Sun. noon–5 p.m., closed on public holidays) is situated in Fort Mason (Building D). It is the only museum in the United States devoted entirely to Mexican art and folk culture from the Pre-Columbian period to the present day. It is particularly rich in ceramics and paintings by Chicanos, the Mexican farm-hands who come to the United States to help with the harvest.

Guided tours
Every second Saturday in the month at 10 a.m. the museum organises a guided tour round the many murals in the Mission District quarter of the city where the museum is situated. Many of these murals show the strong influence of Mexican artists such as Rivera and Orozco.

National Maritime Museum

General
The National Maritime Museum is to be found in the eastern part of the Aquatic Park. Once a prosperous casino, it is now a maritime museum containing models of the different sorts of ships that pass through the Golden Gate – passenger ships, freighters and men-of-war. There is also a library with a collection of historical newspaper cuttings about Californian seafaring, books, pamphlets, log-books, maps and charts. The Photo-

Grace Cathedral on Nob Hill

graphic Archive possesses about 100,000 pictures of sailing vessels, steamers, harbours and views of the port area of San Francisco, the appearance of which is changing all the time.

In the Maritime State Historic Park (Hyde Street) several restored ships are reminders of the time when the harbour was full of sailing ships:

"C. A. Thayer" is a three-masted schooner built in 1895. It was first used in the lumber trade, then carried salmon and finally, until 1950, was used for cod-fishing in the Bering Sea.

"Eureka", a ferry steamer in operation from 1890 to 1957, was in its day the largest passenger ferry in the world. Propulsion was by means of paddles. Also to be seen are the "Wapama", a steam schooner of 1915, the ferry boat "Alma" (1891) and the ocean-going tug "Hercules", which hauled ships into West Coast harbours from 1907 to 1962. The sailing vessel "Balclutha" (1886) is moored at Pier 43 and the submarine "Pampanito" (1943) at Pier 45.

Museum ships

Navy/Marine Corps/Coast Guard Museum

The construction of the Navy/Marine Corps/Coast Guard Museum on Treasure Island was begun at the time of the United States Bi-centennial Celebrations, With displays, documents and pictures the museum illustrates the part played by the US Navy and Marine Corps in the Pacific. A special attraction is the huge mural by Lowell Nesbitt.

Wonderful views of the skyscrapers of San Francisco may be enjoyed during the drive over the San Francisco–Oakland Bridge and especially from Treasure Island. Treasure Island is, it must be added, a man-made island; that is to say, it is a part of Yerba Buena Island which has been reclaimed from the sea. The project was carried out for the 1939 Golden Gate Exhibition.

General

Nob Hill

General

Nob Hill, west of Chinatown, rises to more than 330 ft/100 m and is one of the smartest districts of San Francisco. Before the 1906 earthquake the most prosperous citizens lived here. They began to settle here from the middle of the 19th c. – bankers, industrialists and newspaper owners. They were followed some fifteen to twenty years later by the railroad millionaires who had recently made their fortune, including Charles Crocker, Leland Stanford, Mark Hopkins and Collis Huntingdon.

The name is possibly derived from the word "snob" or – as seems more likely – from "knob", meaning a knoll or rounded hill.

Noteworthy buildings

There are still a number of palatial buildings on Nob Hill which are worth seeing:

Mark Hopkins Hotel (905 California Street): Hopkins Villa stood here until it was destroyed in the earthquake. It was not until 1925 that the 20-storey hotel was constructed. From its "Top of the Mark" bar there is one of the finest views out over the city.

Fairmont Hotel (950 Mason Street): it was financed by James G. Fair, the "Silver King", totally gutted by fire just before its opening in 1906 and later repaired.

The foyer is considered to be one of the finest public rooms in San Francisco. The exterior lift on the tower, added in 1962, is a special attraction.

Pacific Union Club (1000 California Street): San Francisco's most exclusive club for gentlemen; it occupies the villa built in 1886 for James Flood, another "Silver King" and was renovated 26 years later.

Grace Cathedral

On the west side of Huntington Park (1051 Taylor Street) stands Grace Cathedral, built in 1928 in the Neo-Gothic style and obviously influenced by the architecture of Notre Dame in Paris. It is the seat of the Episcopalian Bishop of California. Florentine works of art were the inspiration of the main portals which take the form of casts from Lorenzo Ghiberti's "Gates of Paradise" at the Baptistery in Florence. The interior houses a number of notable original works of art, including a 13th c. Catalonian crucifix, a Flemish altarpiece of the late 15th c., a silk and gold Brussels Gobelin tapestry dating from the 16th c., a terracotta relief of the Madonna and Child by the Renaissance artist Antonio Rossellino and, on the north wall of the ambulatory, a collection of pages from medieval Bibles.

North Beach

General

North Beach stretches north of Chinatown as far as Telegraph Hill, where there was an arm of the bay as recently as 1850. It is one of the most enigmatic parts of San Francisco, and inhabited mainly by Italians and their American descendants.

Washington Square

Washington Square is the centre of the Italian quarter. More than 50,000 Italians live here, and a glance at the shops and restaurants is enough to persuade any visitor that the Italian way of life is still practised in this area. In the sixties and seventies it was where the Hippies ("Flower Children") met; this psychedelic movement started here and in other squares in this quarter of the city. The Church of St Peter and St Paul stands in the square.

Entertainment quarter

The south-east part of this area, especially around Broadway and Columbus Avenue which crosses it, is San Francisco's main entertainment area, with countless night-clubs, jazz-clubs, bars, cabarets, theatres, restaurants and cafés.

Pacific Stock Exchange

Founded in 1873, the Pacific Stock Exchange now occupies buildings designed by the architects Miller and Pflueger and erected in 1930. The

Shopping and leisure centre, Pier 39

exuberant decoration bears witness to the date of construction. The sculptures are by Ralph Stackpole.

During trading hours it is possible to go into the gallery and watch at close quarters the hectic activity of the stockbrokers. However, intending visitors are required to have a recommendation from a San Francisco stockbroking firm.

Pier 39

Near Fisherman's Wharf (see entry) a complex with 130 shops and 23 restaurants was created on the site of a disused pier. On the ground floor and upper storey of this 1000-ft/300-m-long pier all has been activity and bustle since its inauguration in 1978. Pier 39 was completely reconstructed by using timbers from old ships and by tearing down other piers in the vicinity, in order to provide moorings for small boats.

Presidio

The name "Presidio" goes back to 1776 when Spanish troops were first quartered on this site. This wooded stretch of land which covers some 1500 acres/600 hectares lies on the northern extremity of the San Francisco peninsula jutting out into the Pacific. It has always been used for military purposes; at present it is the headquarters of the United States 6th Army, but closure is planned. In the park, to most of which the public is allowed free access and from which there are fine views, stands the Officers' Club. Dating from 1776, it is the only relic of Spanish days.

General

The National Military Cemetery is also part of the Presidio. It has a burial ground where lie more than 15,000 who died in the First World War. Also noteworthy is the gravestone of "Pauline Tyler, Union Spy". She was an

National Military Cemetery

289

St Mary's Cathedral

actress who served as a Union spy during the course of the American Civil War, winning promotion to the rank of major.

Presidio Army Museum

Situated on Lincoln Boulevard (junction with Funston Ave.) is the Presidio Army Museum, housed in an old military hospital dating from 1857. There are exhibitions of relics and documents which illustrate the part played by the military in the development of San Francisco. (Open: Tue.–Sun. 10 a.m.–4 p.m.; closed Thanksgiving, Christmas and New Year; admission free.)

St Mary's Cathedral

St Mary's Cathedral, the third to bear this name, stands on Cathedral Hill (Gough Street and Geary Street) and was built in 1962. It is by far the most impressive of all the churches in San Francisco. (Open: daily 8.30 a.m.– 5 p.m., Sundays and public holidays afternoons only.)

Designed by well-known architects, including Pietro Belluschi and Pier Luigi Nervi, it has a nave without pillars and a dome 198 ft/60 m high, in which 7-ft/2-m-high stained glass windows like great translucent ribbons come together at the top to form a multi-coloured cross. The four windows in the dome symbolise the elements, fire (west), air (north), water (east) and earth (south).

The altar, at which the celebrant faces the congregation in accord with the recommendations of the Vatican Council of 1962, is surrounded by rows of seats on three sides. Above it hangs a cross and a baldacchino.

San Francisco African-American Historical and Cultural Society

The only museum devoted to the culture and history of the African-Americans west of the Mississippi is to be found in San Francisco (Marina

Boulevard, Fort Mason, Building C; open: Tue.–Sat. 10 a.m.–5 p.m.).
Permanent exhibits include documents and pictures relative to their history in California and the part played by them in the American Civil War of 1861–1865.
Temporary exhibitions of works by artists, especially those working in and around San Francisco, are regularly mounted.

San Francisco Fire Department Pioneer Memorial Museum

On Presidio Avenue No. 655, behind the massive doors of this museum, is kept a remarkable collection of photographs, equipment and documents that come from the various fire brigades of San Francisco, especially the Volunteer Fire Brigade which was in existence from 1849 to 1866. Much space is given over to documents concerning events during the disastrous blaze following the 1906 earthquake.
There is a special exhibition devoted to Lillie Hitchcock Coit who paid for the erection of Coit Tower on Telegraph Hill as a memorial in honour of the fire brigade, and was herself made an honorary member of a fire brigade company.

San Francisco-Oakland Bay Bridge

This bridge links the city with Oakland and the towns on the east side of the bay. It was opened in 1936, six months before the Golden Gate Bridge (see entry). The bridge is some 8 miles/13.3 km long, which makes it one of the longest steel bridges in the world. It consists of two interconnected suspension bridges on the San Francisco side, a tunnel through the island of Yerba Buena and a lattice-work bridge on the Oakland side. | *General*

In the earthquake of October 1989 a 50 ft/15 m length of the bridge collapsed and numerous cars were buried in the debris. The 50-year-old bridge was shown not to be earthquake-proof, as the massive concrete construction served merely to intensify the shock waves. A thorough renovation is planned. | *1989 earthquake*

San Francisco Zoological Gardens

San Francisco did not begin to lay out its zoo until quite late (1929), but now it is one of the six most important in the United States (open: daily 10 a.m.–5 p.m.). Its designers took the Carl Hagenbeck Zoo in Hamburg, Germany as their model. The chief attractions are the snow leopards, polar bears, elephants, pigmy hippos, white rhinos and the monkeys which inhabit an island of their own. The enclosure for primates was added in 1985. | *General*

There is also a children's zoo here which is open every day from 11 a.m. until 4.30 p.m. Children are able to play with young animals and feed them. They can also have rides on giant tortoises and on roundabouts. | *Children's Zoo*

Spreckels' Mansion

This mansion is in the Pacific Heights quarter of the city, two blocks away from Van Ness Street. It is worthy of attention on account of the man who had it built, Adolph B. Spreckels, son of Claus Spreckels, an immigrant from Hanover who became the "Sugar King" of California, and also because of its architecture. It was designed by the architect George Applegarth on the lines of a French Baroque palace, and constructed in white stone.

Telegraph Hill with Colt Tower

Colt Tower – old architecture . . .

. . . and new

View of San Francisco from Twin Peaks

Applegarth was also commissioned by Spreckels to build the California Palace of the Legion of Honor in Lincoln Park (see entry).

Telegraph Hill

Telegraph Hill rises 295 ft/90 m on the north side of the inner city. It is one of San Francisco's 43 hills. Rather like Montmartre in Paris, it has many artists' studios on its slopes as well as villas for the well-to-do middle classes.
There is at present no telegraph installation on Telegraph Hill, but the name goes back to the semaphore station erected on what was then a barren hilltop at the time of the Gold Rush.

General

Coit Tower stands 500 ft/150 m above sea-level on the top of Telegraph Hill. The inside of the tower is decorated with 16 monumental murals, the work of 25 painters and their 19 assistants. They were undertaken as part of the work creation scheme designed to alleviate the Great Depression. It is also one of the best vantage points from which to view San Francisco, though it is not quite as high as the Twin Peaks (see entry).
The name "Coit Tower" recalls Lillie Coit (1843–1929), an honorary member of a fire fighting company. She had it built in honour of the fire brigade. The architect Arthur Brown jnr., who was also responsible for the City Hall (see Civic Center) and other public buildings constructed it in 1934. It takes the form of a free-standing column in which many claim they can recognise the valve of a fire hose.
Apart from the murals at ground-level, those inside the tower can be viewed only on Saturday mornings from 11 a.m.

*Coit Tower

Coit Tower is surrounded by Pioneer Park. This was a stony barren hillside until it was laid out as a park when the Centennial Celebrations of the United States took place on Telegraph Hill. The bronze statue of Christopher Columbus is especially noteworthy.

Pioneer Park

*Transamerica Pyramid

Since its completion in 1972 the Transamerica Pyramid, which can be seen from virtually everywhere in San Francisco, has become the new symbol of the city. It is situated at 600 Montgomery Street, north of the Wells Fargo Bank Building, in the middle of the financial quarter. Designed by the architect William Pereira of Los Angeles, it has 48 storeys and reaches up 853 ft/260 m into the sky. It belongs to an insurance and finance company bearing the same name. (Viewing chamber open: Mon.–Fri. 9 a.m.–5 p.m.)

Unlike conventional buildings, the pyramidal tower with its lattice-like cladding, is said to be particularly resistant to earthquake. The main building, square in section, is 150 ft/45 m wide at the bottom and 46 ft/14 m wide at the topmost floor, This section is surmounted by a 150-ft/45-m-high hollow spire illuminated from within. The sides of the pyramidal spire are clad in aluminium sheeting.

The lines of the tall spire are broken by the external lift-shafts (18 lifts) which run up the east and west sides of the building as far as the base of the spire.

Twin Peaks

These two unique and uninhabited hills, almost 1000 ft/300 m high, are not in fact the highest of San Francisco's 43 hills, a distinction belonging to Mount Davidson which is some 33 ft/10 m higher. However, they are easier to get to (No. 37 bus) and offer what is perhaps the finest views out over the city and the bay (there are frequent mists from the Pacific).
Twin Peaks are the only hills in San Francisco not to have been built over and remaining in their original state. From them you can look down over San Francisco and the bay; there is nowhere better than this from which to appreciate the vastness of this impressive city. The Spaniards called the twin peaks "Los pechos de la Chola" (i.e. the Breasts of the Indian Maiden). Even on warm days strong cool breezes blow in from the Pacific, especially in the late afternoon. Warm clothing is therefore recommended.

Union Square

San Francisco really has no central point, but Union Square comes nearest to fulfilling this function. It is here, or in the immediate vicinity, that numerous lines of communication come together, and here are to be found important shops (Macy's, Magnin, Neiman-Marcus, Saks Fifth Avenue) and hotels (Hyatt Union Square, Westin St Francis, Sir Francis Drake); the most important theatres are just a short step away in Geary Street. The southwest corner of the square, where Geary Street and Powell Street meet, is reckoned to be the liveliest spot in all San Francisco.

The site of Union Square was presented to the city by its first American Mayor, John W. Geary. Its ornamental palm trees are unique in central San Francisco. Since 1942 there has been a vast underground car park beneath the square. Union Square received its name during the American Civil War (1861–1865) when mass demonstrations took place here in favour of the troops of the Northern Union and against the secessionist Southern States. In 1902 a Corinthian column of granite with a bronze goddess of victory was erected here in commemoration of Admiral George Dewey's triumph in the Bay of Manila during the short Spanish-American War of 1898.
Political demonstrations still take place in Union Square, where in warm weather most of the benches are occupied throughout the day by strollers and poor people from the slums south of Market Street (see entry).

◀ *Transamerica Pyramid*

Union Square – the centre of San Francisco

*Wells Fargo History Room

Importance

At 420 Montgomery Street, the main street in the Financial District, stands the 43-storey, 564-ft/171-m-high Wells Fargo Bank Building. Its History Room is a rich source of information for all who wish to learn about the early history of California from the time of the Gold Rush (1848) to the 1906 earthquake.

There is a particularly fine example of a Concord coach, in which the Wells Fargo Express Co., founded in 1852, transported passengers and freight, especially gold. A special display is devoted to Black Bart who between 1877 and 1885 ambushed 28 coaches on his own. He often left comic verses at the scene, claming to be a "Robin Hood" figure.

World of Oil

This museum in the Standard Oil Company of California building (555 Market Street; open Mon.–Fri. 9 a.m.–4 p.m.) will fascinate anybody interested in the story of oil from its discovery to the development of its countless by-products.

The history of oil is depicted to visitors by means of models of the equipment used in the oil-fields and by three dioramas. There is also an 18-minute multi-media show called "Magic of a Refinery" which is put on several times a day. It requires no fewer than 26 projectors.

San José

I 1

Santa Clara County
Altitude: 90 ft/27 m
Population: 672,000

Winchester Mystery House – a "witches house"

This rapidly progressing town, situated 37 miles/60 km from San Francisco, is also one of the oldest in the country. Its population has increased ten-fold since the end of the Second World War, and will probably exceed that of San Francisco when the next census is taken. In spite of all its efforts, however, it still does not have a proper town centre; even more so than Los Angeles, it is simply a collection of suburbs strung together.

Location and general

San José was founded in 1777, under the name of Pueblo de San José de Guadalupe. The Mission established 20 years later is now situated outside the town in Fremont, while the Santa Clara Mission built in the pueblo now forms part of the town of Santa Clara (see entry), founded during the Gold Rush period. By 1848 there were still only 700 people living in San José; when it gained the status of a town two years later, however, it boasted 3000 inhabitants.

Origin

San José lies in the extremely fertile Santa Clara Valley, where a great variety of fruit, grapes and vegetables are cultivated. The agricultural products have always been despatched from San José, where the first canning factory was built in 1871. Nevertheless the town could muster only 21,500 inhabitants at the beginning of the 20th c., but 40 years later there were 57,000. Then the real upswing began, giving San José its reputation of being the town with the greatest population growth in the world.
The chief branch of industry continues to be the processing of agricultural products. This is followed by the computer, chemical and engineering industries (especially atomic engineering) which have contributed greatly to San José's economic growth.

Economy

The town's cultural life has not kept pace with its unbridled demographic and economic development, in spite of having a big Performing Arts Center, a Symphony Orchestra and a large Congress Building surrounded by nine hotels which was opened in 1989. The expansion of the nearby airport, which at present deals with six million passengers and is expected

Culture

to be able to take two or three times as many by the end of the century, will not be able to compensate for the town's cultural shortcomings.

Places of interest

Winchester Mystery House

This Victorian gentleman's residence (525 South Winchester Boulevard) with 160 rooms must be the strangest ever. When it was built in 1884 by Mrs Sarah Pardee Winchester, who inherited the Winchester rifle-making firm, it was a farmhouse with eight rooms. For some 38 years carpenters and other craftsmen worked day after day on this house which by the time Mrs Winchester died had been extended considerably but was still unfinished. Mrs Winchester, taken by the building craze, insisted on drawing up all the plans herself, although she was far from being a trained architect. Numerous curiosities were the result: staircases leading nowhere – one even ended at the ceiling – doors opening on to blank walls and windows which are nothing of the sort because they do not look out on to anything. The entrance hall was big enough for her coach to drive into. She bought so much furniture that most of it lay unused in the cellars.

Superstition

The number 13 occurs conspicuously often in the construction of this house. There are 13 bathrooms, many of the rooms have 13 windows, several windows of Tiffany glass exhibit 13 jewels; there are rooms with 13 wooden panels, many of the staircases have 13 steps and 13 coat hooks can be counted in the bedrooms. Superstition? A fortune-teller is supposed to have advised her, following the death of her husband, to build a house to protect herself from the ghosts of all those who had been killed by a Winchester rifle.

Guided tours

From June to September there are tours from 9 a.m. to 6 p.m. Opening times vary during the rest of the year. Information tel. 247-2101.

Rosicrucian Park, Egyptian Museum

In Rosicrucian Park is the headquarters of the Union of Rosicrucians of international freemasonry. The movement owes its origin to anonymous 17th century writings, based on the life of the knight Christianus Rosencreitz (14th c.) and his brotherhood of men and which spread the concept of neoplatonic, alchemic and mystic thought.
The Egyptian Museum in the park possesses a large collection of Egyptian, Assyrian and Babylonian works of art, a reproduction of an Egyptian rock-tomb and French furniture. An adjoining building houses an art gallery and a planetarium which – like the exhibits – are owned by the Rosicrucians. (Open: Tue.–Sun. 9 a.m.–5 p.m.; tel. (408) 287-9171.)

Japanese Garden of Friendship

This 7½ acre/3 hectare garden is a copy of a park in the Japanese twin town of Okayama, and forms an oasis of peace in Kelley Park. There is also a small zoo.

Historical Museum

The San José Historical Museum is also to be found in Kelley Park, near the US 80. Here you can see original buildings and also reproductions of historical buildings, giving you an idea of what San José used to look like. Inside the museum are artefacts relating to San José's Indian, Mexican and early American history. (Open: Tue.–Fri. 10 a.m.–4.30 p.m., Sat. and Sun. noon–4.30 p.m.; tel. (408) 287-2290.)

San Juan Bautista

See Mission Stations

San Juan Capistrano

See Mission Stations

San Luis Obispo

M 1

San Luis Obispo County
Altitude: 230 ft/71 m
Population: 36,000

This town lies about 180 miles/300 km north-west of Los Angeles, at the junction of the US 101 coast road and the CA 1. It is the site of the fifth mission station built by Father Serra (see Mission stations). Serra thought that two volcanic hills nearby resembled a bishop's mitre, and so he gave this otherwise unimportant mission the name of San Luis Obispo de Tolosa (St Louis, Bishop of Toulouse).

Location and origin

Originally the town lived by despatching products from surrounding ranches; gradually tourism and official bodies concerned with the town's development became more important. The California Polytechnic State University, which has about half as many students as San Luis Obispo has inhabitants, boasts important agricultural and scientific engineering faculties.
The first olive trees in North America are said to have been planted in the mission; two of the 200 year-old trees still exist.

Importance

The Ah Louis Store, dating from 1874, is a survival from the time when many Chinese lived in San Luis Obispo. The building originally housed a Chinese bank and post-office, and was where the town's Chinese fraternity used to meet (800 Palm Street; open: daily except Sun.; tel. 543-4332).
The San Luis Obispo County Historical Museum contains artefacts of the Chumash Indians, articles from the ranches, and exhibits from the Victorian period, as well as a library specialising in the history of the county (696 Monterey Street; open: Wed.–Sun. 10 a.m.–4 p.m.; admission free; tel. 543-0638).
12 miles/20 km south of the town stands the Diablo Canyon Atomic Power Station. It is open to visitors twice a day. At 10 a.m. and 2 p.m. the 1½ hour tour starts from the Pacific Gas and Electric Energy Information Center.

Places of interest

San Pedro

See Los Angeles

San Rafael Arcangel

See Mission stations

San Simeon

L 1

San Luis Obispo County
Altitude: 19 ft/6 m
Population: 100

Location and
general

The village of San Simeon lies on the CA 1, almost exactly halfway between San Francisco and Los Angeles, and about 240 miles/400 km from both places. Coming from Los Angeles, take the US 101 as far as San Luis Obispo, and then the CA 1. If you come from San Francisco, take the US 101 south as far as Paso Robles, then the CA 46 west and after that the CA 1. San Simeon consists of one street with motels on both sides, an average-sized beach and some warehouses.

*Hearst Castle

Visitors would hardly bother to stop here were it not for a place of great interest which is at first hidden from view – the famous castle. It was built by the newspaper king William Randolph Hearst (see Famous Personalities), and must surely be the most grandiose and magnificent monument ever erected by a private individual (open: daily from 9 a.m. until 6 p.m.). When Hearst died in 1951 it was still not quite finished, after being in course of construction for 30 years. In spite of having hundreds of rooms there is still not enough space to house all the works of art which Hearst collected during his lifetime.

W. R. Hearst

Hearst's father George, himself not exactly a poor man (he left a fortune of 18 million US dollars when he died in 1891), bought a 40,000 acre/ 16,000 hectare ranch on San Simeon Bay. By buying up more land he enlarged it more than five-fold (230,000 acres/92,000 hectares), until it stretched more than 50 miles/80 km along the Pacific. When W. R. Hearst's mother died in 1919 William Randolph was the sole heir and he decided to build himself a new house on the estate. The official reason given for building this showpiece of a castle was that it was a memorial to his mother. The real reason, however, was the desire of his mistress, the moderately gifted film actress Marion Davies, to acquire a residence "in keeping with her standing". He instructed the Californian architect Julia Morgan (see Famous Personalities) to construct for him, on a hill in the Santa Lucia Mountains 1650 ft/500 m above sea level and almost 6 miles/ 10 km from the coast, a building in which there would be room to house all his art treasures.

The construction
saga

A start was made in 1922. The guest-houses were finished first, and later given the names of La Casa del Mar (The House by the Sea), La Casa del Monte (The House on the Hill) and La Casa del Sol (The House of the Sun). Hearst lived in the first and largest of the three houses himself until the main house, La Casa Grande, was built. The three guest-houses had a total of 46 rooms, and at the time of Hearst's death the main house had 100 rooms, including 38 bedrooms, 31 bathrooms, 14 living rooms, two libraries, a huge refectory (dining room), a cinema, a kitchen and a large reception hall. Hearst named the whole place La Cuesta Encantada (The Enchanted Hill). It was surrounded by a garden covering 120 acres/ 48 hectares with a small zoo. Zebras, mountain goats and Aoudad sheep also grazed on the hill. The last named can still be seen there today.

Hearst State
Historical
Monument

Seven years after Hearst's death the family left the castle to the Federal State of California, which erected the Hearst San Simeon State Historical Monument here and has managed it ever since. Unlike many other histor-

Neptune Bath with neo-antique temple façade

ical buildings, the castle and its contents and fittings have been preserved in their original state, thus giving us an insight into the opulent lifestyle of its erstwhile occupants.

Nobody has ever known for certain how much money it all cost Hearst. Estimates have put it at 30 million US dollars (worth about 300–400 million dollars today). What he paid for the works of art, which he began to collect at the turn of the century, cannot even be guessed at. Many of the paintings from his collection can be seen in other Californian museums, such as the Los Angeles County Museum of Art (see Los Angeles).

How much did it cost?

The Casa Grande is obviously copied from the Cathedral of Seville. The 130-ft/40-m-high tower in the Spanish-Moorish style gives the whole the intended palatial appearance. It is built mainly of reinforced concrete clad with yellow limestone blocks from Utah. Everything had to be transported from the coast to the top of the hill – no light task on roads as they were then (today a made-up road leads to the castle).

Casa Grande

The ground floor of the house contains the dining room, measuring 100 ft/30 m long and 23 ft/7 m high. There are Flemish tapestries on the walls, the hand-carved ceiling imported from Italy portrays saints, and around the room can be seen crests of Sienese families. On this floor also are the reception room, billiard room, cinema, kitchen and pantries.

Ground floor

The first floor houses the main library and the monastic bedrooms. The mezzanine below contains the "Doge's Suite", built in the Venetian style, with the balcony of the living room having four-leaved arches like those at the Doge's palace in Venice.

First floor

On the second floor you will find Hearst's personal suite, also known as the Gothic Suite, with his study and the library where the newspaper publisher liked to relax. The two towers are occupied by the "Celestial Suite", and are

Second floor

Roman swimming bath, with Venetian gold tiles

Dolphin fountain in Santa Barbara

Spanish fiesta in Santa Barbara

connected by a living room from which there is a fantastic view of the Pacific Ocean.

The castle has two swimming pools. One, called the Neptune Pool, is in the open; during Hearst's time it was heated all the year round and was popular with his many guests. It is 105 ft/32 m long and faced with marble. A Greco-Roman temple façade forms the background, while Etruscan columns at each end and statues in white marble complete the antique setting. The other, a Roman bath, is under cover and is so big that Hearst had two tennis courts built on top of it. The concrete building is faced in tiles of brightly coloured Venetian glass and some of gold, a task which took the Italian craftsmen three years to complete. Hearst was said to have derived the inspiration for this from a visit to the 5th c. Galla Placidia Mausoleum in Ravenna.

Swimming pools

There is much more to see, of course. For the most part the guided tours do not give the visitor sufficient time for more than a fleeting glance at the mainly French and Italian furniture, the Gothic and Renaissance tapestries, and the huge fireplaces. There are also exquisite Persian carpets, numerous Roman mosaics, carved ceilings, a fantastic collection of silver and many wooden, marble and stone sculptures.

Guided tours

There are four different guided tours:

Tour No. 1: one of the three guest houses, a small part of the garden, the ground floor of the Casa Grande (reception room, refectory, billiard room and cinema with a short film presentation.

Tour No. 2: "Doge's Suite", three of the monastic bedrooms, the main library (with more than 5000 books and Greek vases), the Gothic and "Celestial" Suites, kitchen and pantries.

Tour No. 3: Casa del Monte, the new wing with its Spanish ceilings over the cinema, Renaissance painting, many beautiful Persian carpets and a video film of a reception Hearst gave for some VIPs.

Tour No. 4: Casa del Mar, wine cellar, the changing rooms of the Neptune swimming pool and the extensive gardens.

During the high season in particular you are recommended to obtain tickets

Drinking fountain

Interior view of County Courthouse

for the tours in advance (each tour lasts about 1¾ hours). The visitor must book for one or two tours on a certain day and at a certain hour; in California, tel. 800/444-7275, from outside the state tel. 619/952-5580. Bookings can be taken by Hearst Castle up to eight weeks prior to the visit. In the high season you should book at least a week in advance, and out of season two days before. If you are already in San Simeon you can buy tour tickets at the Holiday Inn. Mastercard and Visa can be used when booking by telephone. It is also advisable to book a motel room in advance.

Santa Barbara   O 2

Santa Barbara County
Altitude: 36–855 ft/11–259 m
Population: 76,200

General

Location

Santa Barbara lies 92 miles/148 km north of Los Angeles (about two hours travelling time) and 330 miles/530 km south of San Francisco (seven hours travelling). The US 101 passes through the town. Thanks to its favourable position and climate – there is some smog and mist especially in August and September, but the sun shines on 84% of all days – Santa Barbara is a favourite holiday resort.

Ecology

The ecological movement is quite strong in Santa Barbara, because an oil slick in 1969 contaminated the whole beach for a long time. That is one of the reasons why there is a prohibition on extracting more oil from the sea. Even though the state government has repeatedly raised the possibility of a renewal of extraction during the last few years, they have been unable to force it through in the face of local opposition.

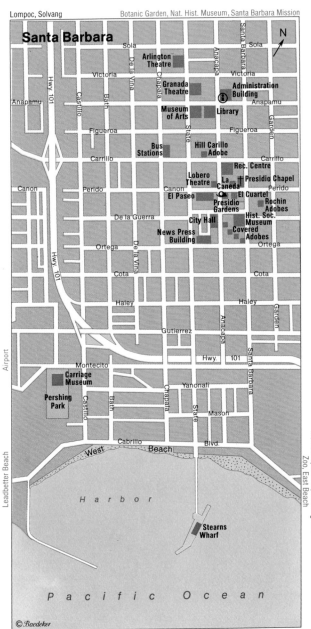

Lompoc, Solvang

Botanic Garden, Nat. Hist. Museum, Santa Barbara Mission

Santa Barbara

N

Sola

Arlington
Theatre

Sola

Victoria

Anacapa

Santa Barbara

Victoria

Hwy. 101

Anapamu

Castillo

Bath

De la Viña

Chapala

Granada
Theatre

Administration
Building

Anapamu

Garden

Museum
of Arts

State

Library

Figueroa

Figueroa

Bus
Stations

Hill Carillo
Adobe

Carrillo

Carrillo

Canon

Perido

Lobero
Theatre

Canon

La
Caneda

Rec. Centre

Presidio Chapel

Perido

El Paseo

El Cuartel

Rochin
Adobes

De la Guerra

Presidio
Gardens

Hist. Soc.
Museum

City Hall

Covered
Adobes

News Press
Building

Ortega

De la Viña

Ortega

Cota

Cota

Haley

Haley

Garden

Gutierrez

Anacapa

Hwy. 101

Hwy. 101

Santa Barbara

Airport

Montecito

Carriage
Museum

Yanonali

Pershing
Park

Castillo

Bath

Chapala

State

Mason

Leadbetter Beach

Cabrillo

West   Beach

Blvd.

Montecito, Oxnard, Los Angeles
Zoo, East Beach

Harbor

Stearns
Wharf

P a c i f i c   O c e a n

© Baedeker

305

View of Santa Barbara, with the County Courthouse in the foreground

History

Origin

Santa Barbara developed around the tenth of the 21 Mission stations (see entry), built in 1786, and around the excellent harbour. Juan Rodriguez Cabrillo had probably already discovered the channel between the mainland and the offshore island in 1542, but it was not until 60 years later that the Spaniard Sebastiano Vizcaino named the settlement "Santa Barbara",

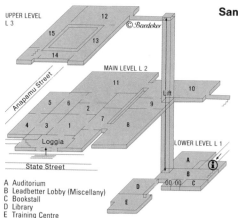

Santa Barbara Museum of Art

1 Ludington Court (Classical sculpture)
2 Thayer Gallery (Classical ceramics, glass, bronze)
3 Campbell Gallery (Asiatic lacquer work, textiles, prints)
4 Sterling Morton Gallery – West (Near East, Japan, China, India)
5 Sterling Morton Gallery – East (European art)
6 Gould Gallery (European art of 19th & 20th c., Impressionists)
7 Von Romberg Gallery (American 20th c. art)
8 Preston Morton Gallery (American art of 18th & 19th c.)
9 Colefax Gallery (miscellany)
10 Park Wing Gallery (modern art)
11 McCormick Gallery (painting, sculpture)
12 Hammett Gallery (prints, textiles)
13 Wood Gallery (photography)
14 Eichheim Gallery (African art)
15 Ala Story Gallery (International European and American art)

A Auditorium
B Leadbetter Lobby (Miscellany)
C Bookstall
D Library
E Training Centre

having landed on the coast on that Saint's Day. A further 180 years went by before Governor Gaspar de Portola landed there with his troops in 1782, and Father Junipero Serra celebrated the first Mass in the recently-built Presidio. Serra did not live to witness the completion of the mission, one of the most beautiful in all California.

Like the rest of California, Santa Barbara was slow to develop. The original Mission Church was destroyed by an earthquake in 1812; the second, with a classical façade and two towers, had just been completed when the Mexicans decided to secularise the mission stations in 1833. Santa Barbara's early history is closely linked with the Spaniards and Mexicans. The town has retained that character to the present day. The first North Americans to come to this area were traders from New England, seeking to buy hides and tallow. On Christmas Day 1846 the town was taken by the Americans without a struggle.

19th century

A second earthquake in 1925 reduced a large part of Santa Barbara to rubble. The Mission station was damaged and took two years to repair (its façade was not finished until 1950).

**Spanish influence

Only a few of the 19th c. Victorian houses are left. Following the earthquake it was decided to rebuild the damaged area in the old Spanish mission style. This gave the town a uniform character unique in California. The most important public buildings in this style are: El Paseo, built round the old "De La Guerra" house, the imposing County Court House and the Santa Barbara Museum of Art.

Many streets also retained their Spanish names. Their Spanish character was further emphasised by fountains, rubbish bins and even letter-boxes being decorated with Spanish tiles, especially in State Street, the town's main thoroughfare.

Places of interest

Today the town is one of the most beautiful in the country and has the great advantage of having most of its places of interest close together, so that they can all be seen quite easily within a short period of time.

General

The Santa Barbara County Courthouse is a Spanish-Moorish building in the style of a palace, completed after the large earthquake of 1929. The tiles lining the staircase are mainly from Tunisia, while those used on the arches are of Californian origin. The entrance hall on the first floor is a strange mixture of styles; the tiles and a passage way to the loggia are Islamic, the pink window is Romanesque and the archway decorated with angels is Byzantine. The County Supervisor's conference hall is entered through a double door; its murals illustrate the history of the county, beginning with the Indians watching the arrival of the first Europeans led by Cabrillo.
A lift goes up to the El Mirador bell-tower, from where you may enjoy a fine view over Santa Barbara. In front of the entrance door is a fountain representing the "Spirit of the Ocean". (110 Ancapa Street, App. 7600; open: daily 9 a.m.–5 p.m.; admission free; tel. (805) 962-6464.)

County Courthouse

The Presidio (fortress), founded by the Spaniards in 1782, was badly damaged in the earthquakes of 1806 and 1812 and became of no importance at all after the American troops entered in 1846. Of the original buildings only El Cuartel, the soldiers' quarters, and the front rooms of the Canedo Adobe remain. The padre's house and the chapel have been restored. (122, 123 and 129 East Canon Perdido Street; open: Mon.–Fri. 10.30 a.m.–4.30 p.m., Sat. and Sun. noon–4 p.m.; admission free; tel. (805) 966-9719.)

El Presidio de Santa Barbara State Historic Park

This U-shaped adobe house was built between 1819 and 1827 as a political and social centre for the community by the fifth commandant of the Presidio. By adding more houses on the north-west and north-east sides it has

Casa de la Guerra

Beach along the Scenic Drive

been made into the El Paseo Complex, a Spanish street which was used as a copy when Santa Barbara was rebuilt after 1925. (11 to 25 East de la Guerra Street.)

Museum of Art

Until 1941 the Santa Barbara Museum of Art was housed in a former post-office, and during its relatively short existence it has assembled an impressive and diverse collection of exhibits. It covers a wide spectrum, ranging from Egyptian works of art, Roman sculptures and an important Asiatic art department, to works by French Impressionists, 20th c. American paintings, photographs, prints, drawings and kinetic art. This little museum is well worth a visit. (1130 State Street; open: Tue., Wed., Fri. and Sat. 9 a.m.–5 p.m., Thur. 9 a.m.–8 p.m., Sun. noon–5 p.m.; admission free; tel. (805) 963-4364.)

Historical Society Museum

This museum is housed in three adobe houses and displays material relating to Santa Barbara's Spanish, Mexican and early American history (including documents and paintings).(136 East de la Guerra Street; open: Tue.–Fri. noon–5 p.m., Sat. and Sun. 1 p.m.–5 p.m.; admission free; tel. (805) 966-1601.)

The following places outside the main town are worth a visit:

Mission Santa Barbara

See Mission Stations

Museum of Natural History

On display are mammals, birds, fish, reptiles, the skeleton of a blue whale, exhibits of plant life and the geology of the Pacific coast and the Channel Islands (see Channel Island National Park), as well as a diorama of prehistoric Indian life. There is also a planetarium with varying displays. (2559 Puesta del Sol, four blocks north of the mission; open: Mon.–Sat. 9 a.m.–5 p.m., Sun. 10 a.m.–5 p.m.; tours of the museum on Sun. at 2 p.m.; tel. (805) 682-4711.)

In the Botanical Garden, covering 65 acres/26 hectares, native trees, bushes, woodland and field flowers and cacti grow in their natural habitat. There are some 5 miles/8 km of easily negotiable paths. A special feature is the dam built in 1806 by Indians under the supervision of the Padre to provide water for the mission and the living quarters. (1212 Mission Canyon Road, about 1½ miles/2½ km north of the mission; open: daily 8 a.m.–sunset. Free guided tours Thur. 10.30 a.m., Sun. 11 a.m.; admission free; tel. (805) 682-4726.)

Botanical Garden

The Zoological Gardens are located in a beautiful setting and include a Children's Zoo as well as elephants, lions, apes, sea-lions and exotic birds. (Ninos Drive, exit to Cabrillo Blvd. east of Milpas Street, near the coast; open: daily 9 a.m.–5 p.m., in summer until 8 p.m.; tel. (805) 962-6310.)

Zoological Gardens

The oldest quay still remaining on the West Coast, Steam Wharf is a continuation, three blocks in length, of Santa Barbara's main street (State Street). It extends out over the Pacific, with restaurants, shops and a pier for fishing. (Open: daily 7 a.m.–midnight.)

Steam Wharf

All these interesting places, apart from the Botanical Gardens, lie along Scenic Drive, a road with blue road-signs. You will pass exclusive residential quarters, such as are to be seen in Santa Barbara's suburbs of Goleta, Carpinteria and Montecito. There is a campus of the University of California in Goleta, as well as a railway museum concerned with the railroad history of Southern California, (open: daily except Sat. 1 p.m.–4 p.m.; admission free). Carpinteria, 12 miles/20 km south-east on the US 101, has the finest bathing beach in the area.

Scenic Drive

Santa Catalina Island

Los Angeles County
Altitude: 20 ft/6 m
Population: 2500

The island of Santa Catalina lies 26 miles/42 km south-west of Wilmington, the port of Los Angeles. It is 21 miles/34 km long and varies between ½ to 9 miles/0.8 to 14 km in width. In the interior there are hills as high as 3135 ft/950 m. The island was discovered by Cabrillo in 1542. He named it "San Salvador" after his ship, but Vizcaino gave it its present name 40 years later, having dropped anchor there on the feast day of Santa Catalina (St Catharine) of Alexandria. The first North American set foot on the island in 1805, and when Governor Pico gave it to an inhabitant of Santa Barbara in 1846 it became first the property of the United States and later was privately owned. Finally it belonged to the chewing-gum manufacturer William Wrigley and his son Philip, who built the main township of Avalon and made the island into a tourist attraction. A casino, deep-sea fishing (tuna, swordfish, sea perch, barracuda and mackerel), diving, swimming, riding and hunting are the main attractions. The interior and most of the coast are uninhabited.
From Long Beach (see entry) and San Pedro (see Los Angeles) there are daily boat and air trips to Avalon.

Location and general

Of the three other neighbouring islands the smallest, Santa Barbara (2 miles/3.2 km long and 1 mile/1.6 km wide), is included in the Channel Islands National Park (see entry), San Clemente is used for naval exercises and San Nicholas, from where all the Indians were taken to the mainland in 1835, is uninhabited.

General map:
see page 99

Surf-rider near Santa Cruz

Santa Clara

Santa Clara County
Altitude: 89 ft/27 m
Population: 88,000

Location and importance

Santa Clara, founded in 1852 and the seat of California's oldest university, lies within the urban complex which stretches along both sides of the US 101 south-east of San Francisco. Today this complex is also known as Silicon Valley because of the large number of industries, both large and small, to be found there. Menlo Park, Palo Alto (see entry), Los Altos, Mountain View, Sunnyvale, Santa Clara and San José (see entry) all run into each other without any apparent boundaries. Santa Clara is the very hub of Silicon Valley. It is also known far and wide for its fruit cultivation, started by the priests at the Santa Clara Mission (see Mission Stations). Today mainly dried fruits, especially apricots and plums, are exported.
The population of Santa Clara has grown so fast within the last few years and other development has been postponed, so that you will look in vain for a town centre. As a result there are few places of interest to visit.

University

Santa Clara's University, founded the year after the town became integrated into the State of California, lies on both sides of the Alameda (poplar grove) which links the towns of Santa Clara and San José. On the campus, which is inhabited by some 7500 students, will be found the ruins of the Mission station destroyed in the first half of the 19th c., as well as the 1928 rebuilt mission close by.

Leisure park

A few years ago a leisure park on the lines of Disneyland was created in Santa Clara, not far from the US 101. Known as "Great America" it covers an area of 100 acres/40 hectares and is made up of five sections (Hometown Square, Yukon Territory, Yankee Harbor, County Fair and Orleans Place).

These depict various aspects of life in America during the 19th and 20th centuries and provide plenty of scope for entertainment of all kinds. (Address: US 101, exit to Great America Park; tel. (408) 988-1776.)

Santa Cruz

Santa Cruz County
Altitude: 20 ft/6 m
Population: 44,000

Santa Cruz, lying about 70 miles/115 km south of San Francisco (on the CA 1), between Monterey Bay and the Santa Cruz Mountains, is very popular because of its 30 miles/46 km of beautiful beaches. For the inhabitants of San Francisco it is the first place south of the city where it is possible to bathe, at least in summer and autumn.

Location and
importance

The mission of the same name (see Mission Stations) was founded in 1791 above where the town now lies. In 1797 the Spaniards created the village of Pueblo Branciforte, the inhabitants of which carried out a series of robberies at the mission which led to its gradual downfall. It was the first of the 21 mission stations to be secularised in 1834.
Santa Cruz developed outwards from the Mission Plaza. Its year of founding is given as 1840, but it did not obtain its charter until 26 years later. The township was initially an important harbour from which redwood felled nearby was shipped all over the world. Gradually it became a holiday resort and spa. The long municipal pier is the only one in California with a leisure park. There is plenty of activity here all the year round. "Miss California" is chosen here every year.

Origin

About 5 miles/8 km north of Santa Cruz, on the CA 9, will be found 1750 acres/700 hectares of forest in which grow some of the most beautiful coastal redwoods (sequoia sempervirens; see entry Redwood Highway, Redwoods). There are also some 15 miles/24 km of trails for walking and riding, as well as camp sites (tel. (408) 335-4598).

Henry Cowell
Redwood State
Park

About 3 miles/5 km north of Santa Cruz, on Branciforte Drive, is one of the strangest places in the whole of California. It was discovered in 1939 and is now privately owned. This is where the laws of gravity no longer seem to apply. Almost all the trees lean to the south-west, balls roll uphill and the nearer you get to the centre of the "Mystery Spot" the more strongly you are pulled magnetically in a south-westerly direction and you can no longer stand upright.

The Mystery Spot

At the northern end of the Henry Cowell Redwood State Park, by the CA 9 road in Fenton, is the start of a 100-year-old narrow gauge railway. Part of its route is through the Redwood Forests and in places it has to negotiate some very steep gradients. Bear Mountain, an old lumberjack village, is worth a short stop.
The trains run throughout the year at varying times (for information about connections: tel. 335-4400).

Roaring Camp and
Big Trees Narrow
Gauge Railroad

The City Museum contains evidence of the history of northern Monterey Bay, Indian artefacts and an aquarium. (1305 East Cliff Drive; open: Tue.–Sun.; admission free; tel. (408) 429-3773.)

City Museum

The Californian Central University's most recent campus lies in the northwest of the town. It was opened in 1965 and already has 9000 students. From the 2000 acre/800 hectare campus there is a splendid view over Monterey Bay. The Joseph M. Long Marine Laboratory is here, with aquaria and a skeleton of a blue whale. (Open: Tue.–Sun. 1–4 p.m.; admission free; tel. (408) 459-2495.)

University of
California

Bodybuilding . . .

. . . on Santa Monica beach

Santa Monica

Los Angeles County
Altitude: 102 ft/31 m
Population: 92,000

Santa Monica was founded in 1886 at the southern end of the mountain range bearing the same name and of Santa Monica Bay. Although linked to the Los Angeles road network it remains an independent town, highly thought of as a residential area and resort. Its name is derived from that of the god-fearing Monica. She was the mother of St Augustine, one of the four Latin Fathers of the Church. In recent years some industrial firms have become established here, the principal one being the Douglas Aircraft Company. The firm's Douglas Aerospace Museum is near the airport (open at weekends only; admission free).

Location and general

The Santa Monica Pier juts out at the end of Colorado Avenue. It has a shopping arcade, a restaurant and a roundabout. You can also fish from this pier. Santa Monica's beach is 3 miles/5 km long and ranks as one of the best in Greater Los Angeles. Palisades Park, with a view over the Pacific, runs along Ocean Avenue between Colorado and San Vincente Boulevards. It is particularly noted for its beautiful gardens.

*Tourist town

The towns of Del Rey and Venice, both south of Santa Monica, belong to Los Angeles and have lovely beaches with many facilities for water sports.

Surroundings

Santa Rosa

Sonoma County
Altitude: 168 ft/51 m
Population: 89,000

The town is situated in the middle of the Sonoma County vine-growing area. There are some 100 wine-producers in the immediate vicinity, and the town is one of the main handling centres for the region's products. As it lies only about 53 miles/85 km from San Francisco and is easily accessible by way of the Golden Gate Bridge and the US 101, Santa Rosa has proved to be a favourite place of residence for commuters who do not mind driving this distance.

Location and general

Luther Burbank, one of America's most important agriculturists (see Famous Personalities), was attracted to Santa Rosa from Massachusetts by the favourable climate and fertile soil. He devoted his life to cultivating new varieties of fruit and vegetables. In the Luther Burbank Memorial Gardens (corner of Sonoma and Santa Rosa Avenues; open: daily from 8 a.m. until 5 p.m.; admission free; tel. (707) 576-5115) you can learn more about the achievements of this man who is buried there under a cedar tree. You can also visit the house where he lived and worked (open: Wed.–Sun. 10 a.m.–3 p.m. in summer, and noon–3.30 p.m. during the rest of the year).

Luther Burbank

The museum is housed in No. 1 Snoopy Place, the address of the well-known American comic artist Charles M. Schulz. Born in Minneapolis in 1922 of German descent, Schulz is the spiritual father of the "Peanuts" family, the main figures of which are Charlie Brown, the dog Snoopy and the sisters Lucy and Linus. Since it first appeared in 1950 it has become one of the most successful of all comic-strips.

Peanuts Museum

Sausalito

Houseboats in Sausalito

Sausalito

Marin County
Altitude: 13 ft/4 m
Population: 7500

Location and general

This former fishing village on San Francisco Bay at the northern end of the Golden Gate Bridge is a favourite place for excursions. It is named after the region's first ranch, Rancho Saucelito. This was the spelling of Sausalito in vogue until 1900; the Spanish word "sauce" means willow, and "sauce-lito" is a small grove of willow trees, for which you will search in vain today. Originally it was a port for whale-hunters and other trading ships.

*House-boats

The numerous house-boats which line the harbour today have become the symbol of Sausalito.

Townscape

The narrow streets, full of little corners and some linked to others by wooden steps, have added to the appeal of Sausalito. Today it is inhabited mainly by commuters from San Francisco. In the upper parts of the town away from the hustle and bustle, a number of artists have settled by the bay. Their work is displayed in the numerous galleries. Most of the shops are on Bridgeway and in Princess Street.

From Sausalito there is a fine view of San Francisco; an impressive scene is when thick mist envelopes the city early in the morning, while Sausalito is enjoying bright sunshine, and only the tips of the skyscrapers can be seen.

Health

Visitors may be interested to learn that it was in Sausalito that a number of moves towards healthier living started, such as holding a national "No Smoking Day". The town council has now decided to make it the first cholesterol-free town in the USA, and in so doing is in competition with Palm Springs (see entry). The latter actually has more restaurants offering fat-free food, such as pizzas made with olive oil and fat-free cheese.

Sequoia National Park

Sequoia & Kings Canyon National Parks   K–M 4/5

In the middle south of the Californian Sierra Nevada the Sequoia and Kings Canyon National Parks cover an area of mountainous land with majestic granite peaks, deep gorges, mountain lakes, rivers and superb forests. The two parks are administered as one. They stretch from the foothills in the west on the edge of the San Joaquín Valley – the longest valley in Greater California – to the main ridge of the Sierra Nevada in the east. Here Mount Whitney (14,495 ft/4418 m) is the highest mountain in the USA (apart from Alaska), and Split Mountain (14,140 ft/4285 m), Mount Goethe (13,350 ft/4047 m) and many others are also over 10,000 ft/3000 m. The John Muir Wilderness Area runs along the eastern flank of the National Park area, which adjoins the Inyo National Forest further east.

Location and
** importance

Sequoia & Kings Canyon National Parks

** Giant Redwoods

The two national parks cover the most impressive section of a vegetation belt which is 250 miles/400 km long altogether and between 4000 and 8000 ft/1200 and 2400 m high. In this area can be found groves and whole forests of mighty redwood trees (see entry for Redwood Highway, Redwoods) of the species sequoiadendron giganteum (sequoia gigantea) or giant sequoia; saplings of which can be purchased at nurseries. Apart from the yew-needled sequoia (sequoia sempervirens) found on the Pacific coast of California, this species is the only surviving member of the genus sequoia belonging to the family of the marsh-cypress (taxodiaceae), which once grew in profusion in the northern hemisphere.

The giant redwood, which can reach a height of 250–300 ft/75–90 m and a diameter of 40 ft/12 m, has flat needles and cones the size of pigeons' eggs. Generally speaking it lives happily with other trees. Its extraordinarily long life span (up to 3500 years) can be attributed mainly to its great resistance to enemies of all kinds and to its astonishing ability to regenerate itself. Its asbestos-like bark, as much as 2 ft/60 cm thick on some older specimens, is an effective protection against forest fire and the high tannic acid content of the wood keeps insects and fungal diseases at bay. Its only real enemy is man. However, the trees can suffer damage from changes in soil conditions, which may occur during the thousands of years of its life as the result of erosion or washing away of the soil around its comparatively shallow root system. The sequoia trees in the national parks are not influenced by arboreal technology.

Climate, flora and fauna

As a result of the marked differences in altitude there are three main climatic zones. The dry lowlands and sloping sites below 1500 ft/450 m above sea level are covered in grass steppes and low scrubland and are free from snow in winter. As well as the extensive native fauna, a large number of animals from the higher regions come here to spend the winter: silver fox, lynx, Californian squirrel, skunk and racoon are often found. The Pacific rattlesnake, which is quite common here, is the only animal in the park which is not a protected species.

The areas at a medium height of between 1500 and 4000 ft/450 and 1200 m are covered in coniferous forests (red and white fir, Ponderosa and Lodgepole pine, cedar and giant redwood). The damp meadows are lined with aspen. Winter wraps this area in a 6–10 ft/2–4½ m blanket of snow. Red deer and black bear are often seen, and occasionally mountain lions (pumas).

The higher mountainous region consists of sparse woodland, mountain meadows and bare rocky and gravel slopes. Here the animal life is less varied, being limited to the hardier species suited to the weather and feeding conditions. In these lonely hills live mountain sheep, the brown wolverine which seeks the lower, milder slopes in winter, and the marmot.

History

In pre-Columbian times this region was inhabited by the Potwisha and Kaweah Indians, two friendly tribes who lived by hunting and fishing and did simple basket-work. They spent the winter on the dry, snow-free lowlands, returning in summer to the cool forests of the central mountain regions. Guided by Indians, Hale Tharp was the first white man to penetrate the sequoia regions of the Giant Forest in 1858. He was followed by large numbers of adventurers and gold-seekers who searched in vain for precious metals (relics in Silver City and Mineral King in the south of the park) and in so doing brought to several thousand Indians living near the Kweah River diseases previously unknown to them, such as scarlet fever, smallpox, measles and fever. Any Indian suffering from these diseases was driven out by white settlers; only ten years after the forest was discovered there were no longer any living in these regions. After the stocks of sequoia had been seriously decimated because of the huge amount of wood obtainable from the trees (one tree was enough to build about 40 houses), the Sequoia National Park was founded in 1890. In the early years the cavalry had to protect the nature reserve from timber thieves.

The species was given the name "sequoia" by the Pressburg botanist Stephan Ladislaus Endlicher (1804–1849), who named it after the Cherokee

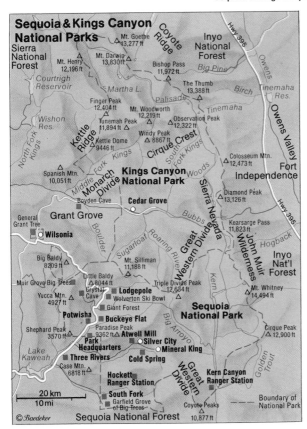

Indian Sequoyah, the creator of an alphabet of symbols representing the sounds of his tribe's language. In 1828 Sequoyah was elected to represent his people in Washington D.C. His statue stands in the National Hall of Statuary in the Capitol. Kings Canyon derived its name from the river which flows through it, which the Spaniards in 1805 christened Rio de los Santos Reyes, (River of the Holy Kings).

Places of interest

The Giant Forest in the west of the Sequoia National Park is one of the few redwood forests where the trees grow so thickly that no others can survive.

* **Giant Forest**

In the north-east of the forest stands the General Sherman Tree; 276 ft/ 83.8 m tall, with a maximum diameter of 36½ ft/11.12 m and 103 ft/31.3 m in circumference at the base, it is one of the mightiest known redwoods. Its age of about 3000 years makes it the oldest living thing on earth. North-east of Giant Forest is Crystal Cave, a marble cave with rich dripstone

* **General Sherman Tree**

317

scenery. (In the summer months there is a guided tour each day of ½ mile/ 0.8 km; warm clothes are advisable).

To the north of this lies Muir Grove, one of the most beautiful sequoia forests with a lot of old trees. In the extreme north-west of the Giant Forest Area will be found Lost Grove, a 50 acre/20 hectare redwood forest with fifteen specimens measuring more than 10 ft/3 m in diameter.

* Muir Grove

From Giant Forest a road branches off south-eastwards to Moro Rock, a vast monolithic block of granite rock (6760 ft/2050 m tall; there is a stony path to the top) from where is a fine panoramic view of forest and mountains as far as Crescent Meadow. From here (also the starting-off point of the High Sierra Trail) a footpath leads to Tharp's Log, a hollow tree trunk used by the discoverer of the Giant Forest as a dwelling-hut.
Immediately north of the Giant Forest lies Round Meadow, surrounded by some beautiful sequoias. Behind it to the northwest stands Sunset Rock (6400 ft/1940 m) from where there is a good view.

Moro Rock

Grant Grove and Redwood Mountain Grove adjoin the Sequoia National Park to the north-west and form a part of the King's Canyon National Park.

* **Grant Grove and Redwood Mountain Grove**

In the north of Grant Grove stands a redwood known as the General Grant Tree. It is 268 ft/81.5 m tall, with a maximum diameter of 40 ft/12.28 m and a circumference at the base of 108 ft/32.8 m. In the south stands Big Stump, the remains of a giant sequoia felled for the World Exhibition in Philadelphia in 1875, and Stump Basin, a redwood forest which had been completely cleared before it was declared a protected area.
The Redwood Canyon Forest on Redwood Mountain is an example of a sequoia forest which is well worth looking at.

* General Grant Tree

Kings Canyon is the valley of the southern arm of Kings River. It is lined with steep walls of rock. The granite peaks of the surounding mountains dominate the floor of the glacial canyon for more than a mile/1.6 km. Easy paths lead from the Cedar Grove Tourist Center to Zumwalt Meadow with its charming scenery and to the impressive waterfalls known as Roaring River Falls and Mist Fall. The high mountain regions are accessible only on foot or on horseback. Tours to Evolution Basin (north), Bubbs Creek Valley (roughly east) or Kern Canyon (south-east) require a high standard of fitness and some mountaineering experience.

Kings Canyon

Tips

There are only tracks through the wilderness of the two parks. You can cross them on foot or on horseback. Although both parks are open throughout the year, the more remote parts are inaccessible in winter. Mountain passes are seldom free of snow before July 1st. The so-called Generals Highway (47 miles/76 km) is blocked by deep snow between December and May. It takes the car-driver to the west of the Sequoia National Park. It leads from the Ash Mountain Entrance through Areale Giant Forest, Lodgepole (winter sports, especially in Wolverton) and Dorst, and leaves the park in the north-west, the far side of Lost Grove. From there it crosses the southern tip of the Sequoia National Forest and meets the US 180 (closed in winter) in the Grant Grove Area. This forms the only approach to the Kings Canyon National Park and links the two national parks together. The Generals Highway ends at Cedar Grove, where a 6 mile/10 km cul-de-sac continues to Cooper Creek.

Roads

There are about 900 miles/1450 km of tracks passing through the two parks. The eastern part of both parks, from which motor vehicles are barred, is crossed by the Pacific Crest Trail (here called the "John Muir Trail"), a

Walks

◀ *Giant redwoods in Kings Canyon National Park*

mountain track which is still being extended. It is 1350 miles/3780 km long, passes through various national parks, and follows the line of the ridge of the Sierra Nevada and the Cascade Mountains all the way from the Mexican to the Canadian borders. In the south of the Sequoia National Park the 40 mile/64 km High Sierra Trail runs eastwards from the Giant Forest Area, through superb countryside by way of Bearpaw Meadow as far as Wallace Creek, where it meets the John Muir Trail.

Coach tours	Sequoia & Kings Canyon Hospitality Service, Sequoia National Park, California 93262.
Events	Campfire programmes: summer evening recitals by the camp-fire in Giant Forest, Lodgepole, Dorst, Grant Grove and Cedar Grove; guided tours there as well; accompanied riding trips from Wolverton, Grant Grove and Cedar Grove (horses for hire at all of them).
Information	The entrances to the parks are 53 miles/86 km south-east of Fresno (see entry) on the CA 190 (Grant Cove Visitor Center) and 35 miles/56 km east of Visalia on the CA 198 (Lodgepole Visitor Center). Both Visitor Centers are open all the year round; they will advise you on the best way to look round the parks. The three motels inside the park are open only from the end of May to the beginning of September; at other times you will have to look for accommodation in Three Rivers, Visalia or Porterville.

Silicon Valley I 1

Location and *importance	At present the name "Silicon Valley" does not appear on any map. It was not until the early seventies that the name was invented by the media as a result of the growing importance of the silicon chip in the expansion of the industry of the Santa Clara Valley southwards along San Francisco Bay. The area along the US 101 between Palo Alto and San José roughly corresponds with Santa Clara County, once very rural indeed, with the mild climate and warm dry summers necessary for the successful growing of fruit and the processing of dried fruits.

Now Santa Clara County, with industries producing semi-conductors, computers and space equipment, has become one of the five most important industrial areas in the USA. In 1985 the average income per household was the third largest in the metropolitan areas of the United States.

American Dream	Silicon Valley has become the symbol of the living American dream of unlimited possibilities. Many of the electronic concerns which are now household names started off in the fifties as a small business in an old garage.
The birth of Hewlett-Packard	A perfect example is the world-famous electronics firm of Hewlett-Packard. In 1939, with capital of 538 dollars, the engineers Dave Packard and Bill Hewlett started to manufacture measuring instruments in the garage behind Dave Packard's house in Palo Alto. This was the date when Silicon Valley was born. After Walt Disney had ordered eight of these temperamental but cheap sound generators there was no holding back this young firm. By investing freely in research and with good market strategy the two engineers succeeded in keeping their products up to date with the latest technology. By the mid-fifties they were able to move into their present main buildings in the grounds of Stanford University.

Their company philosophy, the principles of which were self-responsibility, working together as partners and honest and open dealings, was an example to all. They promoted a team-orientated style of management and a close relationship with their employees.

Model character	As regards its dynamic high-tech development, the Santa Clara Valley conurbation has acquired a model character much imitated elsewhere. It is

fortunate in being near to research, development and educational centres, such as Stanford University, the Universities of Berkeley, San José and Santa Clara, as well as the big research laboratories of private firms such as Lockheed and IBM. These have proved of great value in the exchange of specialised information and is the principal reason for the frequency with which scientists, technicians and managers change jobs.

Moreover, the industrial sites no longer consist of office skyscrapers on the edge of a large city, but are mostly one-storey flat buildings away from the city of San Francisco. There is plenty of room for parking and green open spaces which are earmarked for future expansion. The setting-up of new businesses is made easier by public demand, the supply of land – much of it for residential development with good roads and shopping and leisure facilities – and by state contracts for new electronic products.

Development

In the fifties the building of research and development centres for electronic systems and parts was boosted by state contracts from the Pentagon and NASA for military, space and atomic research. Investment capital came mainly from the big banks in the east of the USA, with quite a lot from the region itself. Most of those who started up firms were college graduates and employees from research and development laboratories.

In the sixties big profits could be made by means of conveyor-belt production and sub-contracting. As early as the seventies, however, over-production and competitive pressures led to many closures and take-overs. Large firms decided on joint research projects; for example, Stanford University, the Pentagon and some private companies got together and built the Stanford Center for Integrated Systems in order to meet Japanese competition.

After the personal computer boom there was a further growth crisis in the mid-eighties. The short life of electronic products, which soon became out of date with new production technology, demanded huge investment in research and development. The firms established in this region have the advantage of being able to benefit from the constant flow of information.

Work and life styles

The fast-moving production cycle goes hand in hand with changing work styles. It is influenced by the constant demand for skilled workers and the resultant high turnover in staff, which leads – as shown at Hewlett-Packard – to a slovenly attitude on the part of the employees.

Also typical is the life style of the young, dynamic and extremely go-ahead technician who is prepared to give up his leisure time and apply himself to his work and vocational training. He is spurred on by the myth of unlimited economic growth reflected in status symbols such as expensive cars (an above-average number of Ferrari sports cars), his own house and a holiday home.

Future outlook

The future prognosis for the Silicon Valley must be based on caution and trying to warn against negative tendencies such as overdevelopment, using too much land by building too densely, and ecological pressures such as pollution of ground water and increasing road traffic. The image of the "cleaner" electronics industry is beginning to wobble a bit.

The so-called County General Plan is intended to combat these crisis symptoms. It has been prompted by self-help groups – mainly academics and women – who demand nil growth, quoting their right to have a say in such matters as further building on open spaces. However, this is likely to be achieved more as the result of long-term changes in thinking patterns than by any centralised measures.

Solvang

Santa Barbara County
Altitude: 495 ft/150 m
Population: 3100

Solvang – Danish windmill

Sonoma – wine-vaults

Location and origin
If you take the US 101 coast road south, and turn off at Buellton on to the CA 164, after a few miles you will reach Solvang, the biggest Danish settlement in the United States of America. It was given its name by the Danish-American Corporation in Chicago, who thought the Danish word "solvang" (sunny meadow) was a fitting description of the little town founded in 1911. Several professors involved in founding the town also set up a college, but this no longer exists.

Danish ambience
Tourism flourishes in this little town with the Danish character on the edge of the Santa Ynez mountains. There are houses in the Danish style and four windmills, and visitors can enjoy cakes and pastries made in the Danish manner and sold in several bakeries and patisseries. In the restaurants you can order karbonader and blomkal and hakkelof med løg (egg). Even a large Sheraton Hotel which opened a few years ago is decorated in the Danish style with Scandinavian furniture. Other hotels in the main street Mission Drive, Copenhagen Street or Alisal Road have such names as Kong Fredrik, Dannebrog, Hamlet, Kronborg and Royal København. A stroll through the little town makes a "velkommen" change.

Every year a three-day Danish Festival is held in the middle of September. The Santa Ines Mission (see Mission Stations), founded in 1804 in Mission Drive, contrasts with the general ambience of the town.

Sonoma

Sonoma County
Altitude: 85 ft/26 m
Population: 6000

Location and general
Sonoma lies some 43 miles/70 km north of San Francisco on the beautifully situated US 12, in the valley bearing the same name. Together with Napa

Vineyards in Sonoma County

Valley this is the most important wine producing region in the United States.

The name "Sonoma" is not, as often assumed, of Spanish origin, but can be traced back to the Wintun Indians who once lived here, and in whose language it meant "nose". However, exactly why this name was chosen when the town was founded in 1835 is uncertain.

The last of the 21 Californian mission stations (see entry) was built in Sonoma in 1823.   History

From June 14th to July 9th 1846 Sonoma was the capital of the short-lived Republic of California. In the morning mist of June 10th 30 cavalrymen from the Sacramento Valley drew up in front of the Casa Grande, the headquarters of the Mexican General Mariano Guadalupe, arrested him and his troops and proclaimed the Republic of California without a single shot being fired. William Ide was made President of the Republic.

An American man-of-war arrived in Monterey on July 7th, the day on which California became part of the United States. Two days later an advance guard arrived in Sonoma, thus finally putting an end to the "Grey Bear Revolution". However, the old bear flag lived on and in 1911 became the official flag of California.

On the eastern edge of Sonoma lies the Buena Vista wine producing   Wine production
concern, founded in 1857 by the Hungarian Count Agoston Haraszthy. He is generally considered to be the father of Californian wine production, even though the Franciscan Fathers had cultivated the first vines for their Communion wine as long ago as 1825. The vineyards in the Sonoma valley today cover an area of 5250 acres/2100 hectares.

The best-known wines, all originally from European vines, include Chardonnay, Pinot Noir, Merlot, Johannisberg Riesling and Gewürztraminer. On the higher slopes will be found Cabernet Sauvignon as well as Zinfandel, a vine developed in America. If you drive up the valley on the CA 12 and CA 128 you will find vineyard after vineyard. In addition to the wine cellars of the Buena Vista you can also visit those of the great Sebastiani and Heywood concerns.

State Historic Park   Also worth seeing is the Sonoma State Historic Park around the plaza. In addition to the San Francisco Solano Mission you will find the former residence of General Vallejos, dating from 1850/1851 (corner of West Spain Street and 3rd Street West), the 1834 Mexican barracks (East Spain Street and 1st Street West), the former Toscano Hotel and a row of interesting houses dating from the town's early days. (Tel. (707) 938-1578.)

Sonora   I 3

Tuolumne County
Altitude: 1825 ft/556 m
Population: 4000

Location and origin
The former gold-mining town of Sonora lies near Big Bonanza, the most profitable mine in Mother Lode County (see entry), west of Yosemite National Park (see entry) at the southern end of the CA 49. One year after it was founded in 1848 it had 5000 inhabitants – more than it has today. The gold-rush had just begun and the district soon turned out to be one of the most profitable. The first gold-miners were Mexican and came from the state of Sonora, after which they named their camp. They were followed by Chileans and Americans, who could not get on with the "latinos" and finally drove them out. A similar thing was happening at the same time in San Francisco, where demobilised soldiers stirred up hatred against the "foreigners".

Mark Twain, Bret Harte
The town, which stretches over seven hills, was the setting for several tales by the American writers Mark Twain and Bret Harte, both of whom stayed here from time to time.

Columbia State Historic Park
About 4 miles/6 km north of Sonora, on the CA 49, lies the Columbia State Historic Park. Here you can admire the once famous gold-mining town in all its old, restored glory. Thousands of hopeful gold-miners lived here at the time. Although restoration is not yet complete you can already visit most of the houses, including an old school-house, a boarding-house, a fire station and a restaurant. (Tel. (209) 532-4301.)

Caves
Within a 13 mile/20 km radius north of Sonora there are some caves well worth a visit. In Moaning Cavern near Vallecito, discovered in 1849, you can see interesting rock-formations from the vantage-point of a 100 ft/30 m spiral staircase.

Those parts of the caves which have not been built over can be seen in the course of a three and a half-hour guided tour (advance booking advisable; tel. (209) 736-2708). The other cave, Mercer Cavern, was discovered in 1885. Here you can see stalagmites, stalactites and aragonites (guided tours lasting three quarters of an hour; to book in advance tel. (209) 728-2101).

The Moaning Cavern is open all the year round, but the Mercer Cavern only from June to September; at weekends only during the remaining months of the year.

South Lake Tahoe

See Lake Tahoe

Stanford University

See Palo Alto

Stockton   H 2

San Joaquin County
Altitude: 13 ft/4 m
Population: 168,000

Founded in 1849, Stockton is linked to San Francisco Bay by a canal
78 miles/125 km long and 30 ft/9 m deep. Today it is an important distribution centre for grain and other agricultural products grown in the fertile
lands around the town.
In its early days it was little more than a place which fortune-seekers passed
through on their way to the gold-mines in Mother Lode County (see entry).
However, a lot of them returned disappointed and decided to remain in
Stockton. It was named after Commodore Robert F. Stockton who had
taken possession of California in the name of the United States of America
in 1846. Since then the town has developed into one of the two largest
inland ports in California (the other being Sacramento). Since the Second
World War, in particular, Stockton has experienced a rapid increase in
population.

Location and
origin

The Magnolia Historic District is well worth a visit. It has some well-
preserved mainly Victorian houses, the oldest dating from 1869.
There is also the Haggin Museum, built in Victory Park in 1931. It displays
works of art of the 19th and 20th c. (Open: Tue.–Sun. 1.30 p.m.–5 p.m.; tel.
(209) 462-4116.)

Places of interest

In Lodi, some 7 miles/12 km north of Stockton on the Joaquin River, can be
found the San Joaquin Historical Museum, where a number of historic
houses display a variety of items which document the county's agriculture
and customs.
Lodi has a dozen vineyards and has become well-known for growing Tokai
grapes and producing the famous Tokai wine.

**Surrounding
countryside:**
Lodi

Tijuana   S 4

Baja California – State of Mexico
Altitude: 16 ft/5 m
Population: 1 to 1½ million

The best way to get to Tijuana from San Diego is by tram. They leave every
15 minutes from behind the Amtrak Station, Broadway and Kettner Boulevard. There are usually parking spaces available at the railway station. The
trams take you as far as the American border town of San Ysidro, where
they turn round. The journey takes about 40 minutes. From there you can
walk to Tijuana over numerous ramps. There are no border-crossing problems in either direction.

How to get there

Tijuana is the most important city on the border between Mexico and the
United States, and is more influenced by the latter than any other Mexican
town. The city lives mainly by tourism and the refining industry. Every year
it attracts many millions of visitors, mainly from the catchment areas of the
cities of San Diego (15 miles/25 km) and Los Angeles (160 miles/260 km).
Therefore it is not surprising that Tijuana claims to be the "most visited city
in the world", for in the last few years it has grown so fast that the actual
size of its population can only be estimated roughly. Certainly, having
completed the 10 to 15 minute walk from the border to the main thoroughfare, Avenida de Revolucíon, the tourist is overwhelmed by the masses of
people pushing their way through the streets; the Americans, intent on
making cheap purchases free of customs duty, and the locals, many of
whom stand around on the sidewalks begging for coins. US dollars are
very popular because 2200 pesos can be obtained for one dollar.

Location and
importance

Tijuana

Tijuana – Fronton Palacio

San Diego

San Ysidro
US Customs

Trolley
Stop

USA

Calle Malinche
(Toll Road)

Mexican Customs

Airport

Pacific Ocean

Bull Ring by-the-Sea

1st.

Downtown
Shopping District

2nd.

3rd.

4th.

5th.

6th.

7th.

8th.

9th.

10th.

Heroes

Niños

Madero

Negrete

Ocampo

Cultural
Center

Jai Alai Fronton

Police

Plaza
Fiesta

Blvd. Agua Caliente

Ave

Tijuana

Calle

Paseo de

Ave

Blvd. Cuauhtémoc

Gral.

Ave Cuauhtémoc de

Padre

Independencia

City Hall

River

Kino

Ave Rodríguez

Heroes

International

Bull Ring

Ave

Rodolfo

Gustavo Salinas

Sánchez
Taboada

16 de Septiembre

Tijuana

Baja California Norte
Estados Unidos Mexicanos
México

(Plan not to scale)

Country Club
& Golf Course

US Consulate

Agua Caliente
Racetrack

© *Baedeker*

MEXICO

326

Tijuana – Mexican traditional art and souvenirs

Tijuana (in the language of the Chochimi Indians "ticuán" means "near water") has a brief history. The city of today developed from a cattle ranch named Tia Juana (Aunt Anna), built by José Maria Echandi in 1829. It began to grow during the Prohibition Period (1920–1933), when the consumption of alcohol was prohibited in the United States and numerous thirsty souls made the short trip across the border.
History

Its importance lies in the great quantity of duty-free goods on offer together with Mexican folk-art and souvenirs, its various festivals and events and its night-life. The place where it all happens, especially at week-ends, is the main square, the Parque Municipal Guerrero, the shopping area around the Avenida de Revolución and the Bulevar Agua Caliente, with their many hotels, restaurants, shops and varieties of sports.
Border town

Tijuana is not just a typical run-down border town with cheap junk-shops, it also shows signs of American influence. There is an American shopping-centre, an international airport and a glass-box of a hotel. The further away from the Avenida de Revolución you get the more you find the slum areas being replaced by new houses. More and more people are streaming into Tijuana from the provinces, but complete redevelopment is not financially viable because new slums keep appearing, together with new factories which find cheap labour here (people call these factories "maquiladoras").

However, Tijuana has kept to the old customs. Bull-fights (no blood is spilled) are still held here on eighteen Sundays in the year: four in each of the months of July, August and September, the rest spread unevenly over the months of May, June and October. They all start at 4 p.m. Tickets can be purchased in advance from Ticketron in Los Angeles (tel. 213/410-1062), in San Diego (tel. 619/231-3554) and at the Amtrak Station, Mexicoach (tel. 619/232-5049).
Bull-fights

In the Hipódromo de Agua Caliente, Agua Caliente Boulevard, there is greyhound racing on Monday, Tuesday, Wednesday and Friday, and horse
Hipódromo de Agua Caliente

Hotel Truckee

racing on Saturday and Sunday. For information in San Diego tel. (619) 299-8518. On this phone number you can also obtain information regarding Jai Alai, with tote-betting, which takes place every day except Thursday in the Fronton Palacio (Avenida de Revolución, corner of 7th Street). Jai Alai is a most attractive sport in which the players hurl a small ball against a wall from a basket on a long stick.

Centro Cultural

One of the first impressions of Mexico is provided by the architecturally interesting culture centre known as Centro, Cultural FONART – which looks rather like a big garage from the outside – on the Paseo de los Heroes and Avenida Independicia. Here short films (multi-media shows) about Mexico are shown and there is an exhibition of Mexico's history (tel. (706) 684-1111).

Tip

As USA Motor Insurance policies are not valid here it is necessary to take one out with a Mexican insurance company. You can obtain further details from the Baja Tijuana Information Center in San Diego, 7860 Mission Center Court; tel. 619/299-8518.

Truckee   G 5

Placer County
Altitude: 5820 ft/1774 m
Population: 2500

Location and general

Truckee, once a little lumberjack village, has developed only slowly, in spite of its strategically favourable position near Lake Tahoe (see entry) and its superb ski-slopes which are among the best in the United States. As a result the small town still provides a good example of a place which has changed but little since the 19th century.

It owes its name to the river called Truckee after the Paiute Indian, who in 1844 led Elisha Steven's group through the Donner Pass (see entry) which they had discovered. Stevens had in fact made up his mind to be the first to cross the Sierra Nevada to Alta California with a covered-wagon trek.

Truckee was founded in 1863 – the same year in which President Abraham Lincoln signed the law which authorised the building of a transcontinental railway. The Central Pacific Railroad Company decided to run the lines right through the middle of Truckee. This led to the development of the timber industry, now long since replaced by tourism as the most important source of income. In 1913 California's first ski-club was formed in Truckee; since then the number has grown to more than twenty. The following ski-slopes are to be found in the immediate vicinity (see Lake Tahoe):

Origin

Boreal, 10 miles/16 km west on the US 80, exit to Castle Peak (Nov.–Apr., tel. 426-3666); Donner Ski Ranch, 10 miles/16 km west on the US 80 (Dec.–Apr., tel. 426-3578); Northstar, 6 miles/9 km on the CA 267 (Nov.–Apr., tel. 562-1330); Tahoe Donor, 6 miles/9 km west on the US 80 (Dec.–Apr., tel. 587-6028).

Ski-slopes

One of the most interesting buildings is the 30-room Truckee Hotel which dates from the year the town was founded. The exterior has barely been changed in the 125 years of its existence. Its name has changed, however, for it used to be called The New Whitney.

Truckee Hotel

It is worth making a trip from Truckee (or Lake Tahoe) to Virginia City, 68 miles/110 km away in Western Nevada. The city was founded in 1859. The best route is the US 80 east, the NV 395 south and then the NV 341. Virginia City lies immediately above Comstock Lode, rich in gold and silver. Comstock Lode covers an area only 2 miles/3 km long and 500 ft/150 m wide, yet within a period of 20 years gold and silver ore worth more than 400 million dollars (in terms of purchasing power at that time) was mined. A point of interest is that the American Civil War (1861–1865) was in part financed by the gold and silver found in this town.

Surroundings: Virginia City

Virginia City is now purely a tourist town which has retained its historical character surprisingly well. Even the "Territorial Enterprise", the news-paper on which Mark Twain began his career as a writer, has now appeared once more in this town of only 800 inhabitants. Ten times as many people lived here between 1860 and 1880; at that time Virginia City was in fact the most important town between San Francisco and Denver.

Ukiah

E 1

Mendocino County
Altitude: 640 ft/195 m
Population: 12,750

Ukiah, 3 miles/5 km from the beautiful Lake Mendocino, lies on the US 101 in a fertile valley which the Indians named Yokaya or Ukiah, meaning roughly south or deep valley. It is the distribution centre for the region's agricultural produce, mainly pears and grapes. The timber industry is also important. In 1898 the International Geodesic Union was founded in Ukiah. It is one of the world's five surveying institutes (all on latitude 39°8' north).

Location and general

Universal City

See Los Angeles

Boat harbour in Ventura

University of California

See Irvine, Los Angeles, Riverside, San Diego/La Jolla, Santa Barbara, Santa Cruz.

Vallejo   H 1

Solano County
Altitude: 50 ft/15 m
Population: 87,000

Location and importance

Situated north of San Francisco on the San Pablo Bay, Vallejo was named after the Mexican General Mariano Guatalupe Vallejo, who tried to persuade the Americans to create the capital of California on his ranch. He did succeed – albeit only for one week from January 5th to 12th 1852 – but the location was found to be inadequate, so the parliament was moved to Sacramento. The politicians were not satisfied with that either and returned to Vallejo again between January 3rd and February 4th 1853, before deciding to move again first to Benicia (see entry) and finally, for the second time, to Sacramento.

Naval dockyard

In spite of all its vicissitudes the town developed, not least because of the purchase of Mare Island, situated between Mare Island Street and San Pablo Bay just before Vallejo. Today submarines fitted with atomic missiles, and other naval vessels are repaired on this 2300-acre/930-hectare site.

Naval Museum

There is also a Marine Academy in Vallejo. The old City Hall now houses an Historical Naval Museum portraying the history of the town and the naval dockyard (734 Marin Street; open: Tue.–Fri. 10 a.m.–4.30 p.m., Sat. and Sun. 1 p.m.–4.30 p.m.; tel. (707) 643-0077).

Ventura   O 2

Ventura County
Altitude: 50 ft/15 m
Population: 75,000

Ventura lies on the US 101 and is 60 miles/96 km north-west of Los Angeles, 30 miles/48 km from Santa Barbara, and about 190 miles/300 km from San Diego. Ventura is an abbreviation for the San Buenaventura Mission (see Mission Stations). Around this centre the town of Ventura has developed over decades. It lies in the middle of an agricultural region. During the previous century people began to grow citrus fruits, avocados and other produce. Today it is the USA's most important area for the cultivation of citrus fruits.
In the early twenties oil was discovered very near to Ventura. This led to the town's economic upswing, and today there is a large oil refinery here.
Since the end of the Second World War holidaymakers have been enticed to Ventura by the superb beaches, especially the San Buenaventura State Beach, a marina which will accommodate 1500 motor and sailing boats, as well as by the excursion boats plying between here and the Channel Islands (see Channel Islands National Park).

Location and importance

Not far from the Mission stands the Ventura County Historical Museum, with artefacts from the Spanish, Mexican and early American periods (100 East Main Street; open: Tue.–Sun. 10 a.m.–5 p.m.; admission free; tel. (805) 653-0323). The Albinger Archaeological Museum is in the same street. It has valuable finds from Indian culture (1500 B.C.), as well as Chinese and Mexican artefacts (113 East Main Street; open: Tue.–Sun. 10 a.m.–4 p.m.; admission free; tel. (805) 648-5823.)

Museums

Weaverville   C 3

Trinity County
Altitude: 2012 ft/613 m
Population: 2800

Weaverville, situated on the CA 299 in North California, is a suitable setting-off point for excursions into the Shasta Trinity National Forest (see Redding). Named after one of the gold miners who established this town outside Mother Lode County (see entry), Weaverville experienced its heyday during the 1850s, when it had more inhabitants than it has now. This was due mainly to the influx of more than 2000 Chinese who worked in the gold mines. In 1854 a feud, called a Tong War, broke out between the Chinese communities, as a result of which part of the Chinese quarter was burned down and a large number of the people left. Only a few Chinese still live in Weaverville.

Location and origin

California's oldest Chinese temple (1874) bears witness to their former presence. It is still used on occasions today. All the objects to be found in this temple, such as valuable carpets and scrolls, were imported from China. The temple stands in the centre of the little town, in Joss House State Historic Park, where an exhibition will tell you all about the life of the Chinese and their contribution to California's development. (Open: daily 10 a.m.–5 p.m.; tel. (916) 623-5284.)
The wild gold-mining period, when anything was allowed, has left its mark.

Chinese Temple

Chinese temple in Weaverville

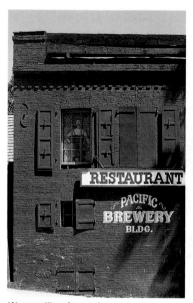

Weaverville – former brewery

Singed redwood

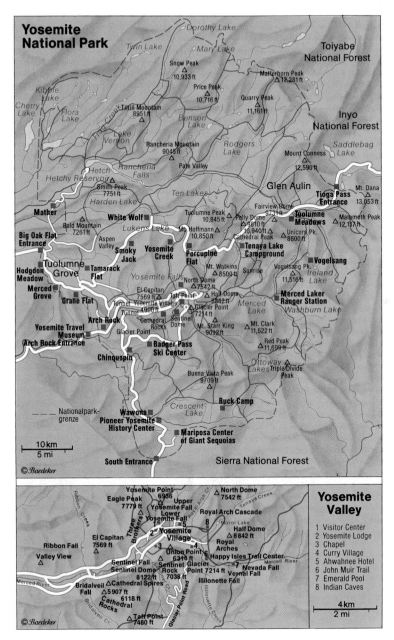

Yosemite National Park

Toiyabe National Forest

Dorothy Lake
Twin Lake
Mary Lake
Snow Peak
10,933 ft
Price Peak
10,716 ft
Matterhorn Peak
△12,281 ft
Quarry Peak
11,161 ft

Kibbie Lake
Cherry Lake
Flora Lake
Tiltill Mountain
8951 ft △

Lake Vernon
Rancheria Mountain
9045 ft △
Benson Lake
Rodgers Lake
Mount Conness
12,590 ft

Inyo National Forest
Saddlebag Lake

Hetch Hetchy Reservoir
Rancheria Falls
Pate Valley
Ten Lakes
Fairview Dome
9731 ft △
Tioga Pass Entrance
Mt. Dana
13,053 ft

Smith Peak
7751 ft △
Harden Lake
Glen Aulin
Tuolumne Meadows

Mather
Bald Mountain
7261 ft △
White Wolf
Tuolumne Peak
10,845 ft △
Polly Dome
△9810 ft
Mammoth Peak
△12,117 ft

Big Oak Flat Entrance
Aspen Valley
Smoky Jack
Lukens Lake
Mt. Hoffmann △
10,850 ft
Mt. Hoffmann
10,940 ft △
Cathedral Peak
Unicorn Pk.
△8600 ft

Hodgdon Meadow
Tuolumne Grove
Tamarack Flat
Yosemite Creek
Porcupine Flat
Tenaya Lake Campground
Vogelsang

Merced Grove
Crane Flat
Yosemite Falls
Mt. Watkins
△8500 ft
Sunrise
Vogelsang Pk.
11,516 ft △
Ireland Lake

Arch Rock
El Capitan
7569 ft
North Dome
△7542 ft
Half Dome
8342 ft
Glacier Point
7214 ft
Merced Lake Ranger Station
Washburn Lake

Tunnel
Yosemite Village
4800 ft
Tunnel
Cathedral Rocks
Sentinel Dome
Merced Lake
Mt. Clark
11,522 ft

Yosemite Travel Museum
Arch Rock Entrance
Glacier Point
Mt. Starr King
9092 ft
Red Peak
△11,699 ft

Chinquapin
Badger Pass Ski Center
Ottoway Lakes
Triple Divide Peak

Buena Vista Peak
9709 ft

Crescent Lake
Buck Camp

Nationalpark-grenze
Wawona
Pioneer Yosemite History Center
Mariposa Center of Giant Sequoias

10 km
5 mi
© Baedeker
South Entrance
Sierra National Forest

Yosemite Valley

Yosemite Point
6936
Eagle Peak
7779 ft
Upper Yosemite Fall
Lower Yosemite Fall
North Dome
△7542 ft
Royal Arch Cascade
Mirror Lake
Half Dome
△8842 ft

Ribbon Creek
El Capitan
7569 ft
Three Brothers
Yosemite Village
Royal Arches
Happy Isles Trail Center
Merced River

Ribbon Fall
Union Point
6314 ft
Nevada Fall
Emerald Pool
Vernal Fall

Valley View
Sentinel Fall
Sentinel Dome
8122 ft
Sentinel Rock
7038 ft
Glacier Point 7214 ft
Illilouette Fall

Bridalveil Fall
△5907 ft
Cathedral Spires
6118 ft
Cathedral Rocks
Taft Point
△7480 ft

Merced River
Bridalveil Cr.
Glacier Point Road
Illilouette Creek

© Baedeker

1 Visitor Center
2 Yosemite Lodge
3 Chapel
4 Curry Village
5 Ahwahnee Hotel
6 John Muir Trail
7 Emerald Pool
8 Indian Caves

4 km
2 mi

For example, there is the picture of a scantily dressed prostitute looking down on passers-by from the window of a former brewery and pub opposite the temple (picture p. 333).

Jackson Museum

The still authentic townscape differs little today from the descriptions given by the American author Bret Harte more than 100 years ago. The items exhibited in the J. J. Jackson Memorial Museum also add to the local colour and history; Indian artefacts, Chinese weapons, fossils and even prison cells brought here from afar can be seen. (Open: May 1st–Oct. 31st daily 10 a.m.–5 p.m.; admission free; tel. (916) 623-5111.)

Yosemite National Park   I/J 4/5

Location and general

Yosemite National Park (pronounced "yossémmitty") was founded in 1890, and extends over 1190 sq. miles/3082 sq. km in the centre of eastern California. It covers a section of the Sierra Nevada rich in forests and lakes, the scenic highlight of which is the Yosemite Valley, measuring some 8 miles/13 km long and some ½-2 miles/1–3 km wide. Swollen by melting snows in spring, numerous waterfalls cascade down the almost vertical granite walls of the Merced River Valley (known to the Spanish as El Rio de Nuestra Señora de la Merced). These walls rise to between 3000 and 5000 ft/900 and 1500 m.

**Flora and fauna

The almost flat valley bottom (at 4000 ft/1200 m above sea-level) is covered in lush flower-strewn meadows, thick bushes and dense clumps of trees. The vastly different levels to be found in the park (between 130 and 1300 ft/400 and 4000 m) produce ideal living conditions for a wide range of animals and plants. Thus wild deer, black bear, coyotes, badgers and numerous rodents roam the lower regions, while marmots frequent the inhospitable mountain heights.

Several clumps of mighty redwoods (sequoia gigantea) are also one of the special sights to be seen in Yosemite National Park.

History

Origin

The Yosemite Valley was formed over millions of years. Originally there was a wide valley here with a river which in time hollowed out a canyon up to 2100 ft/650 m deep. During the Ice Age the canyon became filled right to the top with ice and possibly glaciers. The ice widened the canyon at its weakest points and hollowed out the U-shaped Yosemite Valley. The last glacier filled it to a depth of only about one-third, leaving a moraine of ice behind. Behind this moraine the melting ice formed a lake, which slowly filled with deposits, thus forming the plains in the valley on which meadows and forests are found today.

Development

The first men must have come to the Yosemite Valley 8000 to 10,000 years ago, and Miwok Indians (Ahwahnee) lived there for more than 4500 years before the Europeans came. In the middle of the 19th c., when the gold-rush and its accompanying army of adventurers descended upon California and the villages and hunting-grounds of the Indian aborigines, the latter often carried out bloody reprisal attacks on the white man's mining towns and trading posts. Whilst on a punitive expedition against the Indians on March 25th 1851 the Mariposa Battalion became the first white men to enter the valley. They gave it the Indian name of "U-zu-mate", the name of the grisly bear native to these forests.

The reports made by the Mariposa soldiers quickly aroused public interest in this special and beautiful part of the country and the first visitors were

Gigantic redwoods ▶

Yosemite Valley – El Capitán and Cathedral Rocks

attracted there as early as 1851. In 1864, during the Civil War, President Lincoln signed the Yosemite Transfer of Ownership, which ceded the Yosemite Valley and the Mariposa Grove to California, on condition that it was preserved in its state of natural beauty.

The Scottish naturalist John Muir, who came to the Yosemite Valley four years later, became the chief advocate of the National Park concept. Yellowstone National Park was the first to be created in 1872. It was followed by Yosemite in 1890. California then returned the area to the Federal Government, and with the passage of time it grew to its present size.

Recent history

The first cavalrymen entered the valley along Indian trails; ten years later the first roads were laid and in 1900 the first car came in along the Wawona Road, although cars were not officially allowed until 1913. In 1907 the railway line from San Francisco to El Portal was built along the western boundary of the park, and this remained in use until 1945. The all-weather road from Merced (see entry) was completed in 1926. That was when tourists began to flood into Yosemite National Park; now some 2½ million people visit it every year. In 1984 Yosemite National Park received very special recognition from the United Nations who added it to the list of World Heritage Sites, which includes the natural and made-made Wonders of the World.

Sights in Yosemite Valley

* El Capitán

Coming from Merced your first impressive view of Yosemite Valley is from Valley View Point at the western entrance to the valley. One of the most magnificent and arresting sights is that of the rock massif known as El

Half Dome

Capitán (7572 ft/2307 m), forming in bold relief the very cornerstone of the valley. The impression made by this mighty monolith comes mainly from its dominant position, its majestic shape and its precipitous walls rising 300 ft/100 m above the floor of the valley. Its two end walls facing west and south meet almost at right angles; it is an arduous climb to the top.

Immediately to the west lies the 1612 ft/491 m high Ribbon Fall in Ribbon Creek. East of El Capitán rise the triple peaks of the Three Brothers, the highest of which, Eagle Peak (7780 ft/2371 m), provides a superb view of the valley and Yosemite Falls. *Ribbon Fall

*Eagle Peak

Yosemite Falls are east of Eagle Peak, roughly in the middle of the valley. They are in three parts, with a total overall height of 2425 ft/739 m: the Upper Fall, some 30 ft/10 m wide, plunges down 450 ft/136 m almost vertically; the Middle Cascade consists of a number of small cascades (totalling 680 ft/206 m, and the Lower Fall is 320 ft/98 m high. Yosemite Falls are among the highest in the world and in spring provide the most awe-inspiring sight in the National Park, but they disappear in summer and autumn. In winter a magnificent ice peak, up to 300 ft/90 m in height, forms on the Upper Fall. *Yosemite Falls

East of the Upper Fall, on the end face of the Upper Yosemite Fall Cliff, stands a granite needle known as Lost Arrow. Still further east lies Indian Canyon, the soft stone of which shows more marked signs of erosion than that in the Yosemite valley. The rock-wall on the opposite side of the canyon gets its name of Royal Arches from its semi-circular hollows. On the west side will be found the Royal Arches Cascade, a waterfall about 1000 ft/ 300 m high, which is normally almost dry but which swells considerably in spring and after heavy rain. Royal Arches

East of the Royal Arches, where the valley joins Tenaya Canyon, Washing-ton Column towers above the valley floor. It is a granite tower measuring North Dome

1930 ft/585 m, dwarfed however by the barren North Dome (7545 ft/2299 m).

At its east end the Yosemite Valley forks into two narrow valleys, Tenaya Creek (north-east) and Merced River (south-east). Between the square blocks of rock at the foot of the right-hand wall of the Tenaya Creek Canyon can be found the Indian Caves, where Indians once lived. About 1 mile/2 km upstream the reflection of the North Dome plays on the clear waters of the beautiful Mirror Lake. The best time to see this is during the still hours of morning and evening when the wind has dropped. Tenaya Creek brings great masses of gravel and mud into the lake, so there is a real threat that it may silt up. It dries up almost completely in late summer and does not fill up again until after the autumn storms. There is a 3 mile/5 km path leading round the lake.

Mirror Lake

Opposite the North Dome, and forming the east end of the Yosemite Valley, towers the Half Dome (8850 ft/2695 m) which, as the name suggests, is shaped like a vertically-halved dome. So far it has not been established whether it ever had the other half. It can be climbed from the far side (but only in the warm months of the year) the last stretch to the summit being by cable-car. South of Half Dome is where the Merced River Canyon ends. A little way upstream are Vernal Fall (330 ft/100 m high) and Nevada Fall (610 ft/186 m).

* Half Dome
* Vernal Fall
* Nevada Fall

At the south-east corner of the Yosemite Valley where it joins the Merced Canyon the rocky peak known as Glacier Point (7217 ft/2199 m) reaches towards the sky. This is without doubt the loveliest and most popular spot hereabouts from which to look down over the Yosemite Valley into the Merced Canyon with its waterfalls, and across the High Sierra.

Glacier Point

A valley wall runs in an almost straight line from Glacier Point for about 1 mile/2 km. Its lower regions are covered in boulders. It is dominated by Sentinel Dome (8126 ft/2476 m) and ends in Sentinel Rock (7040 ft/2145 m), the most prominent rock on the south wall.

* Sentinel Rock

Further west you will come to the two slender Cathedral Spires (5900 ft/1800 m and 6120 ft/1865 m high), side by side with the imposing twinned Cathedral Rocks (6630 ft/2021 m) opposite the Capitán. Bridal Veil Fall (50–70 ft/15–20 m wide), cascades down for some 620 ft/189 m on the lower western slopes of these rocks. It is so called because, when the wind is blowing, the waters take on the appearance of a bridal veil. The Ahwahneechee Indians native to the Yosemite Valley named it Pohono, meaning roughly "spirit that blows the air". The wind blows round the waterfall, sometimes making it move sideways. In the summer months, however, it dries up completely.

* Cathedral Rock
* Bridal Veil Rock

The focus of tourism in the valley is Yosemite Village below the main falls. Here you will find the ranger's office, visitors' centre, museum, information centres, accommodation, post-office, shops, riding stables and so forth. In a building west of the Visitor Center is an Indian Cultural Museum with a rich collection depicting Indian cultural history.

Yosemite Village

Roads and Trails

Valley Loop Road runs for 17 miles/27 km along both sides of the Merced River through the Yosemite Valley. In the east a road branches off to Mirror Lake.
From Chinquapin (on the Wawona Road) Glacier Point Road leads to Glacier Point by way of Badger Pass (ski-slopes) and close to the southern edge of the Yosemite Valley.

Roads

◀ *Yosemite Falls*

Half Dome

Mountain paths	Some of the most beautiful places in the valley and its vicinity can be reached by numerous paths of varying difficulty.
Glacier Point Trail	Glacier Point Trail, leading from Yosemite Village and laid down in 1871 before Glacier Point Road was built, is a difficult route (5 miles/8 km) to Glacier Point, with superb views over the valley;
Mirror Lake Loop	A pleasant walk (3 miles/5 km) around Mirror Lake, then ascending Tenaya Creek Valley, past the junction with Snow Creek Trail from Tenaya Lake, and then back to Mirror Lake;
Half Dome Trail	A difficult route (17 miles/27 km; also suitable for horses) from Happy Isles, going first along the upper edge of the Nevada Fall and then up Little Yosemite Valley to the top of Half Dome;
Inspiration Point Trail	A strenuous way round (2½ miles/4 km) from Wawona Tunnel to Old Inspiration Point by the old Wawona Road, which formed the main route to the Yosemite Valley before the Wawona Tunnel was completed;
Vernal Nevada Falls Trail	A mainly difficult road (1½ miles/2½ km) from Happy Isles in the Merced River Canyon uphill to its two waterfalls;
John Muir Trail	The northern end of the trail starts here and it runs for 210 miles/340 km to the Sequoia and Kings Canyon National Parks, through the Californian Highlands as far as Mount Whitney. The trek will take about 20 days, mostly at heights of between 10,000 and 14,000 ft/3000 and 4200 m.
Yosemite Falls Trail	A circular route (7½ miles/12 km) from the camp site near Yosemite Lodge to the upper edge of the Yosemite Falls, with beautiful views over the valley from Yosemite Point and Columbia Rock;

Three Brothers

A difficult route (about 9 miles/14 km) from Glacier Point via Illilouette Creek, near its waterfall, then past Panorama Cliffs and through the Merced Canyon to the Nevada Fall;

Panorama Trail

A strenuous route (14 miles/21 km) from Glacier Point via the southern edge of the Yosemite Valley to the Wawona Tunnel. There are viewing points at Taft Point, Crocker Point and Dewey Point;

Pohono Trail

A steep circular route (1½ miles/2½ km) from Happy Isles to Sierra Point, from where you can see five waterfalls all at the same time (Nevada, Vernal, Illilouette and the Upper and Lower Yosemite Falls).
Footpaths also lead to the floor of the valley, e.g., to the foot of the Yosemite Fall and Bridal Veil Fall.

Sierra Point Trail

Sights to see in the rest of the park area

From the South Entrance the 30 mile/48 km long Wawona Road leads to the Yosemite Valley. About 2 miles/3 km north-east of the park entrance stands the Mariposa Grove of Big Trees (Spanish "mariposa" means butterfly), the largest of the three groups of giant redwoods in the National Park. There are some 500 fully-grown giant redwood trees (sequoiadendron giganteum; see Sequoia and Kings Canyon National Parks) in this forest area which covers about ½ sq. mile/1 sq. km at between 5500 and 7000 ft/1675 and 2135 m above sea level.
In the lower part of this grove stands Grizzly Giant, 210 ft/64 m tall and with a basal circumference of 96½ ft/29.4 m, the biggest tree (about 2700 years old) in Yosemite Park.
In its upper part stands the world-famous "Wawona Tree", the top of which

* Mariposa Grove of Big Trees
* Grizzly Giant

341

broke off under the weight of snow in 1969. A tunnel was made through its trunk in 1881 and the road leads through it.

In the Mariposa Grove Museum there are exhibits on the natural history of the region and its discovery. From Wawona Point (6813 ft/2076 m) in the north of the grove there is a fine view over the High Sierra and into the San Joaquin Valley.

Wawona

The Wawona tourist centre (hotel) lies about 5 miles/8 km north-west of the southern entrance, by the Wawona Road. On both sides of the southern arm of the Merced River will be found the Pioneer Yosemite History Center, an open-air museum with log-cabins, a jail, wagons and a covered bridge dating from the early days of the National Park.

Wawona Tunnel

About 27 miles/43 km north of the southern entrance, on the far side of Chinquapin, where Glacier Point Road turns off to the north-east and just before the entrance to the Yosemite Valley basin, the Wawona Road passes through the Wawona Tunnel, built in 1933 to preserve the landscape. It is 1400 yds/1.3 km long. There are then superb views down into the Yosemite Valley.

El Portal

From El Portal the 9 mile/14 km long Merced Road leads to Valley View Point at the west end of the Yosemite Valley. The El Portal tourist centre was set up in the south-west corner of the park area as a supply centre for park visitors and placed under the protection of the National Park to prevent over-development. Until 1945 this was the terminus of the 78 mile/126 km Yosemite Valley Railroad running from Merced (locomotives and carriages can be seen at the former station, now the El Portal Museum).

Cascade Falls

The Arch Rock Entrance is about 2 miles/3 km north-east of El Portal; 3 miles/5 km further on are the 500 ft/152 m-high Cascade Falls at Cascade Creek and Tanarack Creek.

Merced Grove of Giant Sequoias Tuolumne Grove of Big Trees

From Big Oak Flat Entrance in the west of the National Park Big Flat Oak Road (some 20 miles/32 km long) leads to Yosemite Valley. About 6 miles/ 9 km south-east of the park entrance is the Merced Grove of Giant Sequoias, the smallest of the three groups of redwoods. To the north-east, on the far side of the Tioga Road (one-way approach road from Crane Flat) stands the Tuolumne Grove of Big Trees, the third of Yosemite Park's groves of sequoias.

Tenaya Lake
* Tuolumne Meadows

Tioga Road, 43 miles/69 km long (closed in winter), crosses the central area of the National Park in a roughly west-east direction. It branches off from Big Oak Flat Road at Crane Flat and passes through some magnificent mountain scenery, via the High Sierra past White Wolf (just off to the north is a lodge with cabins and tents; to book tel. 372-13 26) to Tioga Pass (10,000 ft/3030 m). On its way the road passes the north-west bank of the quiet Lake Tenaya, the rocky banks of which show typical signs of glacial abrasion; it also passes through Tuolumne Meadows (8900 ft/2713 m; visitors' centre; lodge with tent site, booking necessary; tel. 372-13 13), upland meadows surrounded by high rounded hilltops; this is the most extensive sub-alpine meadow in the Sierra Nevada. The Tuolumne River flows through it. This river crosses the National Park some 10 miles/16 km north of the Merced River and parallel to it, and on its way it forms a number of waterfalls in the magnificent Grand Canyon of the Tuolumne River. The picturesque May Lake is not far away.

Hetch Hetchy Valley

Further down river is the Hetch Hetchy Valley, somewhat similar to the Yosemite Valley but smaller, with steep rocky walls and high cataracts. Since the completion of the O'Shaughnessy Dam (1923; accessible from Mather) the valley has been filled by the Hetchy Hetchy Reservoir, which supplies drinking water to San Francisco and other towns.

Walks

The northern half of the Yosemite National Park has few roads and can be explored only along footpaths and riding tracks. Tuolumne Meadows is the place to set off from for tours into the mountain wilderness (only in summer). Mountaineering experience and climbing equipment are essential.

Notes

There are three ways to drive to the park: from the south on the CA 141 (66 miles/107 km from Merced; see entry), in the west on the CA 41 (61 miles/ 99 km from Fresno; see entry) and in the west on the CA 120 (12 miles/20 km from Lee Vining); the latter route is closed in the winter months because it leads over the 9900 ft/3000 m high Tioga Pass. From the park entrances it is still a long way to the valley.
On the 120 and 140 roads from San Francisco it is about 200 miles/320 km to the park entrance. It would be very tiring to drive there and back in a day and would leave little time for the park itself. One-day coach tours run from San Francisco, and you can also fly but that is rather expensive.
The Yosemite Transportation System offers tours by coach through Yosemite Valley (2 hours), to Mariposa Grove (½ day), to Glacier Point (½ day) or both combined (1 day).
About 4 miles/7 km south of the South Entrance runs the narrow-gauge Yosemite Mountain Sugar Pine Railroad with old-fashioned trains.

How to get there

Yosemite Lodge and Curry Village in Yosemite Valley.

Horse-riding

A wide range of events and functions awaits the visitor during the summer months. You should consult the park newspaper "Yosemite Guide" which appears weekly. In addition to the numerous ranger programmes (lectures etc.) and campfire talks, there are geology walks (guided tours with geological explanations), ecology float trips (accompanied trips floating down the Merced River with ecological commentaries) and mountaineering, riding and cycling tours (cassette recordings of tours available).

Events

For anyone visiting the Yosemite National Park in the high season, in spring and early autumn, and wishing to stay overnight it is essential to book accommodation in advance. For the hotels and motels inside the park (see Practical Information, Hotels and Motels, Yosemite National Park) there is a centre which will take advance bookings for the Ahwahnee and Wawona Hotels as well as for Yosemite Lodge and Curry Village. If you have to spend the night outside the park you will have the long journey into the park each day.
You can reach the Yosemite Waterfall in a few minutes if you get off the No. 7 bus at Yosemite Lodge.

Accommodation

Yosemite National Park is open 24 hours a day all the year round. You can telephone the Visitor Center on 209/372-0298, ext. 299. The centre will provide information about walks and the maps and permits you will need. (General park information: tel. 209/372-0200 ext. 264. For information about the weather and road conditions: tel. 209/372-4602. To book rooms in advance: tel. 209/252-4848.)

Information

Practical Information from A to Z

Accommodation

See Camping, Hotels and Motels, Youth Hostels

Air Travel

Because of the great distances in the United States in general and in California in particular, air travel is the preferred means of transport. The airports of Los Angeles and San Francisco are among the most important in the country; both are served by some 50 American and international airlines. The airport of San Diego is at present situated near the town but in a few years it will be moved. It does not have the same amount of traffic as the two other cities. In the area of Los Angeles there are in addition to the main airport (International Airport; acronym LAX) four others: Ontario, Hollywood-Burbank, Long Beach Municipal Airport and Orange County Airport. Further information about the airports can be found in the A-Z section under the appropriate heading.

Art Galleries

Beeches Gallery, 7th Avenue, between San Carlos and Mission Street.   Carmel
Connoisseur Gallery I, San Carlos Street, north of 6th Avenue.
Connoisseur Gallery II, Mission Street, between Ocean and 7th Street.
James Peter Cost Gallery, Dolores St. and 6th Ave.
Josephus Daniels Gallery (photograph), Dolores St. near 6th Ave.
Bill W. Dodge Gallery, Dolores St. between 5th and 6th Ave.
Hanson Gallery, Corner Ocean Ave. and San Carlos St.
Miner's Gallery Americana, Corner 6th Ave. and Lincoln St.
Palumbo, Northwest Corner 6th Ave. and Dolores St.
Photography West Gallery, Dolores St. and Ocean Ave.
Simic Galleries, Corner San Carlos St. and 6th Avenue.

Aqua Classics Gallery, 332 First Ave.; tel 494-0138.   Laguna Beach
Austin Galleries, 218 Forest Ave.; tel 497-8300.
Bluebird Gallery, 1540 S Coast Highway; tel 497-5377.
Cove Gallery, 1492 S Coast Highway; tel 494-1878.
Engman Fine Arts, 1492 S Coast Highway; tel 497-7135.
Ruth Mayer Galleries, 550 S Coast Highway; tel 494-8185.
Pacific Edge Gallery, 206 N Pacific Highway; tel 494-0491.
Sandstone Gallery, 384A N Coast Highway; tel 497-6775.

Thomas Babeor Gallery, 7470 Girard Ave.   La Jolla
Contemporary Southwest Galleries, 7863 Girard Ave.
Gallery of Two Sisters, 1298 Prospect St.
Gateway Gallery, 1025 Prospect St.
Jones Gallery, 1264 Prospect St.
Knowles Gallery, 7420 Girard Ave.
La Jolla Fine Arts, 7884 Girard Ave.
Simic Galleries, 7925 Girard Ave.

Ace, 5514 Wilshire Blvd.; tel 935-4411.   Los Angeles
James Corcoran Gallery, 8223 Santa Monica Blvd; tel 656-0662.

◀ *Ventura Marina*

Art Galleries

Art gallery in Carmel

Doizaki Gallery, 244 San Pedro Ave.; tel 628-2725.
Francine Ellman Gallery, 671 N La Cienega Blvd.; tel 652-9285.
E.N.T. Fine Arts, 10450 Wilshire Blvd.; tel 857-0277.
Feingarten Galleries, 8380 Melrose Ave.; tel 655-4840.
Richard Green Gallery, 830 N La Brea Ave.; tel 460-2924.
Jan Kessner Gallery, 164 N La Brea Ave.; tel 938-6834.
Michael Kizhner Fine Art, 748½ N La Cienega Blvd.; tel 659-5222.
Louis Newman Gallery, 322 N Beverly Drive; tel 278-6311.
Neil G. Ovsey Gallery, 703 E 3 Street; tel 935-1883.
Herbert Palmer Gallery, 802 N La Cienega Blvd.; tel 854-0096.
Patti's, 607 W Knoll Drive (West Hollywood); tel 659-3283.
Richard/Bennett Gallery, 332½ N La Brea Ave.; tel 931-4933.
Robertson Gallery, 325 Beverly Drive (Beverly Hills); tel 272-4888.
Jack Rutberg Gallery, 357 N La Brea Ave.; tel 938-5222.
Manny Silverman Gallery, 800 N La Cienega Blvd.; tel 659-8256.
Wade Gallery, 750 N La Cienega Blvd.; tel 652-1733.
Stephen White Gallery (Photography), 752 La Cienega Blvd.; tel 271-3380.

Newport Beach
Art Dimensions, 3134 Via Oporto; tel 675-5377.
Martin Lawrence Galleries, 3439 Via Oporto; tel 673-0171.

Palm Desert
A. Albert Allen Gallery, 73-200 El Paseo Drive; tel 341-8655.
Adagio Galleries, 73-725 El Paseo Drive; tel 346-8816.
Eagle Art Galleries, 72-780 El Paseo Drive; tel 568-5536.

Palm Springs
Adagio Galleries, 193 S Palm Canyon Drive; tel 320-2230.
Clark-Wiggins, 2825 Tahquitz St.; tel 325-8110.
Elaine Horwitch Galleries, 1090 N Palm Canyon Drive; tel 325-3490.
Martin Lawrence Galleries, Desert Fashion Plaza; tel 320-2728.
B. Lewin Galleries, 210 S Palm Canyon Drive; tel 325-7611.
Mayrie Symonds Gallery, 114 N Palm Canyon Drive; tel 325-6152.

Beach with Mediterranean vegetation, near Carmel

Accurate Art Gallery, Corner 12 and J Street; tel 442-1771.   Sacramento

Apache Indian Art Centre, 2425 San Diego Ave. (Old Town); tel 296-9226.   San Diego
Dyansen Gallery, Horton Plaza, 1st Ave. and Broadway; tel 231-2787.
Quinn-Pollack Gallery, W Harbor Drive and Pacific Highway; tel 235-9181.
Tarbox Gallery, McClintock Plaza, 1202 Kettner Blvd.; tel 234-5020.

Allrich Gallery, 251 Post Street; tel 398-8896.   San Francisco
Atelier Dore Inc, 771 Bush Street; tel 391-2423.
John Berggruen Gallery, 228 Grant Ave.; tel 781-4629.
Braunstein Gallery, 254 Sutter Street; tel 392-5532.
Carlson Gallery, 257 Grant Ave.; tel 9823-2882.
Continental Art Gallery, 545 Sutter Street; tel 982-7781.
Fraenkel Gallery, 55 Grant Ave.; tel 981-2661.
Galerie DeTours, 701 Sutter Street; tel 362-0504.
Gump's Gallery, 250 Post Street; tel 982-1616.
Harcourt's Gallery, 535 Powell Street; tel 421-3428.
Kertesz Fine Art Gallery, 521 Sutter Street; tel 626-0376.
Lawrence Ross Gallery, 377 Geary Street; tel 434-3210.
Maxwell Galleries, 551 Sutter Street; tel 421-51931.
Pasquale De Sarthe Gallery, 315 Sutter Street; tel 397-0168.
Pasquale Lanmetti Gallery, 575 Sutter Street; tel 433-2771.
John Pence Gallery, 750 Post Street; tel 885-1182.
San Francisco Art Exchange, 458 Geary Street; tel 441-8840.
Richard Thompson Gallery, 80 Maiden Lane; tel 956-2114.
Vorpal Gallery, 393 Grove Street; tel 397-2200.
Stephen Wirtz Gallery, 345 Sutter Street; tel 433-6879.

Angles, 2230 Main Street; tel 396-5019.   Santa Monica
Robert Berman Gallery, 180 Marine Street; tel 392-4311.
Blum Helman Gallery, 916 Colorado Ave.; tel 451-0955.
Hoffman-Borman Gallery, 912 Colorado Ave.; tel 394-4199.

Michael Maloney Gallery, 910 Colorado Ave.; tel 394-5155.
Pence Gallery, 908 Colorado Ave.; tel 393-0069.

Bathing Beaches

General

Bathing in the Pacific Ocean in the north of California is seldom possible, because of the cool weather and usually rocky coast. Even in San Francisco, which is entirely surrounded by water, there are no bathing beaches. Only south of Santa Cruz (see entry), the town with a great number of beaches, and where there is an amusement park on the beach promenade, are there many bathing beaches. South of Santa Cruz come:

Pacific Bathing
Beaches

Pebble Beach (south of Monterey).
Carmel River State Beach, at the south end of Carmel.
San Simeon State Beach, on the coast of San Simeon a few miles from Hearst Castle.
Cayucos State Beach, Morro Strand State Beach and Atascadero State Beach, all north of Morro Bay.
Pismo State Beach.
Jalama Beach south of Lompoc.
El Capitan, Refugion and Gaviota State Parks, the three beaches of Santa Barbara.
Point Mugu State Park, south of Oxnard.
San Buenaventura State Beach in Ventura.
Malibu Beach (27 m/45 km) from Ventura County to Santa Monica.
County Line Beach, Leo Carillo State Beach, Zuma Beach, Corral Beach, Surfrider Beach, Las Tunas Beach.
Will Rogers State Beach near Santa Monica.
Santa Monica Beach in Santa Monica.
Venice Beach in Venice.
Sunset Beach south of Long Beach.
Huntington City Beach and Huntington Beach State Park in Huntington Beach.
Newport Beach and Balbao Beach in Newport Beach, Laguna Beach.
Aliso Beach in South Laguna.
Dana Point Beach.
Between Carlsbad and San Diego: Carlsbad Beach, South Carlsbad Beach, Ponto Beach, Leucadia Beach, Encinitas Beach, Moonlight Beach, San Elijo Beach, Cardiff Beach, Solana Beach.
Further south in La Jolla and San Diego: Black's Beach, Shell Beach, Marine State Beach, Windansea Beach, Pacific Beach Park, Mission Beach and Ocean Beach Park.

Lakes

Bathing is possible in hundreds of lakes in California. The water is generally unpolluted and there is constant supervision.

Further information about many of these beaches see the A-Z section.

Banks

See Currency

Boat Excursions

Excursions by boat can be made from several towns (see A-Z):
From San Francisco in San Francisco Bay; from San Pedro Harbor in Los Angeles boats operate daily from Santa Catalina Island (see entry). From

Ventura there are occasional boat excursions to the Santa Barbara Islands: From San Diego visitors can make day tours to Ensenada, Baja-California and Mexico, as well as Avalon and Catalina Island. There are also extensive harbour trips and a ferry to Coronado; from Eureka (see entry) there is an excursion in the Humboldt Bay; boat trips on Lake Tahoe and Lake Shasta and on the Sacramento River (see entries); from Morro Bay (see entry) in the Bay of the same name.

Bookshops

As in other parts of the USA there are numerous bookshops in California. In the larger towns there are also specialist bookshops and antique shops, the addresses of which can be found in the "yellow pages". In Los Angeles alone there are 60 branches of the Dalton Bookshops chain and several dozen branches of the Waldenbooks Company.

Business Hours

See entry | Chemists

See entry | Banks

There are no official business hours in the USA. Every shop or restaurant can remain open as long as the proprietor wishes.
Although shops, etc. in smaller places generally close at 7 p.m., some stay open later. In the large cities of Los Angeles, San Diego, San Francisco and San José there are many businesses which stay open until 9 p.m. or later; some supermarkets are open on every day of the week until midnight or even throughout the whole 24 hours. (See also Shopping.) | Shops and offices

The times of opening of museums and similar establishments are given in the A–Z section under their individual names. | Museums

In smaller places restaurants are normally open until 10 p.m. and in large cities until midnight – on weekdays often until several hours later. Most bars and discothèques do not close until 4 a.m. | Restaurants

Camping

There are excellent facilities in California for this popular activity. The National Parks, monuments and forests which are looked after by the Ministry of the Interior, the numerous State Parks for which the California Government is responsible, and the steadily increasing number of private trailer camps (trailer parks) provide more space every year. | General

Advanced booking for a stay in a camp site in a State Park, especially in the main season, is necessary (telephone 1-800-446-PARK); the advanced booking fee is at present $3.75 and the site fee $6 per night. A comprehensive list of these camp sites (California State Camping Guide), can be obtained for $1 in almost all the State Parks, or by post for $2 from the Department of Parks and Recreation, (P.O. Box 94296, Sacramento CA 94296).
Camping in the National Parks, with exception of the Yosemite, does not necessitate prior booking; the rule is "first come first served". A free brochure can be obtained from the US National Park Service, 22900 Ventura Blvd., Woodland Hills CA 91364. | Advanced Booking

Car Rental

Camping Guide	The Rand McNally Company publishes an annual camping guide "Campground and Trailer Directory". There is a full brochure about private camp sites obtainable from Leisure Time Reservation Systems Inc., P.O. Box 1010, Citrus Heights, CA 95600.
Caravanning	See car rental.

Car Rental

General	If you are only visiting San Francisco you will not need a rented car, for the distances are small and public transport is adequate. If you want to travel about the state or stop in either Los Angeles or San Diego a rented car is however essential. You have to be 21 and hold a valid international driving licence and you should also have a credit card – American Express, Mastercard or Visa – (see currency), because with these you do not have to leave a deposit.
Tariffs	Generally tariffs for car rental in the United States of America are lower than those in European countries. However, in any case you should telephone several rental firms and compare their prices. Sometimes there are special offers, particularly for a week's rental. Many firms charge mileage in addition to a daily rental fee; normally the first 750 miles are free and each additional mile costs 30 cents.
Accidents and breakdowns	See Motoring Assistance
Car Rental Firms	Most car rental firms have desks at the airports, and in large cities such as Los Angeles, Sacramento, San Diego and San Francisco offices in the city centre as well. To prevent disappointment, especially in the main season, you should order a car in advance by telephone. All car rental firms have free 800 telephone numbers. The major car rental firms: Ajax Rent-A Car; tel 800/367-2529. Alamo Rent-A-Car; tel 800/327-9633. Avis Reservation Center; tel 800/331-1212. Budget Rent-A-Car; tel 800/527-0700. $ Rent-A-Car; tel 800/421-6868. General Rent-A-Car; tel 800/327-7607. Hertz Corporation; tel 800/654-3131. National Car Rental; tel 800/CAR RENT. Thrifty Rent-A-Car; tel 800/367-2277.
Caravans	Specialised operators – for example Campertours Worldwide (P.O.Box 1549 D-4130 Moers; tel 02841-16464) – offer package tours to California which include return flights by charter aircraft and rental of a caravan.

Chemists

General	American Drug Stores, occasionally called pharmacies, are quite different from European chemists; for most of them dispensing prescriptions is only a very small part of their business. Many are like small supermarkets also selling food and drink and a few also include a snack bar.
Information	You can find most drug stores in the "yellow pages" of the telephone directories which are available in almost every hotel and motel room.
Business hours	Normally from 8 or 9 a.m. until 8 p.m.; some are open until 9 p.m. or even midnight. Most medicaments which are not on prescription can be obtained in supermarkets, many of which, especially in the larger towns, are open throughout the whole 24 hours.

American currency: notes and coins

Clothing

According to the season and region you should take appropriate clothing (see facts and figures, climate). As well as light summer wear a warm pullover for cool evenings and air conditioned buildings is advisable. From May to October no rainwear is necessary except for tours into the mountains where sudden summer storms often occur. For trips into the desert headgear of some kind and sunglasses are absolutely necessary. When using good class restaurants a jacket and/or tie is often demanded; otherwise casual leisure wear is sufficient. Swimsuits should, of course, be taken.

Consulates

The United Kingdom has Consulates General in Los Angeles and San Francisco.
Ahmanson Center, East Building, Suite 312.
3701 Wilshire Blvd., Los Angeles, CA 90010; tel 385-7381 (area code 213).
Suite 850, 1 Sansome Street, San Francisco, CA 94104; tel 981-3030 (area code 415).

Crime

Crime, particularly in the cities of Los Angeles and San Francisco is a problem and there it is mainly carried out by gangs. Whenever possible cars should be parked in an underground garage, for thefts from vehicles (especially in San Diego) are a frequent occurrence. If you have to leave a car during the daytime on the street in a quiet district, it is sensible to put all movable possessions in the boot. After dark you should stay away from parks and beaches. It is also advisable to avoid run-down districts such as Watts in Los Angeles and Western Addition in San Francisco. In the cities it is rare to see police on foot. Police patrolling in vehicles warn tourists in San Francisco not to photograph the Victorian houses with the Transamerica Pyramid in the background from Alamo Square.

Except for valuables which you have to carry about with you, such as a purse, a passport or a wallet, other items should be handed to hotel reception for safe keeping and a receipt for them obtained.

Currency

Currency	The unit of currency in the USA is the US dollar (US $). There are notes with values of 1, 2, 5, 10, 20, 50 and 100 US dollars (in internal banking business there are also larger notes), and coins of 1 (penny), 5 (nickel), 10 (dime) and 25 (quarter) cents; occasionally 50 c (half-dollar) and 1 dollar coins can be found.
Exchange Rates	The exchange rate of the dollar fluctuates against most foreign currencies. Exchanging in America entails accepting a poor exchange rate and greater commission than in Europe, therefore visitors are recommended to change their money into US dollars before they leave Britain, and above all to make sure they have sufficient change (notes of $1 to $10 and coins) available. Shops and restaurants generally do not accept foreign currency; the larger hotels will do so but charge higher commission.
Currency notes	You should note that all American currency notes are of the same size and colour, and can only be distinguished by the value printed on them and by the picture on the black front and the green back of the note. There are no restrictions on the import and export of foreign and US currency, but if bringing in more than 10,000 US dollars you must fill in a customs declaration in the aircraft.
Banks	There are banks in every city in California; they are normally open from Monday to Friday from 9 a.m to 3 p.m.; in larger cities they remain open until 6 p.m. on Fridays for normal banking business but generally not for purchase of dollars against foreign currency. At the international airports of San Francisco, Los Angeles, San Diego and Sacramento most banks have branches which will change foreign currency into dollars. This can also be done at the headquarters of banks such as the Bank of America in San Francisco, 315 Montgomery Street, and in Los Angeles at 117 West 7 Street.
Travellers' Cheques	Since the changing of foreign currency in the USA often causes difficulty (there is no exchange in hotels and time wasting investigations in banks, and in addition this generally leads to a loss on the exchange) it is advisable to obtain US dollars whenever possible before departure. For security reasons you should buy travellers' cheques made out in US dollars by a European branch of American Express, and these can be changed at any bank on production of a passport. For these travellers' cheques a commission of 1% is charged when they are purchased. Euro-cheques are not accepted in the USA. If travellers cheques are lost or stolen they can be replaced by the nearest American Express branch (to be found only in the larger towns) if the control coupon is produced. In other places you will have to telephone the number given in the list accompanying the cheques. You are recommended to take credit cards – American Express, Mastercard and Visa (Diner's Club and Carte Blanche are also accepted in many places). A credit card is often better than a passport as a means of identity. They are useful for paying bills of all kinds – for airline tickets, in hotels and motels,

petrol stations and most shops. When you rent a car credit cards are accepted as a security deposit, whereas cash is not liked.
Many credit cards enable the user to obtain money, using his PIN number, from machines in banks and often in supermarkets.

Customs Regulations

Articles for personal use (clothing, toilet articles, jewellery, photographic and film apparatus, binoculars, portable typewriters, portable radios, video and television apparatus, sports equipment and even a car for 1 year) can be imported without payment of tax. In addition adults can bring in 1 quart (about 1 litre) of alcoholic drink, 300 cigarettes or 50 cigars or 3 pounds of tobacco. In addition every person can import presents up to a value of 100 US dollars including, for adults, up to 1 gallon (3.78 litres) of alcoholic drink and 100 cigars. There are special regulations for the import of live animals, meat, fruit and plants (information can be obtained from customs offices).

Entry into the USA

Distances

See large map at end of book

Emergencies

Emergency Calls: Police, Fire Brigade, Ambulance everywhere 911.

See Motoring Assistance; Information – Motoring Clubs.

Motoring Assistance

Events

Tournament of Roses (parade and game), Pasadena.

January 1st

AG-Expo (Agricultural Fair), Stockton.
South Lake Tahoe Winter Carnival, South Lake Tahoe.

January

Annual National Date Festival, Indio.
Chinese New Year, Chinatown in Los Angeles and San Francisco.
Mounted Police Rodeo and Parade, Palm Springs.
Dog Sleighing, Truckee.
Monterey Film Festival, Monterey.
Almond Blossom Festival, Modesto.
Festival of Whales, (Festival of greeting the grey whales as they migrate to the south), San Juan Capistrano and other places.

February

Santa Barbara International Film Festival, Santa Barbara.
Camellia Festival, Sacramento.
Fiesta de las Golondrinas (return of the swallows), Mission San Juan Capistrano.
Alpine Festival (dog sleigh racing, sculptures in snow, yodelling competitions), Mount Shasta.
Film Festival, San Francisco.
Jazz Festival, Santa Cruz.
Santa Barbara International Orchid Show, Santa Barbara.
Wine Festival, Monterey.
Concert of the Old Fiddlers, Oroville.

March

From January to March the migration of the grey whales to the south can

January-March

353

Events

be observed in numerous places on the coast. (Times can be ascertained from the Californian Office of Tourism in Sacramento; tel 415/391-2000.)

March/April
Easter Sunday Sunrise Services, many places, especially notable in Hollywood and Furnace Creek (Death Valley).
Long Beach Grand Prix (International car race on the streets of Long Beach), Long Beach.

April
Dixieland Jazz Festival, Redding.
Cherry Blossom Festival, San Francisco.
Flower Show, Riverdale.
Apple Blossom Festival, Sebastopol.
Huck Finn Day (Children's Festival), Santa Monica.
Rhododendron Show, Fort Bragg.
Arts Show, Santa Barbara.
National Orange Show, San Bernardino.
Clovis Rodeo, Fresno.
Stockton Asparagus Festival, Stockton.
Whole Earth Festival (alternative technology, music, arts and crafts), Davis.

May
County Fair, La Jolla.
Cinco de Mayo Festival (a celebration of Mexican Independence Day in the Latin communities, especially in Los Angeles, San Diego and San José).
Rhododendron Festival, Eureka.
La Fiesta de San Luis Obispo (Mexican Festival), San Luis Obispo.
Luther Burbank Rose Festival, Santa Rosa.
Fiesta de la Primavera (Spring Festival), San Diego.
Russian River Wine Festival, Healdsburg.
Buck Owen's Rodeo Days, Bakersfield.
Queen Mary's Jazz Festival, Long Beach.
Rodeo, Redding, Ventura.
Creative Rancho Day (exhibition in the Rancho Los Alamitos: the Californian ranch of the 19th c.), Long Beach.
Rodeo Week, Redding.
Spring Fair (three days), Napa.

June
Corpus Christi Fiesta (traditional church procession, 1st Sunday in June), San Diego, Mission San Antonia de Pala.
Santa Monica Arts and Crafts Show, Santa Monica.
Sea Festival, Oakland.
Shasta District Fair (exhibition), Redding.
Napa Valley Wine Auction, St Helena.
Summer Solstice Celebration, Monterey.
Old Globe Festival (Shakespearian), San Diego.
Flower Festival (last weekend in July), Lompoc.
Southern California Exposition, San Diego.
Verdi Festival (in Civic Center), San Diego.

July 4th
Fourth of July Celebration, (Festival of Independence Day), many places.

July
World's Greatest Salmon Barbecue, Fort Bragg.
Japanese Film Festival, Fresno.
Obon Festival (Japanese Buddhist Festival), many places including San José and Stockton.
National Horse and Flower Show, Santa Barbara.
Horse Show (Arab horses), Monterey.
California Rodeo, Salinas.
Lantern Festival, Pacific Grove.
Asian Cultural Festival, West Los Angeles.
Carmel Bach Festival, Carmel.
Sierra Summer Festival, Mammoth Lakes.
Santa Clara County Fair (exhibition), San José.
Flight of Lasers, Newport Beach.

Steinbeck Festival, Salinas.	July/August
Sonoma County Fair (exhibition), Santa Rosa.	
International Surf Festival, Torrance, Redondo Beach, Hermosa Beach, Manhattan Beach.	
El Dorado County Fair (exhibition), Placerville.	August
Mozart Festival, San Luis Obispo.	
San Joaquin Valley County Fair, Stockton.	
San Bernardino County Fair, Victorville.	
Nisei Festival, Los Angeles.	
Monterey County Fair, Monterey.	
Town and Country Fair, Napa.	
Sports and Arts Festival, Santa Monica.	August/September
California State Fair, (one of the greatest agricultural fairs in the USA), Sacramento.	
Nisei Week (Japanese Exhibition), Los Angeles, South Lake Tahoe.	
National Begonia Festival, Santa Cruz.	
Sausalito Art Festival.	September
Los Angeles County Fair, Pomona (L.A.).	
Greek Festival, Modesto.	
Danish Days, Solvang.	
Monterey Jazz Festival.	
Goldrush Days, Mojave.	
Indian Festival, Sacramento.	
Cabrillo Festival (celebrating the discovery of the West Coast), San Diego.	
Jazz Festival, Palo Alto.	
Valley of the Moon Vintage Festival, Sonoma.	
Harvest Festival, many places especially Napa, San José, Monterey.	September/ October
Parade of Champions (historic festival procession and sporting events), Santa Clara.	October
October Festival, many places including Mammoth Lakes.	
Columbus Day Celebrations, including San Francisco (North Beach and Fisherman's Wharf).	
Constitution Day, Monterey.	
Fleet Week, San Francisco.	
Pioneer Day (popular festival with parade, contests and exhibitions), Paso Robles.	
Rodeo, Twenty Nine Palms.	
Hallowe'en Festival, many places including Death Valley, West Hollywood (Los Angeles), Anaheim.	
Silverado Days Celebration, Buena Park.	
Grand National Rodeo, Horse Show and Livestock Exhibition (Rodeo, presentation of horses and cattle), San Francisco (Cow Palace).	October/ November
California International Airshow (the most important airshow in California), Salinas.	
Napa Valley Wine Festival, Napa.	November
Desert Festival (Festival of the onset of winter), Borrego Springs.	
Glass Blowing Exhibitions, Palm Desert.	
Death Valley Encampment (celebrating the first crossing of the desert by American pioneers; popular festival with fiddling competitions, dancing and bonfires).	
Christmas Parade, many places including Hollywood.	November/ December
Christmas tree lighting, many places including Riverside, Ferndale, Fortuna.	

355

Typical American snack-bar

December	California International Marathon, Sacramento.
	Christmas Boat Parade (decorated boats), including Newport Beach and Marina del Rey.
	Christmas and New Year's Festival in Death Valley.
	Queen Mary New Year's Eve, Long Beach.

Food and Drink

Snacks	If you do not wish to eat in restaurants (see entry) because of lack of time or money, you will not go hungry. Typical American snacks – hamburgers, hot dogs and pizzas – can be obtained almost everywhere.
Hamburgers	Most English people are today familiar with hamburgers, a ring of minced meat, usually beef, perhaps flavoured with onion or cheese and sandwiched within a roll.
Hot dogs	A hot dog consists of a sausage with mustard, sandwiched between the two halfs of a long roll.
Pizzas	Pizza consists of a base of thin pastry which is garnished with tomato sauce, slices of sausage, herbs and cheese and is often eaten hot.
Sandwiches	In coffee shops, drug stores and lunch counters a favourite quick snack is a sandwich with corned beef, roast beef or pastrami served on rye bread with a gerkin, together with a cup of coffee.
Drinks	At breakfast and even at other meals the Americans drink lightly roasted and thin coffee or "postum" (caffeine free coffee). A second cup of coffee,

or tea (made with teabags) is often provided without further charge. Drinking chocolate and soft drinks, such as cola, tonic or fruit juice, sodas, club sodas (plain carbonated water) or milk and milk shakes, can be obtained everywhere. These are often served "iced" unless otherwise ordered. Root beer, which was originally made of the root and bark of trees and manufactured after fermentation into a slightly alcoholic drink, can often be obtained in drug stores and from automatic machines. It is now produced from water, sugar, dark dye and various spices, is no longer alcoholic and at first taste not very attractive. Beer is always served cold and is rather lighter than the beers found in Great Britain; it is served by the glass, stein, seidel, schooner or pitcher. Brands often encountered are Budweiser, Schlitz, Falstaff, Pabst, Busch, Lone Star, Coors, La Crosse and Miller as well as the popular and expensive imported beers. Before a meal it is usual to drink a cocktail, a mixed drink based on gin, vodka, vermouth or rum which is often given a fanciful name. Spirits (liquors) favoured by the Americans are: whiskey (Bourbon, Scotch, Canadian, Rye, Irish or blended), vodka, gin, rum, brandy. In restaurants water, generally ice cold, is provided free with meals.

See entry   Wine

Getting to California

Most visitors to California come by air either on direct flights from London and other airports or go first to New York and fly on from there. There are services from New York and other American towns to San Diego, Sacramento, Oakland, and in the season to Palm Springs. Many Californian towns have air services to other places in America (see A-Z Los Angeles, San Diego and San Fransisco, and Practical Information, Air Transport).

Before you begin your journey you should make provision for small pay-   Change
ments (see Tipping, Post, Telephone and Telegraph, Taxis) by having sufficient change with you, especially notes of one and five dollars, as changing larger bank notes is often difficult.

Hotels and Motels

Although in the cities of Los Angeles, San Francisco and San Diego there   General
are a great number of hotels, nevertheless the prices in these cities are
fairly high and it is advisable to stay in smaller places.

Group I+	over $200	Price Categories
Group I	$125-$200	
Group II	$85-$125	
Group III	$50-$85	
Group IV	below $50	

Visitors must expect a sales tax of 6.5% and the so-called occupancy tax   Note
which is levied by towns and communities, and amounts to between 8%
and 12% of the price of the room. It is customary to give tips only when you
stay in a hotel or motel for a fairly long time. The prices given above refer to
a double room; children in the same room as their parents are not charged
extra; for additional adults there is an extra charge which varies between
five and twenty dollars. Breakfast is included in the price of the room only in
exceptional cases.

Hotels and motels belonging to a chain have telephone numbers beginning   Reservations
with 800 which enables the visitor to reserve a room without a telephone
charge. Rooms for one night can also be booked by telephone by quoting a

Hotels and Motels

credit card number. Individual hotels with numbers beginning with 800 are included in the following lists. All hotels with an 800 number can be telephoned from any place in the United States, outside the State of California, by dialling 1 before the 800.

Hotel Chains

Best Western; tel 800/528-1234.
Comfort Inn; tel 800/228-5150.
Embassy Suites; tel 800/362-2779.
Hilton; tel 800/HILTONS.
Holiday Inn; tel 800/HOLIDAY.
Howard Johnson; tel 800/654-2000.
Hyatt; tel 800/228-9000.
Marriott; tel 800/228-9290.
Quality Inn; tel 800/228-5151.
Ramada Inn; tel 800/2-RAMADA.
Rodeway Inn; tel 800/228-2000.
Sheraton; tel 800/325-3535.
Travelodge; tel 800/255-3050.
Vagabond Inn; tel 800/322-1555.
Westin; tel 800/228-3000.

Anaheim
(Area Code 714)

Best Western Stovall Inn, 290 r., III, 1110 W. Katella Ave.; tel 778-1880.
Conestoga, 254 r., II, 1240 S Walnut; tel 535-0300.
Disneyland Hotel, 1174 r., I, 1150 W Cerritos Ave.; tel 778-6600, 800/854-6165.
Emerald of Anaheim, 507 r., I, 1717 W South St.; tel 999-0990, 800 321-8976.
Granada Inn, 80 r., III, 2375 W Lincoln Ave.; tel 774-7370.
Holiday Inn, 312 r., I, 1850 S Harbor Blvd.; tel 750-2801.
Hilton Hotel and Towers, 1600 r., I, 777 Convention Way; tel 750-4321.
Howard Johnson, 320 r., III, 1380 S. Harbor Blvd.; tel 776-6120.
Marriott, 1043 r., I, 700 W Convention Way; tel 750-8000.
Quality Inn, 264 r., III, 616 W Convention Way; tel 750-3131.
Sheraton, 500 r., II, 1015 W Ball Road; tel 778-1700.
Travelodge at the Park, 253 r., III, 1221 S Harbor Blvd.; tel 758-0900.

Avalon-Catalina Island
(Area Code 213)

Pavilion Lodge, 72 r., III, 513 Crescent Ave.; tel 510-2000, 800/428-2506.
St. Laurien, 44 r., II; tel 510-2299, 800/262-5373.
Seaport Village Inn, 28 r., II, 119 Maiden Lane; tel 510-0555.

Bakersfield
(Area Code 805)

Best Western Casa Royale, 119 r., IV, 251 S Union Ave.; tel 327-3333.
Comfort Inn-Central, 52 r., IV, 830 Wible Road; tel 831-1922.
Hilton, 197 r., III, 3135 Rosedale Highway; tel 327-0681.
Holiday Inn, 152 r., IV, 2700 White Lane; tel 832-3111.
Red Lion Inn, 262 r., III, 3100 Camino del Rio Court; tel 323-7111.
Sheraton Valley Inn, 198 r., III, 5101 California Ave; tel 325-9700.

Berkeley
(Area Code 415)

Berkeley Flamingo Motel, 29 r., IV, 1761 University Ave.; tel 841-4242.
Berkeley House Motor Hotel, 112 r., IV, 920 University Ave.; tel 849-1121, 800/528-1234.
Berkeley Marina Marriott, 397 r., I, 200 Marina Blvd.; tel 548-7920.
Berkeley Travel Lodge, 30 r., IV, 1820 University Ave.; tel 843-4262.
Best Western Golden Bear, 42 r., IV, 1620 San Pablo Ave.; tel 525-6770.
Durant, 140 r., II, 2600 Durant Ave.; tel 845-8981.
Shattuck, 170 r., III, 2086 Allston Way; tel 845-7300.

Big Sur
(Area Code 408)

Big Sur Lodge, 61 r., II, CA 1; tel 667-2171.
Glen Oaks Motel, 15 r., IV, CA 1; tel 667-2105.
Ventana Inn, 59 r., I, CA 1; tel 667-2331, 800/628-6500.

Calistoga
(Area Code 707)

Comfort Inn, 55 r., III, 1865 Lincoln Ave.; tel 942-9400.
Mount View Hotel, 44 r., III, 1457 Lincoln Ave.; tel 942-6877.
Roman Spa, 51 r., II, 1300 Washington St.; tel 942-4441.
Wilkinson's Hot Springs, 36 r., III, 1507 Lincoln Ave.; tel 942-4102.

Candle Light Inn, 19 r., II, San Carlos & 5th St.; tel 624-6451.
Carmel Mission In, 165 r., II, CA 1 & Rio Road; tel 624-1841.
Carmel River Inn, 43 r., IV, CA 1; tel 624-1575.
Carmel's Town House Lodge, 29 r., II, San Carlos & 5th; tel 624-1261.
Coachman's Inn, 30 r., II, 7th San Carlos; tel 624-6421.
Cobblestone Inn, 24 r., I, Junipero & 8th; tel 625-5222.
Cypress Inn, 33 r., I, Lincoln & 7th; tel 624-3871.
Dolphin Lodge, 26 r., II, San Carlos & 4th; tel 624-5355.
Highlands Inn, 144 r., I+, CA 1; tel 624-3801.
La Playa Hotel, 75 r., 8th & Camino Real; tel 624-6476.
Lobos Lodge, 29 r., II, Ocean & Monte Verde; tel 624-3874.
Pine Inn, 49 r., II, Ocean Avenue near Lincoln; tel 624-3851.
Quail Lodge, 100 r., I+, 8205 Highland Drive; tel 624-1851.
The Lodge at Pebble Beach, 161 r., I+, 17 Mile Drive; tel 624-3811.
Tickle Pink Motor Inn, 35 r., I, 155 Highland Avenue; tel 624-1244, 800/635-4774.

Carmel
(Area Code 408)

Furnace Creek Inn, 67 r., I, CA 190; tel 786-2345. (Closed from 1 June to 30 September.)
Furnace Creek Ranch, 225 r., III, CA 190; tel 786-2345, 800/528-6367.
Stove Pipe Wells Village, 74 r., IV, CA 190; tel 786-2387.

Death Valley National Monument
(Area Code 619)

Best Western Thunderbird Lodge, 116 r., IV, 5th & Broadway; tel 443-2234.
Carson House Inn, 60 r., IV, 4th & M Street; tel 443-1601.
Downtowner Motel, 70 r., IV, 428 8th Avenue; tel 443-5061.
Eureka Inn, 110 r., II, 7th & F Street; tel 442-6441, 800/862-4906.
Fireside Inn, 63 r., IV, 1716 5th Street; tel 445-0844.
Red Lion Motor Inn, 180 r., III, 1929 4th Street; tel 445-0844.
Royal Pacific Lodge, 50 r., III, 1304 4th Street; tel 443-3193.

Eureka
(Area Code 707)

Best Western Vista Manor, 55 r., III, 1100 N Main Street; tel 964-4776.
Fort Bragg Motel, 49 r., IV, 763 N Main Street; tel 964-4787.
Harbor Lite Lodge, 70 r., III, 120 N Harbor Drive; tel 964-0221.
Quality Inn Seabird, 66 r., III, 191 South Street; tel 964-4731.
Surf Motel, 54 r., III, 1220 S Main Street; tel 964-5361.
Surrey Inn, 53 r., IV, 888 S Main Street; tel 964-4003.
Tradewinds Lodge, 94 r., II, 400 S Main Street; tel 964-4761.

Fort Bragg
(Area Code 707)

Best Western Tradewinds, 112 r., IV, 2141 N Parkway Dr.; tel 237-1881.
Best Western Village Inn, 154 r., III, 3110 N Blackstone Ave.; tel 226-2110.
Best Western Water Tree Inn, 136 r., III, 4141 N Blackstone Ave.; tel 222-4445.
Hyatt Lodge, 60 r., IV, 4290 N Blackstone Ave.; tel 227-4015.
Picadilly Inn University, 196 r., III, 4961 N Cedar Street; tel 224-4200.
Quality Inn Western, 117 r., IV, 2345 N Parkway Drive; tel 268-0711.
Ramada Inn, 167 r., IV, 324 E Shaw Ave.; tel 224-4040.
Sheraton Smugglers Inn, 210 r., II, 3737 N Blackstone Ave.; tel 226-2200.

Fresno
(Area Code 209)

Best Western Date Tree Motor Hotel, 121 r., III, 81-909 Indio Blvd.; tel 347-3421.
Comfort Inn, 63 r., III, 43-505 Monroe Street; tel 347-4044.
El Morocco Hotel, 50 r., III, 82-645 Miles Avenue; tel 347-2306.
Indio Holiday Motel, 38 r., IV, 44-301 Sungold Street; tel 347-0911.
Royal Plaza Inn, 99 r., IV, 82-347 Highway 111; tel 347-0911.

Indio
(Area Code 619)

Andrea Villa Inn, 50 r., III, 2402 Torrey Pines; tel 459-3311.
Colonial Inn, 75 r., I, 910 Prospect St.; tel 454-2181.
Inn by the Sea, 104 r., II, 7830 Fay Ave.; tel 459-4461.
La Jolla Inn, 21 r., III, 5445 La Jolla Blvd.; tel 454-2188.
La Jolla Marriott, 360 r., I, 4240 La Jolla Village Drive; tel 585-1414.
La Jolla Palms Inn, 59 r., III, 6705 La Jolla Blvd.; tel 454-7107.

La Jolla
(Area Code 619)

Hotels and Motels

Hotel Valencia in La Jolla

La Jolla Village Inn, 200 r., I, 3299 Holiday Court; tel 453-5500.
Sands of La Jolla, 38 r., III, 5417 La Jolla Blvd.; tel 459-3336.
Sea Lodge Hotel, 128 r., I, 8110 Camino del Oro; tel 459-8271.
Valencia, 100 r., I, 1132 Prospect Street; tel 454-0771.

Lake Tahoe
(Area Code 916)

South Lake Tahoe
Best Western Lake Tahoe Inn, 400 r., III, 4110 US 50; tel 541-2010.
Best Western Station House Inn, 101 r., II, 901 Park Ave.; tel 542-1101.
Best Western Timber Cove, 261 r., III, 3411 Lake Tahoe Blvd.; tel 541-6722.
Flamingo Lodge, 89 r., II, 3691 Lake Tahoe Blvd.; tel 544-5288.
Holiday Lodge, 165 r., II, 4095 Laurel Ave.; tel 800/544-4095, 544-4101.
Inn by the Lake, 98 r., II, 3300 Lake Tahoe Blvd.; tel 542-0330.
Lakeland Village, 90 r., I, US 50, near Grenze CA-NV; tel 541-4095, 800/822-7711.
Sierra House Inn, 60 r., II, 968 Park Avenue; tel 800/822-5922, 541-4800.
Tahoe Beach & Ski Club, 131 r., II, 3601 Lake Tahoe Blvd.; tel 800/822-5962, 5541-6220.
Tahoe Sands Inn, 109 r., III, US 50 and Ski Run Blvd.; tel 544-3476.
Travelodge South Tahoe, 59 r., III, 3489 US 50; tel 544-5266.

Kings Beach
Crown, 37 r., III, 8200 N Lake Blvd.; tel 546-3388
Falcon Motor Lodge, 31 r., III, 8258 N Lake Blvd.; tel 546-2336.

Tahoe Vista
Cedar Glen Lodge, 32 r., III, CA 28; tel 546-4281.
Charmey Chalet, 20 r., II, 6549 N Lake Blvd.; tel 546-2529.
Tahoe Sands Resort, 34 r., II, 6610 N Lake Blvd.; tel 546-2592.

Tahoe City
Travelodge Tahoe City, 47 r., III, 455 N Lake Blvd.; tel 583-3766.

Caesar's Tahoe Resort, 446 r., I; tel 800/648-3353.
Del Webb's High Sierra, 537 r., II; tel 800/648-3322.
Harrah's Lake Tahoe, 535 r., II; tel 588-6611.
Harvey's Resort Hotel, 575 r., II; tel 800/648-3361.
Lakeside Inn and Casino, 123 r., II; tel 800/523-1241.

Best Western Frontier Motel, 56 r., IV, 1008 Main Street; tel 876-5571.
Dow Villa Motel, 39 r., IV, 310 S Main Street; tel 800/824-9317.
Portal Motel, 17 r., IV, 425 S Main Street; tel 876-5930.

Beachtown, 49 r., IV, 4201 E Pacific Coast Highway; tel 597-7701.
Best Western Willow Tree, 96 r., III, 1919 W Artesia Blvd.; tel 537-6700.
Hyatt Edgewater, 249 r., II, 6400 E Pacific Coast Highway; tel 434-8451.
Hyatt Regency, 531 r., I, 200 S Pine; tel 491-1234.
Marriott Long Beach Airport, 311 r., I, 4100 Airport Plaza; tel 425-5210.
Queen Mary, 390 r., II, Pier J; tel 435-3511.
Ramada Renaissance, 374 r., I, 111 East Ocean Blvd.; tel 437-5900.
Radisson Inn Sea Beach, 71 r., II, 600 Marina Drive; tel 493-7501.
Viscount, 194 r., II, 700 Queensway Drive; tel 435-7676.

Downtown
Alexandria, 500 r., III, 501 S Spring Street; tel 800/421-8815, 626-7484.
Biltmore, 700 r., I, 506 S Grand Street; tel 800/421-0156, 624-1011.
Clark, 500 r., IV, 426 S Hill Street; tel 624-4121.
Figueroa, 280 r., II, 939 S Figueroa Street; tel 800/421-9092, 627-8971.
Holiday Inn/Convention Centre, 201 r., III, 150 Garland Ave.; tel 628-5242.
Howard Johnson, 126 r., III, 1640 Marengo Street; tel 223-3841.
Hyatt Regency, 500 r., I, 711 S Hope Street; tel 683-1234.
Los Angeles Hilton, 1200 r., I, 930 Wilshire Blvd.; tel 629-4321.
Motel de Ville, 61 r., IV, 1123 West 7th Street; tel 624-8474.
New Otani, 446 r., I, 120 Los Angeles Street; tel 800/421-8795, 629-1200.
Sheraton Grande, 470 r., I+, 333 S Figueroa Street; tel 617-1133.
Westin Bonaventura, 1474 r., I+, 404 S Figueroa Street; tel 624-1000.

Hollywood
Bel Age, 200 r., I, 1020 N San Vincente Blvd.; tel 800/424-4443, 854-1111.
Beverly Plaza, 97 r., II, 8384 3rd Street; tel 800/62-Hotel, 658-6600.
Chateau Marmont, 62 r., II, 8221 Sunset Blvd.; tel 656-1010.
Four Seasons, 106 r., I, 300 S Doheny Drive; tel 800/268-6252, 273-2222.
Holiday Inn/Hollywood, 500 r., II, 1755 N Highland Ave.; tel 462-7181.
Hollywood Roosevelt, 450 r., I, 7000 Hollywood Blvd.; tel 800/858-2244,
466-7000.
Hotel Hollywood, 90 r., II, 5825 Sunset Blvd.; tel 800/4457-0021, 462-5400.
Mondrian, 188 r., I+, 8440 Sunset Blvd.; tel 800/424-4443, 650-8999.
Sunset Marquis, 115 r., II, 1200 Alta Loma Road; tel 800/691-2140, 657-1333.
Ramada West Hollywood, 177 r., II, 8585 Santa Monica Blvd.; tel 213-652-
6400.

Beverly Hills & Century City
Bel Air, 92 r., I+, 701 Stone Canyon Road; tel 472-1211.
Beverly Hills Comstock, 73 r., I, 10300 Wilshire Blvd.; tel 275-5575.
Beverly Hillcrest, 150 r., II, 1224 S Beverill Drive; tel 800/421-3212, 277-
2800.
Beverly Hilton Hotel, 625 r., I, 9876 Wilshire Blvd.; tel 274-7777.
Beverly Pavilion, 100 r., I, 9360 Wilshire Blvd.; tel 800/421-0505, 273-1400.
Beverly Rodeo, 100 r., I, 360 N Rodeo Drive; tel 800/421-0545, 273- 0300.
Beverly Wilshire, 454 r., I+, 9500 Wilshire Blvd.; tel 800/421-4354, 275-4282.
Century Plaza, 750 r., I, 2025 Ave. of the Stars; tel 800/228-3000, 277-2000.
L'Ermitage, 105 r., I+, 9291 Burton Way; tel 800/421-4306, 278-3344.
Ramada Inn, 260 r., II, 1150 S Beverly Drive; tel 553-6561.

Westwood and West Los Angeles
Bel Air Sands, 162 r., I, 11461 Sunset Blvd.; tel 800/421-6649, 476-6571.

Del Capri, 80 r., III, 10587 Sunset Blvd.; tel 800/421-3848, 474-3511.
Holiday Inn/Brentwood, 207 r., II, 170 N Church Lane; tel 476-6411.
Los Angeles West Travelodge, 53 r., II, 10470 Santa Monica Blvd.; tel 474-4576.
Westwood Marquis, 250 r., I+, 930 Hildegard Ave.; tel 800/346-0410, 208-8765.
Westwood Plaza, 302 r., I, 10740 Wilshire Blvd.; tel 800/472-8556, 475-8711.

Wilshire
Best Western Executive, 90 r., III, 603 S New Hampshire Ave.; tel 385-4444.
Hyatt Wilshire, 400 r., I, 3515 Wilshire Blvd.; tel 381-7411.
Midtown Hilton, 201 r., II, 400 N Vermont Ave.; tel 662-4888.
Sheraton Town-House, 300 r., I, 2961 Wilshire Blvd.; tel 382-7171.

Airport District
Airport-Century Inn, 150 r., II, 5547 W Century Blvd.; tel 800/421-3939, 649-4000.
Amfac, 751 r., I, 8601 Lincoln Blvd.; tel 800/227-4000, 670-8111.
Best Western Airport Park, 300 r., III, 600 Ave. of the Champions; tel 673-5151.
Embassy Suites, 350 r., II, 1440 E Imperial Ave.; tel 640-3600.
Hacienda, 635 r., II, 525 N Sepulveda Blvd.; tel 800/421-5900, 615-0015.
Holiday Inn/LAX, 612 r., II, 5985 W Century Blvd.; tel 642-7500.
Hyatt House, 600 r., II, 6225 Century Blvd.; tel 670-9000.
L.A. Airport Hilton, 1309 r., II, 5711 Century Blvd.; tel 410-4000.
L.A. Marriott, 1015 r., II, 5855 Century Blvd.; tel 641-5700.
Pacifica, 375 r., I, 6161 Centinela Ave.; tel 800/854-2608, 649-1776.
Ramada Inn LAX, 149 r., II, 9620 Airport Blvd.; tel 670-1600.
Sheraton-Plaza La Reina, 810 r., I, 6101 W Century Blvd.; tel 642-1111.
Stouffer Concourse, 75 r., I, 5400 W Century Blvd.; tel 800/HOTELS 1, 216-5858.
Viscount International, 571 r., II, 9750 Airport Blvd.; tel 645-4600.

Santa Monica - Marina Del Rey
Holiday Inn, 300 r., II, 120 Colorado Ave.; tel 451-0676.
Holiday Inn Bay View Plaza, 309 r., II, 530 Pico Blvd.; tel 399-9344.
Huntley House, 209 r., II, 111 2nd Street; tel 800/556-4011, 394-5454.
Marina Beach Hotel, 350 r., I, 4100 Admiralty Way (MDR); tel 800/421-8145, 301-3000.
Marina Marriott, 284 r., I, 13480 Maxella Ave. (MDR); tel 822-8555.
Miramar Sheraton, 300 r., I, 1133 Ocean Ave.; tel 394-3731.
Pacific Shore, 175 r., I, 1819 Ocean Ave.; tel 451-8711.
Shangri-La, 54 r., I, 1301 Ocean Ave.; tel 394-2791.
Sovereign Hotel, 80 r., III, 205 Washington Ave.; tel 395-9921.

Mammoth Lakes
(Area Code 619)

Alpine Lodge, 62 r., III, Minaret Road, CA 395; tel 800/257-4630, 934-8526.
Best Western Wildwood Inn, 33 r., III, CA 203; tel 934-6855.
Mammoth Mountain Inn, 118 r., II, 1 Minaret Road; tel 800/228-4947, 934-2581.
Sierra Nevada Inn, 158 r., II, 164 Old Mammoth Road; tel 800/824-0583, 934-2551.
Travelodge Mammoth Mountain, 61 r., III, CA 203; tel 934-8576.

Mendocino
(Area Code 707)

Heritage House, 69 r., I, US 1, 5 Miles South; tel 937-5885.
Hill House Inn, 44 r., II, 10701 Palette Drive; tel 937-0554.
MacCallum House Inn, 20 r., III, 45020 Albion Street; tel 937-0289.
Mendocino Hotel, 50 r., I, 45080 Main Street; tel 800/548-0513, 937-0511.
Sea Rock, 17 r., II, 11101 Lansing Street; tel 937-5517.
Stanford Inn by the Sea, 23 r., I, CA 1; tel 937-5025.

Modesto
(Area Code 209)

Best Western Town House Lodge, 50 r., IV, 909 16th Street; tel 524-7261.
Capri Inn, 28 r., IV, 602 McHenry Ave.; tel 524-7374.

The Lodge at Pebble Beach, 17-Mile Drive

Holiday Inn of Modesto, 190 r., III, 1612 Sisk Road; tel 521-1612.
Sundial Lodge, 57 r., IV, 808 McHenry Ave.; tel 523-5642.
Travelers Motel, 53 r., III, 710 N 10th Street; tel 522-7276.
Vagabond Motor Hotel, 99 r., IV, 1525 McHenry Ave.; tel 521-6340.
Western Host Motor Hotel, 100 r., IV, 1312 McHenry Avenue; tel 527-1010.

Arbor Inn, 56 r., III, 1058 Munras: tel 372-3381.
Best Western Monterey Inn, 79 r., II, 825 Abrego; tel 373-5345.
Best Western Park Crest, 53 r., III, 1100 Munras; tel 372-4576.
Cannery Row Inn, 32 r., II, 200 Foran Street; tel 649-8580.
Casa Munras Garden Hotel, 150 r., II, 700 Munras; tel 375-2411.
Cypress Tree Inn, 53 r., III, 2227 Fremont Street; tel 372-7586.
Doubletree Hotel, 374 r., I, 2 Portola Plaza; tel 800/528-0444, 649-4511.
Hilton Monterey, 204 r., I, 1000 Aguajito Road; tel 373-6141.
Hyatt Regency, 579 r., I, 1 Old Golf Course Road; tel 372-1234.
Monterey Beach Hotel, 196 r., II, 2600 Sand Dunes Drive; tel 394-3321.
Monterey Downtown Travelodge, 49 r., III, 675 Munras; tel 373-1876.
Monterey Hotel, 45 r., II, 406 Alvarado Street; tel 375-3184.
Monterey Pines, 34 r., III, 1288 Munras; tel 375-2168.
Monterey Sheraton, 344 r., I, Del Monte & Calle Principal; tel 649-4234.
Pacific, 104 r., I, 300 Pacific Street; tel 373-5700.
Spindthrift Inn, 42 r., I, 652 Cannery Row; tel 646-8900.

Monterey
(Area Code 408)

Chablis Lodge, 34 r., III, 3360 Solano Ave.; tel 257-1944.
Chateau Hotel, 115 r., II, 4195 Solano Ave.; tel 800/253-NAPA, 253-9300.
Clarion Inn, 191 r., II, 3425 Solano Ave.; tel 800/362-6000, 253-7433.
Embassy Suites, 205 r., II, 1075 California Blvd.; tel 253-9540.
John Muir Inn, 59 r., II, 1998 Trower Ave.; tel 257-7220.
Napa Valley Travelodge, 44 r., III, 853 Combs Street; tel 226-1871.

Napa
(Area Code 707)

Four Seasons Hotel, 296 r., I, 690 Newport Centre Drive; tel 759-0808.
Le Meridien Newport Beach, 440 r., I, 4500 MacArthur Blvd.; tel 476-2001.

Newport Beach
(Area Code 714)

Hotels and Motels

Marriott's Resort, Palm Desert

Little Inn on the Bay, 30 r., III, 617 Lido Park Drive; tel 673-8800.
Newport Beach Marriott, 600 r., I, 900 Newport Centre Drive; tel 640-4000.
Rodeway Inn, 45 r., III, 6208 West Coast Highway; tel 642-8252.
Sheraton Newport Beach Hotel, 342 r., I, 4545 MacArthur Blvd.; tel 833-0570.

Oakland
(Area Code 415)

Best Western Thunderbird Lodge, 103 r., III, 233 Broadway; tel 452-4565.
Claremont Resort, 239 r., I, Domingo & Ashby Ave.; tel 843-3000.
Hilton Oakland Airport, 362 r., III, CA 17, Hegenberger exit; tel 635-6000.
Holiday Inn at Airport, 292 r., III, 500 Hegenberger Road; tel 562-5311.
Hyatt at Airport, 335 r., II, 455 Hegenberger Road; tel 562-6100.
Hyatt Regency, 488 r., II, 1001 Broadway; tel 893-1234.
Jack London Inn, 112 r., III, 444 Embarcadero West; tel 444-2032.
Washington Inn, 47 r., III, 495 10th Street; tel 452-1776.

Oroville
(Area Code 916)

Oroville Motor Lodge, 15 r., IV, 711 Montgomery Street; tel 534-9960.
The Plainsman, 42 r., IV, 1835 Feather River Blvd.; tel 533-8201.
Traveler's Motel, 39 r., IV, 1745 Feather River Blvd.; tel 533-2944.
The Villa, 20 r., IV, 1527 Feather River Blvd.; tel 533-3930.
Village Inn, 72 r., III, 580 Oro Dam Blvd.; tel 533-7070.
Wonderland, 22 r., IV, 1475 Feather River Blvd.; tel 533-2121.

Oxnard
(Area Code 805)

Casa Sirena Marina Resort, 274 r., III, 3605 Peninsula Road; tel 985-6311.
Country Inn, 135 r., III, 350 E Hueneme Road; tel 986-5353.
Embassy Suites, 250 r., I, 2101 Mandalay Road; tel 984-2500.
Hilton Financial Plaza, 160 r., III, 600 Esplanade Drive; tel 485-9666.

Palm Desert
(Area Code 619)

Casa Larrea Motel, 20 r., IV, 73-771 Larrea Street; tel 568-0311.
Embassy Suites, 201 r., I, 74-700 CA 111; tel 340-6600.
Eraven Garden Hotel, 222 r., II, 76-477 CA 111; tel 800/237-2926, 346-8021.
Howard Johnson, 130 r., II, 74-675 CA 111; tel 340-4303.
International Lodge, 51 r., III, 74-380 El Camino; tel 346-6161.

La Quinta Resort, 268 r., I, 49-499 Eisenhower Drive; tel 564-4111, 800/472-4316.
Marriott's Resort, 892 r., I+, 74-855 Country Club Drive; tel 341-2211.
Ritz-Carlton, 238 r., I+, 68-900 Frank Sinatra Drive; tel 321-8282, 800/241-3333.
Traveler's Inn, 116 r., III, 71-322 CA 111; tel 341-9100.
Vacation Inn, 130 r., II, 74-715 CA 111; tel 800/231-8675, 340-4441.

Best Western Host, 72 r., III, 1633 S Palm Canyon Drive; tel 325-9177.   **Palm Springs**
Estrella Inn, 75 r., II, 415 S Belardo; tel 320-4177.   (Area Code 619)
Hotel 6 Palms, 124 r., IV, 595 East Palm Canyon Drive; tel 325-6129.
Marquis, 262 r., I+, 150 S Indian Ave.; tel 322-2121.
Marriott's Rancho Las Palmas, 456 r., I, 4100 Bob Hope Drive; tel 568-2727.
Maxim's de Paris, 194 r., I+, 285 Palm Canyon Drive; tel 800/533-3556, 322-9000.
Ocotillo Lodge, 118 r., III, 1111 N Palm Canyon Drive; tel 800/824-4033, 327-1141.
Spa Hotel and Mineral Springs, 230 r., I, 100 N Indian Ave.; tel 800/472/4371, 325-1461.
Plaza Resort, 257 r., I+, 400 E Talquitz Way; tel 320-6868.
Sundance Resort, 57 r., I+, 290 N Avenida Caballero; tel 320-6007, 800/248-2529.
Travelodge, 158 r., III, 333 E Palm Canyon Drive; tel 327-1211
Westward Ho Seven Seas, 210 r., III, 701 E Palm Canyon Drive; tel; 800/472-3313, 320-2700.

Best Western Creekside Inn, 136 r., III, 3400 El Camino Real; tel 493-2411.   **Palo Alto**
Dinah's, 109 r., II, 426 El Camino Real; tel 800/982-5852, 493-2844.   (Area Code 415)
Garden Court Hotel, 61 r., I, 500 Cowper Street; tel 322-9000.
Holiday Inn, 280 r., II, 625 El Camino Real; tel 328-2800.
Hyatt Palo Alto, 200 r., I, 4290 El Camino Real; tel 493-8000.
Hyatt Rickeys, 350 r., I, 4219 El Camino Real; tel 493-8000.
Stanford Terrace Inn, 80 r., II, 531 Stanford Ave.; tel 857-0333.

Gold Trail Motor Lodge, 63 r., IV, 1970 Broadway; tel 622-2906.   **Placerville**
  (Area Code 916)

Best Western Hilltop Inn, 115 r., III, 2300 Hilltop Drive; tel 221-6100.   **Redding**
Best Western Ponderosa Inn, 70 r., IV, 2220 Pine Street; tel 241-6300.   (Area Code 916)
Holiday Inn, 164 r., III, 1900 Hilltop Drive; tel 221-7500.
Imperial Inn, 62 r., IV, 2010 Pine Street; tel 243-3336.
Red Lion Motor Inn, 195 r., III, 1830 Hilltop Drive; tel 221-8700.
Shasta Inn, 144 r., III, 2180 Hilltop Drive; tel 800/258-8555, 221-8200.
Vagabond Inn, 71 r., IV, 536 E Cypress Ave.; tel 223-1600.

American Motelodge, 82 r., IV, 1350 University Ave.; tel 682-1144.   **Riverside**
Best Western Sage and Sand, 45 r., IV, 1971 University Ave.; tel 684-6363.   (Area Code 714)
Best Western Image Suites, 128 r., III, 24900 Elder Ave.; tel 924-4546.
Hampton Inn, 122 r., III, 1590 University Ave.; tel 800/HAMPION, tel 683-1317.
Holiday Inn, 207 r., III, 1200 University Ave.; tel 682-2000.
Howard Johnson, 104 r., III, 1199 University Ave.; tel 682-9011.
Park Inn, 110 r., III, 1150 University Ave.; tel 682-2771.

Best Western Harbor Inn, 99 r., III, 1250 Halyard Drive; tel 371-2100.   **Sacramento**
Best Western Heritage Inn, 127 r., IV, 11269 Point East Drive; tel 641-1076.   (Area Code 916)
Beverly Garland Hotel, 206 r., III, 1780 Tribute Road; tel 800/BEVERLY, 929-7900.
Capitol Plaza Holiday Inn, 368 r., III, 300 J Street; tel 446-0100.
Clarion Hotel, 239 r., III, 700 16th Street; tel 800/CLARION, 444-8000.
Discovery Motor Inn, 101 r., III, 350 Bercut Drive; tel 800/952-5516, 442-6971.

Hotels and Motels

Fountain Suites Hotel, 311 r., III, 321 Bercut Drive; tel 441-1444.
Holiday Inn Holidome, 230 r., III, 5321 Dale Ave.; tel; 338-5800.
Hyatt Regency, 500 r., I, 1209 L Street; tel 443-1234.
Rodeway Inn, 144 r., IV, 3425 Orange Grove Road; tel 488-4100.
Sacramento Downtown Travelodge, 76 r., IV, 1111 H Street; tel 444-8880.
Sacramento Hilton Inn, 334 r., III, 2200 Harvard Street; tel 344-4321.
Sheraton Sunrise Hotel, 265 r., II, 11211 Point East Drive; tel 638-1100.
Vagabond Inn, 107 r., III, 909 3rd Street; tel 446-1481.
Woodlake Resort & Convention Hotel, 314 r., II, 500 Leisure Lane; tel 800/621-0850, 922-6251.

Salinas
(Area Code 408)

El Dorado, 44 r., IV, 1351 Main Street; tel 800/354-9831, 449-2442.
Laurel Inn, 145 r., IV, 841 W Laurel Drive; tel 800/354-9831, 449-2474.
Vagabond Inn, 70 r., IV, 131 Kern Street; tel 758-4693.

San Bernardino
(Area Code 706)

Inland Empire Hilton, 252 r., II, 285 E Hospitality Lane; tel 889-0133.
La Quinta Motor Inn, 153 r., IV, 205 E Hospitality Lane; tel 888-7571.
Maruko Hotel, 238 r., I, 295 N E Street; tel 381-6181.
Quality Inn, 140 r., IV, 668 Fairway Drive; tel 825-7700.
Villa Viejo Motel, 59 r., IV, 777 W 6th Street; tel 889-3561.

San Diego
(Area Code 619)

Bahia, 325 r., I, 996 Mission Bay; tel 800/542-6010, 488-0551.
Bay Club Hotel and Marina, 105 r., I, 2131 Shelter Island Drive; tel 800/833-6505, 224-8888.
Best Western Columbia, 122 r., III, 555 W Ash Street; tel 233-7500.
Best Western Posada Inn, 105 r., III, 5005 N Harbor Drive; tel 224-3525.
Best Western Shelter Island Marina Inn, 97 r., III, 2051 Shelter Island Drive; tel 222-0561.
Dana Inn and Marina, 196 r., III, 1710 W Mission Drive; tel 800/445-3339, 222-6440.
Del Coronado Inn, 400 r., I+, 1500 Orange Avenue, Coronado; tel 435-6611.
Executive Hotel, 102 r., I, 1055 First Ave.; tel 800/932-4848, 232-6141.
Fabulous Inn, 176 r., III, 2485 Hotel Circle; tel 800/647-1903, 291-7700.
Hanalei, 455 r., I, 2270 Hotel Circle W.; tel 800/542-6082, 297-1101.
Hilton Beach and Tennis Resort, 353 r., I, 1775 E Mission Bay Drive; tel 276-4010.
Holiday Inn Embarcadero, 600 r., II, 1355 N Harbor Drive; tel 232-3861.
Horton Grand, 110 r., I, 311 Island Ave.; tel 544-1868.
Howard Johnson Hotel, 136 r., III, 1430 7th Ave.; tel 696-0911.
Humphrey's Half Moon Inn, 141 r., I, 2303 Shelter Island Drive; tel 800/542-7400, 224-3411.
Hyatt Islandia, 347 r., I, 1441 Quivira Drive; tel 224-1234.
Intercontinental, 682 r., I, 333 W Harbor Drive; tel 800/327-0200, 234-1500.
Kings Inn, 140 r., III, 1333 Hotel Circle S; tel 800/542-6089, 297-2231.
Ramada Inn, 184 r., III, 2151 Hotel Circle S; tel 291-6500.
Radisson, 260 r., I, 1433 Camino Del Rio S; tel 800/228-9822, 260-0111.
Rodeway Inn, 45 r., III, 833 Ash Street; tel 239-2285.
Sheraton Grand, 350 r., I, 1590 Harbor Island Drive; tel 291-2000.
Sheraton Harbor Island, 710 r., I, 1380 Harbor Island Drive; tel 558-1500.
Town & Country Hotel, 96 r., II, 500 Hotel Circle No.; tel 800/542-6082, 291-7131.
Travelodge Downtown, 30 r., IV, 1345 10th Ave.; tel 234-6344.
U S Grant Hotel, 280 r., I, 326 Broadway; tel 800/334-6957, 232-3121.
Westgate, 223 r., I, 1055 Second Ave.; tel 800/522-1564, 522-1564.

San Francisco
(Area Code 415)

Luxury hotels
Donatello, 150 r., I+, 501 Post Street; tel 441-7100 or 800/227-3184.
Fairmont Hotel and Tower, 595 r., I+, 950 Mason Street; tel 772-5000 or 800/527-4727.
Four Seasons – Clift, 329 r., I+, 495 Geary Street; tel 775-4700 or 800/268-6282.
Huntington, 143 r., I+, 1075 California Street; tel 474-5400 or 800/227-4683.

Hyatt Regency Hotel: reception hall

Hyatt on Union Square, 693 r., I+, 345 Stockton Street; tel 398-1234 or 800/228-9000.

Hyatt Regency San Francisco, 806 r., I+, 5 Embarcadero Center; tel 788-1234 or 800/228-9000.

Mark Hopkins, 400 r., I+, 1 Nob Hill; tel 392-3434 or 800/327-0200.

Meridien San Francisco, 675 r., I+, 50 Third Street; tel 974-6400 or 800/543-4300.

Nikko San Francisco, 592 r., I+, 222 Mason and O'Farrell St.; tel 394-1111 or 800/NIKKOUSA.

Ramada Renaissance, 1004 r., I+, 55 Cyril Magnin Street; tel 392-8000 or 800/288-9898.

San Francisco Hilton and Towers, 1900 r., I+, 333 O'Farrell Street; tel 771-1400 or 800/4457-8667.

San Francisco Marriott Moscorte, 1500 r., I+, Market and Fourth Street; tel 896-1600.

Sheraton at Fisherman's Wharf, 525 r., I+, 2500 Mason Street; tel 362-5500 or 800/325-3535.

Stanford Court, 402 r., I+, 905 California Street; tel 989-3500 or 800/227-4736.

Westin St Francis, 1200 r., I+, Union Square; tel 397-7000 or 800/327-3608.

Very comfortable hotels
Cathedral Hill, 400 r., I, Van Ness and Geary Street; tel 776-8200 or 800/227-4730.

Clarion Hotel, 435 r., I, 405 East Milbrae Ave., Milbrae; tel 692-6363 or 800/CLARION.

Galleria Park, 177 r., I, 191 Sutter Street; tel 781-3060 or 800/792-9639.

Holiday Inn-Financial District, 557 r., I, 750 Kearny Street; tel 433-6600 or 800/HOLIDAY.

Holiday Inn-Fisherman's Wharf, 580 r., I, 1300 Columbus Street; tel 771-9000 or 800/HOLIDAY.

Hotel Mark Hopkins: entrance

Holiday Inn-Union Square, 405 r., I, 480 Sutter Street; tel 398-8900 or 800/HOLIDAY.

San Francisco Airport Hilton, 541 r., I, San Francisco International Airport; tel 589-0770.

Sheraton Palace, 528 r., I, 2 New Montgomery Street; tel 392-8600 or 800/325-3535.

Sir Francis Drake, 415 r., I, 450 Powell Street; tel 392-7755.

Comfortable hotels
Bedford, 150 r., II, 761 Post Street; tel 673-6040 or 800/227-5542.

Bellevue, 250 r., II, 505 Geary Street; tel 474-3600 or 800/421-8851.

Handlery Motor Inn, 93 r., II, 260 O'Farrell Street; tel 986-2525 or 800/228-0838.

Holiday Inn-Civic Centre, 390 r., II, 50 Eight Street; tel 626-6103 or 800/HOLIDAY.

Holiday Inn-Golden Gateway, 497 r., II, 1500 Van Ness Street; tel 441-4000 or 800/HOLIDAY.

Howard Johnson's Motor Lodge, 128 r., II, 580 Beach Street; tel 775-3800 or 800/654-2000.

Miyako, 208 r., II, 1625 Post Street; tel 922-3200 or 800/228-3000.

Ramada Inn-Fisherman's Wharf, 231 r., II, 590 Bay Street; tel 885-4700 or 800/228-2828.

Raphael, 150 r., II, 386 Geary Street; tel 986-2000 or 800/821-5343.

Good value hotels
Best Western Americana Motor Lodge, 145 r., III, 121 Seventh Street; tel 626-0200 or 800/227-5368.

Best Western Civic Centre Motor Inn, 57 r., III, 364 Ninth Street; tel 621-2826 or 800/227-4368.

Best Western Kyoto Inn, 125 r., III, 1800 Sutter Street; tel 921-4000 or 800/528-1234.

Californian, 250 r., III, 405 Taylor Street; tel 885-2500 or 800/227-3346.

Canterbury/Whitehall, 241 r., III, 750 Sutter Street; tel 474-6464 or 800/227-4788.
Grosvenor Airport Inn, 288 r., III, 380 South Airport Blvd.; tel 873-3200 or 800/528-1234.
Holiday Lodge, 85 r., III, 1901 Van Ness Street; tel 776-4469.
King George, 144 r., III, 334 Mason Street; tel 781-5050 or 800/227-4240.
Quality Inn, 145 r., III, 2775 Van Ness Street; tel 928-5000 or 800/228-5151.
San Francisco, 400 r., III, 1231 Market Street; tel 626-8000 or 800/227-4747.
San Francisco Central Travelodge, 84 r., III, 1707 Market Street; tel 621-6775 or 800/255-3030.
Savoy, 83 r., III, 580 Geary Street; tel 441-2700 or 800/227-4223.
Stewart, 295 r., III, 351 Geary Street; tel 781-7800 or 800/223-0888.
Vagabond Inn, 134 r., III, 2550 Van Ness Street; tel 776-7500 or 800/854-2700.
Villa Florence, 177 r., III, 225 Powell Street; tel 397-7700 or 800/553-4411.

Very good value hotels
Beresford, 114 r., IV, 635 Sutter Street; tel 673-9900 or 800/227-4048.
Beresford Arms, 70 r., IV, 701 Post Street; tel 673-2600 or 800/227-4048.
Best Western El Rancho Inn, 329 r., IV, 1100 El Camino Real, Milbrae; tel 588-2912 or 800/692-3600.
Beverly Plaza, 144 r., IV, 342 Grant Ave.; tel 781-3566 or 800/227-3818.
Cable Motor Inn, 72 r., IV, 2201 Van Ness Street; tel 673-0691.
Carlton, 165 r., IV, 1075 Sutter Street; tel 673-0242 or 800/227-4496.
Cartwright, 121 r., IV, 524 Sutter Street; tel 421-2865 or 800/227-3844.
Cecil, 130 r., IV, 545 Post Street; tel 673-3733 or 800/227-3818.
Chancellor, 150 r., IV, 433 Powell Street; tel 362-2004.
Commodore International, 113 r., IV, 825 Sutter Street; tel 885-2464 or 800/421-0767.
El Cortez, 170 r., IV, 550 Geary Street; tel 775-5000 or 800/821-0493.
Mark Twain, 115 r., IV, 345 Taylor Street; tel 673-2332 or 800/227-4074.
Merlin, 192 r., IV, 85 Fifth Street; tel 424-7500 or 800/227-3282.
Plockwick, 192 r., IV, 85 Fifth Street; tel 421-7500 or 800/227-3282.

Women's hotel
The Women's Hotel, 14 r., IV, 642 Jones Street; tel 775-1777.

San José
(Area Code 408)

Best Western Inn, 70 r., IV, 455 S Second Street; tel 298-3500.
Best Western Sandman Hotel; 149 r., IV, 2585 Seaboard Ave.; tel 435-8800.
Comfort Inn, 58 r., IV, 1310 No. First Street; tel 453-1100.
Fairmont Hotel, 583 r., IV, 170 S Market Street; tel 800/527-4727, 998-1900.
Holiday Inn Airport, 192 r., III, 1355 No. Fourth Street; tel 287-5340.
Holiday Inn Center Plaza, 240 r., III, 282 Almaden Blvd.; tel 998-0400.
Howard Johnson Lodge, 96 r., III, 1755 No. First Street; tel 287-7535.
Hyatt San José, 474 r., I, 1740 No. First Street; tel 993-1234.
Le Baron, 327 r., II, 1350 No. First Street; tel 800/662-9896, 288-9200.
Pepper Tree Motor Inn, 95 r., III, 2112 Monterey Highway; tel 294-1480, 800/845-4041.
Radisson Airport, 200 r., I, 1471 No. Fourth Street; tel 800/228-9822, 298-0100.
Red Lion Inn, 515 r., I, 2050 Gateway Place; tel 800/547-8010, 279-0600.
Sainte Claire Hilton, 184 r., III, 302 S Market Street; tel 295-2000.
Vagabond Inn, 76 r., IV, 1488 No. First Street; tel 294-8138.

Santa Barbara
(Area Code 805)

Best Western Pepper Tree Inn, 150 r., II, 3850 State Street; tel 687-5511.
El Encanto Hotel, 93 r., I, 1900 Lausen Road; tel 687-5000.
El Escorial Hotel, II, Por La Mar Circle; tel 963-9302.
Fess Parker's Red Lion Resort, 360 r., I, 633 E Cabrillo Blvd.; tel 800/547-8010, 564-4333.
Four Seasons Biltmore, 244 r., I+, 1260 Channel Drive; tel 969-2261.
Harbor View Inn, 66 r., II, 28 W Cabrillo Blvd.; tel 963-0780.
San Ysidro Ranch, 56 r., I+, 900 San Ysidro Lane; tel 969-5046.

Hotels and Motels

Santa Barbara Inn, 75 r., I, 435 Milpas Street; tel 800/231-0431, 966-2285.
Sheraton Santa Barbara, 203 r., I, 1111 E Cabrillo Blvd.; tel 963-0744.
Turnpike Lodge, 126 r., III, 4770 Calle Real; tel 800/228-4581, 964-3551.
Upham Hotel, 46 r., II, 1404 De La Vina Street; tel 962-0058.
Villa Rosa Inn, 19 r., I, 15 Chapala Street; tel 966-0851.

Santa Clara
(Area Code 408)

Days Inn, 168 r., III, 4200 Great American Parkway; tel 800/325-2525, 980-1525.
Doubletree Hotel, 502 r., II, 5101 Great American Parkway; tel 800/528-0444, 986-0700.
Edgewater Lodge, 70 r., III, 2930 El Camino Real; tel 800/334-3928, 241-3010.
Embassy Suites, 258 r., II, 2885 Lakeside Drive; tel 496-6400.
Howard Johnson, 96 r., III, 5405 Stevens Creek Blvd.; tel 257-8600.
Mariani's Inn, 120 r., IV, 2500 El Camino Real; tel 243-1431.
Marriott, 755 r., I, Great American Parkway & CA 101; tel 988-1500.
Santa Clara Plaza Hotel, 130 r., II, 2151 Laurelwood Blvd.; tel 800/622-3553, 988-8411.
Woodmark Hotel, 60 r., I, 5415 Stevens Creek Blvd.; tel 800/223-0888, 446-3030.

Santa Cruz
(Area Code 408)

Best Inn, 53 r., IV, 370 Ocean Street; tel 458-9220.
Best Western Torch-lite Inn, 38 r., IV, 500 Riverside Ave.; tel 426-7575.
Candlelite Inn, 42 r., III, 1101 Ocean Street; tel 427-1616.
Casa Blanca Motel, 27 r., II, 101 Main Street; tel 423-1570.
Dream Inn by the Sea, 163 r., II, 175 W Cliff Drive; tel 426-4330.
Holiday Inn, 170 r., III, 611 Ocean Street; tel 426-7100.
Travelodge Riviera, 63 r., III, 619 Riverside Ave.; tel 423-9515.

Santa Monica

(See Los Angeles)

Santa Rosa
(Area Code 707)

Best Western Hillside Inn, 35 r., IV, 2901 4th Street; tel 546-9353.
El Rancho Tropicana, 300 r., III, 220 Santa Rosa Ave.; tel 800/348-4747, 542-3655.
Fountaingrove Inn, 85 r., II, 101 Fountain Grove Parkway; tel 800/222-6101, 578-6101.
Los Robles Lodge, 106 r., III, 925 Edwards Ave.; tel 800/552-1001, 545-6330.
Sheraton Round Barn Inn, 247 r., II, 3555 Round Barn Blvd.; tel 523-7555.
Travelodge, 31 r., IV, 1815 Santa Rosa Ave.; tel 542-3472.
Vintners Inn, 44 r., II, 4350 Barnes Road; tel 800/421-2584, 575-7350.

San Simeon
(Area Code 805)

Best Western Cavalier Inn, 90 r., III, 9415 Hearst Drive; tel 927-4688.
Best Western Green Inn, 115 r., III, CA 1, 3 miles south; tel 927-4691.
Seacoast Lodge, 57 r., III, 9215 Hearst Drive; tel 927-3878.
San Simeon Pines Resort, 60 r., III, 7200 Moonstone Beach Drive; tel 927-4648.
Sands, 33 r., III, 9355 Hearst Drive; tel 927-3243.
Holiday Inn, 120 r., II, 9070 Castillo Ave.; tel 927-8691.

Seqoia & Kings Canyon National Parks
(Area Code 209)

Three Rivers
Best Western Holiday Lodge, 47 r., IV, CA 198, 13 km west of Park entrance; tel 561-4119.
Cedar Grove Lodge, 18 r., III, CA 180 (in park); tel 561-3314.
Giant Forest Lodge, 243 r., III, CA 198, 27 km north of park entrance, in park; tel 561-3314.
Lazy J Ranch, 18 r., IV, 39625 Sierra Drive; tel 561-4449.
Stony Creek Lodge, 11 r., IV, General's Highway (in park); tel 561-3314.

Visalia
Best Western Visalia Inn, 40 r., IV, 623 W Main Street; tel 732-4561.
Lampliter Inn, 100 r., III, 3300 W Mineral King Highway; tel 800/662-6692, 732-4511.
Sundance Inn, 49 r., IV, 1400 Mooney Blvd.; tel 732-6641.

Porterville
Paul Bunyan Lodge, 100 r., IV, 940 W Morton; tel 784-3150.

Best Western King Frederik, 46 r., III, 1617 Copenhagen Drive; tel 688-5515.
Dannerbrog Inn, 75 r., III, 1450 Mission Drive; tel 800/457-5373, 688-3210.
Holiday Inn, 149 r., II, 555 MucMurray Road; tel 688-1000.
Kronborg Inn, 39 r., III, 1440 Mission Drive; tel 800/828-3033, 688-4413.
Petersen Village Inn, 42 r., II, 1576 Mission Drive; tel 800/321-8985, 688-3121.
Royal Copenhagen, 48 r., III, 1579 Mission Drive; tel 800/624-6604, 688-5561.
Sheraton Royal Scandinavian Inn, 135 r., II, 400 Alisal Road; tel 688-8000.
Solvang Inn, 39 r., III, 485 Alisal Road; tel 688-3248.

Solvang
(Area Code 805)

El Dorado, 31 r., II, 405 First Street W; tel 996-3030.
El Pueblo, 38 r., IV, 896 W Napa Street; tel 996-2991.
Sonoma Hotel, 17 r., III, 110 West Spain Street; tel 996-2996.
Sonoma Mission Inn and Spa, 170 r., I, 18140 Sonoma Highway; tel 800/862-4945, 938-1000.
Sonoma Valley Inn, 75 r., II, 550 2nd Street W; tel 938-9200.

Sonoma
(Area Code 707)

Best Western Charter Way Inn, 80 r., IV, 550 W Charter Way; tel 948-0321.
Comfort Inn, 90 r., IV, 1005 No. El Dorado Street; tel 466-2711.
Holiday Harborside, 194 r., III, 221 No. Center Street; tel 466-3993.
La Quinta Motor Inn, 153 r., IV, 2710 W March Lane; tel 952-7800.
National Nine Inn, 207 r., IV, 631 No. Center Street; tel 466-8554.
Ramada Inn, 207 r., III, 111 E March Lane; tel 474-3301.
Stockton Hilton Hotel, 198 r., II, 2323 Grand Canal Blvd.; tel 957-9090.
Stockton Inn Best Western, 150 r., IV, 4219 E Waterloo Road; tel 957-9090.
Vagabond Inn, 100 r., IV, 33 No. Center Street; tel 948-6151.

Stockton
(Area Code 209)

El Conquistador, 110 r., IV, Blvd. Agua Caliente 700; tel 646-4801.
Fiesta Americana Tijuana; 429 r., III, Blvd. Agua Caliente 4500; tel 800/223-2332 or 681-7000.
Nelson, 75 r., IV, Avenida Revolucion 502; tel 85-43-03.

Tijuana-Mexico
(Area Code 706)

Donner Lake Village, 64 r., IV, Eastside Donner Lake; tel 587-6081.
Northstar at Tahoe, 193 r., II, CA 267, 7 miles south; tel 800/822-5987, 587-0200.
Truckee-Tahoe Inn, 100 r., IV, CA 267; tel 587-4525.

Truckee
(Area Code 916)

Best Western Inn, 75 r., IV, 708 E Thompson Blvd.; tel 648-3101.
Clocktower Inn, 50 r., III, 181 E Santa Claus Street; tel 652-0141.
Country Inn, 120 r., III, 298 Chestnut Street; tel 800/447-3529, 653-1434.
Holiday Inn, 260 r., II, 450 E Harbor Blvd.; tel 648-7731.
Pierpoint Inn, 80 r., II, 550 Sanjon Road; tel 643-6144.
Sheraton, 286 r., I, 2055 Harbor Blvd.; tel 643-6000.
Travelodge, 37 r., III, 929 E Thompson Blvd.; tel 648-2557.
Vagabond Motor Hotel, 82 r., III, 756 E Thompson Blvd.; tel 648-5371.

Ventura
(Area Code 805)

Ahwanee Hotel, 121 r., I, CA 140, 1 mile east of Yosemite village; tel 252-4848.
Budget Host Inns John Muir Lodge, 28 r., IV, 22 miles southwest of park entrance; tel 966-2468.
Curry Village, 190 r., III, 1 mile east of the middle of the park; tel 252-4848.
Wawona, 105 r., III, CA 41, 5 miles north of the southern park entrance; tel 252-4848.
Yosemite Lodge, 484 r., III, CA 41 and 140, 1 mile west of the park centre; tel 252-4848.
Yosemite View Lodge, 66 r., II, CA 140, park boundary; tel 379-2661.
Yosemite West Condominiums, 42 r., III, 16 miles south of Yosemite village; tel 372-4711.

Yosemite National Park
(Area Code 209)

Information

Visitor Centers in California

Anaheim	Anaheim Chamber of Commerce, 100 S Anaheim Blvd., Anaheim, CA 92805; tel 714/758-0222.
Bakersfield	Greater Bakersfield Chamber of Commerce, P.O.Box 1947, Bakersfield, CA 933303; tel 805/327-4421.
Barstow	Barstow Chamber of Commerce, 831 Barstow Road, P.O.Box 698, Barstow, CA 92311-0698; tel 619/256-8617.
Berkeley	Berkeley Chamber of Commerce, P.O.Box 210, Berkeley, CA 94703; tel 415/549-7000
Buena Park	Buena Park Chamber of Commerce, 6280 Manchester Blvd., Buena Park, CA 90621; tel 714/521-0261.
Carlsbad	Carlsbad Chamber of Commerce, P.O.Box 1605, Carlsbad, CA 92008; tel 619/729-5924.
Crescent City	Crescent City Chamber of Commerce, 1001 Front Street, P.O.Box 246, Crescent City, CA 95531; tel 707/464-3174.
Eureka	Eureka Chamber of Commerce, 2112 Broadway, Eureka, CA 95501; tel 707/442-3738.
Fresno	Fresno Chamber of Commerce, P.O.Box 1469, Fresno, CA 93716; tel 209/233-4651.
Grass Valley	Nevada County Chamber of Commerce, 248 Mill Street, Grass Valley, CA 95945; tel 916/273-4667.
Indio	Indio Chamber of Commerce, 82-503 Highway III, P.O. Drawer TTT, Indio, CA 922202; tel 619/347-0676.
Lompoc	Lompoc Chamber of Commerce, 9E Cypress Avenue, Lompoc, CA 93436; tel 805/736-4567.
Long Beach	Long Beach Chamber of Commerce, 330 Golden Shore, Suite 50, Long Beach, CA 90802; tel 213/436-1251.
Los Angeles	The Greater Los Angeles Visitors & Convention Bureau, 695 Figueroa Street, Los Angeles, CA 90007; tel 213/689-8822.
Modesto	Modesto Chamber of Commerce, P.O.Box 844, Modesto, CA 95353; tel 209/577-5757.
Monterey	Monterey Peninsula Chamber of Commerce, 380 Alvardo Street, P.O.Box 1770, Monterey, CA 93942; tel 408/649-1770.
Napa	Napa Chamber of Commerce, P.O.Box 0636, Napa, CA 94559; tel 707/226-7455.
Oakland	Oakland Chamber of Commerce, 1939 Harisson Street, Suite 400, Oakland, CA 94612; tel 415/874-4800.
Oxnard	Oxnard Area Chamber of Commerce, 270 W 5th Street, Oxnard, CA 93030; tel 805/487-6305.

Palo Alto Chamber of Commerce, 325 Forest Ave., Palo Alto, CA 94301; tel 415/324-3121. **Palo Alto**

Palm Springs Chamber of Commerce, 190 W Amado Road, Palm Springs, CA 92262; tel 619/325-1577. **Palm Springs**

Pasadena Chamber of Commerce, 171 S Los Robles Ave., Suite 210, Pasadena, CA 91101; tel 818/795-3355. **Pasadena**

Petaluma Chamber of Commerce, 314 Western Ave., Petaluma, CA 94952; tel 707/762-2785. **Petaluma**

Redding Chamber of Commerce, P.O.Box 1180, Redding, CA 96099; tel 916/243-2541. **Redding**

Riverside Chamber of Commerce, 4261 Main Street, Riverside, CA 92501; tel 714/683-7100. **Riverside**

Sacramento Chamber of Commerce, P.O.Box 1017, Sacramento, CA 95805; tel 916/443-3771. **Sacramento**

Salinas Chamber of Commerce, P.O.Box 1170, Salinas, CA 93902; tel 408/424-7611. **Salinas**

San Bernardino Chamber of Commerce, P.O.Box 658, San Bernardino, CA 92402; tel 714/885-7515. **San Bernardino**

The San Diego Convention and Visitors Bureau, 11 Horton Plaza, 1st & F Street, San Diego, CA 92101; tel 619/263-1212. **San Diego**

Visitor Information Center, Corner Market/Powell Street, San Francisco, CA 94102; tel 415/391-2000. **San Francisco**

San José Chamber of Commerce, P.O.Box 611208, San José, CA 95161; tel 408/998-7000. **San José**

San Luis Obispo Chamber of Commerce, 1039 Chorro Street, San Luis Obispo, CA 93401; tel 805/543-1323. **San Luis Obispo**

San Rafael Chamber of Commerce, 818 5th Ave., Suite 101, San Rafael, CA 94901; tel 415/454-4163. **San Rafael**

Santa Barbara Chamber of Commerce, P.O.Box 299, Santa Barbara, CA 930102; tel 805/965-3023. **Santa Barbara**

Santa Clara Chamber of Commerce, P.O.Box 387, Santa Clara, CA 95052; tel 408/296-6863. **Santa Clara**

Santa Cruz Chamber of Commerce, 105 Cooper Street, P.O.Box 921, Santa Cruz, CA 95061; tel 408/423-1111. **Santa Cruz**

Santa Rosa Chamber of Commerce, 637 First Street, Santa Rosa, CA 95404; tel 707/545-1414. **Santa Rosa**

South Lake Tahoe Chamber of Commerce, P.O.Box 15090, South Lake Tahoe, CA 95702; tel 916/541-5255. **South Lake Tahoe**

Stockton Chamber of Commerce, 445 W Weber, Stockton, CA 95203; tel 209/466-7066. **Stockton**

Greater North Lake Tahoe Chamber of Commerce, P.O.Box 884, Tahoe City, CA 95730; tel 916/583-2371. **Tahoe City**

Ukiah	Ukiah Chamber of Commerce, 495 E East Perkins Street, Ukiah, CA 95482; tel 707/462-3091.
Ventura	Ventura Chamber of Commerce, 785 S Seaward Ave., Ventura, CA 93001; tel 805/648-2075.

Automobile Clubs

American Automobile Association (AAA, said "Triple A") World Wide Travel, 8111 Gatehouse Road, Falls Church, Virginia 22042; tel 703/222-6000.
California State Automobile Association, 150 Van Ness Ave., San Francisco, CA 94102; tel 415/5652012.
Automobile Club of Southern California, 2601 Figueroa Street, Los Angeles, CA 90007; tel 213/7413111.

Insurance

It is essential to take out short-term health and accident insurance when visiting the USA, since the costs of medical treatment are high. It is also advisable to have baggage insurance and (particularly if you have booked a package holiday) cancellation insurance. Arrangements can be made through your travel agent or insurance company; many companies organising package holidays now include insurance as part of the deal.
Within the United States foreign visitors can effect insurance through the following companies:

American International Underwriters,
1225 Connecticut Avenue, NW, Suite 414,
Washington D.C. 20036.

Address in the UK:
120 Fenchurch Street,
London WC3M 5BP.

Language

British	American
Autumn	Fall
bill	check
billion – 1000 million (now widely accepted in Britain where traditionally a billion was a million million)	billion
biscuit	cracker, cookie
bonnet	hood (of car)
boot	trunk (of car)
braces	suspenders
caravan	trailer
carry-out	"to go" (in cafeteria, etc)
cinema	movie (theatre)
cloakroom	checkroom
cupboard	closet
dustbin	garbage can
first floor	second floor
flat	apartment
football	soccer
fortnight	two weeks
"gents" (lavatory)	men's room

graduation (university, etc.)	commencement
ground floor	first floor
handbag	purse
label	sticker
"ladies" (lavatory)	ladies' room, powder room
lavatory	rest room
lavatory (roadside)	comfort station
lift	elevator
lorry	truck
luggage	baggage
maize	corn
nappy	diaper
open square	plaza
pavement	sidewalk
personal call (on telephone)	person to person call
petrol	gas, gasoline
post	mail
post code	zip code
queue	stand in line
railway line, platform	track
refrigerator	icebox
return ticket	round trip ticket
reversed charge	collect (on telephone)
ring (up)	call (on telephone)
scone	biscuit
second floor	third floor
shop	store
single ticket	one-way ticket
spanner	wrench
subway	underpass
summer time	daylight saving time
surname	last name
tap	faucett
tin	can (e.g. of food)
tram	streetcar
trousers	pants
trunk call	long distance call
underground	subway
viewpoint, viewing platform	observatory
Whitsun	Pentecost

Spanish Names

Spanish is the second language of the State of California. In the southern part there are more than 3 million Spanish speakers, especially Mexicans. Spanish is also of geographical importance and is met in many variations, for instance in city and street names.

The five largest Californian cities, Los Angeles, San Diego, San Francisco, San José and Sacramento bear Spanish names. In the following list a few of the most important Spanish words are given:

Spanish	English	Spanish	English
água	water	caliente	hot
alameda	poplar hedge	camino real	royal road
álamo	poplar	cañada	valley
alta	high	casa	house
arroyo	workhorse	cerrito	little hill
borego	lamb	cerro	hill
brea	pitch	cienega	marsh, bog
buena vista	fine view	colorado	red
calabasa	pumpkin	costa	coast

Language

Spanish	English	Spanish	English
diablo	devil	nevada	covered with snow
dos rios	two rivers		
el dorado	the golden land	oro	gold
encina	oak	oso	bear
encinita	little oak	palo alto	high tree
escondido	hidden	pescadero	fishing ground
flora (flores)	flower (flowers)	pinos	firs
fresno	ash	playa	beach
gorda	wide	potrero	meadow
hermoso	beautiful	punta	point
hondo	deep	rio	river
laguna	lagoon, lake	salinas	saltmarshes
loma	low hill	san, santa	saint
lobo	wolf	seco	dry
los gatos	the cats	sierra	mountain chain
madera	wood	soledad	loneliness
mariposa	butterfly	sur	south
merced	pretty	tiburón	shark
mesa	table mountain	toro	bull
molino	mill	trinidad	trinity
monte	hedge or thicket	viña	vineyard
morro	round stone block	vista	view, sight

Medical Help

Information can be obtained from hotel or motel reception desks or from local hospitals (see Emergencies).

Motoring Assistance

Breakdowns

If you have a breakdown in a rented car (see Car Rental) you should immediately inform the rental firm and await further instructions. Towing away a car often is a very costly proceeding unless you are a member of the American Automobile Association (AAA) or a similar organisation which offers free repair and towing services. You will find in the "yellow pages", under "automobile repairing services", addresses and telephone numbers of firms which can repair the vehicle if it can be driven to their premises.

Accidents: what to do

Immediate steps Remain calm and polite. Keep a clear head and do the following things in order:

Security 1 Secure the scene of the accident, i.e. switch on hazard lights, set up warning signs (flashing torch, red triangle, etc.) at a suitable distance.

Injury 2 Look after any injured person. Send for an ambulance if necessary.

Police 3 Co-operate with the police.

Details 4 Note the names and addresses of others involved, and the registration number and make of other vehicles involved, together with names and numbers of insurance policies.

Exterior of Los Angeles County Museum of Art

The place and time of the accident and the address of the police station involved are important.

5 Make sure that you obtain evidence. Write down the names and addresses of any witnesses not involved. Make sketches of the scene of the accident or, better still, take a few photographs from different angles.   Evidence

6 Do not admit any blame for the accident or sign any written admission of responsibility.   Responsibility

Museums

For all the following museums see under the relevant place name in A to Z section.

Judah L. Magnus Museum.   Berkeley
Lowie Museum of Anthropology.
University of California Art Museum.

La Jolla Museum of Contemporary Art.   La Jolla
Scripps-Aquarium-Museum.

Long Beach Museum of Art.   Long Beach

California State Museum of Science and Industry.   Los Angeles
Hollywood Wax Museum.
Los Angeles County Museum of Art.
Los Angeles County Museum of Natural History.
Museum of Afro-American History and Culture.

A. Rodin: "The Burghers of Calais" in the Norton Simon Museum

	Museum of Contemporary Art and "Temporary Contemporary". Southwest Museum.
Malibu	J. Paul Getty Museum.
Oakland	Oakland Museum.
Palm Springs	Cabot's Old Indian Pueblo Museum. Palm Springs Desert Museum.
Palo Alto	Stanford Museum of Art.
Pasadena	Norton Simon Museum of Art.
Sacramento	California State Historic Railroad Museum. Crocker Art Museum. Sutter's Fort State Indian Museum.
San Diego	Museum of San Diego History. Natural History Museum. San Diego Museum of Art. San Diego Museum of Man. Timken Art Gallery. Maritime Museum of San Diego. Spanish Village Art Center.
San Francisco	Asian Art Museum. California Academy of Sciences. California Palace of the Legion of Honor. M. H. de Young Memorial Museum. San Francisco Museum of Modern Art.

Egyptian Museum.   San José
Historical Museum of Santa Clara.

Huntington Library, Art Gallery and Botanical Gardens.   San Marino

Santa Barbara Historical Society Museum.   Santa Barbara
Santa Barbara Museum of Art.

Newspapers and Periodicals

Quality newspapers and magazines can be obtained only in the towns of   General
Los Angeles, Sacramento, San Diego, San Francisco and San José. There
are also numerous local newspapers where details of local events can be
found. It is customary in the USA to purchase newspapers almost exclusively from automatic newspaper machines which can be found everywhere.

The most important daily newspapers in California are: in Los Angeles the   Daily Newspapers
"Los Angeles Times" which is among the leading daily papers of the USA,
and the "Los Angeles Herald Examiner"; in San Francisco the "San Francisco Chronicle" and the "San Francisco Examiner"; in Sacramento the
"Sacramento Bee" and in San Diego the "San Diego Union".

The following magazines are very readable: in Los Angeles the monthly   Magazines
"Los Angeles Magazine" and "California Magazine" and in San Francisco
the "Far West" and "Sierra".

Opening Times

See Business Hours

Post, Telephone and Telegraph

As in Great Britain the postal and telephone services are run by separate   General
undertakings.

Post

Postage for letters within the US to Canada and Mexico is 25 cents for the   Tariffs
first ounce (28g), 21 cents for each further ounce; postcards cost 15 cents.
Airmail rates for letters to Europe are 45 cents per half ounce (14g); for
postcards 36 cents.

Visitors are advised to buy stamps at a post office, because in many hotels   Stamps
stamps from automatic machines cost more (so for example for 1 dollar
you will only get three 25 cent stamps). It is advisable to purchase stamps in
small places where the post offices tend to be in the centre; in cities it is
often a long way to the nearest post office.

Post Offices are generally open Monday–Friday 8 a.m–6 p.m.; Saturdays   Post Offices
until 12 noon. Closed on Sundays.

Within the United States the letters must be marked "general delivery" and   Poste Restante
can be collected at main post offices.

The postal code (zip code) is put after the name of the place and the   Postal Codes
shortened name of the state (for California CA). Each code consists of five
digits.

379

Post Boxes   Post boxes are blue with "US Mail" in white lettering.

Telephone

Local Calls   Local calls from coin boxes cost 20 cents, but hotels and motels generally charge double and sometimes three times the price. In small places, however, local calls from hotels and motels can often be made without charge.

Long Distance Calls   It is inconvenient to make long distance calls from telephone boxes because they generally only accept 25 cent coins. However, long distance calls can be made through the operator. You insert a 25 cent coin, dial the desired number with its prefix, and when told the cost of the call insert the remainder of the amount for the first three minutes. If the conversation goes on longer, additional coins must be inserted. The same principle operates for overseas calls, but a large number of 25 cent coins will be needed. It is possible to pay for the call by quoting one's credit card number. Since the telephone service is operated by different private companies long distance calls cannot be made from post offices.

Advice   In order to avoid the excessive costs which hotels charge, you should, if possible, use a private telephone. A call to any country in Europe costs 1.42 dollars from 6 p.m. to 7 a.m., 2.37 dollars from 7 a.m. to 1 p.m., and 1.78 dollars from 1 p.m. to 6 p.m.; plus tax. A three minute dialled call costs from 7.05 to 12.6 dollars.

Dialling codes   From Great Britain to United States   010
From the United States to Great Britain   011 44
followed by the number required, omitting the zero of the local code.

Dialling codes for the most important areas for California are:
Sacramento   916
San Francisco   415
Los Angeles   213
San Diego   619

Telegraph   Telegraph operations are in the hands of private companies. Telegrams within the USA are handled by Western Union, and outside the USA by other companies such as the International Telephone & Telegraph Corporation. To send a telegram it is best to contact the nearest Western Union office (agents everywhere) or to telephone, dialling 0 for the operator and asking for Western Union. Since the night tariff for telegrams was abandoned the costs for fairly long telegrams have risen so much that it is almost as cheap to make a long distance telephone call. As there are only a few telegraphic offices most telegrams are sent by telephone, generally from a hotel (see "Western Union" in the telephone book).

Public Holidays

General   As everywhere else in the United States of America, California has relatively few official public holidays, and even on these, with the exception of Easter Sunday, Christmas Day and New Year's Day, many businesses remain open. However, banks, exchange offices, government and municipal offices and schools remain closed. No extra day is added to the Christian holidays (Easter Sunday, Whit Sunday and Christmas Day). Most of the secular holidays with the exception of Independence Day are fixed anew every year, and in order to lengthen the weekend they are usually on a Monday before or after the actual date of the festival.

Official Holidays   New Year's Day; Martin Luther King Day: 3rd Monday in January; Washington's Birthday: Monday before February 22nd; Easter Sunday;

Memorial Day/Decoration Day: May 30th or the last Monday in May; Independence Day: July 4th; Labor Day: 1st Monday in September; Columbus Day: 2nd Monday in October; Thanksgiving Day: 4th Thursday in November; Christmas Day.

Radio and Telephone

Radio and television sets are provided in almost every hotel or motel room. Apart from news, live radio programmes are rarely transmitted. Most stations make use of records and tapes; some broadcast classical music but the great majority specialise in jazz and rock.

Radio

Some stations transmit programmes intended for one of the many ethnic groups in California, others broadcast news or music all day. Daily programmes can be found in the daily newspapers.

The daily programme of the following television stations can also be found in the daily papers – the weekend programme in the weekend editions – (see Newspapers and Periodicals) which are often provided in hotel and motel rooms. The numerous transmitting stations in the United States are essentially run by three television companies: the National Broadcasting Company (NBC), the Columbia Broadcasting Company (CBS), and the American Broadcasting Company (ABC) which obtain most of their revenue from advertising. In addition almost every large town has a local station which generally transmits repeats of old material. If you wish to avoid the advertising slots (in peak hours every 15-20 minutes) you should switch to the state-run television station Public Broadcasting System (PBS) which normally transmits programmes without advertisements; in Los Angeles this is Channel 28 and in San Francisco Channel 29.

Television

In Hollywood, the television capital of America, visitors can obtain free admission to television broadcasts and can join guided tours of the television studios of NBC and Universal Television. Here are the addresses of some production companies:

Hollywood

ABC Television Network, 4151 Prospect Avenue; tel 557-7777
CBS Television Network, 7800 Beverly Blvd.; tel 852-2345
Fox Television Center, 5746 Sunset Blvd.; tel 462-7111
NBC Television Network, 3000 W. Alameda Blvd. (Burbank); tel (818) 840-4444
Universal Television, 100 Universal City Plaza; tel (818) 777-1000.

Railways

In view of the constantly dwindling rail traffic in the United States, tourists will seldom have the opportunity of using trains. In California, in addition to local trains from the stations of the large cities (except San Francisco which has no station and so it is necessary to use Oakland), there are still a number of useful connections. You can go from Oakland to the capital Sacramento, to Santa Barbara, Los Angeles and San Diego by rail. A Far Western Region Rail Pass for 45 days of unlimited travel, can be purchased outside the US. In addition there is a rail connection from Oakland/San Francisco or from Los Angeles to Chicago (journey time about 50 hours), and you can continue from there to New York. There is no longer any direct connection between the Atlantic and Pacific coasts by rail.

Restaurants

General
There are an enormous number of restaurants in California, ranging from the most expensive high-class establishments with Americanised international cuisine, to the restaurants of country inns. Typically of America are "diners", which are reminiscent of railway dining cars, and drive-in restaurants where you can be served in your car by a "carhop" (generally a girl). No town lacks a snack bar in which hamburgers, frankfurters, pizzas and other typical American dishes are served. Seafood restaurants, most of which are situated on the coast, are especially to be recommended.

Wines
See entry; also A-Z section Sonoma, Napa and other places well known for their wines.

Tips
See entry.

Note
The following list of restaurants is only a selection. The abbreviations in brackets after the name of the restaurant indicate the type of cuisine. The various price groups given before the address comprises an evening meal for one person. The telephone number is intended for telephone reservations which are advisable especially in expensive places.

Abbreviations
A   = American
Ar   = Armenian
B   = Basque
C   = Continental
Ch   = Chinese
F   = Fish
Fr   = French
G   = German
I   = Italian
In   = Indian
J   = Japanese
M   = Mexican
Mo = Moroccan
Pl   = Polish
Pol = Polynesian
Sc   = Scandinavian
Sp = Spanish
V   = Vegetarian

Price Groups
Over $25:   Group I
$20-$25:   Group II.
$10-$20:   Group III.
Under $10: Group IV.

Anaheim
(Area Code 714)
The Catch, (F), IV, 1929 S State Cottage Blvd.; tel 634-1829.
Granville's (A), I, 1150 W Cerrito Ave.; tel 778-1596.
J. W.'s (F-A) II, 700 W Convention Way (Marriott's); tel 750-8000.
The White House (C), III, 887 S Anaheim Blvd.; tel 772-1381.

Avalon
(Area Code 213)
Armstrong's (F), III, 306 Crescent Street; tel 510-0113.
The Palm's (A), III, 2 Country Club Drive; tel 510-2776.
Villa Portofino (I), III, 111 Crescent Ave.; tel 510-0555.

Bakersfield
(Area Code 805)
Lennuchi's Tom O'Shanter (A), I, 2345 Alta Vista Drive; tel 324-6774.
Naitias Basque (B), IV, 3535 Union Ave.; tel 324-4711.
Misty's (A), III, Camino del Rio Ct. (Red Lion Inn); tel 323-7111.
Wool Grower's (F-B), IV, 620 E 19th Street; tel 327-9584.

Garden restaurant in Carmel

Big Daddy's Fish House (F), IV, 249 San Pablo Ave.; tel 848-3959.
Cafe Giovanni (I), IV, 2420 Shattuck Ave.; tel 843-6678.
Chez Panasse (C), III, 1577 Shattuck Ave.; tel 548-5528.
La Mediterranée (C), III, 2936 College Ave.; tel 540-7773.
Spence's Fish Grove (F), IV, 1919 4th Street; tel 845-7771.

Berkeley
(Area Code 415)

Ventana (A), III, CA 1 (Ventana Inn); tel 667-2331.

Big Sur
(Area Code 408)

Calistoga Inn (F), III, 1250 Lincoln Ave.; tel 942-4101.
El Faro (M-A), IV, 1237 Lincoln Ave.; tel 942-4400.
Dining Room (A), II, 1457 Lincoln Ave.; tel 942-6877.
Silverado (A), IV, 1374 Lincoln Ave.; tel 942-6725.
Soo Yuan (Ch), IV, 1354 Lincoln Ave.; tel 942-9404.

Calistoga
(Area Code 707)

André's (A), II, 3770 The Barnyard; tel 625-0447.
Casanova (C), II, 5th Ave., between San Carlos and Mission Street; tel 625-0501.
The Covey (C), I, 8205 Valley Greens Drive (Quail Lodge); tel 624-1581.
Crème Caramel (F), II, San Carlos St. & 7th Ave.; tel 624-0444.
French Poodle (Fr), II, Junipero Ave. and 5th Ave.; tel 624-8643.
Giuliano's (I), II, Mission Street & 4th Ave.; tel 624-2531.
L'Escargot (Fr), III, Mission Street & 4th Ave.; tel 624-4914.
Marquis (Fr), I, San Carlos St. & 4th Ave. (Dolphin Inn); tel 624-8068.
Raffaelo (I), II, Mission Street, between Ocean & 7th Ave.; tel 624-1541.
Shabu-Shabu (J), II, 7th Ave. & Mission Street; tel 625-2828.

Carmel
(Area Code 408)

Inn Dining Room (C), II, Furnace Creek Inn; tel 786-2361. (Closed from mid May to October 1st.)
Oasis Supper Club (C), I, Furnace Creek Inn; tel 786-2361. (Closed from mid May to October 1st.)

Death Valley National Monument
(Area Code 619)

Restaurants

Eureka
(Area Code 707)

Eureka Seafood Grotto (F), II, 605 Broadway; tel 443-2075.
Hunan (Ch), IV, 2912 E Street; tel 444-2214.
Jonah's Seafood Restaurant (F), II, 332 Harris Street; tel 443-2367.
Ramone's Opera Alley Café (C), III, 409 Opera Alley; tel 444-3339.

Fort Bragg
(Area Code 707)

Cap'n Flint's Sea Food (F), III, 32250 N Harbor Drive; tel 964-9447.
The Restaurant (C), III, 418 N Main Street; tel 964-9800.
The Wharf (A), III, 780 N Harbor Drive; tel 964-4283.

Fresno
(Area Code 209)

Estrada's (Sp), IV, 370 Blackstone Ave.; tel 233-1248.
Harris Ranch (A), IV, Coalinga Route 1; tel 935-0717.
Tradewinds (A), IV, 2141 N Parkway Drive; tel 264-5977.

Indio
(Area Code 619)

El Morocco (A), IV, 82645 Miles Ave.; tel 347-2306.
Teresa's Café (M), IV, 45682 Towne Street; tel 347-7411.

La Jolla
(Area Code 619)

Avanti (I), II, 875 Prospect Street; tel 454-4288.
Chart House (A), II, 1270 Prospect Street; tel 459-8201.
El Crab Catcher (F), II, 1298 Prospect Street; tel 454-9589.
Elarios (A), II, 1155 La Jolla Shores Drive; tel 450-0541.
Fisherman's Grille (F), II, 7825 Fay Ave.; tel 456-3733.
George's at the Cove (F), I, 1250 Prospect Street; tel 454-4244.
Gustaf Anders (Sc), I, 2182 Avenida de la Playa; tel 459-4499.
La Valencia Hotel, 1132 Prospect Street; tel 454-0771:
    Café la Rue (A), II.
    Mediterranean Room (A), I.
    Sky Room (A), Tue. to Sat. only, I.
L'Escargot (F), II, 5662 La Jolla Blvd.; tel 459-6066.
Marine Room (F), II, 2200 Spindrift Drive; tel 459-7222.
Sea Grille (C), I, 4240 La Jolla Village Drive; tel 587-1414.

Lake Tahoe
(Area Code 916)

South
Chez Villaret (Fr), II, 900 Emerald Bay Road; tel 541-6603.
Forest Buffet (A-K), II, US 50 (Harrah's Tahoe Hotel); tel 588-6611.
Maison Margitte (A), II, 901 Park Ave. South; tel 542-1072.
Summit Room (C), I, US 50 (Harrah's Tahoe Hotel); tel 588-6611.
Swiss Chalet (C), III, 2540 Tahoe Blvd.; tel 544-3304.
Top of the Wheel (C), I, US 50 (Harvey's Hotel); tel 588-2411.

North
Jackson's Restaurant (A-I), IV, 550 Lakeshore Blvd.; tel 831-1480.
La Cheminée (Fr), I, CA 28, King's Beach; tel 546-4322.
La Playa (F), II, 7046 N Lake Blvd. (Tahoe Vista); tel 546-5903.
Le Petit Pier (Fr-F), II, 7252 N Lake Blvd. (Tahoe Vista); tel 546-4322.

Long Beach
(Area Code 213)

Adolph's (A), III, 700 Queensway Drive (Viscount Hotel); tel 437-5977.
Paradise Café (C), III, 1800 East Broadway; tel 435-8092.
Rusty Pelican (F), III, Marian Drive; tel 594-6551.

Los Angeles
(Area Code 213)

Downtown
A Thousand Cranes (New Otani Hotel) (J), II, 120 S Los Angeles Street; tel 629-1200.
Angel's Flight (A), II, 711 S Hope Street (Hyatt Regency); tel 683-1234.
Edward's Steak House (A), IV, 733 S Alvarado Street; tel 385-0051.
Hanabishi (J), III, 344 East 1st Street; tel 680-1989.
Horikawa (J), II, 111 South San Pedro Street; tel 680-9355.
Lawry's California Center (A-M), III, 570 West Ave.; tel 224-6850.
Little J's (A), III, 1119 S Olive Street; tel 748-3646.
Original Pantry (A), IV, 877 S Figueroa Street; tel 972-9279.
Pacific Dining Car (A), III, 1310 West 6th Street; tel 483-6000.
Rex (I), I, 617 S Olive Street; tel 627-2300.
Top of Five (A), II, 404 S Figueroa Street, (Westin Bonaventura); tel 624-1000.

Los Angeles: restaurant in Chinatown

Velvet Turtle (A), III, 708 N Hill Street; tel 489-2555.
Vickman's (A), IV, 1228 East 8th Street; tel 622-3855.
Clifton's (A), IV, 648 S Broadway; tel 627-1673.

Hollywood
Alouette (Fr), IV, 7929 Santa Monica Blvd.; tel 650-9119.
Amaji (J), III, 6114 Sunset Blvd.; tel 464-7417.
Dar Maghreb (Mo), III, 7651 Sunset Blvd.; tel 876-7651.
Gio's (C), III, 7574 Sunset Blvd.; tel 876-1120.
La Toque (Fr), III, 8171 Sunset Blvd.; tel 656-7175.
Lillian's (A), IV, 962 N Cahuenga Blvd.; tel 462-0435.
Nicky's Bar (C), II, 8730 Sunset Blvd.; tel 659-0929.
Spago (I), III, 8795 Sunset Blvd.; tel 652-4025.
Simply Blues (A), III, 6290 Sunset Blvd.; tel 466-5239.

Beverly Hills
The Bistro (C), I, 246 N Canyon Drive; tel 273-5633.
Café Rocco (C), III, 360 N Rodeo Drive; tel 273-0300.
Chasen's (C), II, 9039 Beverly Blvd.; tel 271-2168.
The Ginger Man (A), II, 369 N Bedford Drive; tel 273-7585.
Jimmy's (Fr), I, 201 Moreno Drive; tel 879-2394.
L'Ermitage (Fr), I, 730 N La Cienega Blvd.; tel 652-5840.
Mr Chow (CH), II, 344 N Camden Drive; tel 278-9911.
Muse (C), II, 7360 Beverly Blvd.; tel 934-4400.
Polo Lounge (C), I, 9641 Sunset Blvd. (Beverly Hills Hotel); tel 276-2251.
The Saloon (A), II, 9390 Santa Monica Blvd.; tel 273-7155.
Trader's Vic (Pol), I, 9876 Wilshire Blvd.; tel 276-6345.

Westwood & West Los Angeles
Alexander's of London (C), III, 8771 W Pico Blvd.; tel 273-1166.
Carl Andersen's Chateau (C), II, 10930 Weyburn Ave.; tel 208-4321.

Restaurants

Damiano's (I), III, 10761 W Pico Blvd.; tel 475-6751.
The Good Earth (V), III, 1002 Westwood Blvd.; tel 208-8215.
La Fondue Bourginonne (Fr), II, 1085 Gayley Ave.; tel 279-1060.
Monty's (A), III, 1100 Glendon Ave.; tel 208-8787.
Paul Bhalla's (In), III, 10835 Lundbrook Drive; tel 208-8535.
West End Garden (C), III, 11835 Wilshire Blvd.; tel 477-2947.

Wilshire
Chianti (I), I, 7383 Melrose Ave.; tel 653-8333.
Citrus (Fr), III, 6703 Melrose Ave.; tel 857-0034.
Giuseppe (I), I, 8256 Beverly Road; tel 653-8025.
Le Chardonnay (Fr), II, 8284 Melrose Ave.; tel 655-8880.
Le St Germain (Fr), I, 5955 Melrose Ave.; tel 467-1108.
Matoi (J), II, 8400 Santa Monica Blvd.; tel 654-0945.
The Windsor (C), I, 3198 West 7th Street; tel 382-1261.

Santa Monica and Marina del Ray
Black Whale (A), II, 3016 Washington Blvd. MDR; tel 823-9898.
Camelions (A), I, 246 26th Street; tel 395-0746.
Chinois on Main (Ch), II, 2709 Main Street; tel 392-9025.
Don the Beachcomber (Pol), II, 13530 Bali Way MDR; tel 823-5435.
The Famous Enterprise Fish Co (F), III, 174 Kinney Street; tel 392-8366.
Knoll's Black Forest Inn (G), III, 2454 Wilshire Blvd.; tel 395-2212.
Les Anges (Fr), I, 14809 Pacific Coast Highway; tel 454-1331.
Le St Michel (Fr), III, 3218 Santa Monica Blvd.; tel 829-3173.
Michael's (Fr), I, 1147 3rd Street; tel 451-0843.
Shanta (In), III, 502 Santa Monica Blvd.; tel 451-9691.
Verdi, Ristorante de Musica (I), I, 1519 Wilshire Blvd.; tel 393-0708.
Warszawa (Pl), III, 1414 Lincoln Blvd.; tel 393-8831.

Mammoth Lakes
(Area Code 619)

Mogul's Steak House (A), III, 10 Mammoth Tavern Road; tel 934-3039.
Mountainside Grill (A), III, 1 Minaret Road, (Mammoth Mountain Inn); tel 934-2581.
Whiskey Creek (A), III, CA 203, 1 mile west; tel 934-2555.

Mendocino
(Area Code 707)

Café Beaujolais (A), II, 961 Ukiah Street; tel 937-5614.
Hill House Inn (C), II, 1070 Palette Drive; tel 937-0554.
MaCallum House Restaurant (A), III, 45020 Albion Street; tel 937-5763.
Mendocino Hotel (F), II, 45080 Main Street; tel 937-0511.

Modesto
(Area Code 209)

Carmen's (M), IV, 1700 McHenry Ave.; tel 329-0208.
Early Dawn Cattle Enterprises (A), III, 1000 Kansas Ave.; tel 577-5833.
Sundial (A), II, 808 McHenry Ave.; tel 524-4375.

Monterey
(Area Code 408)

Cannery (I), II, 652 Cannery Row (Spindrift Inn); tel 372-8881.
Domenico's (F), I, 50 Old Fisherman's Wharf; tel 372-3655.
Fresh Cream (Fr), I, 100 Pacific Street; tel 375-9798.
Old House in Monterey (Fr), II, 500 Hartnell Street; tel 373-3737.
Rappa's (F), III, Old Fisherman's Wharf; tel 372-7562.
Sardine Factory (F), I, 701 Wave Street; tel 373-3775.
Triples (Fr), II, 220 Olivier Street; tel 372-4744.
Whaling Station Inn (C), I, 763 Wave Street; tel 373-3778.

Napa
(Area Code 707)

La Boucane (A), II, 1778 2nd Street; tel 253-1177.
Main Street Bar & Grill (A), III, 902 Main Street; tel 257-7767.
Petri's (C), III, 3342 Vichy Drive; tel 253-1451.
Ricardo's (I), III, 804 1st Street; tel 253-7000.
Ruffino's (I), I, 645 1st Street; tel 255-4455.

Antoine (C), I, 4500 MacArthur Blvd.; tel 476-2001.
Bob Burns (F), II, 37 Fashion Island; tel 644-2030.
The Cabana Café (A), II, 690 Newport Center Drive (Four Seasons);
tel 759-0808.
The Cannery (A), II, 3010 Lafayette; tel 675-5777.
Far Pavilions (In), II, 1520 W Coast Highway; tel 548-7167.
Koto (J), II, 4300 Van Karman Ave.; tel 752-7151.
Nicole's Grill (A), II, 900 Newport Center Drive (Marriott); tel 644-4000.
Rex (F), II, 2100 West Oceanfront; tel 675-2666.
The Ritz (C), II, 580 Newport Center Drive; tel 720-1800.
Royal Kyber Inn (In), III, 1000 Bristol Street; tel 752-5200.
Savannah Grill (A), II, 545 Newport Center Drive; tel 759-0404.
Villa Nova (I), III, 3131 West Coast Highway; tel 642-7880.

Newport Beach
(Area Code 714)

A. J. Topper's (A), II, 1001 Broadway (Hyatt Regency); tel 893-1234.
Emperor (Ch), III, 68 Jack London Square; tel 893-9938.
Il Pescatore (I), III, 57 Jack London Square; tel 465-2188.
Oakland Grill (A), III, 301 Franklin Street; tel 835-1176.
Pavilion Room (A), II, Domingo and Ashby Aves. (Claremont Resort);
tel 843-3000.
The Rusty Scupper (F), II, 15 Embarcadero West; tel 465-0105.

Oakland
(Area Code 415)

The Depot (A), IV, 2191 High Street; tel 534-9101.

Oroville
(Area Code 916)

Cedar Creek Inn (F), III, 73-445 El Pasco; tel 340-1236.
The Grill (A), II, 10805 Palm Drive (Desert Hot Springs Hotel); tel 329-6495.
Manisco's (I-Fr), I, 72-281 Highway 111; tel 340-6610.
Original Mesquite's (A), II, 73-030 El Pasco; tel 340-0999.
Stanley B's (C), III, 73-101 Highway 111; tel 340-6610.
A Touch of Mama's (I), II, 74-063 Highway 111; tel 568-1315.

Palm Desert
(Area Code 619)

Las Casuelas (M), II, 368 N Palm Canyon Drive; tel 525-3213.
Cedar Creek Inn (A), III, 1555 S Palm Canyon Drive; tel 325-7300.
Flower Drum (Ch), II, 424 S Indian Ave.; tel 323-3020.
Ferraro (I), III, 150 E Vista Chino; tel 327-7344.
House of Sensu (J), II, 169 N Indian Ave.; tel 325-0846.
La Vallauris (Fr), I, 385 W Tahquitz Way; tel 325-5059.
Maxim's de Paris Suite Hotel (C), I, 285 N Palm Canyon Drive; tel 322-9000.
Perrina's (I), III, 340 N Palm Canyon Drive; tel 325-6544.
Rennick's (C), II, 100 N Indian Ave. (Palm Springs Spa); tel 325-1461.
Sorrentino's Seafood House (F), II, 1032 N Palm Canyon Drive; tel 325-2944.
Tommy's Pacific Cove (Pol), II, 701 W Baristo Road; tel 323-3100.

Palm Springs
(Area Code 619)

Captain's Cabin Seafood Grotto (F), III, 3295 El Camino Real; tel 493-8233.
Chantilly (Fr), II, 530 Ramona Street; tel 321-4080.
Chez Louis (Fr), II, 4170 El Camino Real; tel 493-1660.
The Good Earth (V), III, 185 University Ave.; tel 321-9449.
The Greenery (A), III, 625 El Camino Real (Holiday Inn); tel 328-2800.
Hugo's Market (A), I, 4219 El Camino Real (Hyatt Rickey's); tel 493-8000.
Scott's Seafood (F), III, 2300 E Bayshore Road; tel 856-1046.

Palo Alto
(Area Code 415)

Beckham's Place (C), III, 77 W Walnut; tel 796-3399.
Cameron's Seafood (F), II, 1078 E Cameron Road; tel 793-FISH.
The Chronicle (C), II, 897 Granite Drive; tel 792-1179.
La Couronne (Fr), I, 142 S Lake Ave.; tel 793-3151.
Maldonado's (C), II, 1202 E Green Street; tel 796-1126.
Merida, (M) IV, 20 E Colorado Blvd.; tel 795-5577.
Ritz Grill (C), III, 168 W Colorado Blvd.; tel 405-0806.
Skylights (C), II, 150 S Robles (Hilton); tel 577-1000.

Pasadena
(Area Code 213)

Georgetown Hotel (A), IV, Main Street; tel 337-4373.
Lillian Russell Room (A), IV, Cameron Park; tel 622-7558.
Zoe's (A), IV, 310 Main Street; tel 622-9681.

Placerville
(Area Code 916)

Restaurants

Redding
(Area Code 916)

Balina's (I-Fr), III, 2703 Churn Creek; tel 221-2612.
Hatchcover (A), III, 202 Hemstead Drive; tel 223-5606.
JJ North's Grand Buffet (A), IV, 2244 Hilltop Drive; tel 221-6200.
Junell's (A), III, 2777 Bechelli Lane; tel 223-2095.
Wintoon's (C), II, 2180 Hilltop Drive (Shasta Inn); tel 221-8200.

Riverside
(Area Code 714)

Cask and Cleaver (F), II, 1333 University Ave.; tel 682-4580.
Lord Charley's (A), III, 1329 University Ave.; tel 686-5040.
Reuben's (A), II, 3640 Central Ave.; tel 683-3842.
Samuel's (A), III, 1200 University Ave.; tel 682-8000.

Sacramento
(Area Code 916)

Aldo's (C), II, Fulton & Marconi Aves.; tel 483-5031.
Café la Salle (Fr), II, 1028 2nd Street; tel 442-7000.
The Firehouse (C), I, 1112 2nd Street; tel 442-4772.
John Q's Penthouse (C), III, 300 J Street; tel 446-0100.
Mansion Court (F-C), II, 700 16th Street (Clarion Hotel); tel 444-8000.
Misty's (C), II, 1401 Arden Way (Sacramento Inn); tel 922-8041.
Ricci's (I), III, 705 J Street; tel 442-6741.
Sakura (J), II, 1111 2nd Street; tel 448-8334.

Salinas
(Area Code 408)

East of Eden (A), III, 327 Pajaro; tel 424-0819.
Italian Villa (I), III, 64 Monterey Highway; tel 424-6266.
Pub's Prime Ribs (A), III, 227 Monterey Street; tel 424-2261.

San Bernadino
(Area Code 706)

Alice's (A), IV, 867 W Jefferson Street; tel 381-2014.
La Potinière, (C), II, 285 E Hospitality Lane (Hilton); tel 889-0133.
Lancers (A), III, 1980 S Waterman Ave.; tel 888-6621.
Oscar's (M), IV, 127 E Highland Ave.; tel 883-9116.
Yamazato (J), III, 289 E Hospitality Lane; tel 888-7708.

San Diego
(Area Code 619)

The Abbey (A), I, 2825 5th Ave.; tel 291-4779.
Anthony's Fish Grotto (F), III, 1360 Harbor Drive; tel 232-5103.
Anthony's Star of the Sea (F), I, 1360 Harbor Drive; tel 232-7408.
Café Pacifica (J), II, 2414 San Diego Ave.; tel 291-6666.
Casa de Bandini (M), III, Old Town Plaza; tel 296-3267.
Crown Room (A), II, 1500 Orange Ave. (Hotel de Coronado); tel 435-6611.
Frenchy Marseilles (C), II, 801 C Street; tel 233-3413.
Grant Grill (A), I, 326 Broadway (U.S. Grant Hotel); tel 239-3121.
Hyatt Islandia (A), I, 1441 Quivira Road; tel 224-1234.
La Pavilion (Fr), I, 500 Hotel Circle North (Town & Country); tel 291-7131.
Lino's (I), IV, 1754 Calhoun Street; tel 299-7124.
Lubach's (A), II, 2101 N Harbor Drive; tel 232-5129.
Old Trieste (I), II, 2335 Morena Blvd.; tel 276-1841.
Sheppard's (A), I, 1380 Harbor Island Drive (Sheraton Harbor Island); tel 291-2900.
Tom Ham's Lighthouse (A), II, 2150 Harbor Island Drive; tel 291-9110.
Tradewinds (A), II, 1775 E Mission Bay Drive (Hilton); tel 276-4010.

San Francisco
(Area Code 415)

Chinatown
Cathay House (Ch), 718 California Street; tel 982-3388.
Empress of China (Ch), 838 Grant Ave.; tel 434-1345.
Four Seas (Ch), 731 Grant Ave.; tel 397-5577.
Imperial Palace (Ch), 919 Grant Ave.; tel 982-4440.
Kan's (Ch), 708 Grant Ave.; tel 982-2388.
Kinokawa (J), 347 Grant Street; tel 956-6085.
Ryumon (Ch), 646 Washington Street; tel 421-3868.
Yamato Sukiyaki (J), 717 California Street; tel 397-3456.

Downtown
Bardelli's (C), 243 O'Farrell Street; tel 982-0243.
Brasserie Chambord (F), 152 Kearny Street; tel 434-3688.
Caravansery (Ar), 310 Sutter Street; tel 362-4640.

Donatello (I), Post & Mason Street; tel 441-7182 (expensive).
Fleur de Lys (F), 777 Sutter Street; tel 673-7779 (expensive).
Iron House (I), 19 Maiden Lane; tel 362-8133.
Lafayette (F), 290 Pacific Street; tel 986-3366.
Donatello (I), Post & Mason Street; tel 441-7182 (expensive).
Fleur de Lys (F), 777 Sutter Street; tel 673-7779 (expensive).
Iron House (I), 19 Maiden Lane; tel 362-8133.
Lafayette (F), 290 Pacific Street; tel 986-3366.
La Mère Duquesne (F), 101 Shannon Alley; tel 776-7600.
Le Central (F), 453 Bush Street; tel 392-2233 (very expensive).
Lefty O'Doul's (A), 333 Geary Street; tel 982-8900.
Lehr's Greenhouse (H), 740 Sutter Street; tel 474-6478.
Le Trianon (F), 242 O'Farrell Street; tel 982-9353 (very expensive).
Little Omar's Café (Ar), 208 Powell Street; tel 781-1010.
The Magic Pan (A), 341 Sutter Street; tel 788-7397.
Marrakech (Mo), 417 O'Farrell Street; tel 776-6717.
Masa's (F), 648 Bush Street; tel 989-7154 (very expensive).
Omar Khayyamm's (Ar), 196 O'Farrell Street; tel 781-1010.
Sam's Grill (F), 347 Bush Street; tel 421-0594.
Tadich Grill (F), 240 California Street; tel 391-2373.
Salmagundi (C), 442 Geary Street; tel 441-0894 (self service).
Trader Vic's (Pol), 20 Cosmo Place; tel 776-2232 (very expensive).

Hotel-restaurants Downtown.
Four Seasons-Clift Hotel (C), 495 Geary Street:
　　French Room; tel 775-4700 (very expensive).
Hyatt on Union Square, 345 Stockton Street:
　　Hugo's One Up (C) (very expensive); tel; 398-1234.
　　Plaza Restaurant (F/I/A); tel 398-1234.
San Francisco Hilton and Tower, Mason Street/O'Farrell Street:
　　Chef's Table (C); tel 771-1400 (very expensive).
　　Henri's Room at the Top (C) (46th floor); tel 771-1400.
St Francis Hotel, Union Square:
　　English Grill, (F); tel 397-7000.
　　Victor's (F); tel 397-7000 (very expensive).
Sir Francis Drake Hotel, Sutter Street/Powell Street:
　　Drake's Tavern (C); tel 392-7755.
　　Carving Board (C); tel 392-7755.
　　Starlite Roof (C); tel 392-7755 (dancing).

Financial District
Carnelian Room (F), 555 California Street; tel 433-7500.
Enzo's Ristorante (I), 3 Embarcadero Center; tel 981-5530.
Ernie's (F), 847 Montgomery Street; tel 397-5969 (very expensive).
Jack's (F), 615 Sacramento Street; tel 421–7355.
Lafayette (F), 290 Pacific Street; tel 986-3366.
Schroeder's (G), 240 Front Street; tel 421-4778.

Hotel Restaurants in the Financial District
Hyatt Regency San Francisco, 5 Embarcadero Center:
　　Hugo's (C); tel 788-1234 (very expensive).
　　Equinox (A); tel 788-1234 (very expensive).
　　Market Place (A); tel 788-1234.

Fisherman's Wharf
Castagnola's (F), 286 Jefferson Street; tel 776-5015.
Franciscan (F), Pier 431-2; tel 382-7733.
Pompei's Grotto (F), 340 Jefferson Street; tel 776-9265.
Scoma's (F), Pier 47; tel 771-4383.
Tarantino's (F), 206 Jefferson Street; tel 775-5600.

Hotel Restaurants at Fisherman's Wharf
Sheraton at Fisherman's Wharf, 2500 Mason Street:
　　Grand Exhibition (A); tel 982-5536 (very expensive).

Restaurants

Ghirardelli Square
Gaylord (In), 900 North Point; tel 771-8822.
Lanzone & Son (I), 900 North Point; tel 771-2880.
Mandarin (Ch), 900 North Point; tel 673-8812.
Paprika's Fono (U), 900 North Point; tel 441-1223.

North Beach
Beethoven (G), 1201 Powell Street at Union Street; tel 391-4488.
Greek Taverna (Gr), 256 Columbus Ave.; tel 362-7260.

Nob Hill
Alexis (F), 1001 California Street; tel 885-6400 (very expensive).
Big Four (A), 1075 California Street; tel 771-1140 (very expensive).
Fournou's Ovens (F), 905 California Street; tel 989-1910 (very expensive).

Hotel Restaurants in Nob Hill
Fairmont Hotel, California Street/Masort Street:
   Venetian Room (C); tel 772-5163.
   The Tonga (Ch); tel 772-5278.
   The Squire Restaurant (F/Ko); tel 772-5211.
   Crown Rooms (Buffet); tel 772-5131 (very expensive).
   Brasserie (A/Ko); tel 772-5199.

Pier 39
Chic's Place (F), Pier 39; tel 421-2442.
Dante's Sea Catch (I/Fi), Pier 39; tel 421-5778.
Neptune's Palace (F), Pier 39; tel 434-2260

Telegraph Hill
Julius's Castle (C), 1541 Montgomery Street; tel 362-3042 (very expensive).

Fort Mason
Green's at Fort Mason, (Building A; V); tel 771-6222.

San José
(Area Code 408)

Belvedere Gardens (A), III, 1350 N 1st Street (Le Baron Hotel); tel 288-9200.
Famous Pacific Fish Co. (F), III, 177 W Santa Clara Street; tel 298-7222.
Hugo's II (C), II, 1740 N 1st Street (Hyatt); tel 993-1234.
Les Saisons (C), I, 170 S Market Street (Fairmont Hotel); tel 998-3250.
Lou's Village (C), II, 1465 W San Carlos Street; tel 293-4570.
Paolo's (C), II, 520 E Santa Clara Street; tel 294-2558.
Le Papillon (Fr), I, 410 Saratoga Ave.; tel 296-3730.
The Velvet Turtle (A), III, 380 S Kiely Blvd.; tel 247-3477.

San Simeon
(Area Code 805)

Corfino's (A), III, 8070 Castillo Drive (Holiday Inn); tel 927-8691.
San Simeon (I), IV, 920 Castillo Drive; tel 927-4604.

Santa Barbara
(Area Code 805)

Andria's Harborside (C), II, 336 W Cabrillo Blvd.; tel 962-8159.
Azuma (J), III, 1024 State Street; tel 966-2139.
China Castle (Ch), III, 1202 Chapala Street; tel 922-6602.
The Epicurean (C), I, 125 W Carillo Street; tel 966-4789.
Four Winds (A), III, 3435 State Street; tel 682-5174.
La Fonda (M), IV, 4141 State Street; tel 964-0917.
Harbor Restaurant (F), II, 210 Stearns Wharf; tel 963-3311.
Joe's (A), III, 536 State Street; tel 966-4638.
Maison Robert (Fr), II, 1325 State Street; tel 962-1325.
Mimosa (Fr), III, 2700 Dela Vina Street; tel 682-1462.
Palace Café (A), III, 8 East Cota Street; tel 966-3133.
Suishin Sukiyaki (J), II, 511 State Street; tel 962-1495.

Santa Clara
(Area Code 408)

Alexander's (C), II, Great American Parkway (Marriott); tel 988-1500.
Arthur's (F), II, 2875 Lakeside Drive; tel 980 1666.
Café Milano (I), II, 5101 Great American Parkway (Doubletree); tel 246-3474.

Fish Market (F), II, 3775 El Camino Real; tel 987-0700.
La Paloma (M), IV, 2280 El Camino Real; tel 247-0990.
Mariani's (I), II, 2500 El Camino Real; tel 243-1431.

Crow's Nest (A), II, 2218 East Cliff Drive; tel 476-4560.
Lilly Marlene (A), IV, 1363 Pacific Ave.
Santa Cruz Hotel (I-F), III, Cedar & Locust Streets; tel 423-7500.

Santa Cruz
(Area Code 408)

See Los Angeles.

Santa Monica

Marshall House (G), III, 835 2nd Street; tel 542-5305.
Matisse (A), II, 620 5th Street; tel 527-9797.
Old Mexico (M), IV, 4501 Montgomery Drive; tel 539-2599.

Santa Rosa
(Area Code 707)

Danish Inn (Sc), II, 1547 Mission Drive; tel 688-4813.

Solvang
(Area Code 805)

Les Arcades (Fr), II, 133 E Napa Street: Tel 938-3723.
The Big Three (A), III, 18130 Sonoma Highway; tel 938-9000.
Depot Hotel (I), III, 249 1st Street; tel 938-2980.
La Casa (M), IV, 121 E Spain Street; tel 996-3406.
L'Esperance (Fr), III, Place des Pyrenées; tel 996-3046.
Magliulo's (I), III, 691 Broadway; tel 996-1031.
Marioni's (A), III, 8 Spain Street; tel 996-6866.
The Grille (A), I, 18130 Sonoma Highway (Sonoma Mission Inn); tel 938-9300.
TJ's Sonoma Grill (A), III, 529 1st Street; tel 938-2122.
The Winemaker (C), III, 875 W Napa Street; tel 996-9799.

Sonoma
(Area Code 707)

Alder Market (C), II, 151 W Alder Street; tel 943-5231.
Arroyos (M), IV, 324 S Center Street; tel 462-1661.
Atrium (C), II, 2323 Grand Canal Blvd. (Hilton); tel 957-9090.
Fish Market (F), II, 445 W Weber Ave.; tel 946-0991.
Le Bistro (C), II, 3121 W Benjamin Holt Drive; tel 951-0885.
Risso's (I), II, 944 Waterloo Road; tel 466-0016.

Stockton
(Area Code 209)

Puerto del Sol (C), IV, General Sanchez Taboada 9; tel 84-01-0147.
Reno (C), III, Calle & Revolucion; tel 85-9210.

Tijuana Mexico
(Area Code 706)

BJ's (A), II, 545 E Thompson Blvd.; tel 643-1212.
Pierpoint Inn (C), III, 550 San Jon Road (Pierpoint Inn); tel 653-6144.
Sportsman (A), III, 53 S California Street; tel 643-2851.

Ventura
(Area Code 805)

Shopping

Although all the large cities still have stores of the traditional type and in the suburbs there are branches of these stores in the large shopping malls, in small places the most important shops are the supermarkets. These sell more than just food, and in some respects are similar to department stores in the range of goods that they have for sale. Opening hours are in general between 9.30 a.m. and 7 p.m., on several days in the week the stores are open until 9 p.m. (See also Business Hours.)

General

Broadway-Southern California, 3880 N. Mission Road; tel 227-2848.
Bullock's, 925 West 8th Street; tel 524-9494.
Bullock's Wilshire, 3050 Wilshire Blvd.; tel 382-6161.
May Company North Hollywood, 6160 Laurel Canyon Blvd.; tel (818) 766-4111.
May Company Wilshire, 6067 Wilshire Blvd.; tel 938-4211.
Nordstrom, Pico and Westwood Blvd, West Los Angeles; tel 470-6155.
Robinson's, 600 West 7th Street; tel 488-5522.
Sak's Fifth Ave., 9600 Wilshire Blvd, Beverly Hills; tel 275-2411.

Los Angeles

Spanish Names

San Diego	Neiman Marcus, Friars Road & Highway 163; tel 692-0100.
	Nordstrom, Horton Plaza, 1st Street & Broadway; tel 239-1700.
San Francisco	Emporium Caswell, 835 Market Street; tel 764-2222.
	Gump's, 250 Post Street; tel 982-1616.
	Macy's, Union Square; tel 397-3333.
	Nordstrom, Market Street, corner 5th Street.
	Neiman Marcus, 150 Stockton Street; tel 362-3900.
	Saks Fifth Ave., 384 Post Street; tel 986-4300.
Specialist Shops	In the large cities there are also numerous speciality shops. You can find their addresses in the yellow pages of the telephone book which is normally to be found in hotel and motel rooms, and which is a very fruitful source of information.

Spanish Names

See Language

Sport

Baseball	In no other state is the American national sport of baseball so well represented as in California, where there are five first-class teams: the Giants (San Francisco) and the Dodgers (Los Angeles) play in the National League; the Padres (San Diego), the Angels (Anaheim) and the Athletics (Oakland) play in the America League. The season lasts from the end of April to the beginning of October.
Football	First-class football teams in California are: the 49'ers (San Francisco), the Raiders (Los Angeles) and the Chargers (San Diego). The season lasts from September to December.
Basketball	Basketball is also widespread in California. The Los Angeles Lakers are perhaps the best known team.
Horseracing	Horseracing with totalisator and bookmaker betting can be found in San Mateo near San Francisco, in Del Mar north of San Diego, in Santa Anita Park in Arcadia and in Long Beach not far from Los Angeles.
Surfing and sailing	On almost all the 75 beaches between Los Angeles and Cambria surfing is one of the most popular sports and very typical of California; originally it came from Hawaii. Surfers – even beginners – practise this sport throughout the year in Ventura. The mighty waves on the cooler northern coast, however, are only suitable for experts. There is good sailing also in the bleak north (including the Bay of San Francisco). Beginners, however, should either sail close to the coast or in the quieter south, perhaps in Mission Bay near San Diego. Sailing craft can be rented from most marinas. Inland waters such as Lake Shasta, Lake Tahoe and the Sacramento River Delta Lands offer equally good opportunities for sailing.
Snorkelling and Diving	For snorkelling enthusiasts the Pacific provides waters full of fish and marine flora (Lovers Cove near Santa Catalina Island). For divers the south coast (sunken ships, starfish in La Jolla Cove near San Diego), and the north coast (Abalone molluscs) are both equally suitable.
Tennis and Golf	Tennis and golf are among the most popular activities. The city of San Francisco has more than 100 public tennis courts; San Diego has 70 golf courses and Los Angeles almost as many.
Winter Sports	Although you would not normally think of winter sports in California there are, in fact, many opportunities for this activity. There are extensive ski areas especially in the Sierra Nevada, Squaw Valley, Mammoth Lakes, Lake Tahoe and Sequoia National Forest. In addition Snow Valley and Green Valley are only about three hours by car from San Diego.

Sailing in California

Golf course in Palm Springs

Swimming

See Bathing Beaches

Taxis

There are numerous taxis at airports, stations, hotels and the special taxi stands. To hire a taxi it is only necessary to stop an empty one. In most cities rates are high because of long distances involved. An exception is San Francisco where the distances are much shorter.

General

The following phone numbers are normally available 24 hours a day:

Beverly Hills Cab Co, tel 273-6611.
Checker Cab Co, tel 481-1234 or 482-3456.
City Yellow Cab Co, tel 870-3333.
Independent Cab Co., tel 659-8294.
Red & White Cab Co., tel 654-8400.

Los Angeles

Diamond or Yellow Cab, tel 234-6161.
Orange Cab, tel 291-3337.

San Diego

Checker Cab , tel 626-2345.
City Cab, tel 468-7212.
Luxor Cab, tel 282-4141.
Yellow Cab, tel 626-2345.

San Francisco

See entry.

Tips

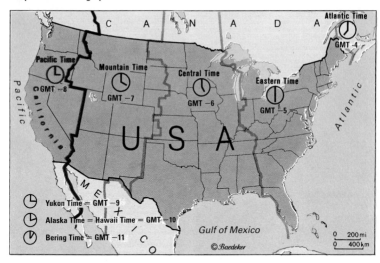

Telephone and Telegraph

See Post, Telephone and Telegraph

Time

Pacific Time	Like the whole of the west of the United States California is in the Pacific Time Zone, that is three hours behind the east coast of America and eight hours behind Greenwich Mean Time.
Summertime	From the last Sunday in April to the first Sunday in October daylight saving time is in operation and clocks are put on one hour.

Tipping

General	In the USA, in contrast to European countries, tips are only rarely included in the total bill and have to be given separately.
Hotels	For items of luggage taken into your room or removed from it the rate is normally 50 cents per item. If you stay more than two days it is normal to give the room maid 50 cents per day in a single room and 1 dollar in a double room. If a porter gets you a taxi you should give him 50 cents to 1 dollar.
Restaurants	The normal tip amounts to 15% of the bill before sales tax (8%) is added. You leave the tip on the table. In the better class restaurants the head waiter and the wine waiter (sommelier) also expect a tip.
Taxis	The driver should have a tip of 15% of the amount shown on the taxi meter and more for a short journey.

Both ladies' and gentlemen's hairdressers expect a tip of 15%. Hairdressers

Normally give 50 cents to the shoeshine boy. Shoeshine

Travel Documents

For a visit to the United States of America you need a passport which must Passport and Visa
be valid for at least six months after the planned date of departure. From
the 15th July 1989 the compulsory visa was abolished, but before arrival in
the USA the tourist or businessman must complete form 1-791 which will
be provided in the aircraft. A visa is still required in the following cases:
people who intend to stay more than 90 days in the USA, students, journal-
ists, exchange visitors, people on official visits, those engaged to American
citizens and members of aircraft crews. Visitors who have an unrestricted
B1 or B2 visa in their passport do not have to complete form 1-791.

Weather Reports

On radio and television (see entry) weather forecasts are regularly given.
Weather forecasts can also be obtained by telephone: in San Francisco by
calling 936-1212 and in Los Angeles 554-1212. In other places you will find
the appropriate number in the general section of the telephone book.

Wine

With a production of 20 million hectalitres the USA takes sixth place in the General
worldwide production of wine; in the western hemisphere it is second only
to Argentina. About 80% of American vineyards are situated in California,
where Spanish missionaries brought the grape (Zinfandel) in 1769, but it
was not until the middle of the 19th c. that vines were grown here in
considerable quantities. Vineyards extended later from California north
into the states of Washington and Oregon.

At one time the vintners endeavoured to produce red, rosé and white wines
of all kinds at the same time and from the same vineyard; they were not
much concerned with the traditional names of the wines and their origins.
Gradually they began to produce top-class wines by specialisation and by
paying regard to the types of grapes and the most favourable ecological
conditions. This development was furthered by the necessity of finding
new sites for vineyards because of the exceptional growth of the cities of
San Francisco and Los Angeles.

It is astonishing that in the land of coca-cola and pepsi-cola wine has New
become so popular. Twenty years ago the Americans still drank up to 70% Developments
of heavy wines and 30% of light table wine; today this situation has been
reversed. Cheap wines which are produced in the Central Valley have
followed this trend and have gradually conformed to it. The considerable
increase in sales of recent years shows that the Americans are drinking
more and more wine, and that Californian wines can be found in Europe.

Twenty years ago Californian wines were scarcely known in Europe. Since Favourable
then more and more top-class wines have gradually become appreciated geographical
by connoisseurs. The reason for this boom is probably to be found in factors
favourable geographical factors, which, in so far as the varieties of grapes
and the areas in which they are grown are together an ideal combination,
have made possible a considerable range of high-class wines. Three factors determine the quality of wine (for example in the Napa valley):

Vineyard in the Napa Valley

The type of soil: sunny slopes with porous gravelly loam produce a better quality wine than the heavy clay in the valley bottoms.

Average temperatures: here there are three temperature zones which are suitable for certain types of grape: warm (Zinfandel, Cabernet Sauvignon, Petite Sirah, Barbera, Grenache, Gamay), fairly warm (Merlot, Gamay, Chenin Blanc, Zinfandel, Cabernet Sauvignon), and cool (Chardonnay, Johannisberg Riesling, Gewürztraminer, Pinot Noir).

Late frost in Spring: this has the worst effect in the valley bottoms.

Modern wine producing technology

What the Californian vintner lacks in experience he makes up for with huge investment and intensive research in the field of wine production technology. An important contribution is made by the University of California which carries out investigation into new methods of cultivation, cellar technology, and improved varieties of grape. Although oak casks are still imported from France, nevertheless far reaching modern technology is employed in the preparation of wine: spraying of mist to cool the vines in hot temperatures, combine-harvesting machines, the most modern riddling implements, stainless steel tanks to protect the wine against acid, and the most modern cooling techniques. Thanks to these methods the brothers Julio and Ernst Gallo in Modesto, for example, have been able to operate the largest co-operative wine producing undertaking in the world.

Wine growing regions

The Californian wine growing regions are, from north to south:

Mendocino and Los Cameros with a cool climate which, however, is favourable for grape varieties which require a cool period for ripening;

Russian River with good table wines which are sold by firms in the Central Valley for blending;

Sonoma Valley with the well-known 19th c. wine cellars of Buena Vista (of Agoston Haraszthy) and Grundlach-Bundschu;

Napa Valley, the centre of Californian high-class wine production with the interesting wine cellars of Robert Mondavi constructed in 1966 in the style of a old mission building. Today this is the most influential wine producing firm in the United States of America;

Rutherford Bench, north of Napa, the "golden area of cultivation" of America which produces the classic Cabernet Sauvignon red wines;

south of the Bay of San Francisco with the small, but very well known, vine growing areas of Livermore Valley and of Paul Macon and Almaden;

South Central Coast with the vineyard areas of Edna Valley (Chardonnay), Santa Maria Valley (Pinot Noir Sanford), Santa Ynez Valley (Firestone) and Paso Robles (Zinfandel of the Martin brothers);

Central Valley with a reliable, often oppressively hot, climate in which grapes with a high sugar content and little acid thrive. Here heavy sweet wines were formally produced, but today thanks to modern technology other wines as well. Almost all the producers of Californian sherry, port and brandy obtain their grapes from the Central Valley.

The Californian wine producing areas can be divided into several climatic zones according to warmth and sunshine. There is first a fairly cool coastal zone, the most important areas of which from north to south are Mendocino, Santa Rosa, Sonoma, Napa, Solano, Alameda, Santa Cruz, Santa Clara, San Benito and Monterey. A warmer inner zone is in the Californian longitudinal valley (Central Valley) with the centres of San Joaquin, Stanislaus, Merced, Madera, Fresno, Tulare and Kern, and the area around Los Angeles including Cucamonga and San Bernadino. In all these areas red, rosé and white wines (and even "champagne") are produced.

The most important wines of California are the following, listed according to the extent of the area in which they are produced (in hectares).

Varieties of Wine

Red Wine

Zinfandel: a spicy red wine with a raspberry bouquet, also called "Californian Beaujolais"; San Joaquin, Sonoma, Monterey, Napa, San Bernadino (10,750 ha).

Carignane: the most important grape variety of the Mediterranean, used in California principally for cheap blended wines but is in decline (8550 ha).

Cabernet Sauvignon: the finest red wine which develops a fruity bouquet as it ages; Napa Sonoma, Monterey, Lake (8285 ha).

Barbera: dark red wine of Italian type, needs a warm climate; Fresno, Madera (7025 ha).

Pinot Noir: light red wine generally not particularly good in California; Sonoma, Napa, Monterey, Santa Barbara (3510 ha).

Petite Sirah: heavy red wine which is rich in tannin but which keeps well; Monterey, San Joaquin, Napa, Sonoma (3340 ha).

Merlot: deep red wine often used to fortify Cabernet grapes; Napa, Sonoma, Santa Barbara (830 ha).

Also ruby Cabernet, Grenache, Gamay Beaujolais and Tinto Madeira.

Rosé

Gamay: genuine French blue grape with white juice which is used here only for rosé wine; Napa, Monterey, Sonoma, Lake (1680 ha).

White wine:

French Colombard: neutral dry white wine for blending, thrives in cooler regions; Madera, Kern, San Joaquin (15,580 ha.).

Chenin Blanc: produced in upland areas, a wine with good body but with pungency; Madera, Fresno, Merced (11,970 ha.).

Chardonnay: the best dry white wine, light, fruity and full bodied; Sonoma, Napa, Monterey (6324 ha.).

White Riesling: (also Johannisberg Riesling), a dry spirited high-class wine; Monterey, Santa Barbara, Napa, Sonoma (3540 ha.).

Sauvignon Blanc: good to very good earthy wine with a fine bouquet; Napa, Monterey, Sonoma (2645 ha.).

Gewürztraminer: a fine species of grape which produces an exceptionally

Wine

full-bodied and spicy wine; Monterey, Sonoma, Napa (1340 ha.).
Also Semillon, Pinot Blanc and Grey Riesling.

Sherry:
Palomino.

Well known Californian wine producers and their products

Area	Vintner	Wines
Santa Rosa	Italian Swiss Colony	Burgundy, Rhineskeller
	F. Korbel & Bros	Korbel Brut ("Champagne")
	Martini & Prati	Sherry
	Parducci	French Colombard
	J. Pedroncelli	Cabernet Sauvignon
	Windsor	Chardonnay
Napa, Sonoma, Mendocino	Beaulieu	Burgundy
		Cabernet Sauvignon
		Grenache Rosé
		Pinot Chardonnay
		Johannisberg Riesling
	Beringer	Pinot Noir
	Buena Vista	Haraszthy Zinfandel
		Gerwürtztraminer
		Pinot Chardonnay
	Chappellet	Chenin Blanc
	The Christian Brothers	Pinot Noir
		Pinot Noir St George
		Gamay Noir
		Napa Rosé
		Chateau La Salle
		Pinot Chardonnay
		Chablis
	Freemark Abbey	Pinot Noir
		Pinot Chardonnay
		Johannisberg Riesling
	Hanzell	Pinot Noir
		Pinot Chardonnay
		Chardonnay
	Joseph Heitz	Pinot Noir
		Pinot Chardonnay
	Ingelnook	Cabernet Sauvignon
		Charbono
		Johannisberg Riesling
	Charles Krug	Cabernet Sauvignon
		Gamay
		Chenin Blanc
		Gewürtztraminer

Area	Vintner	Wines
	Louis M. Martini	Cabernet Sauvignon Pinot Noir Mountain Zinfandel Mountain Barbera Gamay Rosé
	Mayacamas	Cabernet Sauvignon
	Robert Mondavi	Cabernet Sauvignon Chenin Blanc Chardonnay Fumé Blanc Johannisberg Riesling
	Oakville	Cabernet Sauvignon
	Sebastiani	Barbera
	Schramsberg	Blanc de Blancs ("Champagne")
	Souverain	Cabernet Sauvignon Johannisberg Riesling
	Stony Hill	Pinot Chardonnay
Livermore, Santa Clara, Monterey, San Benito	Almaden	Pinot Noir, Gewürztraminer Johannisberg Riesling Blanc de Blancs ("Champagne")
	Chalone	Chardonnay
	Cresta Blanca	Cabernet Sauvignon Premier Semillon
	Concannon	Petite Sirah
	Llords and Elwood	Chardonnay
	Paul Masson	Pinot Noir, Silvaner Emerald Dry
	Mirassou	Santa Clara Zinfandel Cabernet Sauvignon Petite Sirah, Chenin Blanc Monterey Riesling
	Novitiate	Black Muscat
	Martin Ray	Pinot Noir
	San Martin	California ("Champagne")
	Weibel	Pinot Noir
	Wente Brothers	Sauvignon Blanc Pinot Noir, Chablis Dry Semillon Le Blanc des Blancs ("Champagne")
San Joaquin Valley	Famiglia Cribari	Cribari
	Ficklin	Port

Area	Vintner	Wines
	Franzia Brothers	Zinfandel Light Sweet Muscat
	Royal Host	Conti-Royale Burgundy
	Ernest & Julio Gallo	Hearty Burgundy Pink Chablis, Chablis Blanc
Note	Joseph Gazarra	Vin Rosé

As an indication of the provenance and quality of US wines the names of the vintner serve well. Price per bottle varies between 5-20 US dollars. Imported wines are more expensive, there is not much choice and their quality is dubious. Wine (even red wine) is generally served cool in the USA.

Youth Hostels

General

Youth hostels offer economic accommodation especially for younger visitors. You can only stay in any one youth hostel for a limited time. To use youth hostels it is necessary to be in possession of a valid membership card of the American Youth Hostels Federation or of an International Youth Hostel Federation. Prices vary between five and ten dollars per night. Those who are not members of a youth hostels association are charged an additional three dollars per night. There is no restriction on age. Although there are not so many youth hostels in the USA as there are in Europe, there are 28 hostels in California, all but four of which are situated along the coast. The following are the addresses from north to south:

Addresses

Redwood, 30 beds, 14480 Highway 101, Klamath CA 95548; tel (707) 482-8265.
Eel River Redwoods, 34 beds, 70400 Highway 101, Legett, CA 95455; tel (707) 925-6469.
Two Springs, 5 beds, Oroville, CA 95965; tel (916) 534-0157.
North Lake Tahoe, 30 beds, 10015 W River Street, Box 1227, Truckee, CA 95734; tel (916) 587-3007.
Anderson Valley, 4 beds, P.O. Box 555, Boonville, CA 95734; tel (707) 895-2138.
Point Reyes, 44 beds, P.O. Box 247, Point Reyes Station, CA 94956; tel (415) 663-8811.
Golden Gate, 60 beds, Bldg 941, Fort Barry, Sausalito, CA 94965; tel (415) 331-2777.
San Francisco International, 160 beds, Bldg 240, Fort Mason, San Francisco, CA 94123; tel (415) 771-7277.
Long Valley, 10 beds, Rt. 1, Box 189 B, Mammoth Lakes, CA 93546; tel (619) 935-4377.
Point Montara Lighthouse, 45 beds, 16th Street at Hwy. 1, Montara, CA 94307; tel (415) 728-7177.
Hidden Villa Ranch, 29 beds, 26870 Moody Road, Los Altos Hills, CA 94022; tel (415) 941-6407.
Pigeon Point Lighthouse, 50 beds, Pigeon Point Rd/Hwy 1, Pescadero, CA 94060; tel (415) 879-0633.
Sanborn Park, 40 beds, 15808 Sanborn Road, Saratoga, CA 95070; tel (408) 741-9555.
Tree House, 6 beds, P.O.Box 173, Midpines, CA 95345; tel (209) 742-6318.
Santa Cruz, 16 beds, 511 Broadway, Santa Cruz, CA 95060; tel (408) 423-8304.

Monterey High School, 50 beds, Hermann Drive, Monterey, CA 28148, San José, CA 95159; tel (408) 298-0670.

Lemoore, 4 beds, 525 Lombardy Lane, Lemoore, CA 93245; tel (209) 924-2835.

Bill's Home Hostel, 4 beds, 1040 Cielo Lane, Nipomo, CA 93444; tel (805) 929-3647.

Singing Pines, 10 beds, 657 Modoc (P.O. Box 1082), Big Bear Lake, CA 92315; tel (714) 866-2532.

Santa Monica, 1436 Second Street, Santa Monica, CA 90401; tel 213/393-9913.

Hollywood YMCA, 29 beds, 1553 N Hudson Ave., Hollywood, CA 90028; tel (213) 467-4161.

Westchester YMCA, 50 beds, 8015 S Sepulveda Blvd., Los Angeles, CA 90045; tel (213) 776-0922.

Los Angeles International, 60 beds, 3601 S Gaffey Street, Bldg 613, San Pedro, CA 90731; tel (213) 831-8109.

Fullerton Hacienda, 15 beds, 1700 N Harbor Blvd., Fullerton, CA 92635; tel (714) 738-3721.

San Clemente, 40 beds, 233 Avenida Granada, San Clemente, CA 92672; tel (714) 492-2848.

Elliott International (Point Loma), 60 beds, 3790 Udall Street, San Diego, CA 92107; tel (619) 223-4778.

Index

Index

Notes

Notes

Notes

Notes

Notes

Notes